Canada's Rights Revolution

Canada's Rights Revolution
Social Movements and Social Change, 1937-82

Dominique Clément

UBCPress · Vancouver · Toronto

16 15 14 13 12 11 10 09 08   5 4 3 2 1

Printed in Canada on ancient-forest-free paper (100% post-consumer recycled) that is processed chlorine- and acid-free, with vegetable-based inks.

Library and Archives Canada Cataloguing in Publication

Clément, Dominique, 1975-
   Canada's rights revolution: social movements and social change, 1937-82 /
Dominique Clément.

   Includes bibliographical references and index.
   ISBN 978-0-7748-1479-9

   1. Human rights movements – Canada – History – 20th century. 2. Human rights advocacy – Canada – History – 20th century. 3. British Columbia Civil Liberties Association – History. 4. Civil Liberties Union (Montréal, Québec) – History. 5. Canadian Civil Liberties Association – History. 6. Newfoundland-Labrador Human Rights Association – History. I. Title.

| JC599.C3C54 2008 | 23.0971 | C2008-901773-0 |

Canadä

UBC Press gratefully acknowledges the financial support for our publishing program of the Government of Canada through the Book Publishing Industry Development Program (BPIDP), and of the Canada Council for the Arts, and the British Columbia Arts Council.

This book has been published with the help of a grant from the Canadian Federation for the Humanities and Social Sciences, through the Aid to Scholarly Publications Programme, using funds provided by the Social Sciences and Humanities Research Council of Canada.

UBC Press
The University of British Columbia
2029 West Mall
Vancouver, BC V6T 1Z2
604-822-5959 / Fax: 604-822-6083
www.ubcpress.ca

To Derek and Vicki

Contents

Acknowledgments

Sigh. Where to begin. As often happens, this book is a product of hard work, dedication, and, to no small degree, simple luck. I have had the good fortune of working with the right people at the right time. When I began my master's degree at the University of British Columbia in 1998, I struggled to find a topic. George Egerton was assigned as my thesis supervisor, and he quickly grasped the potential of my undergraduate thesis on the 1945-46 royal commission on espionage. He encouraged me to develop this research and to expand my ideas about the role of civil liberties associations in the debate surrounding the commission's controversial actions. Over time my interests in rights advocacy would culminate in this book. I suppose this book, then, began with an innocent suggestion by a well-placed thesis supervisor in 1998.

After Vancouver I left for the shores of Newfoundland, and at Memorial University I was once again fortunate to work with the right people. Christopher English taught me the importance of clear and concise writing, while James Overton introduced me to a wonderful literature on social movements. James Walker, Robin Whitaker, and A.A. den Otter sat on the examination committee and provided excellent suggestions for turning the thesis into a book. Greg Kealey, though, really deserves the credit for much of this work. He provided invaluable feedback on writing and preparing this research project, combined with a stream of precious advice on the vagaries of academic life. Without his support this work would never have seen the light of day.

I am indebted to many people for allowing this project to come to life. Behind every good historian is a friend with a spare bedroom near an archives. I shudder at the thought of how I would have completed so many weeks of research in Ottawa without my folks (Jean-Pierre and Patricia), who not only gave me a place to crash but drove me back and forth to the Library and Archives of Canada. The staff at the Service des archives et de gestion des documents de l'Université du Québec à Montréal were wonderful; they quickly mobilized to make the files of the Ligue des droits de l'homme available to me during my short visit. Bernice Chong at the Law Society of British Columbia Archives and Bert Riggs at Memorial University's Centre for Newfoundland Studies went out of their way to make sure I had access to all the sources I needed for this project. I must also thank Danielle McLaughlin, who worked diligently to ensure my access to the Canadian

Civil Liberties Association papers, and Ivan Morgan, who answered my torrent of questions about the Newfoundland Labrador Human Rights Association. Both the Newfoundland Human Rights Commission and the British Columbia Teachers' Federation opened their doors to me in the waning hours of the work day to scour stacks of old documents. More than two dozen people were interviewed for this book, and I am grateful to them for their time and frankness in helping guide me to this point.

The last two years of my PhD were spent as an instructor at the University of British Columbia, and this was followed by a two-year postdoc at the University of Victoria. The two history departments provided a congenial atmosphere dedicated to quality scholarship. People like Robert Macdonald, Eric Sager, and Tom Saunders spent a great deal of time nurturing me as a scholar and as a teacher. I spent six months at the University of Sydney, where Greg Patmore encouraged me to do transnational comparative research, and years later he continues to support my work. The faculty in the Department of American and Canadian Studies at the University of Birmingham also encouraged me to consider these issues from a broader perspective. I am particularly indebted to Steve Hewitt for reading an earlier draft of this book. Bob Ratner, Reg Whitaker, and Gary Teeple also read portions of this work and suggested critical revisions. Once the book was ready for publication, I found an eager and receptive publisher in UBC Press and, particularly, in Melissa Pitts, who helped shepherd *Canada's Rights Revolution* to the shelf where it sits today. The anonymous readers played a key role in guiding this manuscript into its final form. Their time and energy is greatly appreciated.

Finally, this book would not have been possible without support from the Social Sciences and Humanities Research Council, the Association of Rhodes Scholars in Australia, the International Council for Canadian Studies, the Association for Canadian Studies, the J.R. Smallwood Foundation, the Osgoode Society for Canadian Legal History, Memorial University of Newfoundland, and a grant from the Canadian Federation for the Humanities and Social Sciences through the Aid to Scholarly Publications Program. Their financial support was, I hope, well spent.

Abbreviations

BCCLA	British Columbia Civil Liberties Association
CBA	Canadian Bar Association
CBC	Canadian Broadcasting Corporation
CCF	Co-operative Commonwealth Federation
CCLA	Canadian Civil Liberties Association
CCLU	Canadian Civil Liberties Union
CJC	Canadian Jewish Congress
CLAT	Civil Liberties Association of Toronto
CLAW	Civil Liberties Association of Winnipeg
CLC	Canadian Labour Congress
CLDL	Canadian Labour Defense League
CPC	Communist Party of Canada
ECCR	Emergency Committee for Civil Rights
FLQ	Front de libération du Québec
ICCPR	International Covenant on Civil and Political Rights
ICESCR	International Covenant on Economic, Social and Cultural Rights
JLC	Jewish Labour Committee
LDH	Ligue des droits de l'homme
LSBCA	Law Society of British Columbia Archives
LOOT	Lesbian Organization of Toronto
MCLA	Montreal Civil Liberties Association
MDPPQ	Mouvement pour la défense des prisonniers politiques québécois
NAC	National Action Committee on the Status of Women
NCHR	National Committee for Human Rights
NDP	New Democratic Party
NGO	non-governmental organization
NLHRA	Newfoundland-Labrador Human Rights Association
OCLA	Ottawa Civil Liberties Association
ODD	Office des droits des détenu(e)s
RCMP	Royal Canadian Mounted Police
RIN	Rassemblement pour l'indépendance nationale
SMO	Social Movement Organization
SOS	Secretary of State

SUPA	Student Union for Peace Action
TLC	Trades and Labour Council
UBC	University of British Columbia
UCHR	United Council for Human Rights
UDHR	Universal Declaration of Human Rights

Canada's Rights Revolution

1
Introduction

Two events, separated by time and geography, symbolize the central themes of this book. In 1945 a young, frightened Russian cipher clerk working in the Soviet embassy in Ottawa left one night with several top-secret documents clutched secretly beneath his coat. Igor Gouzenko carried a terrible secret with him, one he hoped would buy him asylum: evidence of a Soviet-led spy ring operating in Canada. In response, the federal government instituted a royal commission to track down the spies. In October 1970 the Front de libération du Québec (FLQ) kidnapped James Cross, the British High Commission's senior trade commissioner in Montreal, and Pierre Laporte, a Quebec cabinet minister, in an effort to promote Quebec independence. These are the only two moments in Canadian history when the War Measures Act was employed in peacetime. Habeas corpus was suspended, people were arrested and interrogated by the police for weeks without access to legal counsel, and reputations were sullied as a result of the stigma attached to being associated with an act of treason. The state's response to the Gouzenko Affair and the October Crisis was met with profound opposition from people across the nation, and it stimulated the formation of new human rights and civil liberties associations. The history of these "rights associations" is the subject of this work.

The sixties has been characterized by one of Canada's leading scholars of social movements as "the climax of a period of social movement activism in Canada."[1] Never before, nor since, has the country experienced such an explosion of activism. *Social movement organizations,* groups dedicated to realizing the goals of a particular social movement, were integral to these movements. Gay men in Vancouver and Toronto met in their homes to form the country's first gay rights groups; women came together in community centres to develop a program of action to raise awareness of such issues as abortion and equal pay; students congregated outside classrooms in universities to organize campus demonstrations to demand a say in the governance of the university; and in Vancouver, men and women concerned about the impact of nuclear testing on the environment united to form what would become one of the most recognized advocacy groups in the world. These patterns were repeated, time and time again, in the homes, offices, and street corners of cities and towns in Canada, bringing together people concerned with everything from Aboriginal issues to the treatment of prisoners. Social movement activism defined the sixties and seventies.

Many of these activists clothed their demands in the language of human rights. These activists, and the beliefs they promulgated, constituted a genuine human rights movement. Organizations dedicated to realizing the rights of homosexuals (e.g., Gay Alliance towards Equality, 1971), women (e.g., National Action Committee on the Status of Women, 1972), or African Americans (e.g., Urban Alliance on Race Relations, 1975) were among the many different kinds of social movement organizations that represented the advocacy aspect of the human rights movement. But among all of these groups was a unique collection of social movement organizations that stood out from the others: rights associations. Dedicated to realizing the dreams of the modern human rights movement, rights associations differ from, for instance, women or gay rights groups in several critical ways. Rights associations are self-identified "civil liberties" or "human rights" associations (e.g., the Alberta Human Rights Association or the Nova Scotia Civil Liberties Association). Unlike organizations dedicated to defending women or homosexuals (or children, prisoners, African-Canadians, etc.), rights associations do not claim to speak on behalf of a specific constituency but, rather, seek to defend the rights of all citizens. Each one is fervently non-partisan; the preservation of human rights, and not political power, is their only goal. Finally, one of the more curious aspects of these associations is that they are not mass-based organizations and attract only a small number of members. Prior to the sixties, there had been only a sprinkling of such organizations across Canada, barely a dozen groups active at one point in time. By the 1980s, more than forty rights associations had emerged.

Canada's Rights Revolution is a history of the sixties and seventies seen through the eyes of a generation of human rights activists. As such, it has two primary objectives. The first is to explore some of the most controversial human rights violations identified by rights associations. Given the immense impact of the October Crisis of 1970, it is surprising how little literature is available on the crisis aside from the predictable spate of speculative works arising in the wake of an event of such magnitude. The same could be said for the Gastown Riot or illegal RCMP activities in the 1970s. Human rights activists saw their communities bitterly divided on how to deal with drug addicts, police violence, censorship, abortion, the health and welfare of prisoners, and religion in public schools. Each of these controversies highlights how people struggled to apply vague human rights principles to concrete issues facing their community.

The second objective is to study a unique phenomenon emerging during this period: professional social movement organizations. Although not constitutive of the human rights movement, social movement organizations were important vehicles for promoting social change. But how did they conceive of social change? In an era made famous by activism and social ferment, what challenges faced social movement organizations? To answer these questions, this book examines the evolution of four case studies: the British Columbia Civil Liberties Association, the

Ligue des droits de l'homme, the Canadian Civil Liberties Association, and the Newfoundland-Labrador Human Rights Association. Six key themes are explored in detail: the impact of state funding on social movement activism; the differences between the first generation (1930s-50s) and second generation (1960s-80s) of rights associations; the strategies for change deployed by activists; the obstacles involved in forming a national social movement organization in Canada; the ideological divisions between activists dedicated to the same cause; and the relationship between social movement organizations representing different movements. Microstudies of social movement organizations are rare in Canada – an unfortunate oversight considering their significant influence during this period.

Ultimately, though, *Canada's Rights Revolution* is about asking a more fundamental question: To what degree can rights discourse promote social change? Part of the answer lies in studying how activists used human rights principles to identify problems in their community and guide their ideas and strategies for change. For this reason, rights associations are the ideal case study, even though many of the people who led these organizations were not themselves targets of human rights abuses. Social movement organizations serving a particular constituency are informed by a host of other ideologies, from feminism to gay liberation. Rights associations espoused human rights as a universal idiom, and, as Evelyn Kallen notes, "rights predicated on any other attribute, such as race, class, or gender, are not human rights."[2]

Rights associations offer us a window into how people have sought to define and apply ideas about human rights. Movements are defined by the beliefs they propagate, but they are composed of the people who articulate and shape, sometimes imperfectly, those beliefs. Rights associations were sites of contestation in which individuals from an array of social backgrounds struggled to apply vague principles to concrete issues that were affecting people's everyday lives. A history of rights associations is a history of a small but integral manifestation of the human rights movement.

Before we proceed, some conceptual issues should be addressed. The international human rights system, and the organizations that form the basis of this work, are guided by the principles of freedom, equality, and dignity. As philosopher Jack Donnelly notes, human rights, which are the rights one has simply by virtue of being human, are the "highest moral rights, they regulate the fundamental structures and practices of political life, and in ordinary circumstances they take priority over other moral, legal, and political claims."[3] Human rights are grounded on the presumption of the equal worth and dignity of all human beings. Ronald Dworkin posits that states must treat all persons as moral and political equals, and not distribute goods on the basis that some citizens are entitled to greater resources because they are more worthy, or constrain liberty because one's conception of the good life is superior to another's.[4] Canadian sociologist Evelyn Kallen views the underlying principles of the international human rights system in terms of social equality and social justice. In addition to the right to life and human dignity, freedom to decide and determine one's own destiny as well as equality of opportunity are elemental human rights principles. These principles are not absolute, but they are universal, inalienable, and exist prior to law.[5]

These principles are enshrined in every international human rights treaty and can be found in the constitutions of every rights association in Canadian history. But principles are not easily translated into practice. One of the first explorations into the history of human rights in Canada was penned in 1966 by Walter Tarnopolsky in a work entitled *The Canadian Bill of Rights*. From the outset he made it clear that he used the terms "civil liberties" and "human rights" interchangeably.[6] Rights associations of the sixties and seventies, however, considered the differences between human rights and civil liberties to be quite serious. In the early 1970s, when a federation of rights associations was formed, the members believed that the distinction was significant enough that they felt the need to burden the organization with a painfully cumbersome title: the Canadian Federation of Civil Liberties and Human Rights Associations. Clearly, rights activists identified themselves in ideological terms, and, as we shall see, these distinctions also reflected differences in the nature of their activism.

Any attempt to define separate categories of rights is a risky endeavour. A great deal of the literature dealing with human rights depends on the Universal Declaration of Human Rights (UDHR) and the two covenants, the International Covenant on Civil and Political Rights (ICCPR) and the International Covenant on Economic, Social and Cultural Rights (ICESCR), as reference points for distinguishing between differing categories of rights. Yet, the right to self-determination in the ICCPR (1.1) requires some recognition of the economic, social, and cultural rights in the ICESCR; the right to family is enshrined in both the ICCPR (23.2) and the ICESCR (23.2); and the right to join a union in the ICCPR (10.1) is also entrenched in the ICESCR (8.1). Categorizing rights is therefore an artificial exercise at best, and we should appreciate that these boundaries "can obviously be blurred and quite arbitrary."[7]

Civil rights were among the first rights to emerge historically, a product of bloody revolutions and challenges to monarchical power. Civil rights are herein understood as property rights and the rule of law. These rights include freedom of contract and the right to property (and to not be deprived of property without compensation), to withhold one's labour, and to join a trade union. Civil rights also encompass basic legal rights such as a fair trial, an independent judiciary, access to counsel, the presumption of innocence, habeas corpus, double jeopardy, and, most important, equality before the law. In contrast, *political rights* are defined as those rights that are required for the operation of a modern liberal-democratic state, including the right to free speech, free press, assembly, association, and religion. Lyman Duff, speaking from the bench of the Supreme Court of Canada in 1937, proclaimed that it "is axiomatic that the practice of this right to free public discussion of public affairs, notwithstanding its incidental mischiefs, is the breath of life for parliamentary institutions."[8] Political rights provide citizens with control over the state. For example, individuals have the right to vote, to be elected, and to petition the government. Political rights serve to mediate relations between civil society and the state.

Social, economic, and cultural rights have primarily been associated with the welfare state, including health services, social security mechanisms (e.g., old age pensions, employment insurance), and state-subsidized education. Other social and economic rights include the right to work, a decent standard of living, food, housing, and favourable working conditions. Cultural rights have manifested themselves in a variety of forms in Canada, from multiculturalism to language rights.

An interesting theme in the history of rights associations in Canada has been the decision by *human rights* associations to embrace economic, social, and cultural rights, while *civil liberties* associations have generally avoided this type of advocacy. One way of explaining this divergence is to distinguish between negative rights and positive rights.[9] When civil liberties activists argue that people must be free from restraint to carry out their desires (e.g., freedom from restrictions on personal behaviour), these activists are articulating a conception of liberty based on *negative* rights. Civil libertarians abhor unnecessary restrictions on individuals in their pursuit of the good life, such as imposing the same religion on individuals. This does not mean that civil libertarians oppose, for instance, progressive income taxes, but they oppose restrictions on our ability to formulate our own conception of the good life, such as limits on the press, religion, association, assembly, or speech. In contrast, Canadian human rights associations have historically forwarded a more robust definition of freedom that includes both negative and positive freedom. An advocate for *positive* freedom seeks to ensure individuals' capacity to formulate their desires, values, and goals. In this sense, liberty is defined as the freedom to act and to make claims against the state – the right to provisions of basic goods or the right to equal access to employment. Whereas negative freedom is rooted in equality of opportunity, positive freedom assumes the individual's right to bring about what she or he desires. Lack of training is thus a restriction on one's positive freedom. As Jerome Bickenback suggests, the "value of negative freedom must be derivative from positive freedom."[10] Social, economic, and cultural rights (positive rights) are critical in ensuring individual freedom.

Maurice Cranston, among others, has argued that positive freedoms are not true human rights because they require support from the state, and it is unreasonable and costly to characterize the provision of aid as a right. Such a formulation is problematic. Civil and political rights are principally defended through expensive legal systems and often require the state to act in a positive manner to ensure their protection. Social and economic rights are no less enforceable. We have the ability to provide all Canadians with a minimum of food and housing, but we choose not to because of resistance to extensive redistribution and structural change. Even Isaiah Berlin, one of the most well-known philosophers on the question of negative-positive rights and a staunch opponent of the idea of positive freedom, acknowledged that "to offer political rights, or safeguards against intervention by the state, to men who are half-naked, illiterate, underfed, and diseased is to mock their condition; they need medical help or education before they can understand, or make use of, an increase in their freedom."[11]

Another way of explaining the ideological differences among rights activists is to characterize some as libertarians and others as egalitarians.[12] In theory, libertarians believe in liberty and egalitarians believe in equality. A libertarian embraces negative freedom: freedom exists in the absence of coercion. In contrast, an egalitarian believes in positive freedom: freedom is derived not only from the lack of an intentionally created obstacle, but it is also violated by unintended obstacles, such as being born into a poor family. Therefore, egalitarians claim that the poor in capitalist societies are unfree, or less free than the rich, and libertarians claim that the poor are equally as free as the rich.

Both terms can be highly misleading. For instance, right-wing libertarians embrace extreme notions of self-ownership and reject any kind of redistribution of wealth; in contrast, left-wing libertarians support the division of resources equally among all individuals and, in some cases, oppose inherited wealth. No rights association in Canada could be honestly characterized as libertarian in either sense. However, as *descriptive* terms they can be useful in explaining the emergence of contrasting objectives between civil liberties (libertarian) and human rights (egalitarian) associations. Egalitarian activists favour positive rights and advocate for economic, social, and cultural rights (but not to the detriment of other rights). A libertarian approach, by contrast, is characterized by a concern for equality of opportunity and protecting individuals' negative rights. In practice, these divisions are constantly blurred, but the dichotomy between negative and positive rights partially explains why human rights associations have, unlike civil liberties associations, considered the elderly's need for inexpensive drugs or access to low-income housing for the poor as human rights.

Human rights advocates thus do not reject civil liberties but, rather, embrace a broader conception of rights, which is more inclusive. Still, at times, the two ideological camps come into conflict. For instance, it is not uncommon for civil liberties groups to tolerate hate speech as an exercise of free speech, whereas human rights associations demand that hate speech be censored. A libertarian approach would lead someone to oppose any abuse of an individual liberty; hate speech would be tolerable only because the alternative would be a violation of the individual's liberty to speak freely. The same approach informs opposition to laws that restrict drug use or consensual and private sexual relationships (including gay sex). Egalitarians also oppose state regulation of private sexual relationships, but they argue that equality can only be achieved through positive state action. In theory, minorities cannot participate equally in society if they are victims of hate propaganda or live in fear of becoming targets of violence promoted by hate-mongers. The difference between libertarian and egalitarian approaches to rights advocacy represents an important ideological dispute over the nature and function of human rights.

In the following work, the term "civil liberties" is associated with negative freedom and "human rights" with positive freedom; and, by extension, civil liberties are associated with civil and political rights while human rights are associated with economic, social, and cultural rights.[13] Human rights, however, are not *separate* from civil liberties. As Supreme Court of Canada justice Rosalie Abella once noted, "human rights start where civil liberties end ... Human rights are not only about civil liberties' emphasis on individuals in their relationship with the State, they are more emphatically about individuals in their relationship to one another, relationships that invoke the State's intervention and assistance, and request different treatment to narrow the gap."[14] In the following study, "human rights" is used broadly to refer to all forms of rights advocacy, whereas "civil liberties" is narrowly applied.

Human rights is a highly malleable term. Such ideological distinctions are a useful tool for explaining the nature of rights advocacy, but they should not be mistaken for an unbending ideological predisposition among activists. Ideology did not predetermine the activities of rights associations. There have always been individuals within human rights organizations who opposed censorship of pornography and individuals among civil liberties groups who support legislation banning hate speech. Attempting to sort out this conceptual minefield through a study of the practices of social movement organizations is an important goal of this work.

The vast majority of Canadians instinctively see human rights as an inherent good. We applaud national leaders when they raise concerns over human rights violations in China, and we accept the need to go to war to defend these principles, as was the case with the NATO intervention in Kosovo. But how are human rights enforced? By what mechanism do we articulate and understand such a vague concept? And what are the implications of these methods? Speaking before crowds of people in New York's Central Park in 1945, American jurist Learned Hand reminded Americans about the true source of liberty in the modern age: "I often wonder whether we do not rest our hopes too much upon constitutions, upon laws and upon courts. These are false hopes; believe me, these are false hopes. Liberty lies in the hearts of men and women; when it dies, no constitution, no law, no court can save it."[15]

The history of the human rights movement is closely tied to the evolution of the modern state, but scholars have too often adopted a top-down approach, examining the evolution of human rights from the point of view of state actors and the courts.[16] Only recently has work emerged on the role of non-state actors in framing rights discourse, but, even outside Canada, scholars have yet to vigorously pursue studies linking human rights to social movement activism. This is unfortunate. As Todd Landman and Joe Foweraker assert, the "discourse of rights has no independent capacity for action, and cannot simply 'shower meanings on the society below' ... this discourse can only be effective when attached to social actors and organizations. Social movements, for their part, do not merely perceive or receive rights as symbols, but are active in discovering, shaping, and disseminating these rights."[17]

Canada's Rights Revolution is based on two fundamental assumptions about the nature of human rights activism. First, the idea of human rights as it has evolved in the twentieth century is intimately linked with the state. Human rights activism is primarily, but not exclusively, focused on the state; activists seek to protect individuals against state abuse of human rights or to mobilize the state to protect human rights. As Miriam Smith has suggested, the link between rights and the state is inherent in the nature of rights discourse: "Rights talk assumes that changing or strengthening the law is in itself a means to [achieve] social change and that legal changes are thus the proper goal of political struggle and organizing. Rights talk thus defines social and political change as legal change."[18] When four black freshmen from the North Carolina Agricultural and Technical College in Greensboro sat down at a whites-only lunch counter at Woolworths demanding to be served, their goal was to pressure a private business to change its policies. Obviously, such activism was not state-oriented. Yet, when merchants agree to serve blacks or when neighbourhoods remove restrictive covenants, they are not conferring *rights* upon others. A voluntary act by private individuals is not a recognition of a right.

The second assumption, which derives from the former, is that human rights are only tangibly realized through laws or regulations. Individuals and groups can make rights-claims and such claims have a powerful moral force, but they are not *rights* until recognized as such by the state. As James Walker posits in his seminal book on human rights and the Supreme Court of Canada, "rights are what the law says they are."[19] Human rights activists will eventually seek out the state to have their rights-claims recognized. Thomas Hobbes once suggested that covenants without the sword are but mere words. One could say much the same about human rights.

Human rights thus encourage social activists to think of social change as legal change. The danger of such an approach is that it may be self-defeating. Martha Minow raises serious concerns about the rhetoric of rights in her study of the disabled and the law in the United States. She claims that inequality is rooted in knowledge-constructed differences based on "labels" and ideas of the "norm" that are accepted as natural and immutable. Rights discourse obscure these knowledge-power relationships by offering the veneer of formal equality when, in reality, treating everyone equally blinds us to the social handicaps caused by labelling. She found that rights rhetoric underscores the power of the established order to withhold recognition of the claims of disabled individuals.[20]

Human rights activism can also be highly elitist. Rainer Knopff and F.L. Morton have accused Charter-enthusiasts of hijacking the democratic process by using the Charter and the Supreme Court to adjudicate important social issues through an unelected judiciary. Such a process, according to Knopff and Morton, is profoundly anti-democratic. It favours a cadre of educated middle-class elites who seek to impose their ideas on public policy without having to lobby governments and mobilize public opinion.[21] Knopff and Morton, of course, blame the political left for this travesty, but critics of human rights activism can be found across the political spectrum. Miriam Smith has pointed out that, in the case of the gay rights movement, activists initially used litigation and advocacy to mobilize grassroots support, whereas Charter litigation made legal reform, not mobilization, the central goal of the movement. Tom Warner, an accomplished gay rights activist from Ontario, has argued that pre-Charter campaigns to have sexual orientation included in human rights codes had a dampening effect on the movement by redirected resources towards litigation and away from grassroots mobilizing.[22]

It is also questionable whether human rights activism is capable of confronting systemic inequalities. Using Amnesty International and Human Rights Watch as case studies, Gary Teeple concludes that they "absorb ... the energies of individuals, groups, sectors, and classes that might otherwise have presented a challenge to state policies; and they dampen a possible critical awareness about the link between the problems they are supposedly addressing and the nature of the economic and political system itself."[23] Nelson Lichtenstein is one of the few historians to have grappled with the implications of human rights discourse on social activism. In the context of the American labour movement, Lichtenstein has suggested that certain aspects of union activity have been displaced by a state-run human rights apparatus in the form of agencies, such as the Occupational Safety and Health Administration, that encourage workers to seek out individual, as opposed to collective, solutions. Rights discourse has proven incapable of dealing with the structural crisis facing the United States because a "rights-based approach to the democratization of the workplace fails to confront capital with demands that cannot be defined as a judicially protected mandate."[24]

Clearly, there is a basis for raising concerns about the implications of human rights activism. But recognizing the drawbacks of human rights activism does not vitiate its potential to promote social change. Canadian historians such as James Walker have argued that the courts can, at times, be a forum for systemic social change through the construction of new cultural codes.[25] Even a negative decision by a court is fruitful if the court becomes a forum for challenging, or at least questioning, common sense notions of, for instance, racial hierarchies.

Many of those who have mounted sustained criticisms of human rights activism are not prepared to reject it outright. Minow, for instance, rescues rights discourse from the very critique she has proffered. According to Minow, rights discourse has the potential to constrain those with power by exposing and challenging hierarchies of power.[26] Miriam Smith also believes in the potential of rights discourse to empower oppressed minorities. People outside the hegemonic classes can politicize their grievances and gain recognition from mainstream members of society by making their demands in the language of rights. Similarly, Lichtenstein, who fears the continued dominance of rights consciousness in its current form, has faith in the potential for human rights activism to challenge inequality and exploitation, but rights discourse should not be employed to the detriment of other, complementary, forms of collective action. Even Teeple, who derides the work of Amnesty International and Human Rights Watch, accepts that if human rights associations defended social rights with as much vigour as they do civil and political rights, they would invariably raise questions about social and economic inequalities.[27]

The primary obstacle to effective human rights activism may therefore be the adoption of a minimalist approach to human rights. Human rights defined as civil and political rights offer, at best, only formal equality and, at worst, the illusion of freedom and equality. The history of rights associations in Canada is a history of a rights culture struggling over competing ideas of human rights, and this has, more often than not, resulted in the adoption of a minimalist approach to human rights. In other words, human rights has often been interpreted by state actors and social activists as simply political and civil rights. Not all rights associations fit this mould. Some groups insisted that human rights had to include social, economic, and cultural rights. In doing so, these activists soundly rejected a minimalist approach to human rights. And yet, as the case studies demonstrate, even those who embraced social rights conceived of social change as legal change and, therefore, employed strategies capable of achieving only limited reform.

The history of rights associations in Canada is not that of a linear, clearly evolving movement. There have been two identifiable generations of civil liberties and human rights associations in Canadian history. The first generation had its roots in the 1930s and peaked in the 1940s; the second generation emerged in the 1960s and peaked in the 1970s. Within the international literature on human rights, the term "generations" is often used to explain changing ideas about rights, such as references to a generation of civil and political rights followed by a generation of social and economic rights. Generations, in the context of this book, however, is a reference to the activists themselves and to the historical context in which they lived.

Karl Manheim, one of the original thinkers on the question of "generation" as a historical concept, suggests that belonging to a generation is analogous to belonging to a class: "both endow the individuals sharing in them with a common location in the social and historical process, and thereby limit them to a specific range of potential experience, predisposing them for a certain characteristic mode of thought and experience, and a characteristic type of historically relevant action."[28] Manheim was careful to qualify his comments. A generation should not be seen as a social group that acts in unison or, necessarily, as a progressive outgrowth of previous generations; instead, to use generation as an analytical concept is to recognize that a community of people who are all born within the same short span of years share a common historical and cultural experience that collectively shapes their lives (e.g., similar schools, common family structures, comparable economic opportunities, exposure to ideas about patriotism and politics). In essence, to quote Anthony Esler, they are "products of a common cultural environment."[29]

A generation is also partly defined by biology and demographics. For Doug Owram, the baby boom encompassed people born in Canada in the late forties and coming to maturity in the sixties. Rights associations of the 1960s and 1970s were dominated by the baby boomers. Walter Thompson was fresh out of law school in 1972 when he joined the Nova Scotia Civil Liberties Association (and became president a few years later), and Norman Whalen, a founding member and future president of the Newfoundland-Labrador Human Rights Association, was on the cusp of finishing his articling position in St. John's when he became involved in the association. None of the individuals who attempted to form a national rights association in 1946 were present in 1971, when a national federation of rights associations was born in Montreal.

The activists who form the backbone of this story believed that they represented a new generation, a break with the past. By challenging the perceived values and beliefs of the previous generation, the baby boomers constituted themselves as a historically specific generation. Baby boomers also shared a common historical experience. Among other things, the boomers witnessed the expansion of the welfare state, the Quiet Revolution, and rising concerns over the use of illegal narcotics among middle-class youths. These and other crucial experiences shaped the boomers' activism. In Montreal, a group of people politicized by the Quiet Revolution and new ideas about human rights purged the organization of the old guard, which was tied to traditional notions of civil liberties. When Irving Himel was quietly encouraged to leave the newly formed Canadian Civil Liberties Association, it was a signal that a fresh cohort of activists with a new agenda had taken over.

The concept of a movement, not generations, is the primary category of organization for this book, but it is important to acknowledge that not everyone has a voice in this account. As a universal idiom, human rights is inclusive; it does not recognize racial, ethnic, gender, and other barriers. In practice, however, rights associations rarely represented the diverse communities they claimed to speak for. Rights associations have historically been led by middle-class activists and often white men (with some significant exceptions). Still, through them we hear the stories of blacks abused by police in Toronto, religious minorities marginalized in Newfoundland, political radicals repressed in Montreal, and poor drug addicts in Vancouver. As non-partisan organizations that did not represent a specific constituency, rights associations were drawn to issues that affected everyone in the community, from abusive police practices to limits on free speech. At times, these organizations were alone in speaking out on these issues.

Given the proliferation of rights associations in the sixties and seventies, it would be impossible to examine every organization in detail. Four rights associations have been carefully selected as case studies. The case study approach allows for an in-depth discussion of the inner workings of social movement organizations.[30] Sociologists often use case studies in the study of social movements. Unfortunately, sociologists depend primarily on interviews and published materials, whereas historians have been more successful at employing archival materials in examining social movements. People who have historically been marginalized in Canadian society have often used rights associations as vehicles to give voice to their demands. The case study approach provides an avenue for historians to gain access to the voices (albeit, mediated through middle-class activists) of individuals who rarely appear in state records. Single mothers on welfare in Toronto, for instance, used the Canadian Civil Liberties Association to challenge degrading welfare policies. Case studies can help us understand how individuals struggled to understand and articulate the ideals of a particular movement, without falling into the trap of depending on abstract reasoning common to studies that lack a microscopic approach. To be sure, the case study approach raises the spectre of making broad generalizations from a narrow sample, and *Canada's Rights Revolution* makes no claims to being exhaustive. Yet, by placing the experiences of these activists within their historical context and choosing a broad sample of case studies, we can catch a glimpse of the human rights movement as a whole. These case studies were specifically chosen not only because of their longevity but also because they represent the same goals and objectives embraced by other rights associations. The four case studies are diverse in size and origins, represent different regions and ideologies of rights, and include francophone and anglophone organizations.

Chapter 2 examines the intellectual foundations of the rights revolution, although such a monumental task can only receive a cursory examination in this context. Chapter 3 offers a brief survey of the first generation of rights associations in Canada, from the 1930s to the 1950s, while Chapter 4 offers a short introduction to the phenomenon of "professional social movement organizations" in order to set the stage for analyzing the case studies as social movement organizations. Chapters 5 through 8 are the case studies. Each chapter presents the early history of the four oldest and most active rights associations in Canada, and the chapters are organized chronologically from the point of each group's inception: the British Columbia Civil Liberties Association (Vancouver, 1962), Ligue des droits de l'homme (Montreal, 1963), the Canadian Civil Liberties Association (Toronto, 1964), and the Newfoundland-Labrador Human Rights Association (St. John's, 1968). All four associations are still active today, but this study ends in the early 1980s. Cuts to government funding and a lack of volunteers forced most rights associations to fold by the early 1980s. Moreover, the 1982 Charter of Rights and Freedoms fundamentally altered the strategies and orientation of many social movement organizations. Rights associations, for instance, energetically embraced the Charter and shifted most of their resources to instigating court challenges. I leave it to future historians to consider the impact of Charter litigation and constitutional rights on social movement dynamics in Canada.

Several of the issues dealt with in this work are specific to the history of rights associations, but they are also a manifestation of other developments in Canada. In the latter half of the twentieth century, new human rights issues caught the imagination of Canadians, and the positions adopted by rights associations, as well as the ideological divisions among them, were partly an expression of these new developments. In addition, the organizational concerns facing rights associations were consistent with the experience of many professional social movement organizations. For instance, the history of these associations challenges the assumption that state funding, at a time when government funding for social movement organizations reached unprecedented levels, necessarily limits or constrains social activism. Similarly, new communications technology, cheaper air travel, and an expanding pool of individuals interested in participating in social movement organizations created new opportunities for organizing at the national level. One of the key issues dealt with in *Canada's Rights Revolution* is the inability of rights associations to form an inclusive national association. Their failure is, among other things, a testament to the obstacles facing all social movement organizations seeking to form a national association in a physically immense, regionally divided, and culturally diverse nation. Some of these topics are addressed in the theoretical literature on social movements and human rights, particularly by sociologists in the United States and Europe, but what is lacking is an intensive, long-term empirical study of the activities of social movement organizations that only a historical study can offer.

Each case study exemplifies one theme in particular. The ideological differences between civil liberties and human rights are embodied in the extensive array of position papers developed by the British Columbia Civil Liberties Association and the philosophy articulated by the new cadre of leaders who took over the Ligue des droits de l'homme in the early 1970s. The Canadian Civil Liberties Association's claims to national status offer a rare opportunity to discuss national social movement organizing. The Newfoundland-Labrador Human Rights Association's dependence on state funding sets the stage for a broader discussion of the role of state funding for social movement organizations in Canada in the seventies.

Historians have paid little attention to the history of social movement organizations in Canada except for political associations, and few scholars have attempted to chart an entire network of organizations dedicated to the same cause. Historical work on the human rights movement often focuses on the state and the role of state actors in promoting and defending human rights. This is certainly the case with early scholars of human rights in Canada, particularly legal scholars and political scientists. Almost as if the state alone were responsible for human rights innovations.[31] The history of these four organizations offers an opportunity to witness how non-state actors have struggled with varying notions of rights and have played a key role in pressing the state to recognize human rights claims. A study of human rights at this particular juncture is propitious in the context of the global war on terror and constant attempts by the state to constrain individual rights. The history of rights associations is a history of lessons already learned.

2
Canada's Rights Revolution

In the 1950s the small town of Dresden, Ontario, was one of the most racially segregated communities in Canada. Blacks, who constituted about 20 percent of the population in Dresden, were banned from most white churches and were refused service by white merchants. One of the more notorious violators of Ontario's weak anti-discrimination legislation in the 1950s was Morley McKay, a restaurant owner who refused to serve blacks. When the Jewish Labour Committee sent black volunteers to test the law, McKay would either openly refuse them service or quickly close the restaurant when they approached from down the street. At one point, one of the volunteers was "seriously concerned that he might be attacked by the restaurant owner, who was wielding a large meat cleaver and appeared to be having trouble controlling his notorious temper."[1]

Dresden was symbolic of a broader phenomenon at this time. The deportation of Japanese Canadians in 1946 was the ultimate example of the limits of Canada's rights culture. Immigration policies were explicitly racist until 1962, and restrictive covenants (restrictions on the ethnic, racial, or religious mix in a neighbourhood) were common in the first half of the twentieth century. During the Second World War, Canada was among the world's least hospitable destinations for Jewish refugees, allowing barely five thousand Jews to enter the country during the course of the war. Blacks and many other minorities who sought to enlist were rejected by recruiting centres. Women did not get the vote in Quebec until 1940, and several minority groups, including Aboriginals, were denied the provincial and federal franchise until well after the war. Without the franchise, individuals could not hold public office or serve on a jury. Minorities were regularly denied licences to operate businesses. Anti-Semitism, segregation among blacks and whites in Nova Scotia and southern Ontario schools, limited economic opportunities for women, and widespread discrimination among Native peoples was a basic reality of life in Canada.

Many scholars have identified a "paradigm shift" in human rights taking shape in the aftermath of the Second World War.[2] Horrified by the implications of the Holocaust and the abuses committed by a state on its own citizens, it became increasingly difficult to claim that discrimination was simply a manifestation of aberrant individual behaviour. People began to seek broader solutions. Within a generation the relationship between individuals and the state had fundamentally altered, and the role of the state with regard to private relationships within civil society had also evolved. Canadians, irrespective of their ideas or physical characteristics, became assertive rights-bearing citizens. In 1947, Parliament repealed the Chinese Immigration Act, which had virtually banned Chinese immigration, and enfranchised people of East Indian and Chinese descent. By 1949, all legal restrictions on Japanese Canadians had been removed. And this was just the beginning. The postwar welfare state established certain basic social rights for all Canadians, from free health care to accessible education. Privacy acts were passed in most jurisdictions to protect citizens against spurious wiretaps or limiting disclosure of their personal information. Children, prisoners, mental patients, welfare recipients, the disabled, and a host of others asserted their rights as never before. Linguistic rights were given added protection with the passage of the Official Languages Act in 1969. Restrictions on women serving on juries were removed by the 1980s, as were requirements for women to leave the civil service after they were married (this requirement remained on the statute books in Newfoundland until the 1980s). Prisoners were granted the vote in Quebec in 1979.[3]

Developments in Canada reflected similar international phenomena. The Charter of the United Nations stated the organization's intention "to reaffirm faith in fundamental human rights, in the dignity and worth of the human person, in the equal rights of men and women and of nations large and small." Canada's human rights movement predated international developments, but the international community provided domestic activists with greater ammunition for making human rights claims.[4] The UDHR, ICCPR, and ICESCR, for example, went further than the Charter. The first two documents not only asserted basic civil and political rights but the UDHR and the ICESCR also characterized leisure time, education, fair wages, and working hours as basic rights. Individuals, and not just states, were now the subject of international law. As Marc Bossuyt notes, it is "fair to state that nothing came even close to an international system of protection of human rights before the founding of the United Nations."[5]

The rights revolution in Canada has had profound political, legal, social, and cultural ramifications. Four developments in particular symbolize the central themes of Canada's rights revolution: (1) challenges to parliamentary supremacy, (2) the expanding role of the state and innovations in public policy, (3) the explosion of social movement activity in the sixties, and (4) changing attitudes towards freedom and equality. Each of these developments was part of a human rights movement sweeping across the country by the 1960s. This "rights revolution" represented an important shift not only in the relationship between citizens and the state but also within civil society.

The Politics of Rights: Parliamentary Supremacy and the Bill of Rights Movement

As with any revolution, the rights revolution deeply affected political discourse in Canada. In 1922, Prime Minister Mackenzie King expressed concern about Anglo-Saxons becoming "debased" if lower races were allowed to mingle freely in Canada. Twenty-five years later, King suggested that "the people of Canada do not wish, as a result of mass immigration, to make a fundamental alteration in the character of our population."[6] Within a couple of generations after the Second World War, however, such views were marginalized in political debate.

The rights revolution entailed an important change in the role of the state in Canada; governments became active agents in protecting and enforcing a new rights regime. In 1867, the newly formed Dominion of Canada had virtually no rights built into the Constitution except for a few references to language and denominational education. The fathers of Confederation had little stomach for the constitutional rights favoured by their southern neighbours, and the decision to avoid entrenching a bill of rights was perfectly consistent with the British tradition of parliamentary supremacy.[7] In a way, the movement for a bill of rights and its challenge to parliamentary supremacy represented the ultimate triumph of the rights revolution in Canada.

At the close of the war in 1945, Alistair Stewart, recently elected member of the Co-operative Commonwealth Federation (CCF), presented before Parliament the first resolution to create a Canadian bill of rights.[8] In the Regina Manifesto, the CCF's founding document in 1933, the organization had called for amendments to the Constitution to protect racial and religious minorities, and to offer greater protection for freedom of speech and of association. Only a year before Stewart introduced his motion, the civil liberties subcommittee of the Canadian Bar Association had recommended entrenching certain rights in the Constitution.[9]

Stewart's motion, with no support from the ruling Liberals, was little more than symbolic and was destined to fail, as was a similar attempt by John Diefenbaker to introduce a bill of rights into the proposed Citizenship Act in 1946. Diefenbaker, a leading figure within the Conservative Party and prime minister-elect in 1957, would lead the passage of a statutory bill of rights in 1960 (unlike a constitutional amendment, a statute can be revoked by Parliament).

Opponents of a bill of rights appealed to notions of parliamentary supremacy. Parliament was held to be the defender of personal freedoms, as enshrined in the 1689 Bill of Rights. A.V. Dicey, possibly the most important thinker in British legal history and a mainstay of law school curriculum in Canada for most of the twentieth century, held that the "principle of parliamentary sovereignty means neither more nor less than this, namely, that Parliament thus defined has, under the English constitution, the right to make or unmake any law whatever; and, further, that no person or body is recognised by the law of England as having a right to override or set aside the legislation of Parliament."[10]

Appeals to parliamentary supremacy were often invoked by power-holders concerned with any proposed limits on their ability to legislate. The Liberals had ruled almost continually since 1921, with brief interludes of Conservative rule under Arthur Meighan (1926) and R.B. Bennett (1930-35). During the Second World War, the executive governed by orders-in-council passed by the federal cabinet; in essence, an enormous amount of power was concentrated within the cabinet, and there were few checks on its authority. For the CCF and Conservatives like Diefenbaker, a bill of rights was an attractive solution to the potential abuses arising from the exercise of virtually unfettered executive power. During the debates over the espionage commission (discussed in the following chapter), the Liberals defended their unilateral suspension of civil liberties in Canada in 1945-46 by appealing to the principle of parliamentary supremacy. Minister of Justice J.L. Ilsley claimed that "those principles resulting from Magna Carta, from the Petition of Rights, the Bill of Settlement and Habeas Corpus Act, are great and glorious privileges; but they are privileges which can be and which unfortunately sometimes have to be interfered with by the actions of Parliament or actions under the authority of Parliament."[11] A bill of rights, in Ilsley's view, threatened to Americanize the Canadian political system.[12]

Support for legislating human rights was growing by the 1940s. Alberta attempted to pass a bill of rights in 1946, but it was struck down by the Supreme Court of Canada. In order to enforce new laws relating to pensions and labour, the Social Credit government of Alberta had attempted to take control of banks and credit institutions within the province through its abortive Bill of Rights, a blatant violation of federal jurisdiction over banking.[13] A breakthrough occurred in Saskatchewan in 1947 when the CCF, led by Tommy Douglas, introduced the country's first Bill of Rights.[14] As Carmela Patrias notes in her recent article on the origins of the Saskatchewan Bill of Rights, it was a product of the CCF's long-standing commitment to minority rights and the efforts of minorities suffering from discrimination. Written by Morris Shumiatcher, a Jewish lawyer with strong ties to the CCF, the legislation purported to protect such rights as due process, speech, religion, association, assembly, and press while prohibiting discrimination. Since the statute did not provide for an enforcement mechanism, and it was unclear at the time which level of government had jurisdiction over civil liberties, the bill was more a symbol than an instrument for defending human rights. Nonetheless, it was a landmark achievement. As Patrias notes, "at a time when denial of employment, refusal to sell or rent housing and provide service in restaurants and hotel accommodation, on religious or racial grounds, were all legal elsewhere in Canada, the significance of Saskatchewan's enactment of a bill with such a comprehensive list of rights appears undisputable."[15]

The movement for a national bill of rights continued to grow in the wake of the initiative in Saskatchewan. Tommy Douglas had already expressed, at a Dominion-provincial conference in 1945, his support for adding anti-discrimination provisions and basic civil liberties to the Constitution.[16] The Canadian Congress of Labour began advocating for a national bill of rights as early as 1947, and the Trades and Labour Congress followed suit in 1948.[17] Among the few active civil liberties associations in Canada, support for a bill of rights was virtually unanimous. At a December 1946 conference in Toronto to discuss common strategies, civil liberties groups from Ottawa, Montreal, and Toronto all expressed their support for a constitutionally entrenched bill of rights.[18]

Yet, when the Universal Declaration of Human Rights was being negotiated in 1948, Canada was one of the few countries initially opposed to the Declaration. Prime Minister Mackenzie King was concerned, among other things, that the Declaration could be used to pressure the federal government into acceding to unwanted reforms. In the end, it was a combination of American influence and the distasteful prospect of voting alongside the Soviet block, South Africa, and Saudi Arabia that led Canada to support the initiative during the final vote before the General Assembly.[19]

Both domestic and international developments contributed to the government's decision to institute a series of parliamentary committees to consider the possibility of creating a bill of rights. In 1947, 1948, and 1950, joint committees of the House of Commons and Senate conducted investigations into the feasibility of a national bill of rights. But after more than twenty years of continuous rule and the imposition of extensive economic and social controls during the war, the Liberals had little reason to welcome a bill of rights. Neither the 1947 nor the 1948 committee led to any substantial action on the part of the federal government. The provinces were even less enthusiastic about the prospect of a constitutional rights regime. Except for the attorney general from Saskatchewan, provincial leaders warned the committees that they were treading on dangerous ground. Any bill of rights would violate provincial jurisdiction and would be vigorously resisted by the provinces.[20]

Only the 1950 House and Senate committee, led by Liberal senator Arthur Roebuck (who held the unenviable distinction of being the most outspoken Liberal in favour of a bill of rights), held public hearings and considered the issue in-depth. The presentations before the Roebuck committee offer some insight into how state and non-state actors viewed a potential bill of rights. In describing the types of rights appropriate for adding to the Constitution, there was an unspoken consensus in favour of civil and political rights. Irving Himel of the Association for Civil Liberties and representatives from the Department of External Affairs were sceptical of placing economic and social rights in the Constitution. Even organized labour was divided on the question of economic and social rights. Eugene Forsey, speaking for the 350,000 workers of the Canadian Congress of Labour, believed that a bill of rights was only capable of defending negative rights and that the rights to work or education required positive action by the state, best left to federal and provincial governments.[21] In contrast, the Trades and Labour Congress called for the entrenchment of economic rights in the Constitution. For instance, it argued that employment should be a recognized constitutional right, although the Congress was vague on precisely which level of government was responsible for creating employment.[22]

Roebuck must have been disappointed with the results of his own committee.[23] The committee recommended passing a declaration of human rights but only after the federal and provincial governments had agreed on an amending formula for the Constitution (a highly unlikely prospect in the near future). In a letter to Irving Himel in June 1950, Roebuck spoke of the divisions between the English- and French-speaking members of the committee; the latter were hesitant to support a bill of rights that could result in a derogation of provincial powers.[24] French-Canadian MPs' opposition had denied Roebuck the opportunity to present to the Senate a confident recommendation for a constitutionally entrenched bill of rights. Mackenzie King's earlier hesitancy to support the UDHR out of concern for offending provincial rights clearly had some basis in fact. Any attempt by the federal government to claim jurisdiction over fundamental freedoms could be seen as an attempt to steal powers from the provinces.

Despite entrenched opposition, there was growing support for some kind of bill of rights. The movement for a bill of rights was an important step in acknowledging the compatibility of constitutional rights with the Canadian political system. It represented a meaningful alteration in political debate in the context of an evolving welfare state in which governments were increasingly responsible for ensuring social and economic security. By 1960, as the Conservative government prepared to enact its own bill of rights, the notion of parliamentary supremacy was waning. Davie Fulton, Diefenbaker's minister of justice, was not opposed to a constitutional amendment and, in fact, favoured a bill of rights binding on the provinces. In his presentation to the parliamentary committee considering the government's proposed legislation, Fulton did not resort to appeals to parliamentary supremacy to explain his government's decision to introduce a statute instead of a proposed constitutional amendment; rather, he discussed the legal and political obstacles to amending the British North America Act. Specifically, Fulton was concerned with the lack of an amending formula and the implications of having Britain amend the Constitution for Canada, which was moving itself out from the shadow of the British Empire.[25]

At the same time, the position of the Liberal Party had begun to change. During the debate over Diefenbaker's proposed bill of rights in 1960, Lester B. Pearson, leading the Liberals, was quick to distance the party from the actions of the King government in 1946: "I wish to say for myself and for those associated with me in this House that we do not believe that certain of those actions were really necessary, or that they should be repeated in any similar situation in the future."[26] Instead of opposing a bill of rights in principle, as the Liberal government had done in the 1940s, Pearson criticized Diefenbaker for not consulting the provinces. Parliamentary supremacy was slowly losing its influence among the ranks of the Liberal elite, a fact Pearson acknowledged when he pointed out that "new circumstances, new difficulties and new pressures may justify some such departure [from parliamentary supremacy]."[27]

Still, these were baby steps. Early political debates clearly reflected a minimalist view of human rights. The Saskatchewan and federal bills of rights did not go far beyond freedoms of press, assembly, speech, association, and religion as well as due process and anti-discrimination provisions.[28] Classical liberal values dominated the politico-legal order of the country. Statesmen favoured trial by jury, rule of law, freedom of contract, and minimal government interference in their basic freedoms. Even the socialist CCF approached rights from a minimalist perspective. Tommy Douglas and the CCF created the first public health care program in the country, but their 1947 Bill of Rights did not suggest that health care was a human right. In 1955, the federal CCF, led by M.J. Coldwell, proposed a motion in Parliament to work with the provinces to entrench human rights in the Constitution. His motion referred to free speech, assembly, association, free press, religion, equality under the law, privacy, and prohibiting excessive bail and the suspension of habeas corpus.[29] The CCF was unique in its unwavering dedication to a constitutionally entrenched bill of rights. And yet, at a time when the Universal Declaration of Human Rights spoke of employment and social security as human rights, the CCF limited its vision of a national bill of rights to basic civil and political rights.

By the late 1960s, the Liberal Party no longer represented a serious obstacle to the bill of rights movement. Pierre Elliott Trudeau became the leader of the Liberal Party in 1969 and used his position to promote his vision of a bill of rights. In a speech before a conference of federal and provincial first ministers on the anniversary of the UDHR, Trudeau called for a constitutionally entrenched bill of rights to "identify clearly the various rights to be protected, and remove them henceforth from governmental interference."[30]

A special joint committee on the Constitution, established by the federal government in 1970, recommended adding a bill of rights to the Constitution. In terms of which rights should be included, little had changed in twenty years. With the exception of adding protections for language rights, the committee envisioned doing little more than entrenching those rights found in the 1960 Bill of Rights. But a look at the reasoning offered by the committee reveals the fundamental shift that had been emerging in recent years. In sum, the committee rejected parliamentary supremacy as an obstacle to entrenching rights in the Constitution:

> Parliamentary sovereignty is no more sacrosanct a principle than is the respect for human liberty which is reflected in a Bill of Rights. Legislative sovereignty is already limited legally by the distribution of powers under a federal system and, some would say, by natural law or by the common law Bill of Rights. The kind of additional limit on it which would be imposed by a constitutional Bill of Rights is not an absolute one, for a Bill of Rights constitutes rather a healthy tension point between two principles of fundamental value, establishing the kind of equilibrium among the competing interests of majority rule and minority rights which is in our view of the essence of democracy.[31]

Why did the committee reject a core precept of British political tradition? The committee's position reflected a much broader trend emerging throughout the country as a whole. Some have argued that the movement away from parliamentary supremacy represented the influence of American political culture in Canada. Others credit Trudeau's own political philosophy or the influence of the political left in Canada, which had long advocated for constitutional rights. James Kelly credits the 1980-81 Special Joint Committee on the Constitution with helping undermine support for parliamentary supremacy: "The new constitutional politics of citizen participation rejected the intention of the premiers to preserve significant aspects of parliamentary supremacy, and this had a direct impact on the textual evolution of the Charter."[32] Certainly one of the most potent forces in Canada at this time was found in the increasing assertiveness of French Canadians. Terrified at the implications of the Parti Québécois victory in 1976 and stunned at the growing support for the Yes side in the 1980 referendum, federalists pledged constitutional reform during the referendum campaign. Two years later, the Constitution was patriated, with an entrenched Charter of Rights and Freedoms. For federalists, the Charter was a powerful weapon to be used for promoting national unity.[33] The Charter paid homage to the civil and political rights that advocates such as Stewart and Diefenbaker had long envisioned for the Constitution. However, it was a testament to the changes occurring within Canada at this time that sections on equality, multiculturalism, and Aboriginal rights were included in the Charter. Most important, language rights were added to the Constitution and placed beyond the purview of the notwithstanding clause.

The Charter of Rights and Freedoms ushered in a new era and was, in many ways, the ultimate manifestation of the rights revolution in Canada. With some notable exceptions, particularly in the form of some recognition of minority rights, the Charter focused primarily on civil and political rights. The absence of any extensive recognition of economic, social, and cultural rights was a manifestation of the minimalist approach to human rights evident in much of the political discourse on human rights in Canadian history. Nonetheless, the break from parliamentary supremacy was a significant development in the evolution of Canada's rights culture.

The Human Rights State: Human Rights and the Law

The rights revolution went far beyond constitutional debates. Up until the war there was little legal recognition of the rights of minorities, but within forty years a massive human rights program was initiated by federal and provincial governments in Canada, creating a veritable "human rights state." The human rights state was an institutional infrastructure designed to protect human rights through various state institutions.

Anti-discrimination legislation was the most visible pillar of the state's human rights program. Ontario's 1944 Racial Discrimination Act banned discriminatory signs and publications in an effort to prohibit the use of "Whites Only" or "No Jews or Dogs" signs. Saskatchewan's 1947 Bill of Rights also prohibited discrimination with respect to accommodation, education, and employment.[34] Both statutes lacked an enforcement mechanism and were weak instruments for protecting citizens against discrimination. Judges, who found it difficult to conceive of discrimination as a criminal act, were reluctant to convict. Fines did little to help victims find new jobs, and most minorities were unaware of the legislation.[35]

It would take the combined efforts of dozens of advocacy groups (discussed in Chapter 3), from churches to civil liberties advocates, to convince governments to enact legislation with some teeth. Ontario took tentative steps in this direction in 1950, with an amendment to the Labour Relations Act to withhold legal protections from collective agreements that discriminated on the basis of race or creed, and soon after it introduced a bill that prohibited the enforcement of restrictive covenants. Within a year, the Conservative government of Leslie Frost passed the country's first Fair Employment Practices Act and Female Employees Fair Remuneration Act. A Fair Accommodation Practices Act soon followed in 1954. These were significant milestones in the history of the human rights movement in Canada, and Ontario's foray into the field of human rights legislation had a snowball effect. Within five years, similar laws were enacted in five other provinces.[36]

These initial steps represented a significant transformation in the role of the state. Governments directly intervened in everything from business practices to rental accommodations to discourage discrimination. Nonetheless, many people looked upon these early advances as a pitiful beginning; the legislation lacked any kind of effective enforcement mechanism or penalties. David Orlikow, a New Democratic Party (NDP) member of the Manitoba Legislative Assembly in 1960 and a local human rights activist, decided to take action. He teamed up with Gerri Sylvia, an African-Canadian woman living in Winnipeg, and drove her around town to a series of restaurants to apply for employment. Her applications were quickly rejected, and, in some cases, merchants did not even bother to ask about her qualifications. The next day, Orlikow sent two Caucasian women to the same restaurants to apply for the same jobs, and they were promptly offered the positions. Faced with such blatant examples of racial discrimination, the government decided to appoint a commission under the Fair Employment Practices Act to investigate the complaint. After numerous delays, the commission concluded that there was insufficient evidence to prove discrimination, and the charges were dismissed.[37] The case highlighted the difficulties involved in proving cases of discrimination, and, in fact, the legislation was rarely used. Between 1953 and 1969, for instance, only twenty complaints were adjudicated under various anti-discrimination statutes in British Columbia; more than 70 percent of these complaints were dismissed.[38]

At the federal level, the 1960 Bill of Rights was a dismal failure. Frank Scott noted in 1964 that "that pretentious piece of legislation has proven as ineffective as many of us predicted."[39] The Bill of Rights suffered a painful reception at the hands of the judiciary. In *Robertson and Rosetanni v. The Queen* (1963), the Supreme Court of Canada rejected arguments that the Lord's Day Act (banning the operation of a business on a Sunday) violated freedom of religion under the Bill of Rights. According to Ronald Ritchie in his decision for the majority, the Bill of Rights only enshrined *existing* rights when it was passed in 1960. The statute did not create any new rights, and since freedom of religion already existed before 1960, when the Lord's Day Act was enforced, there was no basis for making the law inoperative.[40] By 1969, the Court had yet to use the Bill of Rights to assert an individual's civil liberties against the state. Even the famous *Drybones* case in 1970, in which the Court ruled Section 94(b) (prohibiting Aboriginals from being intoxicated off reserves) of the Indian Act inoperative because it violated the equality under the law clause of the Bill of Rights, failed to set an effective precedent. In 1974, the Court effectively reversed itself in *Attorney General of Canada v. Lavell*, where the Court refused to accept a section of the Indian Act that required women (but not men) to surrender their Indian status if they married a non-Indian violated equality under the law. Once again writing for the majority, Ritchie suggested that to accept Lavell's claim would essentially invalidate the federal government's ability to designate special treatment for Native people and thus render it impotent in carrying out its responsibilities under the Constitution.[41] In effect, the judgment meant that Indian women could be discriminated against so long as all Indian women were discriminated against equally.[42]

Subsequent attempts in the 1970s to use the Bill of Rights' "equality under the law" clause to render legislation inoperative were equally unsuccessful.[43] Out of this failure, however, came success. The inability of the Bill of Rights to provide concrete protection for human rights led activists and policy makers alike to demand a constitutional amendment in 1982. The Charter of Rights and Freedoms would transform the courts into a far more active agent in combating human rights violations.

While the Court remained unimaginative in its approach to human rights issues in the 1960s, a more effective pillar of the human rights state was the ombudsman. The role of the ombudsman was to "generate complaints against government administration, to use its extensive powers of investigation in performing a post-decision administrative audit, to form judgements that criticize or vindicate administrators, and to report publicly its findings and recommendations but not to change administrative decisions."[44] Canada's first ombudsman appeared in Alberta in 1967, followed by New Brunswick (1968), Quebec (1968), and Manitoba (1969). Ombudsmen were available in almost every jurisdiction by the end of the 1970s (except in Prince Edward Island and the federal government).[45] While ombudsmen had no direct link to human rights legislation, they clearly played a role in defending individuals from the state by establishing machinery in which citizens could pursue claims against the government. This process included complaints not falling under the jurisdiction of human rights legislation, such as the case of a civil servant abusing his or her power.

In addition to the ombudsmen, Canada's two largest provinces initiated major investigations in the 1960s to revise their laws to conform with current standards of human rights. The Ontario Royal Commission Inquiry into Civil Rights was appointed in 1964 and was chaired by former chief justice of the High Court, James McRuer.[46] For the next seven years, the McRuer Commission examined hundreds of Ontario statutes, received thousands of submissions, and heard hundreds of witnesses. All told, the commission's reports contained 2,281 pages and 976 recommendations. As McRuer's biographer has suggested, "nothing quite like McRuer's inquiry into civil rights had been seen before in Canada."[47]

While McRuer was preparing his first report, another major commission was announced by the Quebec government in 1967, led by lawyer and former minister of municipal affairs, Yves Prévost. The Commission of Enquiry into the Administration of Justice on Criminal and Penal Matters in Quebec investigated the application of criminal and penal law in Quebec. If McRuer's report was a monumental effort that produced a massive tomb to occupy policy makers for years, then Prévost's report was almost biblical in proportions, with enough recommendations to keep policy makers busy for another generation. The commission produced five volumes (some as long as 1,500 pages), with more than a dozen subvolumes and appendices. It represented the most comprehensive analysis of Quebec penal law ever conducted by the provincial government.

It would be impossible to summarize the hundreds of recommendations and analyses presented in these two voluminous reports in this space. McRuer and Prévost dealt with such issues as ombudsmen, legal aid, provincial bills of rights, the operation of juvenile and family courts, coroner's inquests, the provision of bail for poor people, providing compensation to victims of crimes, and making the judicial system more efficient in processing appeals. Both resulted in the implementation of widespread reforms.

While McRuer and Prévost were busy transforming the statute books that would affect two-thirds of the population, human rights legislation was undergoing a significant transformation. Fair Employment Practices and Fair Accommodation Practices laws were consolidated into human rights codes. Ontario led the way with the country's first Human Rights Code in 1962, and by 1977 every jurisdiction in Canada had a code and a full-time human rights commission.[48] Human rights codes were expansive statutes prohibiting discrimination on numerous grounds (e.g., race, religion, ethnicity, national origin, age) in accommodation, services, and employment. Codes differed by province (Newfoundland, for instance, also prohibited discrimination on the basis of political opinion), but in each case the state paid full-time human rights officers to enforce the code and appointed a commission to spread awareness about it. In British Columbia, for instance, the Human Rights Code was enforced by the Human Rights Branch and the Human Rights Commission. The branch was responsible for investigating and conciliating human rights complaints. Any complaint that could not be informally adjudicated was sent to a board of inquiry to either impose a settlement (e.g., fine, offering the complainant a job, posting a notice promising to abide by the code, etc.) or dismiss the complaint. The Human Rights Commission initiated education programs, instigated complaints, and represented complainants before boards of inquiry. Until 2002, when British Columbia disbanded its Human Rights Commission, and 2006, when Ontario followed suit, these commissions remained a mainstay of the state's human rights program in every jurisdiction across Canada.[49]

Human rights commissions were at the forefront of challenging traditional ideas about human rights. Rights discourse and the role of the state had traditionally favoured the discriminator; the rights to freedom of speech or association were interpreted to mean the right to refuse service to certain peoples or to express prejudicial ideas. In contrast, anti-discrimination legislation "represented a fundamental shift, a reversal, of the traditional notion of citizens' rights to enrol the state as the protector of the right of the victim to freedom from discrimination. It was, in fact, a revolutionary change in the definition of individual freedom."[50] The first tentative steps towards the human rights state included policies designed to end legal distinctions among citizens in areas such as immigration and the franchise. Eventually, however, the human rights state matured with prohibitions on overt acts of discrimination and state policies designed to "correct systemic conditions that produce discriminatory results even in the apparent absence of overt prejudicial acts."[51]

Another facet of the human rights state was law reform commissions. Law reform commissions were responsible for conducting extensive research and study into provincial and federal laws in their respective jurisdictions and, as was the case with the McRuer Commission and Prévost Commission, offering recommendations to improve the law in ways that could better respect individual rights. Ontario began the trend by appointing a law reform commission under McRuer in 1964 at the same time as it appointed the Royal Commission Inquiry on Civil Rights; and, by the end of the 1970s, most of the provinces had similar institutions. The federal Law Reform Commission was created in 1971.

Law commissions, human rights codes, ombudsmen, and royal commissions were only the most visible manifestations of the human rights state. A myriad of new initiatives were undertaken by the state to deal with human rights issues. The Canadian Association of Statutory Human Rights Agencies was created in the seventies to act as a national coordinating committee for human rights commissions. A conference on human rights ministers was held for the first time in British Columba in 1974. An interdepartmental committee on human rights emerged from the conference to organize task forces within the federal government to study human rights issues.[52] These and numerous other initiatives represented a significant shift from the days when governments actively discriminated against minorities.

With the introduction of the Charter in 1982, the deficiencies of the Bill of Rights were overcome and the human rights state was fully entrenched. Numerous other pieces of legislation, royal commissions, and bureaucratic structures were created to promote the state's human rights agenda. The rights revolution thus entailed a significant transformation in the law from the pre-Second World War period, when, as one scholar has suggested, "the violation of civil liberties in Canada did not seem to be of serious concern."[53]

Strategies for Change: Human Rights Activism

The impact of the rights revolution was felt outside the realm of policy making and the courts. Social movement activism reached a fevered pitch in the sixties and seventies, and thousands of Canadians eagerly formed social movement organizations to promote the ideals of their respective movements. Many, but not all, of these organizations represented a human rights community, a collection of activists and organizations employing human rights discourse. Political lobbying and legal reform was only one form of activism. True equality for gays or women, for example, could not be achieved simply by adding new sections to human rights codes. Education programs, women's centres, gay pride parades, civil disobedience, and a multitude of other forms of activism forced Canadians to confront new ideas about equality, and activists did not always employ rights discourse. Nonetheless, social movement activists were an integral a part of the rights revolution.

One of the most powerful movements to sweep Canada, and most of the Western world, in the 1960s was the New Left and the student movement. Within ten years the student movement peaked and declined. Organizations such as the Student Union for Peace Action (the successor to the Combined University Campaign for Nuclear Disarmament) mobilized university students across the country to work with disadvantaged communities, protest the Vietnam War, and raise awareness on a variety of social issues. It was "the single most important New Left organization in Canada."[54] The Company of Young Canadians (created by an Act of Parliament in 1965), which absorbed the leaders of the Student Union for Peace Action as it declined in the late 1960s, continued to mobilize youths until the 1970s, when it became defunct.

In the midst of an expanding student movement, the women's movement experienced its own resurgence. By the sixties increasingly larger numbers of women were joining the workforce and receiving a university education. Branches of the Voice of Women, formed in 1960, began campaigning for the legalization of the birth-control pill as early as 1962 – a position the country's largest women's organization, the National Council of Women, was slow to accept. The contradictions between the promise of education and the reality of the labour market, as well as changing attitudes towards sexuality and the family, contributed to the revitalization and radicalization of the women's movement. The Royal Commission on the Status of Women, established in 1967, was a watershed for the women's movement and a symbol of second wave feminism, a critical juncture characterized by Naomi Black as the "first success of the second wave of Canadian feminism."

When the Royal Commission on the Status of Women published its report in 1970 it provided a rallying point for women and led to the formation of a new national federation of women's organizations. Those feminists who had been central in lobbying the government to create the commission formed the National Action Committee on the Status of Women (NAC) in 1971. NAC's primary mandate was to ensure the implementation of the commission's recommendations. By 1972, NAC represented more than forty-two associations.

The women's movement expanded exponentially in the 1970s. British Columbia's feminists claimed two established organizations in 1969; by 1974 they could boast more than a hundred. There were at least thirty-nine women's centres across Canada by 1979. National conferences were held by lesbians in 1973 in Toronto and by rape crisis centres in 1975. International Women's Year, proclaimed by the United Nations for 1975, contributed to the continued mobilization of women and their entry into various organizations and activities. The expansion of women's rights groups created a veritable mosaic of organizations. Women organized their own unions, political parties, and advocacy groups; opened women's centres, bookstores, publishing houses, hostels, and transition houses; and held cultural events such as women's music festivals. Radical feminists came together in groups such as the Lesbian Organization of Toronto (LOOT), which was formed in the early 1970s and rejected any working relationship with men on the basis that such relationships were inherently unequal.[55] An apartment rented in downtown Toronto for LOOT meetings became, in part, a physical sanctuary for lesbians, a place where they could socialize, share stories, and plan political action away from the scrutiny of a community that, at the time, was ill-prepared to accept alternatives to heterosexuality. One of the most difficult issues the women's movement had to grapple with was the place of lesbians. Mainstream women's groups were either uninterested or sometimes outright hostile towards lesbians, leading lesbians to form their own separate organizations.[56] The proliferation of gay and lesbian groups is another example of a social movement dramatically coming to life in the 1970s.

As one historian has suggested, the "1970s are hailed as the decade of gay rights in North America."[57] Several small gay liberation groups appeared in Canada's larger cities in the early 1970s, groups such as the Front de libération homosexual in Montreal, in reaction to the closure of gay bars under the War Measures Act. Gay liberationists challenged established moral codes (e.g., heterosexuality) by living an alternative lifestyle and articulating a new set of values. During this same period, gay rights activists (including, for example, those involved in Gay Alliance Towards Equality in Vancouver and Toronto) called for legal protections for gays and lesbians; a gay and lesbian journal, *The Body Politic,* emerged in Toronto.[58] These organizations were at the forefront of the gay rights movement, which sought, among other things, to secure protections for homosexuals in human rights legislation. While there are no statistics on the number of organizations formed in the seventies, there is no doubt the number was quite substantial. Even a national organization was formed – the National Gay Rights Coalition – in 1975.[59]

Aboriginals were also highly active in forming social movement organizations. Between 1960 and 1969, four national Aboriginal associations and thirty-three separate provincial organizations were born.[60] Many of these groups were pioneers in organizing Aboriginals beyond the local level for the first time. For instance, the Union of Nova Scotia Indians (1969) was Nova Scotia's first province-wide Aboriginal association. At the national level, one of the most influential Aboriginal organizations was the National Indian Council of Canada (1961), which disbanded when the National Indian Brotherhood was formed in 1968. The National Indian Brotherhood was the first national Aboriginal organization run by and for Aboriginals and would later evolve into the Assembly of First Nations.[61] Indian friendship centres multiplied across the country thanks to substantial financial support from the federal government's Secretary of State. As David Long notes, a significant aspect of this revived Aboriginal activism was "the expansion of the term 'aboriginal rights,' which by 1981 had been revised from its original focus on land rights to include the rights to self-government."[62]

Human rights activism was only one part of the "Red Power" movement, which called for a fundamental realignment of Aboriginals' relationship with Canadians through an aggressive assertion of Aboriginal identity. Louis Francis, a Mohawk, had been purchasing goods in the United States and bringing them to Canada for years without paying customs duties thanks to the provisions of the eighteenth-century Jay Treaty, which guaranteed Mohawks' open access across the border. When Francis tried to bring a used washing machine across the border in 1968, he discovered that a 1956 Supreme Court of Canada ruling had opened the door for the government to charge duties, although it had taken customs officials over a decade to decide to enforce it. Within weeks, a group of Mohawk from the St. Regis reserve, led by a charismatic young female activist named Kahn Tineta Horn, blockaded the Seaway International Bridge near Cornwall, Ontario, to protest the imposition of cross-border taxes. Protestors raised barricades and Horn purchased a Native headdress in the United States and flouted the law by carrying it over the bridge and refusing the pay duties. It took the combined efforts of the RCMP, the Ontario Province Police, and the Cornwall police to raid the barricades, take them down, and arrest thirty-five protestors. The incident was as much an exercise in promoting collective identity as it was in using civil disobedience to assert Aboriginal interests.[63] However, by the mid-seventies much of the radicalism that had blossomed in the sixties was on the decline. In its place was an increasingly bureaucratic movement dominated by hierarchical organizations employing interest group tactics.[64]

Ethnic minorities also mobilized in unprecedented numbers. Associations for the Advancement of Coloured People proliferated in the late 1950s and 1960s.[65] These black rights organizations employed tactics similar to those of NAC, the Gay Alliance towards Equality, and the National Indian Brotherhood, focusing primarily on political lobbying, educational programs within the African-Canadian community, and providing services to their members.[66] Some of the more active of the new groups representing African Canadians included the Black United Front in Nova Scotia, the Urban Alliance on Race Relations (Toronto), and the National Black Coalition. The Black United Front, formed in 1969 at a meeting of seven hundred mostly young black militants, is a good example of the increasing assertiveness of African Canadians.[67] Black United Front activists rejected the assumption that discrimination was a result of individual acts, and they located the problem in systemic obstacles to black equality. They sought to promote a collective sense of identity, to develop programs to enhance the economic and political power of African-Canadian people, and to improve their self-image. These organizations provided African Canadians with a stronger voice on the local and national stage than they had ever had before. Empowering black people was at the heart of their activism.[68]

By the mid-1980s, the Secretary of State was providing funding to 3,500 separate organizations across the country.[69] Greenpeace was founded in 1971 when a group of people from Vancouver rented a boat and set off to protest the testing of atomic bombs in Amchitka, Alaska. Children's rights, prisoners' rights, animal rights, and advocates for peace and official language groups are just a few other examples of the many social movement organizations active across Canada during this period.

Human rights discourse pervaded these social movements, but not all social movement organizations could be characterized as human rights advocates. Important distinctions divided many of these activists. Gay *reformers* sought amendments to human rights statutes while gay *liberationists* encouraged people to openly declare their sexual orientation. At times, liberationist militancy on such issues as pornography and removing the age of consent "grated on assimilationist, equality-seeking advocates, who saw them as impediments to securing legislative reform."[70] Several activists have also, in retrospect, criticized rights-based reformers. As Tom Warner notes in the case of gay rights groups, "pursing human rights amendments would lead ultimately to the dominance of conservative voices and assimilation with heterosexuals on their terms, rather than the liberation sought by more radical proponents."[71]

A similar dichotomy divided the women's movement. Faith in the human rights agenda was perhaps the most critical factor distinguishing liberationist feminists from reformers. One of the first books produced by the women's liberation movement, *Women Unite!*, published in 1972, introduces women's liberation by distinguishing it from reformers' concern with equal rights: "The philosophy of the women's rights groups is that civil liberty and equality can be achieved *within* the present system, while the underlying belief of women's liberation is that oppression can be overcome only through a radical and fundamental change in the structure of our society."[72] Becki Ross, in one of the few exhaustive studies of a radical women's organization in Canada, offers the same distinction. In her discussion of the Lesbian Organization of Toronto's clashes with the International Women's Day coalition, Ross notes that "in both 1978 and 1979, lesbian feminists criticized the way in which a civil-rights approach to lesbianism revealed the coalition's liberal-individualistic approach to the terrain of sexual politics. By directing its inventory of anticapitalist and antipatriarchal demands at the state, the coalition reduced lesbian oppression to the rights of lesbian mothers in child-custody battles and the inclusion of anti-discrimination protection in the Ontario Human Rights Code."[73] For activists who adopted a radical or liberationist approach, while the rights revolution promised a new era of equality, it was not without its limitations.

The massive expansion of social movement organizations was an important aspect of the rights revolution. Previously marginalized and powerless members of

Canadian society were employing rights discourse to make claims for equality and fair treatment. It is interesting to note, however, that rights associations were bastions of white, Christian, male activists. As the case studies demonstrate, it is surprising how consistently most rights associations, from Newfoundland to British Columbia, tended to attract mostly men and few visible minorities. The proliferation of identity-based movements undoubtedly drew women, visible minorities, and others away from rights associations and contributed to this lopsided demographic trend. But the nature of human rights discourse, a discourse that was embraced by reformers employing conservative tactics, may have further discouraged people with more radical aspirations from participating in organizations dedicated purely to the pursuit of a rights agenda.

Canada's Rights Culture

Demands for a bill of rights, law and policy reform, and social movement activism offer only a glimpse into the profound impact of the rights revolution on Canadian society. Fundamentally, however, the rights revolution was about new ideas. Human rights are intimately linked with changes in the law, yet at the same time they are informed by the cultural context of the community they serve. In 1914, for instance, the Supreme Court of Canada upheld a Saskatchewan statute banning white women from working for Chinese men. As James Walker notes in his study of the case, the entire issue was reduced to a debate over the right of Chinese men to hire white women; no one raised the issue of a woman's right to choose her own employment. In the case of a Jewish man who, in 1951, challenged a restrictive covenant that barred Jews from owning property in a Toronto neighbourhood, "the Court allowed the respondents' argument – that racial discrimination was both morally and legally acceptable – to pass without contradiction, and declined to confirm the appellants' assertion that racial distinctions were contrary to public policy."[74] Within a generation, racial and religious discrimination would be considered not only illegal but also morally reprehensible.

Human rights are a powerful force because the source of human rights lies not in the law but in human morality.[75] A society with a strong rights culture allows individuals to make rights claims even though, at the time, they are not recognized by the state or even the community around them.

Canadians have come to view themselves as rights-bearing citizens, and this has had a profound impact on the relationship between the state and civil society. With the hardships of the Great Depression still fresh in the minds of many Canadians, the government's successful prosecution of the war both at home and abroad convinced many people that the role of the state had to change. Laissez-faire economics gave way to the modern welfare state. And if the state could protect citizens against old age and unemployment, why not protect them against discrimination? Over time, Canada's rights culture has evolved from simply prohibiting overt acts of discrimination. Cynthia Williams suggests that Canada's rights culture has shifted from a traditional focus on negative rights towards egalitarian and cultural rights. According to Williams, the "preoccupation with procedural equality in the 1950s centred on equality before the law ... During the 1960s and later, however, popular equality claims turned to more substantive concerns, and a new focus on equality of opportunity included the demand that citizens be guaranteed equal benefits from society."[76] Sections in the Charter on language rights, multiculturalism, and Aboriginals are only one manifestation of this new era. By the 1980s, Canadians increasingly considered access to education and health care as rights. In many ways, the pillars of the welfare state, from employment insurance to workers compensation, were as much a manifestation of Canada's rights culture as was the right to vote and the right to equal pay. The welfare state is rooted in a powerful belief in the legitimacy and necessity of social rights.

A unique rights culture has evolved in Canada. According to Michael Ignatieff, Canada's rights culture is today defined by three qualities: "First, on moral questions such as abortion, capital punishment, and gay rights, our legal codes are notably liberal, secular, and pro-choice ... Second, our culture is social democratic in its approach to rights to welfare and public assistance ... The third distinguishing feature of our rights culture, of course, is our particular emphasis on group rights."[77] This rights culture has found expression in many forums other than the courts. Ignatieff goes on to suggest that skyrocketing divorce rates since the 1970s is about more than the introduction of new divorce legislation; the endorsement of individual autonomy through rights talk partly eroded the assumption of female self-sacrifice that bound many families together. The power of rights discourse is also based on its ability to empower marginalized and powerless people in the community. They may be denied legal recourse for their claims, but rights discourse provides them with a legitimate forum in which to advance their claims in ways that are not easily ignored. Such is the case with the battle for sexual equality for gays and lesbians, in which human rights claims are used consistently, and sometimes effectively, to challenge the power of the sexual majority to define what is normal.[78]

The legal, political, social, and cultural manifestations of the rights revolution were thus part of a fundamental shift in Canadian society. Human rights discourse was mobilized to challenge basic notions of common sense. Ideas about racial hierarchies and parliamentary supremacy were discarded, and new conceptions of the role of the state and the law emerged. The human rights movement altered Canadians' perception of what was right and fair.

A rights revolution had occurred in Canada.

3
The Forties and Fifties: The First Generation

Stimulated in part by the Russian Revolution in 1917 and the subsequent geopolitical developments, the spread of communism concerned Canadian political leaders, and their fears had a trickle-down effect. In 1933, Constable Joseph Zappa of the Montreal police force shot an unarmed Pole, Nick Zynchuck, in the back during an eviction proceeding in Montreal. When asked to account for his actions, Zappa shrugged his shoulders and replied "He's a Communist."[1] With its rejection of capitalism and private property, and its dedication to the overthrow of the state, communism represented a fundamental challenge to the status quo. The Canadian state became an active participant in the persecution of communism at home. In time, the state's campaigns against communism would lead to the formation of the country's first rights associations.

Victims of discrimination played a crucial role in mobilizing the human rights movement in Canada. To be sure, the state had its own role to play in fomenting the rights revolution. Political leaders such as Tommy Douglas, John Diefenbaker, and Pierre Trudeau were influential advocates for reform, and, as the following chapters reveal, the state was responsible for funding numerous social movement organizations. These organizations, many of which could not possibly have survived without state funding, were at the forefront of innovations in human rights reforms, from lobbying for human rights legislation to educating the public.

But victims of oppression have always been the best advocates for reform.[2] A Jew banned from a law school can become a symbol of the hypocrisy in a society that espouses liberal principles while denying equal opportunities to all of its citizens. Individuals who suffer the shame and frustration of discrimination are not only motivated to advocate for change but are also in a better position to mobilize others who have been targets of similar treatment. It is thus hardly surprising to see the first rights associations emerge from the ranks of communists, political radicals, and trade unionists who were the targets of the most extreme forms of government repression. Meanwhile, visible minorities, women, and other targets of oppression began to organize themselves and became powerful advocates for change. By the 1950s, rights associations would prove to be useful allies for minority advocates who had the resources to mount campaigns for reform but lacked the privileged access to the corridors of power enjoyed by many rights associations.

The first generation of rights associations set the stage for the emergence of their successors in the 1960s. Many parallels exist between the two generations.

Ideological divisions among activists, debates over a national rights association, and a concern for legal reform were common among both generations. Key figures within rights associations during the 1940s and 1950s would also play a prominent role in establishing new organizations in the 1960s. A complete history of rights associations in the sixties and seventies, therefore, begins with the first rights associations in Canada, which emerged a generation earlier.

Criminalizing Communism

Section 98 of the Criminal Code was one of the earliest and most direct means employed by the federal government to stamp out communism. It was added to the Criminal Code in the wake of the Winnipeg General Strike in 1919. The sheer size and range of the general strike had demonstrated the enormous power of organized labour in the aftermath of the First World War. Essential services were stopped, newspapers closed down, police went on strike, and a central strike committee effectively took control of the city. Thirty-five thousand workers were on strike in Winnipeg, with thousands more in sympathy strikes across the nation.

Section 98 was designed to forestall any similar action in the future by disposing of radical union leaders and foreign agitators. Under Section 98, a judge could impose a penalty of up to twenty years in prison for individuals who were members or officers of an unlawful association (defined as an organization seeking to overthrow the state or promote economic change through force or violence). The Royal Canadian Mounted Police (RCMP) was empowered to seize, without warrant, all property belonging or suspected of belonging to an illegal organization, and any owner of a hall who provided premises to such a group could be imprisoned for up to five years and fined up to $5,000. Frank Scott, writing in 1932, noted that the "permanent restriction on the right of association, freedom of discussion, printing and distribution of literature, and fear of severity of punishment, is unequalled in the history of Canada and probably any British country for centuries past."[3] Section 98 was complemented by an amendment to the Immigration Act in the same year, which allowed officials to deport any alien or citizen not born in Canada for advocating the overthrow of the government by force.

Section 98 of the Criminal Code was used throughout the 1920s and 1930s by the police to harass the Communist Party of Canada (CPC), break up meetings, disperse audiences, raid offices, confiscate literature, and detain activists. Three prosecutions were brought under Section 98, the most notable being the trial of eight leaders of the CPC in 1931. One of the most vocal critics of Section 98 was the Canadian Labour Defense League (CLDL). Founded in 1925 in Toronto, the CLDL was arguably the CPC's most effective front organization. The central aim of the CLDL was to defend the civil liberties of workers and protect strikers from prosecution. By 1927, fifty-two groups were associated with the CLDL, with a combined membership exceeding three thousand people. The CLDL achieved prominence during the worst years of the Great Depression by agitating on behalf of the CPC and defending thousands of workers in court who were prosecuted for their militant labour activity.[4]

The CLDL became moribund in the late 1930s, and the federal government formally banned the organization in 1940 in the midst of attempts to revive the group during the war. In searching for early manifestations of rights associations, the CLDL represents the crucial difference between early civil liberties advocates and the modern rights associations that would emerge soon after its demise. Instead of defending the rights of all Canadians, CLDL's advocacy was limited to the working class. The organization "did not pretend to follow the dictum of making no distinctions about whose liberties [it] defended."[5] Unlike contemporary rights associations, the CLDL made no secret of its partisan affiliations and its preference for the rights of the working class.

In contrast, there were two attempts in the 1930s to form a true rights association dedicated solely to the preservation of civil liberties for all citizens. The Canadian Civil Liberties Protective Association was organized by members of the League for Social Reconstruction, a think tank of leftist intellectuals with ties to the Co-operative Commonwealth Federation, in 1933. Frank Scott was part of another initiative in 1934 called the Emergency Committee for the Protection of Civil Liberties, an organization that was formed in response to a law in Quebec requiring individuals to receive permission to distribute circulars on city streets. Neither group lasted for more than a few years.

The Padlock Act and the Canadian Civil Liberties Union

Mackenzie King's decision to revoke Section 98 of the Criminal Code in 1936 had a domino effect destined to eventually stimulate the formation of Canada's first generation of rights associations. Soon after the elimination of Section 98, the CPC began distributing leaflets in Quebec, to the ire of the premier and attorney general, Maurice Duplessis. Deeply anti-communist, Duplessis quickly acted to fill the void created by the revocation of Section 98 by passing An Act to Protect the Province against Communist Propaganda (a.k.a. the Padlock Act) in 1937. This statute made it illegal to print or publish any newspaper, periodical, pamphlet, circular, or document propagating communism or bolshevism and to accommodate any organization propagating these views. The attorney general was empowered, upon receiving satisfactory proof of these activities, to order the closing of the accommodation for up to one year. Since the act did not define Bolshevism or communism, it was easily abused by Duplessis, who used his powers under the act against the CCF and trade unions, and even closed down Jewish and Ukrainian community centres.[6]

The Padlock Act was the mid-wife to the first rights associations in Canada.[7] In Montreal, a branch of the Canadian Civil Liberties Union (CCLU) was formed in

1937. A collection of autonomous organizations across the country from Vancouver to Montreal, the CCLU soon had branches in Toronto and Ottawa, stimulated in large part by opposition to the Padlock Act. Additional groups were formed in Winnipeg and Ottawa in 1938-39. The branches of the CCLU were the first rights associations in Canada. They were non-partisan and dedicated to protecting the rights of all citizens; their goal was to incorporate people from varying ideological camps. Montreal's CCLU quickly garnered support from the Student Christian Movement, the Fellowship of Reconciliation, the League for Social Reconstruction, the CCF, the Montreal Presbytery of the United Church, and local trade unions in their call for disallowance of the Padlock Act.[8] Within a few years the Montreal branch had recruited one thousand members.

CCLUs quickly mobilized their fellow citizens in an effort to pressure the federal government to use its power of disallowance on the Padlock Act. In 1938, for instance, the Toronto CCLU sent a delegation of groups representing 100,000 Canadians to Ottawa. Their call was refused by the minister of justice, Ernest Lapointe, the cabinet's leading political figure from Quebec. Several attempts by the Montreal CCLU to challenge the legislation in court failed, and it was not until 1956 that a decision of the Supreme Court of Canada found the legislation ultra vires and rendered it inoperative.

The Line in the Sand: Communists and Social Democrats

With the onset of another world war in 1939, a new host of human rights issues came to the fore. According to historian Ramsay Cook, the Defence of Canada Regulations "represented the most serious restrictions upon the civil liberties of Canadians since Confederation."[9] An entire apparatus designed to protect national security was expanding under the pretext of how best to fight the war. Loyalty to the state was paramount. To question the prevailing orthodoxy was to risk becoming the target of police surveillance, losing a government job, being purged from a trade union, or facing deportation proceedings. In the rush to protect the nation from various threats identified by the popular media, RCMP, and political leaders, it did not take long for minorities and controversial groups to become targets.

The Liberal government that was in power during the Second World War was far more repressive than the Conservative government that was in power during the First World War. King and his cabinet were responsible for censoring 325 newspapers and periodicals in the early stages of the Second World War (compared to a total of 184 under Borden). Wartime propaganda was promoted through the National Film Board and the Wartime Information Board. More than thirty political, social, religious, and ethnic organizations were banned, and internment camps housed approximately 2,423 Canadians.[10] Habeas corpus and many of the rights designed to protect citizens from arbitrary state action were suspended.

Surprisingly, civil liberties groups avoided the internment issue; instead, they focused their energies on the Defence of Canada Regulations. In Vancouver, a branch of the CCLU devoted its efforts to defending a bookstore owner from prosecution for selling subversive material of a communistic nature.[11] The Toronto CCLU, renamed the Civil Liberties Association of Toronto (CLAT) in 1940, organized a massive rally of five thousand people on 17 July 1942, with Arthur Roebuck, a Liberal senator, and Arthur Garfield Hays of the American Civil Liberties Union addressing the crowd. Among the central demands raised at the rally was to lift the ban on the CPC. A second rally, on 10 February 1943, called for the restoration of the Ukrainian Labour Farmer Temple Association, another victim of Defence of Canada Regulations.[12]

But underneath the veneer of a united front among civil libertarians lurked bitter rivalries and divisions, which came to the fore during the war. CLAT's activism was tempered by its members' unwillingness to work with communists. B.K. Sandwell (editor of *Saturday Night*) and the liberal moderates in CLAT fought off an attempt by communists to take control of the group in 1942. The battle scarred the leaders of CLAT and opened a rift that would eventually lead several members to leave CLAT and form their own organization.[13]

Divisions within the left were acrimonious, and the refusal of many social democrats to work with communists compounded a similar refusal among prominent liberals like Sandwell to be seen cooperating with communists. Before and during the war, defending communists absorbed a great deal of the energies of civil liberties associations such as the CCLU and CLAT. But the defence of communists was not undertaken without some difficulties. Communists dominated the CCLUs in Montreal and Vancouver, and they were active in the Toronto group. However, the Ottawa CCLU, formed with the support of David Lewis of the CCF, was disbanded in 1939 out of concern that communists were gaining too much control of the organization. Winnipeg's CCLU barely lasted a year, and, in 1939, the newly constituted Civil Liberties Association of Winnipeg refused to allow communists to join. An attempt to form a national civil liberties association initiated by the Montreal CCLU in 1941 failed when other groups refused to work with known communists.[14]

Many CCF'ers were ardent civil libertarians who were appalled by the persecution of communists, yet their suspicion of communism prevented them from working with any organization linked with communists.[15] The CPC's attempts to work with the moderate left in Canada in the 1930s, and its calls for a united front with the CCF (a call that was quickly rejected by the CCF), led to bitter conflicts within the labour movement. During this period the labour movement was shaken by "internecine warfare inside the trade unions and the central labour bodies. It was the confrontation of two inflexible strategies, with the trade unions as the battleground."[16] The ideological divisions within the labour movement and the political left spilled over into civil liberties organizations and would raise significant obstacles to cooperation among rights associations.

"A farce of citizenship": Japanese Canadians and the Espionage Commission

Only three rights associations were still active after the Second World War: CLAT, the Civil Liberties Association of Winnipeg (CLAW), and the Vancouver branch of the CCLU. Two incidents at the close of the war were to have a major impact on rights associations and led to a peak of human rights activism in the late 1940s. The first was the scandal surrounding the deportation of Japanese Canadians.

In British Columbia, Asians had a long history of being discriminated against. All manner of policies, from immigration restrictions, head taxes, and restrictions on work and trade to denial of the franchise were part of the Oriental experience in British Columbia from the 1800s to the Second World War. In a culmination of decades of discrimination, in 1942, thousands of Japanese Canadians were detained in internment camps or expelled from the west coast and relocated in other parts of the country.[17] Surprisingly, few civil libertarians spoke out against the expulsion. Many felt it was a necessary measure to protect national security (and Japanese Canadians themselves) during the war, even though the prime minister admitted that not a single Japanese Canadian had been charged for an act of sabotage. The decision to disenfranchise Japanese-Canadian citizens during the war, however, elicited strong opposition; letters and petitions from outraged Canadians, church groups, and civil liberties associations piled up in Ottawa.[18] To compound an already tense situation, on 15 December 1945 the cabinet passed three orders-in-council to repatriate over ten thousand Japanese Canadians back to Japan, a country many of them had never seen. Three-quarters of them were citizens, half of whom were born in Canada. As James Walker notes, opponents to the policy of disenfranchisement and the deportation orders, including leading figures within the Liberal Party, argued that the racism that informed these policies was in conflict with the principles guiding the Allies' war effort to defeat fascism: "the identification of racial discrimination with the wartime enemy had been established in the prevailing rhetoric."[19]

Rights associations may not have reacted to the evacuation and internment of Japanese Canadians, but the deportation orders roused civil libertarians to action. In a letter sent to fifty-five newspapers on 4 January 1946 (published in eleven papers), Frank Scott vigorously condemned the deportation of Canadian citizens as "a farce of citizenship ... To find it sponsored by a government bearing the name Liberal and not objected to by a vigorous public protest, warns us how far our standards have sunk during these past years."[20] CLAW, CLAT, and the Vancouver CCLU raised a public outcry. The prominent Canadian historian Arthur Lower (CLAW), for instance, sent letters to members of Parliament and a brief to the prime minister opposing the orders.[21] Civil libertarians added their voice to a groundswell of opposition to the drastic measures. Members of the Anglican, United, Roman Catholic and Baptist churches warned King that that the orders were "an act of indefensible tyranny and folly"; CCF'ers lambasted the government in Parliament; and Japanese Canadians mobilized opposition to the government's policies.[22] CLAT joined a coalition of groups formed in 1945 (the Cooperative Committee for Japanese Canadians), which was opposed to the deportation orders that brought together unions, women, and social gospel advocates. They carried a case all the way to London to the Judicial Committee of the Privy Council in a failed attempt to have the orders ruled illegal.[23]

The experience of Japanese Canadians was to have a profound impact on the human rights movement. When civil liberties groups met at a conference in Toronto in 1946, the deportation orders were considered among the three leading issues facing rights association at the time, the others being the Padlock Act and the Gouzenko Affair (discussed below).[24] The press, particularly in the East, was highly critical of the policy. One editorial in the *Globe and Mail* insisted that these "ill-conceived orders should be revoked forthwith," and numerous papers encouraged the government to disregard the Privy Council's ruling.[25] Walker suggests that the deportation orders roused the "public consciousness," and, following the success of a coalition of Canadian groups in pressuring the federal government to abandon the plan, others across the country were encouraged to organize and fight discrimination. Students in Toronto protested against facilities that denied access to blacks; labour and church groups united with Chinese Canadians to demand equal treatment; and public opinion polls revealed growing support for enfranchising East Indians and Chinese.[26]

The state's treatment of Japanese Canadians during and after the war would continue to preoccupy future generations of Canadians and act as a constant reminder of the need for safeguarding human rights. Japanese Canadians became a powerful voice among advocates for a national bill of rights soon after the war.[27] During the hearings of the Special Committee on the Constitution in 1980-81, which considered amendments to the proposed Charter of Rights and Freedoms, memories of the war haunted the proceedings. As Thomas Berger, a noted lawyer and human rights activist in the 1980s, pointed out, it was generally conceded during the hearings that the treatment of Japanese Canadians during the war "represented an evil instance of mass racial hysteria, made worse by the pusillanimity of the federal government. All agreed that it was an event which must never be repeated."[28]

One other issue stands out as a critical factor in mobilizing human rights advocates during this period. If the deportations raised the ire of civil libertarians, the espionage commission of 1946 facilitated the mobilization of rights associations in a way no other issue had done before.[29] Igor Gouzenko's defection on 5 September 1945 has been referred to by many authors as the instigating event of the Cold

War. Hiding classified documents under his coat as he exited the embassy, Gouzenko, in order to gain asylum, offered the federal government evidence of a Russian spy ring operating in Canada. While the RCMP interrogated Gouzenko, the cabinet passed a top secret order-in-council (PC6444) empowering the minister of justice under the War Measures Act to investigate Gouzenko's allegations. Unbeknownst to Canadians, the government had just suspended several of their basic rights two months after the end of hostilities in August 1945. PC6444 allowed the minister of justice to suspend habeas corpus and to detain suspects indefinitely without access to lawyers or family.[30]

The defection became public on 4 February 1946, when a popular American talk show host, Drew Pearson, claimed to have evidence of a Russian defector in Canada. Realizing there was little he could do to keep the defection hidden, King gathered his cabinet together the next day to pass order-in-council PC411, creating a royal commission to investigate Gouzenko's claims. Ten days later, on the heels of thirteen early-morning RCMP raids against suspected spies (including one raid on the wrong person's apartment!), King announced to the world that his government was investigating allegations of espionage.[31] The decision to use a royal commission was a conscious attempt to avoid the pitfalls of procedural protections in the judicial system. In a top-secret memo to the prime minister on 5 December 1945, E.K. Williams, president of the Canadian Bar Association, warned that "criminal proceedings at this stage are not advisable. No prosecution with the evidence now available could succeed except one of Back, Badeau, Nora, and Grey."[32] A strict police investigation followed by a trial would likely fail to convict most of the suspects. Williams favoured a royal commission as "it need not be bound by the ordinary rules of evidence if it considers it desirable to disregard them. It need not permit counsel to appear for those to be interrogated by or before it."[33]

The proceedings of the 1946 espionage commission rank alongside the October Crisis of 1970 as the most extensive abuse of individual rights in Canadian history in peacetime. When the federal government passed an order in council in 1945 under the War Measures Act to aid the investigation of a royal commission – an investigation that continued long after the war had ended – the government effectively suspended the fundamental rights of every Canadian. At least sixteen individuals were arrested and held incommunicado (no access to lawyers or family and friends) in the RCMP's Rockliffe Barracks in Ottawa, some for up to five weeks. Each was placed in a cell under suicide watch, with an RCMP guard near the cell at all times. The cell was small, nine feet by eight feet, with a window opening three feet wide and a 100-watt light bulb shining twenty-four hours a day. They were interrogated several times in secret by RCMP officers and encouraged by their "cell-mates" to cooperate with the commissioners, two Supreme Court of Canada justices, Robert Taschereau and Roy Lindsay Kellock. When they were finally brought before the commission, where the proceedings were held in camera, suspects were questioned about their political beliefs, links to communist reading groups, feelings about the USSR, and their recent activities. Suspects were threatened with contempt of court and six months in jail if they did not testify before the commission. Some were repeatedly interrogated after refusing to speak without access to a lawyer, a right reserved to the commissioners under the Public Inquiries Act.[34] After a failed hunger strike, one of the detainees, David Shugar, wrote to Minister of Justice Louis St. Laurent on 9 March 1946, claiming that "if I am to judge by the treatment accorded to me yesterday afternoon before your Royal Commission, I can only come to the conclusion that, as a Canadian citizen, I have been completely stripped of all my rights before the law."[35]

If the government had limited itself to a secret inquiry, the backlash would have been much less severe. The decision to prosecute the suspects using the commission's transcripts represented for many an attempt by the state to circumvent the judicial system.

Civil libertarians reacted strongly to the dangerous precedent set by the espionage commission. Three new groups emerged in 1946. With the demise of the communist-led Montreal CCLU during the war, an opening existed for the rise of the Montreal Civil Liberties Association (MCLA).[36] This new body was composed primarily of social democrats, including Frank Scott, who were opposed to the deportations and to PC6444. Perhaps the last attempt to form a civil liberties organization with communists and social democrats was initiated in Ottawa with the birth of the Ottawa Civil Liberties Association (OCLA). Harry Southam, editor of the *Ottawa Citizen,* was the OCLA's honorary president, and the founding meeting was attended by such luminaries as Arthur Roebuck, John Diefenbaker, M.J. Coldwell, and Cairine Wilson.

A third association was spawned in Toronto, but this one represented an extreme expression of the divisions within the left. The Emergency Committee for Civil Rights (ECCR) was led by a splinter group of communists frustrated at the dominance of liberals like Sandwell in CLAT.[37] The creation of the ECCR did not forego total cooperation between rival groups. Both organizations participated in conferences and rallies together in 1946.[38] These instances appear to have been uncommon examples of cooperation between communists and social democrats/liberals among rights associations. In 1946, a second attempt (following the Montreal CCLU's efforts in 1941) in Ottawa to form a national civil liberties association failed and has been characterized by Frank Clarke as a "rancorous affair."[39] C.S. Jackson of the ECCR called for a broad-based organization to include organized labour, while J.P. Erichsen-Brown of the OCLA rejected the idea of a communist being a legitimate civil libertarian. The conference broke down and no consensus was reached.

The Vancouver CCLU and CLAT were relatively silent regarding the espionage commission (although Sandwell vigorously attacked the commission in the pages of the magazine he edited, *Saturday Night*), and the MCLA limited its activities to publishing an advertisement in the *Montreal Star* condemning PC6444 (but not the commission). Scott and his colleagues' dislike of communists and worries of being seen defending accused communist spies likely dampened their enthusiasm.

The OCLA and the ECCR, and to a lesser degree CLAW, entered the fray enthusiastically. They sent letters to politicians, published advertisements in newspapers, produced reports through detailed research, and distributed literature. Extensively researched reports produced by the OCLA and the ECCR detailed the implications of the government's actions: accounts of RCMP officers' tearing up letters from family members and suggestions of psychological abuse were among the more graphic incidents recounted in the reports. Advertisements financed by the ECCR appeared in the *Toronto Daily Star,* one of the country's largest newspapers, on 15 June and 29 June 1946. Motions passed by the Ottawa and Winnipeg groups denounced the use of wartime powers in peacetime and the circumvention of the judicial process, and were forwarded to the Minister of Justice. They also hoped to convince the minister to stop distributing the report because it contained accusations of guilt against individuals already acquitted in court.[40] As Sandwell attacked the commission in *Saturday Night,* Arthur Lower of CLAW expressed similar concerns in the pages of the *Winnipeg Free Press*. Several groups also had their correspondence read before Parliament, where the CCF and Conservative Party were hammering the Liberals over the commission.[41] Within a few weeks the ECCR had accumulated $9,000 and had an office with a paid secretary from which it mailed 15,000 pieces of literature, including a regular bulletin.[42]

To the disgust of its critics, the commission achieved some of its goals. Thanks to the commission's transcripts, several individuals were successfully prosecuted for conspiracy to violate the Official Secrets Act. For others, their reputations were tarnished or they lost employment. Israel Halperin, a math professor at Queen's University, would have been dismissed had it not been for the intervention of Chancellor Charles Dunning – who feared embarrassment to the university should Halperin be dismissed despite being acquitted in court – before the Board of Trustees. Another acquitted suspect, David Shugar, lost his position with the Department of National Health and Welfare.

Three key themes emerge from the events of 1945-46. First, the debates in Parliament, the media, the Canadian Bar Association, and the creation of three new rights associations represented one of the most intense public debates on a human rights issue ever seen in Canada. Debates surrounding individual rights and the role of the state became a significant question of public discussion in the postwar period, stimulated in large part by the espionage commission and the treatment of Japanese Canadians.

Second, it was at this stage that social democrats and liberals increasingly came to dominate rights associations. The Vancouver CCLU, MCLA, CLAW, and CLAT were all led and dominated by social democrats or liberals, and the ECCR (re-named the Civil Rights Union in 1947) was the only communist-inspired associa-tion. Divisions among civil liberties associations were a reflection of the impact of the Cold War. As one scholar has noted, the "Communist and social demo-cratic rivalries of the 1940s exhibited a vehemence seldom witnessed in Canadian labour."[43] Communist purges soon became the order of the day within the country's leading labour organizations – the Trades and Labour Congress and the Canadian Congress of Labour.

Civil liberties associations faced similar divisions. Attempts to bridge these ideo-logical camps in the OCLA failed, and its president's refusal to work with com-munists at the 1946 meeting in Ottawa represented the rising domination of non-communists in the OCLA. The refusal of leaders in the OCLA, CLAW, and the MCLA to work with communists, the ascendancy of Garnett Sedgewick and social democrats to the leadership of the Vancouver CCLU, and the split in CLAT had effectively sidelined communists within rights associations. Politically, com-munists were reeling from the ban on the CPC during the war, and the creation of the Labour Progressive Party to replace the CPC had little success. The Labour Progressive Party was further tarnished by the conviction of the party's only elected MP (Fred Rose) as a result of the espionage commission's investigation. Rights associations of the immediate postwar period had undergone a significant ideo-logical shift from the days of the CLDL and the CCLU.

Third, the philosophy of parliamentary supremacy was the central obstacle facing rights associations during this period. Louis St. Laurent and J.L. Ilsley (who replaced St. Laurent as minister of justice in late 1946) used the language of parlia-mentary supremacy to justify the government's actions in the wake of Gouzenko's defection.[44] In court, judges refused to accept defence counsel objections to the use of the commission's transcripts. One of the earliest rulings, set by James McRuer (future chief justice of Ontario) of the Ontario High Court, concluded that it was not "at all clear that this court has, in these proceedings, any jurisdiction to review the conduct of the commission or to decide that a commission acting with appar-ent lawful jurisdiction has at any time by its conduct deprived itself of jurisdic-tion."[45] Judicial decisions in the spy trials reflected a clear deference to Parliament and the inherent limitations of the courts to act as a forum for the defence of individual rights.[46]

Public opinion also reflected a deference to legislative authority when the ques-tion of preserving individual rights was raised. A poll by the *Toronto Daily Star* following the espionage commission determined that 93 percent of respondents had heard about the Gouzenko Affair and that 61 percent approved of the government's tactics.[47] Another Gallup poll taken in 1949 asked respondents if they believed in complete freedom of speech and if people should be allowed to say anything at any time about government and the country. Of the 2,019 respondents,

36.2 percent said no and another 15 percent had no opinion or had a qualified answer.[48] Four years later, another poll found that 62 percent of respondents favoured limiting the speech of communists and only 26 percent considered it a fundamental democratic right.[49] Opinion polls were still in their infancy at this time and were a crude measurement of overall opinion, and yet these few examples demonstrate, at the very least, an undercurrent of opinion sympathetic to state-imposed limitations on individual rights.

Anti-Discrimination Legislation

There is no question that the Gouzenko Affair and the treatment of Japanese Canadians were dramatic and controversial scandals that shook the nation and had a lasting impact on the human rights movement. But for many Canadians, the most pressing human rights issue of the period was something affecting their daily lives: discrimination. Battling discrimination became a hallmark of the early human rights movement. Rights associations, staffed primarily by white, middle-class men, were not as central to early anti-discrimination campaigns as organizations led by victims of discrimination. Nonetheless, rights associations played an integral supporting role in campaigns to secure anti-discrimination legislation in Canada.

James Walker has identified three stages in the movement for racial equality beginning in the mid-twentieth century. The first phase, for "equal citizenship," sought to end legal distinctions among citizens in areas such as immigration and the franchise; the second phase involved demands for "protective shields" that led to the anti-discrimination legislation noted earlier; and the third phase, the "remedial sword," was characterized by state policies designed to "correct systemic conditions that produce discriminatory results even in the apparent absence of overt prejudicial acts."[50] These "phases" often overlapped, and campaigns for equal citizenship and protective shield policies were prevalent by the 1950s. Each phase was informed by changing common-sense notions about race and the nature of prejudice. Anti-discrimination legislation campaigns in the wake of the Second World War, for instance, were guided by a belief that discriminatory acts were the result of individual aberrant behaviour or psychological problems attributed to pathological individuals. These individuals influenced popular notions of what was right and moral (like a contagious disease). The solution, therefore, was to stop the disease at its source by mobilizing the state to prevent individual acts of discrimination. One of the most vocal advocates for anti-discrimination legislation in the 1950s was the Association for Civil Liberties, a Toronto-based organization created from the ashes of CLAT. But the Association for Civil Liberties lacked the resources to mount an effective campaign of its own.

The solution was an alliance with representatives of a community with a direct interest in seeking anti-discrimination legislation. Jews were particularly well placed to combat discrimination. Jewish lawyers and academics conducted human rights research and acted as spokespersons for various campaigns, while Jewish workers within the labour movement and the political left represented a large and out-spoken ethnic minority in organizations such as the CCF. Jews were able to draw upon an extensive network of Jewish organizations, from community groups to unions, which formed a "province-wide communication network unparalleled by any other minority group."[51] Possibly the most important organization in this net-work was the Jewish Labour Committee (JLC).

Few other organizations in Canadian history can claim to have had such a crit-ical impact on fighting discrimination. Formed in 1936, the JLC and the Joint Pub-lic Relations Committee (formed in 1938) of the Canadian Jewish Congress were front-runners in the push for anti-discrimination legislation in Ontario. Kalmen Kaplansky, a Polish-born Jew who was a member of the International Typographical Workers' Union, was the JLC's executive director for combatting racial discrimi-nation in the labour movement and was instrumental in the formation of the Joint Labour Committees to Combat Racial Discrimination in Toronto, Windsor, Montreal, Vancouver, and Winnipeg.[52] The Joint Public Relations Com-mittee and the JLC, initially competitors, joined forces in 1947 under the Joint Advisory Committee on Labour Relations, with Kaplansky as its leader.

Both the Trades and Labour Council and the Canadian Congress of Labour provided funding and support to Kaplansky's network of labour committees. La-bour's participation in the Joint Advisory Committee on Labour Relations rep-resented a significant shift in its attitudes towards racial minorities. For most of the first half of the twentieth century, labour was a strong proponent of closed borders, and it considered immigrants and racial/ethnic minorities, most notably the Chinese in British Columbia, who earned significantly lower wages than did people of European descent, as potential strike-breakers and as a threat to the power of organized labour.[53] Changes within the labour force and the realization that racism was a significant obstacle to working-class unity had a profound im-pact on the labour movement. Well over 2 million immigrants entered the coun-try between 1946 and 1961, and a significant percentage of the growing labour force was made up of new Canadians. Postwar prosperity also led to higher wage levels among immigrants, who began to swell the ranks of organized labour.[54] Through its support for the JLC, labour had become one of the most outspoken advocates for tolerance and fair practices in the country.

As early as 1946, the Canadian Jewish Congress (CJC) had committed itself to pursuing the realization of fair employment practices legislation in Ontario. Co-operation between the Association for Civil Liberties and the labour committees in Toronto was essential to the campaign for anti-discrimination legislation. With such prominent members as Sandwell, Andrew Brewin, Charles Millard, and Rabbi Abraham Feinberg who had access to members of the government, the Association for Civil Liberties was the ideal front-runner for the coalition. The Association for

Civil Liberties could provide the Kaplansky network with a group of middle-class, non-communist advocates of racial equality with access to Canada's political elite. Meanwhile, the Kaplansky network enjoyed access to the resources of organized labour. Kaplansky provided the funds and resources for public opinion polls, research, publications, and sending delegations to Toronto.[55] The alliance soon proved successful. As noted in the previous chapter, Ontario led the country in passing anti-discrimination legislation thanks to the efforts of activists from groups like the JLC and the Association for Civil Liberties.

The campaign for anti-discrimination legislation was clear evidence of the small but critical role played by rights associations in the early human rights movement. Throughout the 1940s, rights associations had been at the forefront of numerous campaigns against human rights violations. These primarily white, male, middle-class organizations were composed of people who were themselves occasionally targets of state oppression, especially political radicals or socialists who were victims of the Padlock Act and other draconian measures. Beginning in the late 1940s and culminating in their efforts during the 1950s in securing anti-discrimination legislation, rights associations made their mark less as vehicles for voicing the discontent of victims of rights violations and more as allies for victims seeking redress. Whether it was supporting a coalition to challenge the deportation orders or providing the JLC with access to the corridors of power, rights associations could be valuable allies in the struggle for social justice.

A National Rights Association

Social movements often produce national organizations, and this was no less the case with the human rights movement. Over the years the human rights movement has inspired the creation of hundreds of national organizations, from the National Action Committee on the Status of Women to the National Black Coalition. The attraction towards forming a national body is obvious: in a federal system certain powers are reserved for the federal state, and a national body is in a strong position to complement the work of local groups. Simple geography dictates that having a social movement organization in Ottawa will not only offer activists greater access to the corridors of power but also help link people across a vast territory. Rights associations, however, have historically struggled to create a national body. As noted above, attempts to create a national rights association in the 1940s floundered due to ideological divisions between communists and social democrats.

By the 1950s, most of the rights associations that had emerged since the war were largely inactive or defunct. The Vancouver CCLU, CLAW, OCLA, and MCLA had quickly dissolved. The Association for Civil Liberties had been formed out of members from CLAT eager to create a national civil liberties association, but it never expanded outside Toronto. Among the leadership were Toronto lawyers

Irving Himel and Andrew Brewin (future New Democratic Party MP) as well as Sandwell and Charles Millard of the United Steelworkers of America. They expended most of their energies combatting restrictive covenants, censorship, and police powers, while agitating for provincial anti-discrimination legislation and a bill of rights.[56]

One of the requirements for membership in the Association for Civil Liberties was not having membership in any other civil liberties association, a measure designed to exclude communists. The League for Democratic Rights was formed in 1950 out of a merger of the Civil Rights Union of Toronto (formerly the ECCR), the newly formed Montreal Civil Liberties Union, and a group in Timmins. As was the case with the Association for Civil Liberties, the League for Democratic Rights was an attempt to form a national rights association, but one inclusive of communists. In this regard, the League was more successful than its liberal counterpart. With funding coming in from chapters as far away as Vancouver and Halifax, the League could legitimately claim to be the closest manifestation to a national rights association the country had ever seen. But it was a short-lived initiative that was largely unsuccessful in most of its campaigns.[57] The fact is that neither the Association for Civil Liberties nor the League for Democratic Rights were highly effective. Whether a symptom of Cold War politics or their choice of issues, it was the Association for Civil Liberties and its ability to ally with other organizations that made it the more effective of the two groups.

To find the beginnings of a stable and effective national rights association in Canada, it is necessary to go a bit further afield. True, the National Committee on Human Rights (NCHR) and the Jewish Labour Committee were not, by definition, rights associations. In addition to not being self-identified human rights or civil liberties associations, rights associations are defined as independent groups that did not represent a specific constituency. The NCHR and the JLC were intimately tied with the labour movement. Support for the JLC in particular came primarily from working-class organizations, and the mandate of both organizations was undeniably influenced by the priorities of organized labour. When rights associations across Canada attempted to form a national group in the 1940s (and, later, in the 1960s), no one thought to call either the NCHR or the JLC to sign up. Yet their willingness to advocate on behalf of all individuals and to establish a national network of human rights committees merits a brief comment on their contribution to the human rights movement alongside rights associations. Moreover, the labour movement was a powerful force in the early human rights movement. By the fifties, combined with the efforts of the Jewish Labour Committee, which had become integral to labour's human rights activities since the 1950s, labour's efforts represented the most well-organized and prolific national non-state human rights program.

When the Trades and Labour Council and the Canadian Congress of Labour merged in 1957 to form the Canadian Labour Congress (CLC), each had its own human rights committee with mandates to battle racial discrimination in the labour movement.[58] A new national committee for human rights was formed following the merger. The NCHR's mandate was to focus on the "elimination of racial and religious discrimination in all areas of Canadian society and the promotion of equality of opportunity in employment, housing, and public accommodation for all residents of Canada."[59] The NCHR worked with local and regional human rights committees in the labour councils and federations to campaign for anti-discrimination legislation, education, and research; investigated cases of discrimination; and worked with governments and non-governmental organizations to promote tolerance and fair practices. By 1957, seven municipal labour councils with human rights committees were located in Nova Scotia, Ontario, Quebec, Manitoba, and British Columbia.[60] Provincial labour federations in British Columbia, Manitoba, Ontario, and Quebec also had their own human rights committees. The role of the NCHR was to coordinate the activities of these various labour committees and advise the CLC executive on how best to lobby the federal government.

Most of the NCHR's work in the fifties and early sixties involved funding local labour committees. Through the CLC it was also able to secure an amendment to the National Housing Act to prohibit government contracts to companies that discriminated in their employment practices.[61] When the country was celebrating the International Year for Human Rights (1968), in its most ambitious project yet the CLC funded a newly graduated social worker, Pat Kerwin, to work in Kenora, Ontario. Kenora was one of the poorest regions in Canada, and the Natives residing in reserves around the town lived in deplorable conditions. More than six thousand Aboriginal people inhabited reserves surrounding a city of only twelve thousand people. Alcoholism was rampant, the quality of local housing was poor, there was a lack of basic services such as electricity and telephones, relations with police were strained, and Aboriginals were discriminated against in services and employment in Kenora. As one reporter noted, the town's "principal claim to fame is its Indian problem."[62] By 1963, the average lifespan for a male Aboriginal in the region was thirty-three years, while that for a female Aboriginal was thirty-four years.

The Kenora project was an $11,000 investment by the CLC and proved to be a valuable contribution to the Aboriginals in and around Kenora. Kerwin helped Aboriginals submit complaints to the appropriate agencies and acted as a type of ombudsman with the government, most often through the Department of Indian Affairs, asking for things such as building new houses on reserves, continued employment of Aboriginals in specific government projects, and getting higher rates paid to an Aboriginal corporation for laying gravel. Several projects, from the building of an ice rink to constructing dams to protect wild rice crops, were designed to enhance community activities; chiefs would work to secure the supplies, volunteers from the community would do the work, and the state would offer funding. By the time Kerwin had left in 1970 to work with the CLC's Department of Social Action and Community Affairs, he had convinced the federal government to fund one staff person in the region to work with the Aboriginals and to assess their needs. Eventually, the project expanded to a staff of eighteen people, who operated out of Kenora.[63]

The Kenora project was a unique initiative and was never replicated despite its apparent success. Part of the reason why Kenora was never repeated lies with the CLC's declining interest in channelling scarce resources into human rights activism after 1968. As the leader of the labour movement in Canada, the CLC continued to play a significant role in lobbying for rights-related issues. The CLC was one of the few organizations outside Quebec to oppose the use of the War Measures Act in 1970, and it continued to lobby on issues including abortion, capital punishment, wiretapping, RCMP activities, and the federal Human Rights Act. But the NCHR was unquestionably playing a diminished role. Its publication, *Human Rights Review,* would be discontinued in 1977, and around the same time the CLC stopped providing grants to the provincial labour committees. While its advisory role to the CLC executive on human rights issues continued, and remains today, the new Department of Social Action and Community Affairs (created in 1970) took over responsibility for a variety of human rights issues, notably Indian affairs.[64] By the late 1970s a separate women's bureau had been created, taking even more responsibility away from the NCHR. Whereas the labour movement had been one of the most vocal advocates of an entrenched bill of rights in the 1940s and 1950s, it was absent from the special joint committees on the Constitution in 1970 and 1981 when hundreds of other groups presented. With the exception of a few organizations, most notably the Canadian Civil Liberties Association, the CLC had virtually no relationship with any rights association.[65]

The decline of the NCHR was linked with the parallel disintegration of the JLC. Since the JLC had combined the human rights work of the CLC and the Canadian Jewish Congress in the 1950s to combat discrimination, the activities of labour and the JLC were intimately connected. Such was the success of the JLC by 1960 that Frank Scott was led to state he knew "of no single body in the whole of Canada doing as much continuous and consistent work for civil liberties."[66] At the heart of the JLC's human rights program was the work of its labour committees to combat racial intolerance. Another noted civil liberties lawyer in the sixties claimed that "every major effort to get civil rights legislation, most of the leading cases and surveys, have been organized and initiated by one of our labour committees for human rights."[67] The JLC virtually monopolized labour's human rights program; reports of the NCHR were simply verbatim reports of local JLC committees. With operations in five urban areas by 1959 (Vancouver, Winnipeg, Windsor, Toronto, and Montreal), the JLC had a large network of rights associations. For most of the fifties and sixties the JLC-CJC alliance remained a powerful force in the slowly evolving human rights movement and was the country's closest approximation of a national rights association.

Activists in the JLC were involved in some of the most comprehensive anti-discrimination battles in Canada. In Montreal, the United Council for Human Rights (the JLC's local labour committee) regularly badgered the provincial government to pass a bill of rights. In 1962, Alan Borovoy was briefly dispatched to Halifax to help organize a human rights committee to deal with one of the most blatant examples of racial segregation in Canada: Africville. A study published in the same year found that, in this Halifax suburb of several hundred African Canadians (which included only two white families), 35 percent of residents earned less than $1,000 annually in wages. Six to nine people lived in the average Africville household (compared to two to three in Halifax), and it was not unusual for a home to be without running water or public sewage disposal, requiring residents to use wells and outside toilets.[68] Through Borovoy, the JLC played a marginal but constructive role in helping the residents of Africville seek fair compensation. He gave speeches, met with reporters in his hotel room, spoke before city council, and created a local JLC committee to help the impoverished African-Canadian residents of Africville who were being forcibly relocated by the municipal government. Alongside the JLC's work with Aboriginals, the Africville project was consistent with the group's desire to help empower minorities to fight discrimination and to defend their interests. The most active committee in the country was easily the Ontario Labour Committee for Human Rights. In his time with the Ontario committee Borovoy resolved dozens of cases of discrimination across the province and organized a large number of surveys to highlight instances of discrimination.

By the early 1970s, the work of organized labour and the JLC was eclipsed by a burgeoning number of rights associations following the creation of new groups surrounding the International Year for Human Rights and the maturing of rights associations created in the sixties. None of the labour committees was active after 1972, and, although the JLC national committee was revived in the late 1970s, it was a shadow of its former self. The JLC was effectively moribund by the mid-1970s, and the NCHR, whose main activity was consulting the CLC executive and supporting the JLC, followed the latter into obscurity.

If there is any single event linked with the decline of the JLC, it would be the decision of Alan Borovoy to quit as director in 1968 and join the Canadian Civil Liberties Association (CCLA). It was a symbolic switch, given how rights associations were slowly eclipsing the work of the JLC. Borovoy had agreed to leave the Toronto section to take over leadership of the national JLC in 1967, but it struggled to find a replacement for him in Ontario, a clear sign of an organization on the decline. In addition, while the number of labour committees alone would suggest that the JLC continued to be a dynamic organization into the sixties, this was in large part an illusion. At one point, Borovoy was the associate director of the NCHR; the director of the JLC; and the staff person for the Ontario Labour Committee for Human Rights (OLCHR), the human rights committees of the Ontario Federation of Labour, and the Toronto and District Labour Council. These five committees were in effect doing all the same work out of one office in Toronto led by a single individual who would don whatever "hat" was most appropriate to the situation.[69] Borovoy's predecessor as director of the JLC, David Orlikow, an NDP MP by the 1960s, agreed to return and take temporary control of the JLC after Borovoy's departure. It was readily apparent that Orlikow could not devote much time to the JLC, and for years he struggled to find a suitable replacement. Not only had the JLC lost its most dynamic activist, but the NCHR had also begun conducting its own human rights activities and had stopped working with the JLC.[70]

Demographic factors and changing attitudes towards minorities further contributed to the fall of the JLC. Whereas the Jewish working class had been a major force in establishing the JLC and the Joint Public Relations Committee in the 1940s, it was a declining constituency by the 1970s.[71] James Walker has also recently suggested that the nature of the "problem" the JLC was designed to combat had changed. The JLC had been created to deal with discrimination derived from pathologically prejudiced individuals (thus necessitating anti-discrimination legislation to ban such behaviour), but by the seventies discrimination was increasingly characterized as "institutional racism" or "systemic racism."[72] As a result, a new set of strategies and organizations was needed to deal with more systemic forms of discrimination.

But perhaps the most convincing explanation for the decline of the JLC was simply that it had accomplished many of its goals. Canada was no haven of tolerance by the seventies, but overt racism was clearly on the decline. Anti-discrimination legislation had been passed in every province and would soon be implemented at the federal level; most of the provinces had active human rights commissions, several with full-time staff. For more than twenty years the labour committees of the JLC had been fighting discrimination, and it could be fairly said that at the time of its demise, racism in employment, services, and housing was at a historic low.

For the human rights movement the 1950s was, to say the least, a watershed. Organized labour had emerged as the most powerful force within the human rights movement, and the Jewish Labour Committee, by the early 1960s, could honestly claim to be one of the leading forces for promoting tolerance in the country. At the same time, however, in their success lay the seeds of their decline. Human rights commissions were doing much of the work the JLC had done years earlier. By the late sixties it became increasingly apparent that the JLC had lost its lustre, and no other organization could take up the mantle of a national rights association; instead, out of this decade would emerge a series of local rights associations that were destined to have a deep impact in Canada.

4
Social Movement Organizations: A Brief Introduction

A typical strategy employed by activists and advocacy groups is to claim to speak on behalf of people they have never met. In truth, few organizations have historically had a legitimate claim to speak on behalf of a majority of the people who adhere to the principles of any movement. Unfortunately, many scholars therefore consider the study of organizations as a distraction from what they see as the real transformation occurring during the sixties; namely, the formation of new cultural codes.[1] Such disregard for the study of organizations ignores the important historical shift that began in the sixties with the rise of professional social movement organizations (SMOs) in unprecedented numbers. A strong argument can be made that SMOs, such as the four case studies presented in the following chapters, can tell us a great deal about the nature of a social movement.

Classical social movement theories view social movements as deviant behaviour or, to borrow from Emile Durkheim, as expressions of *anomie*. More recently, scholars of social movements have premised their work on the recognition that social movements are the product of normal (non-deviant) social behaviour. Social movements are a typical and healthy part of any society. A key subject in the sociological literature arising from resource mobilization theory is the study of formal organizations as "carriers of social movements." Mayer Zald, John McCarthy, Jo Freeman, Doug McAdam, R.A. Cloward, and Francis Fox Piven are among those scholars who have led the field in the study of professional social movement organizations, particularly in the Untied States.[2]

Resource mobilization theorists have attempted to explain the tremendous expansion in the number of social movements and SMOs in the sixties and seventies, particularly in the United States. This development, a historically unique phenomenon, is less the result of a confluence of specific issues than it is of structural changes. American society, as well as Canadian society, was increasingly wealthy by the 1960s, and the middle class was expanding. Affluence creates discretionary income, which can support social movements. Educational attainment and economic success also led larger numbers of people from the middle class to participate in voluntary associations and political activities. While the working class may have had as much leisure time as the middle class, the latter enjoyed greater discretionary income, which allowed it to participate more in SMOs (i.e., through dues instead of direct participation). Further resources were increasingly available through foundations, churches, and governments, which, since the sixties, have provided more funding for SMOs than ever before. Finally, new technologies allowed the media to have a disproportionate impact in the formation of various organizations designed to encourage individuals to participate in social movements. Television brought riots in Alabama and police violence in Georgia to the homes of millions of Americans whose support for a movement no longer depended on personal experience and immediate situational context. Thus, the expansion of social movement activity during this period was a result of structural changes that allowed movements and organizations to thrive.

SMOs are composed of various classes of participants, from *adherents,* who embrace the goals of the movement, to *constituents,* who also provide resources. Professional SMOs draw most of their resources from a membership base with which they have limited contact, and they are composed of a full-time expert staff, whose central objective is to ensure the group's survival. Media campaigns, mass mailings, and other activities allow groups to mobilize support and encourage adherents to become constituents. Activities such as these will inevitably lead to competition among SMOs for a finite number of resources. The lack of face-to-face interaction with adherents or constituents requires SMOs to place a priority on public education campaigns, or tools such as the media and mass mailings, in order to spread their message.[3]

Professionals (lawyers, doctors, social workers, journalists, professors, etc.) played a central role in leading the second generation of rights associations. One of the reasons for the preponderance of professionals in SMOs generally is the power of experts in contemporary debates on issues such as abortion or human rights. It is a feature of contemporary movements that they depend on expert opinion: "Analysing the interplay of causes, costs, consequences, and options requires extensive knowledge of esoteric subjects, unavailable to even relatively well-educated laymen. In modern societies experts play a role in defining facts and issues for many movements, from tax redistribution to the impact of pornography on individual behaviour."[4]

SMOs have become the institutional forum for mobilizing resources, including labour or money, and expressing grievances arising from a social movement. An SMO is not, in itself, a movement, but an SMO and the movement's grassroots adherents form an important dynamic. Jo Freeman explains the importance of studying SMOs in order to understand social movements:

A social movement has one or more core organizations in a penumbra of people who engage in spontaneous supportive behavior which the core organizations can often mobilize but less often control. When there is spontaneous behavior with only embryonic organization, there may be a premovement phenomena awaiting the right conditions to become a movement, but there is no movement per se ... An organization that can mobilize only its own members, and whose members mobilize only when urged to action by their organisation, is lacking a key characteristic of movements. Regardless of whether structure or spontaneity comes first, or if they appear simultaneously, the important point is that both must exist.[5]

The following case studies are presented as social movement organizations that are a manifestation of the human rights movement. By the end of the seventies, more than forty rights associations had been independently formed across the country. These groups, which had few ties to each other, were linked by the ideas and beliefs born of the human rights movement.[6]

SMOs, like traditional interest groups, generally pursue their interests against the state. There are some exceptions. As Mayer N. Zald and John D. McCarthy note, SMOs "include in some degree radical and clandestine terrorist groups, retreatist sects that revalue the world, reform-oriented political action groups, and interest groups aimed at changing a law or policy to benefit its members."[7] Becki Ross has produced a detailed history of the Lesbian Organization of Toronto, a seventies organization composed mainly of "small friendship circles of largely young, white, middle-class lesbian feminists [which] set out to create social and support-oriented settings wherein they could explore the precious opportunity to come out and invent themselves anew."[8] The purpose of LOOT was to provide lesbians with a visible presence in the community and to challenge dominant heterosexual cultural mores. Notwithstanding some rare exceptions, however, most SMOs either directly or indirectly engage with the state.

To be sure, SMOs consider policy or legislative change a victory, but activism takes a myriad of forms, and not all SMOs will use litigation or lobbying to achieve social change. SMOs employ a variety of strategies and tactics to get their message across to the public, and, at times, promoting tolerance or understanding is more valuable than legislative success. Bill Ratner and William K. Carroll have compared three different SMOs in Vancouver to demonstrate how each of the three groups employed radically different tactics and strategies for change. End Legislated Poverty, an umbrella organization for anti-poverty groups, attempts to empower the poor and shine light on their plight through a variety of tactics, including rallies, picketing, boycotts, letter-writing campaigns, leafleting, producing media (e.g., newsletters), street theatre, and social events. British Columbia's Coalition of People with Disabilities condemns the marginalization of disabled people and lobbies policy makers through position papers and briefs. In an attempt to undermine the normative assumptions attached to disabled/abled, the disability group avoids affirming a distinctive disabled identity, which stands in marked contrast to the objectives of the Centre. The Centre is a service-oriented organization that provides a physical space for promoting gay/lesbian/bi/transsexual identity. Activists encourage activities that promote a common identity in order to empower sexual minorities and to raise their self-respect in a society in which many face discrimination and marginalization. The Centre offers peer counselling, a library, a speakers' bureau, a legal clinic, youth and coming-out groups, and a state-funded health clinic that provides HIV and sexually transmitted disease tests.[9]

Ratner and Carroll's study is an example of the "dual strategy" model employed by many social movement organizations born since the sixties. A key feature of social movement activism, encouraged and organized by SMOs, is direct action. Environmentalists, for instance, have spiked trees or chained themselves to trees to protest clear-cut logging and to "create dramatic media footage that can be used to promote the values of the movement." Instead of "conforming to the ideal type description of social movement political behaviour, many movements may follow a dual strategy of influencing the state and society. Environmental groups may lobby government while engaging in activities that are designed to influence public opinion and to change social attitudes."[10] Dual strategies have the potential to be far more effective than conservative state-oriented tactics, which are at the mercy of policy makers and do not lead to mobilizing large numbers of people for political action and consciousness raising.

A critical aspect of social movement activity, therefore, is grassroots mobilization and a willingness to employ direct action in conjunction with traditional interest group tactics. SMOs, which are central to mobilizing the resources and adherents of a social movement, are an integral part of this process. As Naomi Black has pointed out in her analysis of the Voice of Women, SMOs employ a mix of strategies. Some of the Voice of Women's tactics included anti-nuclear vigils, protest marches, international conferences, knitting clothes for children in North Vietnam, and boycotting war toys. Several of these activities were designed to promote a culture of pacifism or to help victims of war, while others were directly oriented towards the state. At one point, the group sought to pressure the Canadian government to oppose nuclear testing by presenting officials with thousands of baby teeth to demonstrate the impact of the fallout from nuclear testing.[11] The success of the Voice of Women relied not on its ability to develop a small core group of professional experts working the system but, rather, on a host of strategies of which a key factor was mobilizing and engaging with large numbers of people. Warren Magnusson has identified similar strategies in other SMOs; the Raging Grannies (peace activists), for instance, focus less on the state and more on promoting their political and cultural sensibilities to others.[12]

SMOs are thus not predisposed to working directly through political and legal institutions, even if their objective is legislative change. In fact, several social movement scholars have questioned the inevitability of SMOs' adopting conservative tactics. In their study of SMOs in the United States, Roberta Ash Garner and Mayer N. Zald have concluded that SMOs employ both radical and conservative tactics, and the direction taken by an individual SMO depends on internal and external developments. Similar conclusions have been reached by Stephen W. Beach, Joseph

R. Gusfield, and William A. Gamson, to name a few. In his study of tenants associations in New York, David P. Gillespie demonstrates how the decision to avoid using radical tactics (e.g., mass rent strikes) in favour of conservative tactics (e.g., litigation and bargaining with individual landlords) was the result of a conscious decision by activists regarding the feasibility of radical tactics in a particular situation.[13]

One of the most important advances in social movement studies over the past generation has thus been to highlight the important (if not central) role of SMOs in social movements. By studying the organizational manifestation of a social movement, historians can extrapolate many of the goals and objectives of a particular movement as well as how a movement's principles are shaped by historical context. This framework is a useful guide for placing rights associations within the larger context of the social movement industry in Canada. Rights associations were typical of the professional SMOs that proliferated across North America in the sixties and seventies and that were influenced by such factors as rising educational levels, an expanding middle class, state funding for advocacy groups, and new technologies.

Social movement theory also provides a useful framework for analyzing the strategies and tactics of advocacy groups. Although SMOs are more likely to focus on the state in their attempt to promote social change and to employ conservative tactics such as lobbying and litigation, many organizations have historically employed dual strategies that involve direct action and the mobilization of grassroots activists. In this book, any organization that was a self-identified civil liberties or human rights association, was non-partisan, and was not organized around a specific constituency or issue (e.g., environmental rights) is included under the rubric of "rights association." As social movement scholars have demonstrated, professional SMOs, such as the rights associations examined in the following chapters, had a variety of strategies from which to choose and were not predisposed to conservative tactics by virtue of being organized. And yet, although the definition of "rights association" employed in this book embraces dozens of organizations that had no ties to each other, rights associations did share a significant trait. As the case studies demonstrate, rights associations have rarely embraced the dual strategies utilized by other SMOs and have seldom employed mass mobilization tactics or direct action strategies. The reason for this lies as much in the nature of their advocacy – human rights – as in their organizational form.

5

The British Columbia Civil Liberties Association

The Sons of Freedom was a minor sect of the Doukhobours in southwestern British Columbia, at most numbering a couple of hundred members. Zealous traditionalists, they rejected materialism and encouraged their Doukhobour brethren to adopt a more religious lifestyle and avoid the trappings of modern society in everything from exploiting animals to the use of electricity. This "encouragement" went far beyond simply adopting a particular lifestyle for themselves: bombing and destroying Doukhobours' property, burning symbols of materialism, and engaging in nude parades to demonstrate Adamite simplicity were among the Freedomites' more notorious activities from the 1930s to the 1960s as they waged a virtual guerrilla war in southwestern British Columbia.

From 1923 to 1962, the Freedomites were responsible for over 1,100 arsons and bombings. The federal government and the RCMP struggled to deal with the violence, beginning with imposing harsh sentences of up to three years in jail for nude paraders and, in a series of raids between 1954 and 1960, seizing Doukhobour children, who were then sent to state institutions. But the violence continued, culminating in a string of 259 bombings and arsons in 1962 alone in the Kootenay region.[1] On 24 March 1962, the RCMP's new tactic was revealed. One hundred and fifty officers (out of total of seven hundred stationed in British Columbia) raided the town of Krestova to arrest fifty-seven members of the Fraternal Council of the Sons of Freedom, having already detained ten others and issued warrants for three more.[2] The charge: conspiracy to intimidate the Parliament of Canada and the Legislature of British Columbia.

The Freedomites' tactics had earned them little public sympathy, despite the loss of their children and the imprisonment of hundreds of nude paraders. Coverage in the *Vancouver Sun* and the *Province* in 1962 suggests that the media approved of the police's determination to contain the sect through rigid law enforcement. The decision to use the extraordinary charge of intimidating Parliament and the Legislature, however, had lasting repercussions in the province long after the Freedomites had disappeared. In reaction to the raids, a civil liberties committee was formed in Vancouver to raise money for the defence of those Doukhobours charged. The British Columbia Civil Liberties Association (BCCLA) was thus born from a concern over excessive police powers and the state repression of an unpopular minority group, a dominant theme in the organization's activities for the next twenty years.

The BCCLA was the first attempt to form a civil liberties association in the province since the demise of the Canadian Civil Liberties Union's Vancouver chapter. It began as a small collection of academics meeting in the halls of the University of British Columbia (UBC) and has evolved into an outspoken and respected community group active in the defence of individual rights. From the perspective of the BCCLA, the sixties and seventies was not only a period in which the expanding activities of the state threatened fundamental freedoms but it was also a period in which ideas about rights were changing.

Each case study highlights several key human rights issues. The BCCLA, for instance, dedicated itself to defending against censorship, the use of the War Measures Act in 1970, abuse of police powers, and compulsory treatment of drug addicts. Each controversy offers insights into the strategies deployed by rights associations and acts as a window onto how groups such as the BCCLA struggled to understand and apply complex ideas about rights to concrete social issues. Each case study chapter also touches on five key themes: strategies for change; a national rights association; state funding; relations with other social movement organizations; and ideologies of rights. In the case of the BCCLA, its single-minded focus on civil and political rights distinguished it from advocates who embraced a broader conception of rights. Moreover, the association's total dependence on state funding, coupled with its aggressive attack on the state's human rights record, supports the contention that social movement organizations are not necessarily co-opted by state funding. Finally, the history of the BCCLA tells us a great deal about the role of the legal system as an agent for social change in the seventies. While the association would prove highly successful in many of its endeavours, it chafed at the inability of the courts to act as an effective forum for the defence of fundamental freedoms.

A New Era Begins: The Proliferation of Rights Associations

The creation of the BCCLA in 1962 inaugurated a new era of advocacy on the part of rights associations. Between 1960 and 1982, a wave of rights associations swept across the country; at least forty-one organizations were created during this period, compared to scarcely a dozen in the first generation.[3]

Some of these organizations barely lasted a year, whereas others continue to be active today. Three of the four case studies in this book – the BCCLA (1962), the Ligue des droits de l'homme (1963), and the Canadian Civil Liberties Association (1964) – were among the first groups to emerge in the sixties. By 1970, civil liberties associations had popped up in Halifax, Windsor, Ottawa, Victoria, and Hamilton. Within a decade, at least one civil liberties association had been active at one point in time in every province. Although their origins were far from similar and few of these organizations had any ties with each other, it is interesting to note that most civil liberties organizations were created in reaction to specific human rights abuses on the part of the state. For instance, the Civil Liberties Association-National Capital Region was formed in response to police harassment of youths who were selling an alternative newspaper.[4] Police had decided to harass and seize copies of a paper called *Octopus*, which was being distributed on the Sparks Street Mall, a pedestrian walkway in downtown Ottawa. Although in theory no one could peddle or conduct business on the mall without a permit from the Pedestrian Mall Authority, in practice the mainstream newspapers never bothered to obtain one. *Octopus* was the only paper targeted by officials, who prosecuted people for illegally distributing it on the mall. After twenty months of negotiations with the mall authority, the capital's civil liberties association was finally able to convince the latter to allow *Octopus* to be distributed so long as the vendors did not harass people.[5] Such stories characterize the early history of most civil liberties associations.

In contrast, many human rights associations began as an initiative of the state. The International Year for Human Rights, the twentieth anniversary of the UDHR, would leave an indelible mark on Canada's human rights movement. Human rights committees with a mandate to promote this anniversary were established in every province by either the federal or provincial government, and from these committees was born a new breed of rights associations. These new groups quickly severed their ties with the state and became non-governmental organizations. Unlike their civil liberties counterparts, organizations such as the Newfoundland Labrador Human Rights Association embraced a broader conception of individual rights. As the case studies demonstrate, the ideological divisions between human rights and civil liberties associations would prove to have significant repercussions.

By 1970, the enthusiasm surrounding the anniversary celebrations led to the formation of human rights associations in Vancouver, Edmonton, Saskatoon, Charlottetown, Winnipeg, Owen Sound, Yellowknife, and Kitchener-Waterloo. Soon enough, others followed suit, and rights associations were created in London, Saint John, Sudbury, Whitehorse, Fort McMurray, Lethbridge, and Grand Prairie. Some of these groups emerged in the wake of the anniversary, while others were a grassroots response to a perceived human rights violation. A group of young men and women in Edmonton, many of whom were parents, were disgusted to learn that some schools in their city still practised corporal punishment (e.g., striking students' hands with rulers) and formed a civil liberties group to successfully put a stop to the practice. In London, Ontario, a law professor at the University of Western Ontario, Carl Grindstaff, discovered upon reading his morning paper that the local police had decided to arrest ten people for shoplifting near Christmas and keep them in jail over the holidays as an example to other potential shoplifters. Grindstaff was outraged at the decision to imprison people for stealing forty dollars' worth of merchandise; he called together a group of leading activists in the city to form a civil liberties association, which unsuccessfully sought a Writ of Prohibition to prevent further detentions for shoplifting.[6]

And this was just the beginning. The number of rights associations in the sixties and seventies was staggering compared to the number in the first generation. British Columbia, in particular, proved to be a hotbed of human rights activism. People came together in their homes or local meeting halls to form rights associations in Powell River, Kamloops, Penticton, Quesnel, Prince George, Comox-Strathcona-Courtenay, Kelowna, and Williams Lake as well as in the north-central and south Okanagan regions. These rights associations identified themselves as either civil liberties or human rights groups or, in some cases, as both. The ideological divisions between civil liberties and human rights associations were no more evident than in the decisions by several rights associations to pay homage to both concepts (e.g., the Alberta Human Rights and Civil Liberties Association and the New Brunswick Human Rights and Civil Liberties Association).

Several rights associations also created chapters. By the early 1970s, the CCLA alone had affiliates in Fredericton, London, Moncton, Kingston, Regina, Saint John, Winnipeg, and Timmins. Not to be outdone, provincial rights associations in Newfoundland (Northern Labrador, Gander, and Corner Brook); Nova Scotia (Pictou County, Truro, Cape Breton, and Yarmouth); Prince Edward Island (Summerside); New Brunswick (St. Quentin-Kedgwick, Dalhousie, Caraquet, Bathurst, Tracadie, Shippegan); Quebec (Quebec City, Estrie, and Sept-Îles); Manitoba (Brandon); Saskatchewan (Moose Jaw and Esterhazy); and Alberta (Calgary, Lethbridge) attempted to create their own chapters. The BCCLA refused to create chapters and, instead, encouraged the formation of independent associations across British Columbia. Several chapters would manage to survive the test of time and become independent organizations; however, by and large, such efforts proved ineffective. Barely a dozen rights associations remained active by the early 1980s. The proliferation of rights association was unique to the seventies.

Table 5.1

Individual paid memberships in civil liberties and human rights associations, 1971-77

	1971	1972	1973	1974	1975	1976	1977
Newfoundland-Labrador HRA	40	120	120	119	130	125	117
Prince Edward Island CLA	NF	100	65	80	35	119	250
Nord-est du Nouveau Brunswick	NF	300	200	400	250	30	30
Sud-est du Nouveau Brunswick	NF	NF	1,500	10	10	IN	IN
CCLA,* Fredericton	60	40	60	35	52	IN	10

◄ *Table 5.1*

	1971	1972	1973	1974	1975	1976	1977
Nova Scotia CL and HRA	233	230	75	125	120	IN	IN
Ligue des droits de l'homme	350	300	550	750	750	738	487
CLA, Cornwall	NF	NF	20	55	30	25	20
CLA, National Capital Region	160	150	38	72	79	68	113
CLA, Hamilton	40	20	92	90	90	150	NA
CCLA,* Toronto	2,000	4,000	2,750	4,000	4,000	3,000	3,000
CCLA,* London	20	20	IN	6	20	IN	IN
Kitchener-Waterloo HR Caucus	NF	NF	14	35	30	40	27
HR Committee, Sudbury Region	NA	30	40	IN	35	25	NA
Owen Sound HR Committee	20	20	IN	IN	IN	IN	IN
Kenora Area Civil Liberties Group	NF	NF	NF	NF	NA	IN	IN
CCLA,* Windsor	75	50	IN	IN	10	10	10
CCLA,* Manitoba	200	100	40	10	IN	IN	IN
Manitoba CL and HRA	NF	NF	NF	NF	NA	NA	NA
Winnipeg CLA	NF	NF	NF	NF	NF	NF	14
Saskatchewan Association on HR	75	75	200	235	475	456	480
CCLA,* Regina	60	60	75	18	12	12	NA
Alberta HR and CLA	200	200	250	150	250	50	75
Alberta HR and CLA, Lethbridge	NF	NF	25	24	IN	25	IN
Fort McMurray HR Council	NF	NF	NF	NF	NF	NF	20
Lethbridge Citizens HR Council	NF	NF	NF	NF	NF	NF	25
British Columbia CLA	500	450	500	463	364	268	259
British Columbia HR Council	NF	45	80	72	103	100	85
Williams Lake HR and CLA	NF	NF	30	30	30	7	36
Comox-Strathcona CLA	NF	NF	NF	NF	41	IN	IN
Quesnel CLA and HRA	NF	NF	NF	30	70	18	60
Kamloops Civil Liberties Society	NF	NF	NF	NF	22	41	35
Abbottsford CLA	NF	NF	NF	25	IN	IN	IN
Powell River CLA	NF	NF	NF	NF	NF	57	29
South Okanagan CLA	NF	NF	NF	NA	26	38	100
North Central CLA	NF	NF	NF	NF	NF	NA	NA
Fair Practices Comm., Whitehorse	NF	NF	NF	NA	IN	IN	IN
Yukon HRA, Whitehorse	NF	NF	NF	NF	NA	IN	IN

* Chapters of the Canadian Civil Liberties Association.
HRA: Human Rights Association.
CLA: Civil Liberties Association.
NF: Not Formed / NA: Not Available / IN: Inactive/Defunct.
Source: Rights and Freedoms, no. 21, March 1976, and no. 25, March 1977.

The Birth of the BCCLA

On 9 December 1962, a public meeting held at International House on the campus of the University of British Columbia, attended by eighty people, led to the creation of the BCCLA.[7] The original Board of Directors consisted mainly of university professors and lawyers, led by Philip Hewett, a well-known Anglican minister in Vancouver. They immediately established a committee to examine the Freedomite issue and created a "Doukhobour defence fund" for litigation and investigation into the conditions at Agassiz prison, where at least 104 Doukhobour, men, women, and children were held.

The conspiracy charges levelled against the Fraternal Council had been dismissed months prior to the formal creation of the BCCLA. In July 1962, at a preliminary hearing, Sid Simons, one of the group's founders, convinced a judge to dismiss the charges because there was no direct evidence of a conspiracy and the mere association with the council was not sufficient to warrant conviction or even a trial.[8] More than one hundred Doukhobours continued to be held at Agassiz prison under deplorable conditions, and the newly minted BCCLA successfully lobbied the provincial government for several early releases. The conspiracy charges were eventually dropped, with no one having been brought to trial.

Academics have long played a key role in the leadership of the BCCLA, and this was reflected in the group's first executive board. Hewett soon stepped down as president due to other commitments and was replaced by James Foulks, a professor of pharmacology at UBC. The remaining executive included John Fornataro (vice-president, professor), Michael Audain (executive secretary, student), Margaret Erickson (recording secretary, housewife), and Fritz Bowers (treasurer, professor).[9] The original constitution limited the group's operations to those "chiefly carried on in the Province of British Columbia" and drew upon the UDHR, French Declaration of the Rights of Man and the bills of rights in the United States, Britain, and Canada as its guiding principles.

A key figure in the association's early history was Reg Robson, a sociology professor at UBC, whose major publications focused on the effectiveness of alcohol treatment centres and the sociological factors affecting professional recruitment for academics and nurses. One of the founders of the association, Robson sat on the Board of Directors well into the 1980s and served in various executive positions, including executive secretary (1969-72, 1978), president (1972-75, 1980-82), and treasurer (1975, 1979). No member was more dedicated than Robson, who served in these various capacities when no one else was available and helped to ensure the viability and institutional memory of the association. He resisted the CCLA's attempts to form a national rights association headquartered in Toronto and played a central role in the creation of a rival organization, the Canadian Federation of Civil Liberties and Human Rights Associations. Robson took the lead in doing media interviews on behalf of the BCCLA during the October Crisis, oversaw the creation of new rights associations across British Columbia, and was a key player in the association's most active campaigns, including its reaction to the Gastown riot and its challenge of the Heroin Treatment Act. It was thanks to his dedication and perseverance that the association thrived and became an effective rights advocate both provincially and nationally.

Robson personified many of the characteristics that defined the BCCLA in its early years. Not only did the organization play host to a cadre of west coast academics but it was also a predominantly male organization. By the early 1980s, the vast majority of the directors were, like Robson, white, middle-class, male professionals living in the Lower Mainland. More than 80 percent of the directors were either lawyers, professors, or social workers, with a scattering of journalists, housewives, and students. Robson had also been active throughout his life in several left-wing causes and, although membership was open to anyone who supported the group's principles and was staunchly non-partisan, the BCCLA was far more likely to attract left-wingers, including future MLA's in the NDP.[10] Harry Rankin, a Vancouver city counsellor and a communist who never joined the Communist Party of Canada, noted the lack of minorities represented on the BCCLA's board and warned the organization against becoming too academic.[11] An editorial in the *Vancouver Sun*, heralding the creation of the BCCLA, similarly cautioned the group that "this academic, left-wing orientation should not be reflected in the causes the [BCCLA] chooses to defend. Trade unionists or Doukhobours ... are not the only people whose liberties are occasionally threatened."[12] Although the BCCLA's activities were never constrained by any kind of partisan bias, its first twenty years were characterized by close ties with the NDP and an inability to construct a leadership structure that reflected the broader community.

"It's simple common sense": Defending Free Speech in British Columbia

Censorship is the most direct challenge to free speech, which is arguably the most fundamental right in a democratic society. And yet censorship was so widespread in Canada by the 1960s that defending free speech occupied the BCCLA for at least a generation.

The provincial government was occasionally active in censorship. The minister of education, for instance, banned Philip Roth's *Defender of the Faith* from being distributed to Grade 12 students in 1967.[13] The film censor was a powerful force for censorship in British Columbia. Under the 1913 Moving Pictures Act, a censor was hired to regulate the distribution and content of films in the province. Section 5 of the act allowed the censor to "permit or absolutely to prohibit the exhibition of any film or slide which it is proposed to exhibit in the Province." Seventy-four films were censored in 1931, although, by the 1960s, only two or three films on average each year were being censored.

Local governments and officials, however, were by far the most prolific censors. Stewart McMorran, the notorious Vancouver city prosecutor with the dubious distinction of having sought a record number of habitual criminal rulings, was equally zealous in clamping down on obscenity. By 1966, McMorran's attempts to use various provisions in the Criminal Code to censor obscene materials in Vancouver had infuriated several local judges, and he was barred from eight of ten magistrate's courts for disrespect and bad behaviour. In 1968, Bill Deverall, the BCCLA's vice-president, defended Doug Hawthorn, who had been indicted for selling Kama Sutra calendars in his Vancouver psychedelic shop.[14] Deverall was a criminal lawyer and a future best-selling novelist whose first novel, *Needles,* pitted a heroin-addicted prosecutor against a psychopathic drug dealer on the streets of Vancouver. In 1969, New Westminster passed a bylaw banning the distribution of newspapers on city streets. In practice, the bylaw did not affect mainstream media such as the *Vancouver Sun* and the *Province,* which were left unmolested while vendors selling alterative papers were harassed and denied licences. The BCCLA announced that it would challenge the bylaw in court but was hard-pressed to catch a police officer enforcing the law in order to take the city to court. Not to be outdone, the association decided to send its own directors to sell alternative newspapers on the street in New Westminster in order to force the Crown prosecutor to act; however, the latter subsequently claimed that the bylaw did not apply to newspapers.[15] Darwin Sigurgeirsson represented the BCCLA in the BC Supreme Court in 1971, when the Court upheld a Surrey bylaw giving the City Council control over special events, a law primarily designed to prohibit rock concerts.[16] As late as 1978-79, Vancouver's mayor was threatening to require licences for merchants selling pornography, and Penticton banned the distribution of pamphlets on its streets.[17] The *Georgia Straight,* in particular, raised the ire of local officials. By 1968 the paper had been banned in New Westminster, Surrey, White Rock, North Vancouver, West Vancouver, Squamish, and Haney.[18]

Producers of potentially obscene or contentious literature and art had to face a myriad of potential obstacles in Vancouver. Under the City Charter, the chief licence inspector had the power to suspend the licence of any business that, in his opinion, was guilty of "gross misconduct."[19] Furthermore, bylaw 2944 provided the chief licence inspector with explicit power to censor theatre: "It shall be deemed cause for the cancellation, suspension or revocation of any license granted, hereunder for any person to produce in any building or place in the City any immoral or lewd theatrical performance or exhibition of any kind, and the Inspector shall have full power to prohibit or prevent any indecent or improper performance or exhibition." Neither the city charter nor the bylaw defined gross misconduct or immoral material, a decision left up to the subjective analysis of the inspector. In a 1969 interview, Chief Licence Inspector Milton Harrel claimed to use "simple common sense" in determining whether a production was obscene.[20] He was also in a position to pressure theatres or newspapers to change their format by simply threatening a ban or the removal of their licence.

It was the censoring of local theatre that eventually cost the chief licence inspector some of his broad powers of censorship. Harrel was targeted by the BCCLA for threatening to remove the licence of David Gardner, who ran the Vancouver Playhouse, if he presented the rock musical *Hair*, whose final scene depicted people in the nude. Despite offers of free legal counsel from the BCCLA, Gardner chose to acquiesce rather than to take on the city, and the play was removed.[21] Inspector Harrel also imposed a fine on the Gallimaufry troop's performance of *The Beard* at the Riverqueen Coffee House. When the proprietors of the Riverqueen were arrested on obscenity charges, the BCCLA provided legal counsel to appeal their convictions.[22] On 8 July 1969, Harrel shut down a production of *Camera Obscura*, a Gallimaufry Theatre production at the Arts Club in which actors wore transparent clothing. In addition to providing the theatre with free legal counsel, the association contacted Charles Fleming (deputy cooperation counsel for Vancouver) in an effort to convince him that the bylaw empowering the inspector to close down theatre productions was ultra vires the city's jurisdiction since it involved the use of federal criminal power. Fleming agreed and suggested to council that the section be rewritten. On 15 July 1969, City Council voted to instruct Fleming to remove theatre censorship from the section in bylaw 2944, thus limiting the power of the licensing inspector. Unfortunately for the BCCLA, it was less successful in having the entire bylaw amended. Harry Rankin, a member of the BCCLA and an alderman, pushed Fleming to further recommend the removal of Section 277(c) dealing with gross misconduct, which Fleming supported and, in turn, recommended to council. Section 277(c), however, was upheld by the provincial Supreme Court, and the censor continued to threaten Gallimaufry with the loss of its operating licence if it did not stop presenting obscene productions.[23]

The private sector had its own role to play in censoring unpopular ideas. In 1970, the *Victoria Times* was unwilling to print articles on homosexuals, and thirteen other papers similarly refused to publish a copy of an article being circulated to papers across the province.[24] In the late 1960s, several store owners in Vancouver agreed to voluntarily remove copies of *Playboy* from their shelves. None of these incidents attracted nearly as much attention, however, as did the BCCLA's challenge to a regulation imposed by the Pacific National Exhibition (PNE) in 1969.

The amusement park passed a regulation in 1969 prohibiting booths that served partisan or political purposes.[25] The BCCLA could accept a ban on political parties if it applied equally to all parties, but it was initially concerned that the regulation could be applied indiscriminately to censor attempts at social activism. Its fears were quickly proven justified. Among those banned from setting up booths at the PNE were the People's Co-operative Bookstore, China Arts, and the Combined University Campaign for Nuclear Disarmament. When the BCCLA was refused a meeting with the PNE Board of Directors, it set up a picket in front of the parade grounds. The picket – and this was the only time the group had ever used such a tactic – was supported by the BC Federation of Labour and the Vancouver Labour Committee for Human Rights (the local JLC committee). It received coverage in the newspapers and television media, particularly once the groups began calling for a labour boycott of the PNE. The picketers directed their criticisms against the PNE as well as against the Vancouver City Council, which provided the grounds free of charge. After the picket was moved to City Hall, Mayor Tom Campbell intervened to mediate the dispute, and the ban was soon lifted.[26] The BCCLA had achieved an important, and very public, victory against censorship.

Despite the BCCLA's success with the PNE, the issue paled in comparison to the virtual war of survival fought by the *Georgia Straight*. In 1970, a Senate committee report on the mass media expressed what could be described as nothing less than utter disgust with the unofficial censorship practised in British Columbia against the *Georgia Straight:*

> There are tens of thousands of people who think Vancouver's underground news-paper, the *Georgia Straight,* is a marvellous publication – provocative, funny, thought-ful, courageous, honest and joyous. There are probably hundreds of thousands of people in Vancouver who, whether or not they've read a copy, think the *Straight* is obscene, immoral, scurrilous, and subversive – an all-round menace to youth. This latter-judgement appears to include most of Vancouver's municipal and law-enforcement Establishment, for the *Straight* has been subjected to intimidation and harassment, both legal and extra-legal, that we can only describe and shocking.[27]

The BCCLA would play a critical role in defending the right of the *Straight* to be distributed in Vancouver.

The *Georgia Straight* was an alternative paper, part of the hippie youth culture that was challenging conformity and authority. Founded in 1967, the paper soon had a circulation of 60,000 to 70,000.[28] One of the paper's founders later admitted to not knowing "any particular reason for the founding beyond a general perva-sive desire to annoy establishment institutions in general and established news-papers in particular. Also, if one wished to be flowery, to provide a local voice for whatever counter-culture exists in Vancouver."[29] According to a more recent ac-count: "The precise circumstances of *Georgia Straight*'s birth, however, remain the subject of grave dispute and much conjecture. Poets were involved in it ... The whole thing might have arisen from a discussion that followed a reading by Leonard Cohen at the University of B.C. ... Drugs were involved. Confusion persists to this day."[30]

On the same day the *Straight*'s office opened (a week after the first issue appeared), the police arrived at the doorstep in a patrol wagon to pick up the publisher, Dan McLeod, to investigate him for vagrancy (a comfortably nebulous charge commonly used by the police to harass undesirables).[31] It took less than six weeks for Mayor Campbell to attack the new paper. He urged the city licensing inspector to use his power under Section 277(c) of the City Charter to suspend the paper for gross misconduct. Campbell described the paper as "filth" and made it clear that "as far as I'm concerned, this was a 'rag' paper; it was a dirty paper; it was being sold to our school children; and I wouldn't tolerate it on the streets any longer." Within weeks the paper was suspended, and the BCCLA unsuccessfully attempted to have the suspension lifted. Justice Thomas Dohm, presiding over the BCCLA's challenge to the suspension order, went so far as to praise the mayor for his actions. The case was appealed before the provincial Appeals Court, with a representative from the attorney general of Canada appearing to defend the *Georgia Straight*. The appellate court decided to ignore their freedom-of-the-press argument and instead voided the suspension on the grounds that the city licensing inspector should have provided a hearing to explain why the paper was suspended. However, the Court's ruling was mooted by an earlier decision of the licensing inspector to lift the ban after he was satisfied the content of the paper had changed.[32]

Not to be deterred, the mayor asked City Council to reinstate the suspension, and when the council refused, at a meeting attended by the BCCLA, he hired a private law firm to consider an injunction. The firm recommended that the mayor wait to see the results of an obscenity charge against the *Straight* in the hopes that they would deter the publishers from allowing contentious material to appear in the paper.[33]

Overturning the suspension in court was only the beginning. During the first two years Dan McLeod, the *Straight*'s publisher, was in a constant battle to keep the paper alive:

Municipalities prohibited the sale of the newspaper on their streets; McLeod and the *Straight*'s vendors sold the paper openly and courted arrest. For poking fun at a judge, the *Straight* was charged with criminal libel, sparking a legal battle that lasted years. For the ribald humour of its comics pages, the *Straight* fought nine obscenity charges. For printing instructions on marijuana-growing, the *Straight* was charged with "inciting to commit an indictable offence." A sex-advice column from a hippie doctor brought four separate obscenity charges. For running an excerpt from a novel, the *Straight* faced another obscenity charge. In March 1968 the *Straight* was found guilty for defamatory libel when it awarded Magistrate Lawrence Eckhardt the Pontius Pilate Certificate of Justice for sending a group of hippies to jail for hanging around outside the courtroom. All this took place within two years of 5 May 1967.[34]

The paper could not even find a local printer to publish the early issues and had to seek out printers in Victoria. The University of British Columbia's bookstore refused to distribute the *Georgia Straight*.[35] In 1969 alone, the paper faced twenty-two criminal charges against its editor and employees.[36]

The BCCLA was not involved in the libel suit but was occasionally successful in having local bans removed. Relations between the BCCLA and the *Straight* were often strained, and the two frequently acted independently in challenging the bans. The BCCLA was still considered by many in Vancouver, including writers for the *Straight*, as a middle-class organization lacking proper representation by women or minorities. Another alternative newspaper in Vancouver, *The Grape*, described the association's meetings as boring and academic, remote from city life, and dominated by Americans, with little interest in social welfare issues.[37] It was thus not uncommon for the *Straight* to refuse the BCCLA's offers of assistance.[38] Nevertheless, in at least one case, the BCCLA provided McLeod with legal counsel to defeat an obscenity charge. In May 1969, McLeod was charged with obscenity under Section 150(1)(a) of the Criminal Code for various pictures published in the *Straight* and two articles entitled "Penis De Milo Created by Cynthia Plaster-Caster," and "Young Man Wants to Meet Women 30 yrs Old for Muffdiving, etc." Thomas Berger defended McLeod and used Fritz Bowers (one of the founders of the BCCLA) to testify to the publication's literary merit. The original trial judge had dismissed the charges because undue exploitation of sex, which formed the basis of the Crown's obscenity charge, was not part of the test established by the Supreme Court. He also refused to rule the pictures published in the *Straight* obscene and "dismissed the charge, having no evidence before him of what the word 'muffdiving' means, and declining to take judicial notice of a word that he has never heard before." The ruling was upheld on appeal, although only grudgingly, by the presiding judge, who held "the view that there will always be those few in society who will continue to abuse civil rights and liberties and to confuse freedom with licence to print anything, forgetting that the rest of society has a right to be protected against unwarranted shock or abuse ... But I find that there is no undue exploitation of sex in the article, and that the article in the context in which it is written does not amount to an obscene publication."[39]

In dismissing the charges in *R. v. McLeod*, Judge Isman also suggested that the city prosecutor, McMorran, was perhaps a little too eager and inconsistent in deciding who to prosecute for obscenity. For the BCCLA and the *Straight*, the reprimand and the dismissal of the charges was just one more victory in a long string of attempts by the state to suppress the newspaper. But censorship could take a myriad of forms in a city with energetic and creative prosecutors. McLeod was soon convicted of growing marijuana and was fearful of providing the police with a reason to charge him with a parole violation. As a result, his lawyers regularly read and censored samples of the *Straight,* while vendors were harassed by the police and accused of vagrancy or drug use.[40]

The mainstream media remained silent throughout most of these developments, perhaps because they cared little for hippies or were intimidated by the possibility of being charged with libel. Their silence led the Senate committee on mass media to comment as follows: "It saddens us to report that most daily papers have been either lukewarm in their editorial approach to this issue, or have ignored it altogether."[41] The coverage provided by the mainstream press in Vancouver was limited to discussing why the *Straight* had been charged with libel, and no critical commentary or discussion on freedom of the press was raised in either the *Vancouver Sun* or the *Province.*[42] It was not until 1973 that Allan Fotheringham, a popular columnist for the *Vancouver Sun,* commented on the court's imposition of a $1,500 fine against the *Georgia Straight.* Fotheringham lamented the inability of the mainstream media to raise their voices against a campaign of injunctions and suits directed at other members of the press: "Some day some scholar interested in the law and its abuse is going to do a serious study of how authorities in this town – particularly [Stewart] McMorran – have attempted to intimidate and to bust the *Straight* by persistent harassment and prosecutions which more often than not failed. The documentation will cause a scandal and everyone will ask what the rest of us were doing – including the newspapers – while this was going on."[43]

The October Crisis
Soon after Berger had successfully appealed the obscenity charge against the *Straight,* the BCCLA found itself embroiled in the October Crisis. Trudeau's decision to invoke the War Measures Act received a quick condemnation from the association, which could find no evidence of a legitimate insurrection or inadequacies in the Criminal Code to justify the use of war powers.[44]

Opposition to the federal government was a bold move, given the amount of support the prime minister's action enjoyed in British Columbia. The same newspapers that had remained silent about attempts to suppress the *Straight* were quick to support the use of war powers. As with most Canadian newspapers, the *Province* and the *Vancouver Sun's* headlines were dominated by the October Crisis from October to December 1970. The *Vancouver Sun,* by far the largest paper in the province and having the highest distribution west of Toronto, offered virtually uncritical support to Trudeau for most of the crisis.[45] The powers were described in a 19 October editorial as a "temporary measure, to be lifted when its purpose is achieved and possibly replaced by a new act designed to stamp out revolutionary violence of the kind typified by the Front de libération du Quebec. The pledge to restore normal democratic liberties when the danger is past is explicit enough for most Canadians to take it on faith." Concerns raised by the BCCLA received little attention in the *Vancouver Sun* (none in the *Province*), although on 22 October the paper noted that it was "disquieting to know so many Canadians have been jailed without probable cause."

Soldiers did not patrol the streets of Victoria, yet the crisis atmosphere caused by the invocation of the War Measures Act was not unfelt in British Columbia. Seven members of the Vancouver Liberation Front, a fringe group sympathetic to the aims of the FLQ, were arrested and detained for distributing copies of the FLQ manifesto in Vancouver.[46] The RCMP also paid a visit to the editors of the University of Victoria's student newspaper and ordered them not to publish a letter written by philosophy professor Ronald Kirby, who claimed that, because he supported the cause of the National Liberation Front in Vietnam, he had to support the FLQ.[47]

The mainstream press reserved their criticism of the use of war powers for two other developments that were closer to home. The first controversy was a minor one. Mayor Campbell proved, once again, his talent for infuriating civil libertarians. In April 1971, he proposed to use the War Measures Act to run hippies and draft dodgers out of town. A few of his colleagues were also eager to exploit the situation. At a City Council meeting, Alderman Halford Wilson introduced a resolution that would have banned public meetings on city-owned property, while various members of the council tried their best to prevent a parade that had been held annually for the previous five years.[48]

Neither the *Vancouver Sun* nor the *Province* had any kind words for such blatant attempts to exploit the situation to pursue interests predating the crisis and totally unrelated to the terrorist activities. The *Vancouver Sun* was particularly virulent in its condemnation, suggesting that "the least responsible reaction to be found anywhere in Canada was that of Vancouver's own mayor. At a time when the country was in the grip of horror, Campbell tried to capitalize on the invoking of the War Measures Act to further his vendetta on local hippies and draft dodgers. His personal politicking with such a sad affair can only be described as damnable."[49] None of the proposals came to fruition.

The second controversy was a great deal more serious. The provincial cabinet, under the leadership of W.A.C. Bennett, passed an order-in-council calling for the dismissal of any teacher who expressed sympathies with the FLQ or who called for the overthrow of a democratically elected government.[50] The order was prompted by the actions of Arthur Olsen, a Dawson Creek high school teacher, who reportedly expressed sympathy for the FLQ.[51] Universities, colleges, and school boards were included in the order, and the implicit threat was that any institution failing to apply the new regulation would lose its grant from the government. In a province so distant from, and untouched by, the October Crisis, the declaration was little more than a show of force by a Social Credit Party that was soon to be defeated in an upcoming election. The papers quickly distanced themselves from the order.

The *Vancouver Sun* characterized the decision as "an overreaction which serves to emphasize the very dangers that Mr. Trudeau was so anxious to guard against," and the *Province* considered the order a far-reaching abuse of human rights.[52]

For the BCCLA, the order and Bennett's threats to refuse grants to schools with teachers sympathetic to the FLQ represented a blatant attack on freedom of speech and offended one of the association's most basic principles. It sought to challenge the validity of the order in court (once again represented by Thomas Berger) and was refused a hearing because the organization had no direct standing. In effect, until someone was actually dismissed under the authority of the order in council, the legislation could not be challenged.[53]

Once again, the courts proved a difficult venue for the defence of fundamental freedoms. The unwillingness of judges to accept interveners was compounded by the court's decision that the regulation could not be challenged until it was applied. Yet, the threat of dismissal alone was an infringement on freedom of speech; the cabinet did not have to dismiss anyone to exercise a degree of control over the rights of teachers to speak freely. While it is unlikely many teachers, if any, were affected by the order, the defeat established a poor precedent for future confrontations between the BCCLA and the cabinet. With the exception of the dismissed obscenity charge against McLeod, the courts had proven to be a limited forum for the defence of civil liberties.

Violence in the Streets: The Gastown Riot

Symbols of authority are often the central target of protest movements. The *Georgia Straight* was used as a forum for criticizing the mainstream press and openly mocking the legitimacy of the courts. The most visible symbol of authority in any society, however, is the police. Limiting the gamut of police powers has been one of the key objectives of civil liberties associations since their inception.

During this period, the BCCLA was the only organization consistently concerned with police-community relations in British Columbia. It was mildly successful in convincing the police to change tactics and accept new procedures, but in most cases the group could only hope to bring public attention to police activities through the press or a court challenge. Suppression of the Sons of Freedom by the RCMP and the provincial government had led to the creation of the BCCLA. The Schuck trial (discussed below) was an attempt by the BCCLA to convince a judge to award damages as a result of abusive police tactics. The police were launched into the headlines once again in 1971, when Fred Quilt, an Aboriginal in northern British Columbia, died while in police custody for drunk driving. The BCCLA worked successfully with Native groups to have an inquest called over the circumstances of Quilt's death, although the investigation subsequently rejected claims of police brutality as the cause of death.[54]

Each year, the association uncovered dozens of cases of police abusing their powers. A group of teens was pulled over by police in 1970 near Saanich for having "suspicious materials" in their vehicle (an empty oil can and some tubes). The three teens had their car impounded and were forced to walk home in the middle of winter.[55] To discourage prostitution, the police would sometimes target suspected pimps with continuous fines and parking or speeding tickets to put them out of business.[56] Accusations of police abuse were also raised following drug raids in Coquitlam and Port Moody. Interrogating children in schools, equipping officers with mace and riot sticks, unfairly suspending drivers' licences, raiding book sellers, conducting searches without warrants, and harassing juveniles were among the many serious accusations the BCCLA laid against the police.

Tensions between youths and police climaxed in the Gastown riot of 7 August 1971. The riot was, in some ways, just another addition to the list of police abuse of powers during this period, but it also brought to the fore the conflicts between institutions of authority and various movements in the province. In the context of the seventies, the riot was another manifestation of the battles being fought by the *Straight*, the Doukhobours, and the BCCLA against the courts, the municipal government, and the police.

It was a smoke-in. Prompted by articles in the *Georgia Straight* hundreds of youths had converged on Maple Tree Square in the popular area of Gastown in downtown Vancouver. For the previous week, writers Kenneth Lester and Eric Sommer had been promoting the gathering to protest drug laws and recent drug raids in the area (Operation Dustpan). Hundreds of young people, many described by the media as hippies, had assembled in the square; some were smoking pot, others were playing music or just wandering around. By 10:00 a.m., combined with people on the street, the crowd had expanded to almost two thousand. Inspector Abercrombie, who was the senior officer in charge at the scene, decided to clear the crowd after receiving false reports of windows being broken. He ordered the crowd to disperse within two minutes. When his first warning was ignored, Abercrombie ordered four policemen on horseback with riding crops to disperse the throng. They were followed by police officers in riot gear who were supported by plainclothes officers scattered among the crowd. Absolute pandemonium broke out. People coming out of stores and restaurants in Gastown found themselves caught up in a battle between police and youths, some of the latter throwing rocks, pieces of cement, and bottles.[57] Abercrombie realized he was facing a riot in the making.

The violence quickly got out of hand. Observers were available from the BCCLA and the media, having followed the calls issued through the *Georgia Straight* by Lester and Sommer. Officers used their horses to pin people into doorways and hack at them with their sticks; a woman, screaming, was pulled by her hair across shards of broken glass by two police officers; a police officer was struck by a brick, which led to the crowd cheering; and youths shouting obscenities were beaten by police.[58] A clash between police and youths had unexpectedly erupted into uncontrolled violence in the heart of Vancouver.

Seventy-nine people were arrested and thirty-eight were charged with various offences. There was an immediate public backlash. Newspapers lined their front pages with details on the riot and its aftermath. The *Vancouver Sun* called for an inquiry, noting that the "volume of rhetoric and abuse that has been pouring out ever since [the riot] ... has so confused the public that only a detached, impartial and coherent assessment of the whole affair will now suffice to put blame where it belongs."[59] The *Province* was convinced there would be "deepening suspicion and hostility between young people and the police – unless Attorney General Peterson steps in at once and orders an independent investigation of the whole affair."[60] Naturally, the *Georgia Straight* was quick to condemn the police and point to the riot as evidence of a police force hostile to youths. Mayor Campbell defended the police and claimed that a conspiracy by Sommer and Lester was responsible for the violence; however, he publicly stated his support for an inquiry into alleged police abuses.[61] Gastown merchants, sympathetic with those caught in the riot, organized a bail-fund and planned a social gathering for protestors and police to ease tensions within the community.[62] Campbell, the BCCLA, and the media (including the *Georgia Straight*) were all calling for a provincial inquiry, and, as a result, in late August, the Attorney General ordered Justice Thomas Dohm (a provincial Supreme Court judge) to investigate the causes of the Gastown riot.

The Dohm inquiry lasted for ten days and heard forty-eight witnesses. Joseph Laxton represented the BCCLA, which had managed to raise $1,200 to cover his legal fees. Its position centred on the use of excessive force by the police. For the past few years the association had opposed the acquisition of more riot sticks by the local police force, fearing an increase in confrontations between police and youths, and the riot seemed to have confirmed its earlier concerns. A public statement released by James Wood of the BCCLA criticized the tactics employed by the police, their use of plainclothes officers, and the prejudice displayed by officers in targeting youths with particular haircuts and clothes.[63]

As the inquiry progressed, two different interpretations over the causes of the Gastown riot emerged. On one side was the BCCLA, supported by the BC Federation of Labour and other advocacy groups. It saw the riot as a reflection of underlying tensions between youths and police that had been building for years.[64] Youths were frustrated with strict drug laws while police harboured negative and prejudicial attitudes towards hippies – an attitude encouraged by the rhetoric and blustering of local politicians like Campbell. Research conducted by the BCCLA concluded that police officers were increasingly alienated from the community due to the use of patrol cars rather than foot patrols, distinguishing uniforms, lack of civilian participation in the administration of the police force, and a poor system for handling complaints. These factors all contributed to a fundamental problem between youths and symbols of authority; since March 1970, twenty-five separate youth demonstrations had taken place in Vancouver and Victoria alone.[65]

On the other side of the debate were the policemen's union, municipal politicians, the media, and the Dohm Report. Dohm acknowledged Abercrombie's overzealousness, and he agreed that the crowd had not degenerated into a mob and that individual officers used "unnecessary, unwarranted and excessive force." His recommendations to the Board of Police Commissioners included banning demonstrators from taking over public streets, training squads of police officers specifically for crowd control duty, using horses for crowd control except on sidewalks and store fronts, and eliminating the use of plainclothes officers for crowd control.[66]

Responsibility for the riot, however, was placed squarely on the shoulders of Sommer and Lester, whose "true motivation is their desire to challenge authority in every way possible ... Any popular cause serves their purpose if it enables them to gather a gullible crowd who may act in such a way as to defy any authority. The harassment of young people by the drug squad police and the resultant hostility was grist to their trouble-brewing mill." Dohm, George Murray of the policeman's union, and Mayor Campbell all blamed the riot on an anarchist conspiracy to cause havoc on the streets. The *Province* considered the "root cause of the whole ugly business ... two dangerous yippies [trying] to use a protest against marijuana law as a means of gathering a crowd for a confrontation with police."[67] This sentiment was shared by the *Vancouver Sun,* which lambasted Campbell for his inflammatory rhetoric but which laid blame at the feet of a small group of troublemakers.[68]

Compared to riots in American cities, the Gastown riot was a minor affair, small both in numbers of people involved and in degree of violence. For the City of Vancouver, and to a lesser extent for the province as a whole, no event better represented the divisions within the community. Institutions of authority focused on the superficial causes of the riot and were unwilling to consider the broader implications of the conflict. The BCCLA and other advocacy groups sought a deeper explanation. They pointed to the underlying strain emerging from the nature of the youth protest movements, with their illicit drug use and hippie culture, and the attitudes of the state and media towards them. By the early 1970s, the police were a little more open to suggestions from the civil liberties association. The BCCLA was involved in drafting a new procedures manual for the Vancouver police and was invited to the opening of the new police college in 1975. Frustrated with its inability to curb police abuses through individual cases, the association had turned to working with the police on procedures, training, and policies.[69] The willingness of the police to entertain feedback from community groups was most likely prompted, however, by the fallout from the riot.

Taking the Government to Court: The Heroin Treatment Act

Illegal narcotics and their popularity among youths was undeniably one of the central causes of the Gastown riot and had been an issue for the BCCLA since the mid-1960s. The association framed the debate as a question over the role of the state in regulating behaviour versus the right of an individual to determine her/his own lifestyle. With the highest number of drug addicts in the country, Vancouver loomed large in the war against drugs. The BCCLA's battle against the Heroin Treatment Act was its last major initiative at the end of the seventies, and it represented the organization's most concerted effort to use the courts to defend individuals from state abuse of their civil liberties. The history of the Heroin Treatment Act also highlights one of the most divisive public debates on a civil liberties issue in the province, if not the country as a whole, during this period.

Treatment was the new catch word in the 1950s and 1960s. Attempts to use criminal sanctions were giving way to a recognition that the use of illegal narcotics had increased despite already existing draconian measures (a conviction for simple possession of marijuana, even for first-time offenders, could lead to a prison sentence). The Narcotic Addiction Foundation was set up in British Columbia on 13 September 1955 to provide homes in which drug users could work off their addiction.[70]

Compulsory treatment was an important aspect of the new treatment approach. The federal government passed the Narcotic Control Act in 1961 to replace the existing legislation dealing with illegal drug use. It was the first major revision of the drug laws since the 1920s. The legislation maintained most of the provisions of the original Opium and Drug Act. Part 2 of the act, however, which never passed into law, provided for compulsory treatment followed by ten years of parole for first-time offenders. In theory, treatment could stem the flow of illegal drugs into Canada by eliminating the demand for drugs. This new law, based on the desire to reform rather than to punish addicts, was unquestionably a major step and had the potential to completely reverse the traditional law enforcement paradigm. But none of these provisions was ever employed; the institutions designed to treat addicts were never built, and Part 2 was never proclaimed.[71]

A new problem born in the sixties revitalized the debate on how to deal with drug addiction. Marijuana use increased exponentially during this period, notably among middle-class youths and on university campuses. Unlike the previous generation of users, portrayed as poor, downtrodden, and marginalized, these new users were part of mainstream society and used drugs as a form of social protest against prevailing social norms. Attempts to deal with this new problem through traditional law enforcement techniques failed completely. In 1965 there were only sixty convictions for possession of marijuana, a figure that increased to over six thousand by 1970, with no noticeable deterrent effect on users.[72] The Gastown

Riot was the perfect example of the new drug culture among youths and its clash with police.

In 1969, the federal government implemented a royal commission (chaired by Gerald LeDain) to investigate the use of narcotics in Canada. A majority of the commission's members, including the chair, recommended that the federal government remove criminal penalties for possession of cannabis and provide a system of compulsory treatment for addicts (administered by the provinces).[73] But the commission was divided on the issue. A minority dissent by Professor Marie-Andrée Bertrand, a criminologist, rejected compulsory treatment because the psychological aspects of addiction could not be properly dealt with through a regimen of forced treatment rejected by the patient. She called for the complete decriminalization of cannabis and a system to provide for its legal distribution.[74] In retrospect, the report accomplished very little. Few of the recommendations were adopted, and, as Marcel Martel notes in his recent book on national debates over the regulation of marijuana, except for reducing penalties relating to possession, the federal government made virtually no changes to the laws dealing with illegal narcotics (although the federal government did abolish writs of assistance in the 1980s).[75]

The BCCLA had maintained a consistent interest in drug laws dating back at least to 1966, when the association hosted a well-attended seminar on the question of illegal narcotics. When the LeDain Commission held hearings in Vancouver in 1969 and 1970, hundreds of people attended and dozens made presentations. The police called for greater regulation of the drug trade, and various individuals demanded the state not interfere with their chosen habits.[76] The BCCLA's position reflected its civil libertarian ethos. Individual actions, not conditions, should be illegal. An alcoholic caught driving or a drug addict stealing to pay his/her habit should be the target of criminal proceedings, but criminalizing the possession of non-medical drugs violated the individual's right to live her or his chosen lifestyle. The association also noted the failure of criminal laws in the United States and other countries to discourage drug use. LeDain's final report supported greater state regulation of drugs because addicts were a strain on public funds, but the BCCLA quickly dismissed the idea since the same point could be made for smoking tobacco. According to the BCCLA, the Narcotic Control Act "creates a legal fiction. It transforms a relatively harmless substance into the equivalent drug such as opium and heroin."[77]

For years, provincial politicians had been talking about dealing with the drug problem in British Columbia. An attempt in 1969 to legislate a ban against LSD (unless its use was approved by the health minister) was struck down by the Supreme Court of Canada for invading federal jurisdiction over criminal law. Malcolm Matheson, a member of the Attorney General's Office under the NDP in 1973, recommended compulsory treatment and the creation of quarantines for addicts.[78]

Outside occasional comments by individual members of government, however, there is no evidence the NDP seriously contemplated new legislation to implement the recommendations of the LeDain Commission. It would take the election victory of the Social Credit Party in 1975 to open the new front on the war against drugs.

The decision to act on the LeDain Report drew the Social Credit government into a major political controversy that would last for years. In 1977, the province introduced the Heroin Treatment Act to provide for compulsory treatment of heroin addicts.[79] Heroin use had reached remarkable levels by the late seventies in British Columbia. The heroin trade alone was estimated at $255 million per annum, the fifth largest industry in the province. Sixty-one percent of all heroin addicts in the country were in British Columbia, an increase of 167 percent since 1970 and 586 percent since 1956.[80]

The Heroin Treatment Act provided for the creation of area coordinating centres, a commission to administer the act, and evaluation panels consisting of medical practitioners and psychologists. Under Section 13, the act gave police the power to require suspected drug addicts to present themselves at area coordinating centres to be evaluated by a panel of experts as to the extent of their addiction. Once the panel decided that treatment was required, the act empowered the commission to apply to a court to forcibly detain the individual for up to three years, of which six months could include incarceration. Appeals against the detention order were available through the appellate court, although the onus of proof was reversed to require the defendant to demonstrate that she/he was not in need of treatment. Having been defeated in 1969 in their attempt to ban LSD, the government was careful to focus on treatment, not criminal sanctions, as the basis of its new drug legislation.

Opposition members in the Legislature accused the government of using the bill as a political tactic by playing off public fears of drug use and drug-related crimes. It was perhaps the most vigorous public debate in the province on a civil liberties issue for the entire decade. Due process concerns loomed large in the debate. One member characterized the medical board as a disguised judicial hearing and condemned the decision to reverse the onus of proof. Others suggested that the bill was unconstitutional and violated the federal bill of rights. The Canadian Bar Association took the position that the bill was criminal law dressed up in the guise of health legislation. Since voluntary treatment had failed in several other jurisdictions, many people questioned the viability of a compulsory system. Norman Levi, a former cabinet minister and member of the BCCLA, declared his opposition to spending "billions of dollars of scarce resources fighting an impossible war. I'm not prepared to do that at all ... But this idiocy of trying to beat something that we can't beat ... If you are going to look at it from the medical position, what we have to do is follow it through logically."[81]

The government stood fast against mounting criticism towards the bill. Supporters of the legislation claimed that it would protect not only the safety of the community but also, in an excellent example of the flexibility of rights discourse, the civil liberties of drug addicts. Introducing the legislation in second reading was Minister of Health Robert H. McClelland. He acknowledged how

> one of the most overriding concerns that has been expressed to date, at least, of those opposed to this proposed health legislation is the infringement upon the civil liberties of known heroin users. I can't repeat this often enough, but anyone with any knowledge of the nature of narcotic dependency is fully aware of the lack of normal civil liberties to which narcotic-dependent individuals now have access ... This plan is designed to help individuals retain a state of being where the same civil liberties that most people ordinarily enjoy are accessible ... A sincere desire to improve one's lot in life is paired with an insatiable thirst for immediate gratification ... The coercive aspect of the heroin plan would immediately address and remedy this dynamic.[82]

The government's case rested on the failure of previous voluntary treatment programs to deal with heroin addicts and the overriding needs of the community over the individual. Kenneth Rafe Mair, minister of consumer and corporate affairs, believed that allowing addicts who were called before the Board of Review to have access to counsel and the appeals process were sufficient provisions to satisfy due process. He accepted that "the Mental Health Act is [not] easy legislation ... I don't pretend that they do not in some way erode what we consider to be the pure civil liberties to which we are entitled. But to the extent that it varies from those principles, I am convinced it is justified in light of the ill that we seek to cure."[83] It was an emotionally charged exchange in which threats to civil liberties clashed with heartfelt concerns about the lot of drug addicts. Walter Davidson's appeal to the opposition's sympathy for the plight of the weak exemplified the deep-seated moral issues facing the province's political leaders:

> I really wonder how many people debating this bill today have had the opportunity, as I have had, to interview 14-year old girls addicted to heroin and forced into a life of prostitution to support their habit. I wonder how many members who oppose this bill have had the opportunity, as I have had, to find a young girl or a young man dead in a fleabag hotel, the victim of an overdose; or to see the results of a lifetime of heroin abuse in the form of total human degradation; or have come into contact with the pushers and the pimps who live in the lap of luxury off the avails of human misery; or have sensed the frustration felt by every law enforcement officer who, because of our insufficient laws and our sharpie lawyers, is unable to obtain a conviction for trafficking in narcotics. I want to assure you that those who have experienced this

feeling share a hatred for those associated with the narcotics industry, and a contempt for our legislators who refuse to take a real stand and provide meaningful legislation for the benefit of those coming along and entering the mainstream of life.[84]

Among the many groups opposed to the proposed legislation were the Canadian Bar Association, the Elizabeth Fry Society, the BC Corrections Association, the Narcanon Society, and former chair of the BC Police Commission, John Hogarth. Gordon F. Gibson, the lone Liberal in the Legislature, presented a petition from nine thousand of his constituents in Langley who opposed the legislation.[85] The most extensive media coverage appeared in the *Vancouver Sun*. The paper was adamantly against the legislation, particularly because of the threat it represented to civil liberties. In the midst of the debate in mid-June, the paper concluded that relevant statistics did not "provide a rationale for a multi-million dollar treatment program – such as that proposed by McClelland – that denies due process of law, turns policemen into health officials and health officials into judges, and has every chance of failing to achieve its goal, and may not be within the jurisdiction of the province to enact."[86]

The Heroin Treatment Act was the perfect issue for the BCCLA. The association had been debating the issue for years and had a clear stance against any form of compulsory medical treatment. The legislation had the potential to affect everyone in the community, not only minority groups. Programs such as affirmative action raised difficult questions over the scope of civil liberties, whereas the Heroin Treatment Act was a simple question of negative rights. It also pitted the BCCLA against a political party whose policies it generally opposed,[87] and it immediately provided them with such allies as the NDP, the Canadian Bar Association, the Elizabeth Fry Society, and the media. The controversy also had the potential to provide the association with publicity and a forum in which to promote its views. Throughout the debate in the Legislature, NDP politicians quoted from BCCLA briefs, and the *Vancouver Sun* noted the association's opposition in articles and editorials.[88] When the act became law on 29 June 1978, the BCCLA prepared its court challenge to the constitutionality of the legislation.

Jim Dybikowski, a philosophy professor at UBC with legal training, appeared before the BC Supreme Court on behalf of the BCCLA in June 1979. Requests to the provincial and federal government to have the legislation reviewed by the courts were rebuffed, and the association was forced to bring the legislation to court on its own. Judge Allan McEachern heard the case and initially refused the group standing because, as in the teacher's case during the October Crisis, Dybikowski was not directly affected by the legislation. Brenda Ruth Schneider, a heroin addict, replaced Dybikowski as appellant, and the judge allowed the case to go forward with Dybikowski as legal counsel. Since there was no constitutional basis upon which to challenge the legislation for violating Schneider's civil liberties, the BCCLA's case rested on whether or not the province had the appropriate jurisdiction to pass the Heroin Treatment Act.

Counsel for the Attorney General stressed that the act was designed to treat heroin addicts and fell under comparable jurisdiction, such as the provincial Public Health Act. Treatment, not punishment, was the purpose of the legislation, and it therefore also fell under provincial jurisdiction over "property and civil rights" and not federal criminal law. In contrast, Dybikowski claimed that the pith and substance of the legislation was punishment because it provided for incarceration and compulsory detention in the guise of treatment. Due process rights were at stake. Persons tested under the act had no power to examine or question the results. They were barred from choosing their own medical examiner. Accused could not introduce or collect evidence themselves, and upon detention a person lost all liberty and was at the mercy of the director's discretion. Another key component of the BCCLA's defence was the federal Narcotic Control Act. Phase 2 of the federal anti-drug legislation (which was not yet activated) was proof that Parliament already had legislation for the treatment of addicts.[89]

McEachern decided in favour of the appellant. The case was the greatest court success the BCCLA achieved prior to the passing of the Charter. It was a high profile case, initiated and funded by the association, against a major piece of provincial legislation. The judge considered the legislation criminal law because health legislation was meant to apply equally to all residents rather than to target a particular subset within the community. His decision revolved around the question of jurisdiction in relation to the treatment of addicts. According to McEachern, the federal Narcotic Control Act was also designed to deal with treatment, and, this being the case, the province could not legislate in this area.[90]

After succeeding in the provincial Supreme Court, the *Schneider* case faced an uphill battle. In 1981, the British Columbia Court of Appeal unanimously struck down the lower court decision and ruled the legislation intra vires. The appellate court rejected McEachern's analysis of the Narcotic Control Act and claimed that the act had no relevance to the provincial legislation by virtue of Phase 2 not being declared. Focusing on the narrow language of the statute, the appellate judges noted the legislation's references to dependency, patients, and treatment and concluded that it was designed to help addicts, not punish them.[91]

Within a year the BCCLA funded an appeal to the Supreme Court, where another unanimous decision found the legislation intra vires. Brian Dickson, in presenting the decision for the entire court, believed that the Heroin Treatment Act did not fall under any all-encompassing federal residuary power. Since Phase 2 of the federal legislation was not yet declared, the paramountcy argument was rejected. The due process argument put forth by the appellant raised some concerns for Dickson as the legislation dealt with "local evils" and curtailed the individual's freedom, but this was not enough to place the treatment of drug addicts under the criminal law power. There were already several provisions for appeal available under the legislation, and a written statement from the director of the review board was necessary to commit a patient, satisfying the requirement for due process. Quoting the LeDain Report, the judge concluded that narcotics were a medical, not a criminal, condition and that the Heroin Treatment Act was firmly within the realm of public health.

Due process arguments aside, the BCCLA also objected to the Heroin Treatment Act because it violated some of the fundamental principles upon which the organization was founded. The law was being used to punish people for their state of being, not their actions, and it refused individuals the right to choose their own form of medical treatment. Moreover, the legislation violated the integrity of the judicial system by establishing a non-judicial decision-making body with the power to incarcerate and detain people for years, allowing only for an appeal against the question of whether or not treatment was needed – a question the BCCLA felt was unsuitable for provincial Supreme Court judges. Unfortunately, until the advent of the Charter, the BCCLA could not present a case before the courts based on the violation of a fundamental freedom.

The BCCLA: A Case Study in Negative Freedom

Each of the four case studies in this work offers its own insights into the evolution of social movement organizations in Canada. The four associations had to grapple with the question of whether or not to accept funding from the state, whether or not to form relationships with other social movement organizations, whether or not to participate in a national body, and how to develop strategies for change. The BCCLA is particularly useful for understanding how activists applied vague human rights principles to a wide array of social issues without favouring any particular constituency in the community. It dedicated a great deal of resources and energy to developing position papers and briefs on numerous issues from a civil libertarian perspective.

State Funding

Unlike many of the small rights associations that emerged during this period, the BCCLA had a relatively strong membership base. Sixty members in 1962 rose to more than five hundred by the late 1970s; in 1972, it collected $4,509 in dues, and this rose to $7,416 by 1979. But not until the early 1980s did membership dues exceed more than 10 percent of the budget. At best, the BCCLA could boast an annual revenue of approximately $10,000 in a good year, exclusive of government grants.[92] Ten thousand dollars hardly constituted prosperity, and, limited to these funds, the BCCLA's services would have been severely curtailed had it not been for state funding.

The BCCLA was completely dependent on state funding. Reg Robson was proficient in securing state funding and played a key role in convincing city councils, the provincial government, and the secretary of state to provide financial support. The federal government proved to be, at times, a generous supporter of the BCCLA's activities. Regular grants of $5,000 or more were provided to the association by the secretary of state for operational funding alone. In 1973, the organization landed a major victory with a $35,000 grant from the federal Local Initiatives Program to expand its operations beyond Vancouver.[93] The association immediately hired a group of field workers to travel across the province to create local rights associations. Field workers provided paralegal services to inform people about the availability of legal aid (created under the NDP government in 1972) and alternative avenues for redress; they also secured counsel and contacted relatives for bail. The explosion of rights associations in British Columbia in the seventies was, in no small part, a result of this initiative. Unfortunately, it soon became evident that the local associations depended heavily on the field worker, and, once he/she moved on to a new city, several associations quickly withered away.[94]

At one point, in 1975-76, the BCCLA enjoyed a revenue base of almost $150,000. Most of these monies were government grants directed at specific projects, mainly educational work in schools and field workers, not legal services. Despite its dependence on state funding, however, there is no evidence the organization ever shied away from an issue to avoid insolvency. The BCCLA never avoided taking on unpopular issues that could have cost them members, such as the Ku Klux Klan's right to free speech. In fact, most of the association's work during these years was directed against the same governments that provided funding to the BCCLA, whether this meant taking on state censorship, legislation compelling addicts to seek treatment, or the government's overreaction during the October Crisis. The BCCLA targeted all three levels of government, but at no time was the association threatened with losing its funding as a result of its activities.

"Another unwelcome organization issuing press releases": Strategies for Change
The BCCLA's earliest activities were by necessity limited, with a budget of less than $2,000 in the first few years, rising to $6,230 in 1969, at which point the group appointed its first part-time assistant and secured an office in downtown Vancouver. The association initially provided free legal advice over the phone and formed several committees to conduct research, although, as many of its former leaders have wryly noted in retrospect, the existence of a committee was no assurance of anything actually being done. Dependence on volunteer work was a significant obstacle. Few of the committees did anything more than provide a report, and most became moribund within a few years.

The committee on religious education is a perfect example of the group's early activities and the difficulties facing a new social movement organization that is trying to make a name for itself. British Columbia operated a secular education system, with no publicly funded religious schools. Only the Lord's Prayer was permitted in public schools, and clergy were banned from the positions of superintendent, teacher, trustee, or inspector. In an attempt to combat demands by religious groups for separate schools, the provincial government amended the Public School's Act in 1944 to require readings from the Bible and the Lord's Prayer in all public schools. One of the BCCLA's original committees was given a mandate to look into strategies to eliminate the 1944 amendment. It was not until 1969, however, that action was finally taken. One of the directors, Herschel Hardin, tabled a report recommending that the organization seek an amendment to the Public Schools Act to ban any religious practices in public schools, while encouraging the secular study of religion.[95] The report was forwarded to the provincial government but received no response. Hardin then sought out his only natural ally outside the BCCLA with the resources to mobilize people around this issue: the British Columbia Teachers' Federation.

The teachers' federation had been grappling with this issue since at least 1958, when local federation leaders raised concerns over religious practices in schools. In a response to a letter in 1958 from Vaughan Lyon of the United Church, J.A. Spragg of the teachers' federation claimed that "many of the active advocates of religious education seem to be interested primarily in using the time, authority, and the influence of the public schools to further the specific dogma of their particular denomination or sect."[96] In 1964, the teachers' federation adopted an official position against all religious exercises in BC schools. A committee was immediately struck to examine the issue, and it concluded that teachers felt a degree of coercion in following religious exercises, despite the option to be exempted under the legislation, and that teachers felt unqualified to discuss the theological aspects of Bible readings.[97]

These developments did not inspire change. While there was a degree of consensus in the teachers' federation against religious practices in schools, it was not a priority for the union. A later report, compiled by Philip Hewett in 1968, concluded that, while a majority of teachers opposed the practice, it had broad public support and that the teachers' federation could alienate large segments of the public if it challenged it.[98] The union corresponded briefly with members of the provincial cabinet about considering amendments to the Public Schools Act; however, this met with little success, and the union's executive quietly dropped the issue.

'In 1969, Hardin attempted to reignite the debate within the BC Teachers' Federation and the BC Parent-Teachers' Federation through correspondence with the executive and a request that he be allowed to address the latter's annual meeting. The teachers' federation and the parents' association had the resources and public profile to raise a serious public debate on this issue in a way that the BCCLA, still a young organization, could not do alone. His request to speak was quickly rebuffed, with the parent-teachers' association spokesperson's noting the failure of a local federation's motion two years earlier to ban Bible readings in schools.[99] The lack of interest on the part of the BC Teachers' Federation and parent-teachers' association's executives, and the failure of both the BCCLA and the union to push the government to consider amending the legislation, left no more options for action. The committee on religious education soon collapsed.

Alongside its advocacy program, the BCCLA immediately began organizing educational activities. In addition to seminars and public lectures, the group published a monthly newsletter, *Democratic Commitment*, beginning in 1967. By the late seventies more than four thousand copies were being distributed, and the organization's booklet, *Arrest,* was published continually for the next two decades. In 1980 alone, the BCCLA sold ten thousand copies of its three booklets, *Arrest, Discrimination*, and *Youth and the Law*.[100]

The stage was thus set for the next twenty years. Throughout most of its history, the BCCLA has primarily focused its activism on seeking legal reform and, to a lesser degree, education. With stable funding, the association was able to engage in extensive educational work and research.[101] A *Vancouver Sun* editorial serenading the young organization in 1962, however, not only warned the BCCLA to ensure the protection of everyone's civil liberties whatever their political leanings but also encouraged it to focus on the courts in order to avoid becoming "another unwelcome organization issuing press releases."[102] Undoubtedly, Robson and his cohorts would have wholeheartedly agreed with this assessment. For most of its early history, the BCCLA constantly sought out lawyers who were willing to provide free legal support or, in some cases, create a legal defence fund. Board members were often called upon to provide free legal services, and a network of about eighty volunteer lawyers was available to defend people abused by the police or jailed demonstrators, usually students or the poor, with no means to hire their own lawyers. As the BCCLA matured, however, it discovered two important obstacles to using the courts as a defence against attacks on civil liberties.

The first obstacle was financial. Most of the organization's funding came from the state, and grants were usually project-specific or provided a shoe-string budget for administration. Any funds to hire lawyers would have to come out of donations or membership dues left over from administrative costs. A legal defence fund was established in 1970-71, with a few thousand dollars available for costs and for hiring a lawyer. The funds were used in 1978 for a civil case when a couple sued the Vancouver police for physical abuse. The Schucks were grabbed by undercover police, roughed up, and arrested on suspicion of purchasing illegal narcotics simply because they happened to be caught walking near a known drug dealer.[103] In 1982, the BCCLA funded its first Supreme Court challenge over the legality of the provincial Heroin Treatment Act, which imposed compulsory treatment on heroin addicts. The *Schuck* case alone cost $1,000, and the Supreme Court appeal cost almost $9,000.[104] Both cases were lost. The high cost of any court action made it difficult for the BCCLA, with most of its $150,000 trapped in administration or government project grants, to contemplate taking a case to court.

The second obstacle was institutional. Until the advent of the Charter of Rights and Freedoms, judges generally frowned upon requests by third parties for intervener status. Many judges, for instance, were concerned about the possibility of interveners turning their courtrooms into public forums comparable to royal commissions.[105] There was nothing peculiarly Canadian about this philosophy. Australian and English human rights associations also found the courts hesitant to allow them to submit factums, even in appeals to the High Court or Privy Council.

A bias against interveners was only one of several obstacles facing activists in the courts. When the provincial government threatened British Columbia teachers with dismissal in 1970 if they expressed sympathy with the Front de libération du Québec, several university professors in the BCCLA sought to challenge the legislation in court. It came down to a question of who had legal standing. The judge found "no question whatsoever of the plaintiffs being in jeopardy. I think jeopardy must mean actual jeopardy not hypothetical jeopardy, which could arise only if the plaintiffs advocated one or other of the policies specified in the impugned Order in Council ... There is no suggestion they have or wish to do so."[106] Activists were thus prevented from challenging offensive legislation unless they were directly affected, even though the very existence of the regulation as a threat hanging over the heads of the province's teachers was enough to stifle free speech. Nonetheless, hippies, protestors, and students alike enjoyed free legal advice and assistance in bail hearings or magistrates' courts thanks to the volunteer work of members of the BCCLA, even if in most cases the attempt to convince a judge that the police had overstepped their bounds was a futile gesture.[107] In general, the BCCLA found the courts to be a limited forum for defending civil liberties.

"A pitiful record for an association that claims national status": The National Question

The BCCLA played a central role in the creation of the Canadian Federation of Civil Liberation and Human Rights Associations (hereafter the Federation) in the early seventies. The Federation was an umbrella organization of rights associations with an office in Ottawa. In essence, it was a forum for networking among rights associations and a vehicle for advocacy at the national level. The Federation was, in many ways, a product of Reg Robson's vision of a national rights association, and Robson would become a leading force in its creation (the history of the Federation is detailed in Chapter 7). It was Robson who secured funding to organize meetings in Winnipeg and Montreal, initiated the first cooperative actions during the October Crisis, corresponded with rights associations, chaired the meetings, wrote the constitution, and provided leadership on the Federation's Board of Directors. Had Robson and his allies managed to convince the Canadian Civil Liberties Association to join the Federation, it would have been a truly inclusive national rights association. But divisions among rights associations, and particularly between the BCCLA and the CCLA, made such unity difficult.

The relationship between the BCCLA and CCLA has always been strained due to the latter's pretensions to national status. The BCCLA letterhead in 1967 indicated that it was formally affiliated with the CCLA, although, except for doing some research under the CCLA's Ford Grant, there is no evidence of the two groups' having worked together. Affiliation, even if it existed in practice, was quickly dismissed by the membership and the BCCLA executive in 1968 and was never again reconsidered. The Board of Directors decided that the CCLA was "primarily an Ontario Association [and] there would be some reluctance on the part of the BC Association to regard it as an appropriate Federal organization of which they would become an affiliate."[108] Nonetheless, the BCCLA accepted funding from the CCLA to conduct a survey on due process in British Columbia. The report produced by the BCCLA in 1970 was the only project that saw the associations work together towards a common goal.

Tensions between the BCCLA and the CCLA were a problem as early as 1970. At this time, on behalf of the BCCLA, Robson thwarted Alan Borovoy and the CCLA's attempts to create an informal network of rights associations coordinated by the CCLA. He believed that Borovoy's proposal would have created a paper organization dominated by the Toronto group, and he wanted, instead, to create a more concrete and independent association.[109]

In fact, the CCLA's efforts to evolve into a national rights association often rankled members of the BCCLA. In the BCCLA's newsletter, *Democratic Commitment,* several contributors expressed frustration with the CCLA's practice of "poaching" BCCLA members in British Columbia. By refusing to explicitly acknowledge in its solicitation campaigns that it was not affiliated with the BCCLA, the CCLA was signing up members who believed they were joining the Vancouver association.[110] In effect, the CCLA was stealing members from the BCCLA. The leadership of the BCCLA also accused the CCLA of falsely laying claim to national status, when, in reality, it was nothing more than an Ontario organization with a scattering of members outside the province. Hugh Keenleyside, a former ambassador and UBC professor with a reputation for advocating western Canadian interests in federalist circles, relinquished his membership in the CCLA because of poor geographic representation on the Board of Directors (out of thirty-two, twenty-two were from Toronto and five were from elsewhere in Ontario).[111] According to Keenleyside, "even for Canada this is a pitiful record for an association that claims national status ... I shall ... confine myself to working with the [BCCLA] which makes no pretence to a status it cannot justify."[112]

Despite its difficulties with the CCLA, the BCCLA was active in working with other rights associations. It was represented on the Federation's national executive almost continuously throughout the seventies. The Federation could also count on the expertise of the BCCLA for its national agenda; at one point, Robson appeared before the House of Commons Standing Committee on Justice and Legal Affairs to discuss wiretapping.[113] As one of the larger rights associations in the country, the BCCLA was able to provide some additional support for the Federation, such as printing five thousand pamphlets in 1976 at no charge.[114] Support for the national federation was, nevertheless, qualified. In 1978, the BCCLA could not afford to send a delegate to the national conference without financial assistance, and it debated the possibility of leaving the Federation if changes to the fee structure required larger groups to contribute more. Limited finances and a focus on local issues often constrained the BCCLA's ability to function at the national level.

The BCCLA also did not hesitate, when appropriate, to involve itself in key national debates outside the Federation. The BCCLA made representations to the LeDain Commission (1973) on illegal narcotics and the McDonald Commission (1979 and 1980) on national security. Such endeavours remained a peripheral activity for a group whose priority remained the defence of civil liberties in British Columbia. The nature of these activities, however, depended largely on how the organization understood and conceived of the nature of civil liberties.

Ideological Foundations[115]

In forming an organization dedicated to individual rights, members of the new association found themselves facing important ideological and conceptual challenges. The international debate over the nature of individual rights, symbolized in the UDHR and the two covenants, raised serious questions about the importance of economic, social, and cultural rights. Should a civil liberties association advocate for a minimum standard of living and access to education in addition to free speech? The positions adopted by the BCCLA not only reflect these ideological challenges over the meaning of human rights, but they also offer an interesting overview of some of the most offensive human rights violations across the country and in British Columbia during this period.

Since the 1960s, rights associations have faced an expanding bureaucracy and administrative tribunals on a scale never before seen in Canada. These tribunals represented a potentially serious threat to individual rights. For instance, immigration review boards had enormous influence over the process for admitting people to Canada, and the BCCLA was quick to lobby the federal government to expand opportunities for claimants to appeal decisions of the board. Some of the other positions adopted by the association with regard to administrative tribunals included the creation of a crimes compensation board to provide relief for victims of a criminal offence, an ombudsman's office, and adequate safeguards against the forced government expropriation of property. However, the BCCLA was solely concerned with the *administration* of these services, not with their nature. Its positions were consistent with the idea of negative freedom: preventing the arbitrary exercise of state power.

In the field of administrative decision making, the BCCLA did not hesitate to consider important social and economic issues, from the provision of social welfare to industrial relations. When legislation dealing with landlord-tenant rights was introduced in 1970, the BCCLA feared that landlords would exploit tenants desperate to find homes in Vancouver's ferociously competitive housing market. The brief recognized tenants' problems as rooted in the larger social and economic problems facing the community, but its recommendations were limited to procedural matters. In conceptualizing rights as civil liberties, the association went far beyond the basic freedoms of speech, assembly, association, press, and religion. This was inevitable within the context of an expanding welfare state and government regulation. Yet the solution was always conceived in the form of government regulation or some form of judicial or administrative review of state agencies. Thus, the civil liberties association concerned itself solely with the role and responsibilities of the state. It was a philosophy rooted in the perception of civil liberties as negative rights, free from government interference, except through regulation or appeal to ensure equal access to everyone.

The same philosophy informed the association's approach to issues of discrimination. Restrictive covenants (a compact among neighbours that most often banned individuals of certain races or religions from purchasing property in a community) were illegal in British Columbia by the mid-1960s. The lack of legislation specifically banning restrictive covenants forced some individuals to cover the cost of court proceedings to have existing covenants declared void, and the BCCLA intervened in 1968 to remove a covenant attached to lands owned by British Pacific Properties Limited (the covenant was remarkably detailed, and it specified latitudinal and longitudinal coordinates of regions in the world to indicate those people who were restricted from buying their properties). A more contentious issue was the BCCLA position on the Ku Klux Klan, which received widespread attention in the press in 1981 following reports that someone was distributing racist flyers in a Vancouver high school. The BCCLA reacted by sending a speaker to Argyle High School to speak on the evils of discrimination. In principle, the BCCLA supported the right to free speech no matter how heinous the ideas, and it promoted education (as opposed to criminal sanction) as the only way to combat discriminatory ideas.

Whereas free speech issues easily generated consensus among the directors of the BCCLA, the entire question of affirmative action was highly divisive. A brief presented to the board in 1980 recommended promoting affirmative action programs that would require employers to notify minority applicants of potential job openings and actively seek to correct any imbalances in the representation of minorities in certain sectors of the economy. The board debated the question for weeks, but its members were unable to come to an agreement over whether or not to support affirmative action – an unusual situation for an organization accustomed to working by consensus.[116] While restrictive covenants and free speech for the Ku Klux Klan fit comfortably within the framework of negative freedom, the idea of positive programs designed to favour particular groups in order to counter discrimination did not conform to the group's conception of civil liberties. Affirmative action expanded the concept of rights beyond what most civil liberties advocates, who were concerned with ensuring equality of opportunity and not positive state action, were willing to accept.

The BCCLA's central focus during this period – due process rights – reflected the priority its leadership placed on negative rights. Due process rights generally referred to the administration of justice, such as access to legal aid, court proceedings, provisions for bail, and protections against self-incrimination. The BCCLA spent years attacking the habitual criminal provisions of the Criminal Code, which dated back to 1947. These provisions allowed for anyone charged three times before turning eighteen years old and then charged with a fourth crime to be imprisoned for life. Such people were at the mercy of the National Parole Board, which alone could allow habitual criminals to go free while remaining on parole for the rest of their lives. By the 1960s, there were few such prosecutions in Canada, but in 1963 Stewart McMorran, the Vancouver city prosecutor, began a series of prosecutions against habitual criminals. By 1968, British Columbia was the unquestioned leader in charging people as habitual criminals, with seventy-five convictions; the next largest number of convictions was sixteen, and this occurred in Ontario, a province with a substantially larger population than British Columbia.[117] One of these cases, in which the defendant was represented by Thomas Berger, a well-known criminal attorney (and future judge) in Vancouver, involved a three-time shoplifter and petty drug user who was prosecuted by McMorran and sentenced as a habitual criminal. In his memoirs, Berger notes how those "who were liable to find themselves targeted called it 'The Bitch.'"

Habitual criminal laws, according to the BCCLA, were anathema to natural justice. The idea of imprisoning an individual for what he or she *might* do in the future was reprehensible to civil libertarians. To make matters worse, the habitual criminal section of the Criminal Code allowed the judge to consider the kind of people with whom the accused associated in order to determine whether or not to assign her/him habitual criminal status. In effect, the provision allowed for a form of guilt by association.

The BCCLA's official positions reflected a conception of rights as negative rights. Civil liberties were rights derived from the state, protected through judicial review or regulation. An individual's freedom was threatened by the arbitrary exercise of state power (such as when welfare officers abused their power) or by the lack of procedural safeguards in areas in which people are easily exploited (such as landlord-tenant relations). The organization's agenda prioritized issues such as due process, discrimination, and administrative decision making. When measured against the UDHR or the International Covenant on Economic, Social and Cultural Rights, the BCCLA's agenda clearly reflected a minimalist approach to human rights advocacy. The latter covenant encourages its members to provide access to education, a minimum standard of living, health care, and fair wages. The BCCLA never addressed these issues, and its positions in such areas as social assistance were careful not to specify what minimum standard of support was appropriate. Its focus on negative rights represented the kind of approach to rights advocacy derided by critics who claim that human rights activists are primarily concerned with civil and political rights.

Relations with Other Social Movement Organizations

The BCCLA may be one of the oldest and most active SMOs in British Columbia, but by the early 1980s it had largely failed to develop lasting relationships with other advocacy groups. A key obstacle was ideological. Feminists, for instance, had little sympathy for an organization that was defending pornographers' right to free speech. As one of the BCCLA's presidents, John Dixon, once quipped: "It was very soon the case that we got to be called unconscious exploiters only on our luckiest days."[118] Throughout its history the BCCLA has been scrupulously non-partisan, a position that often made it difficult for it to join coalitions. In 1984, organized labour and a host of SMOs throughout British Columbia came together to form a massive coalition to oppose the Social Credit government's "austerity package," a budget based on extensive funding cuts to welfare and social services (including the Human Rights Commission). Initially, the BCCLA was a member of the Solidarity Coalition, but the Coalition's links to the NDP and its political opposition to the Social Credit government proved unpalatable to the non-partisan BCCLA, and it soon abandoned it.[119]

The BCCLA found common ground with SMOs on numerous issues. In challenging the Heroine Treatment Act, the BCCLA found eager allies among the Elizabeth Fry Society and the Canadian Bar Association. Women's groups and organized labour often echoed the BCCLA's demands for reforms to provincial human rights legislation.[120] Common ground, however, did not lead to long-term cooperation, and these moments were the exception that proved the rule. In its first twenty years of activity, the BCCLA formed no strong relationships with other organizations. Perhaps because the BCCLA occupied a relatively unique place in the community, as a non-partisan association concerned with issues such as censorship and police violence, it simply had limited opportunities to work with others.

By the early 1980s, the BCCLA had grown from an association of sixty members with a budget of a few hundred dollars to one of over one thousand members and a budget of $150,000. During this time the BCCLA was an active defender of individual rights both locally and nationally. Although it was a young organization, struggling year by year simply to stay afloat, the BCCLA was successful in employing rights discourse to defend the interests of the marginalized. Its appeal was consistent in each case: every individual had fundamental freedoms, such as free speech, and the community had a moral responsibility to respect these rights. At a time when the mayor of Vancouver was waging a virtual war on hippies and the *Georgia Straight,* and the Ku Klux Klan was promoting hate-mongering, it was the rare organization that was willing to come to the defence of those who were easy targets for vilification and state suppression.

At the same time, the first twenty years of the BCCLA's existence was marked by constant failures to achieve its own goals. Unlike its predecessor, the Vancouver CCLU, the BCCLA could draw on a new legal regime designed to protect individual rights, from international treaties to provincial human rights codes and the federal Bill of Rights. And yet the courts were poor forums for the defence of civil liberties. Two of the most controversial state policies that violated civil liberties – the order-in-council directed against teachers in 1970 and the Heroin Treatment Act – survived legal challenges. The history of the BCCLA also reflected a minimalist approach to rights activism. At no time did the group embrace positive rights or promote economic, social, and cultural rights. The repertoire of strategies employed by the BCCLA involved working directly with state officials or state institutions, in contrast to other SMOs, which were willing to employ civil disobedience or mass mobilization.

In terms of strategies for change, the BCCLA was not much different from the Vancouver CCLU, but this was no classical liberal association; the BCCLA readily accepted a proactive role for the state in protecting human rights. As James Walker notes, liberals had traditionally favoured the discriminator; the rights to freedom of speech or association were interpreted to mean the right to refuse service to certain people or to express prejudicial ideas. In contrast, anti-discrimination legislation "represented a fundamental shift, a reversal, of the traditional notion of citizens' rights to enrol the state as the protector of the right of the victim to freedom from discrimination. It was, in fact, a revolutionary change in the definition of individual freedom."[121] The BCCLA was a manifestation of this new liberal ethos: a belief in equality of opportunity policed by the state. Although the Vancouver CCLU and other rights associations in the forties and fifties were proponents of anti-discrimination legislation, rights associations in the sixties and seventies were faced with new challenges. Unlike the Vancouver CCLU, the BCCLA's focus on the due process rights of workers and welfare recipients reflected the new issues facing human rights activists under the welfare state. Civil liberties advocates were ideally suited to raise concerns about abuses of power derogated to welfare state agencies. The organization was also the leading community group in Vancouver intent on policing the police. The BCCLA remains active today, and it is the oldest operating civil liberties association in Canada.

6
La Ligue des droits de l'homme

Trudeau: It's true that there are a lot of bleeding hearts around who can't stand the sight of soldiers with helmets and guns. All I can say is: go on and bleed. But it's more important to maintain law and order in society than to take pity on people whose knees start to quake as soon as they see the army ... Society must take every means available to defend itself against the rise of a parallel power which would defy the power of the people's elected representatives, and I believe that there are no limits on this obligation. Only cowards would be afraid to go all the way.

Reporter: How far would you go?

Trudeau: Just watch me.

Pierre Elliott Trudeau's famous words during the October Crisis in 1970 continue to reverberate today as evidence of his unwavering hostility to those who openly challenged his decision to invoke the War Measures Act. His reference to "bleeding hearts" was directed to, among others, those rights associations that were among the most vocal opponents of the government's actions during the crisis. Surprisingly, Quebec's only rights association was noted not for its actions but for its silence. When the ultimate challenge to the rights of Canadians and Quebeckers from the state presented itself, the Ligue des droits de l'homme (LDH) failed to distinguish itself and fulfill its central mandate. The failure of the LDH during the October Crisis would lead to profound changes in the structure and orientation of the association.

The experience of the LDH is unique among rights associations. While the BCCLA was grappling with censorship, police powers, and the rights of drug addicts, the LDH focused its energies on due process violations by the courts, the rights of prisoners, and, most important, a provincial bill of rights. The LDH evolved into the most egalitarian rights association in Canada; its mandate to promote social justice led it to advocate for social, economic, and cultural rights. In many ways, it is the ideal contrast to the BCCLA's civil libertarian approach to rights. The LDH is also the only rights association to deal with the question of collective rights as they pertain to minority language and cultural rights. Finally, as the second largest rights association in the country and extensively funded by the state, it struggled over the implications of state funding, particularly when it raised the ire of the state with its controversial language policy.

The LDH is a perfect case study for showcasing the differences between the two generations of rights associations. The years from 1963 to 1970 were the "law years" of the LDH, a time when legal reform and a concern for civil liberties dominated the association's agenda. Led by Frank Scott, a prominent figure among the rights associations in the forties and fifties, this early stage in the history of the LDH represented a brief continuation of the policies of the first generation. From 1970 to 1975, however, the group embraced a radically new approach to rights advocacy. By the mid-1970s, the LDH's new leaders had made a decisive break with the previous generation. And yet, despite achieving a major victory in 1975 with the passing of the Quebec Charter of Human Rights and Freedoms, an internal crisis brought the organization to the brink of disaster. By 1982, it had become clear that the LDH, like many rights associations of the period, had peaked in the late 1970s.

"An anachronism failing to function properly": The Law Years, 1963-70

In contrast to the three other case studies, no specific event triggered the creation of the Ligue des droits de l'homme. Its origins can be traced to several leading intellectuals in Quebec in 1963 who envisioned a modern rights association that would serve Quebec and possibly the nation as a whole. It was an initiative of Father Gérard Labrosse, a French-speaking Jesuit priest, who recruited Pierre Elliott Trudeau, Jacques Hébert, and J.Z. Léone Patenaud to help form a provisional committee alongside nineteen others. Included in this collection of prominent figures was Frank Scott, a renowned constitutional scholar, and Thérèse Casgrain, a powerful leader in the women's movement and a key figure in the successful drive in 1940 to grant women the vote in Quebec. At the group's inaugural meeting, a Montreal lawyer, Alban Flamand, was elected the first president. It was a comfortable affair among a group of intellectual elites, many of whom were close friends. The only real debate arose over what to call the new organization. Originally, it had been dubbed the Ligue des droits de l'homme de la Province de Québec, but Trudeau, determined to have the group play a national role, insisted that the provincial reference be eliminated. Thus was born the Ligue des droits de l'homme/ Civil Liberties Union.[1]

A concern with civil liberties was expressly articulated in the group's constitution, a document strongly reflecting the ideas of Frank Scott and those who had spearheaded the first generation of rights associations. Article one of the constitution defined the association's mandate in terms of protecting individuals' rights to speech, assembly, association, religion, and equal treatment through law reform. Of the individuals chosen to lead the association, eight were lawyers, eight journalists, two union organizers, one a professor, one an economist, two business leaders, and two student leaders. As with other rights associations in Canada, the membership of the LDH was composed primarily of well-educated professionals. Eight of the twenty-five initial members were English speaking. Few minorities or women were brought into the fold, and the organization would have to claim to speak on behalf of people who were not active within it. A recruitment campaign prepared in February 1966 qualified the group's interest in being "plus sur la qualité que la quantité" of its membership.[2] In addition, all new members to the association had to be approved by the administrative council. By requiring all new members to be approved in a vote, the LDH could effectively filter potentially contentious members.

It is interesting to note that there was no real discussion of language rights in these early years. While in 1963 this was consistent with the political context of the period, even though the issue had begun to dominate Quebec politics in the late 1960s, the LDH refused to adopt a position on language rights until 1972. Perhaps out of a concern for implicating itself in one of the most controversial issues of the period, the LDH never explicitly asserted language rights at this stage of its history. Most likely, however, members such as Scott would have wanted the Ligue to focus on individual rights issues as opposed to entering into the debate over language rights as collective rights (in the 1930s, Scott had made it clear that he believed that a civil liberties association should focus almost exclusively on freedoms of speech and association).[3] In addition, as was the case with the BCCLA, the constitution of the new LDH focused on equality of opportunity, political and civil liberties, and anti-discrimination. There was no reference to the social and economics rights of youths, women, the elderly, Aboriginals, or the disabled. These issues would not mobilize the organization for another decade.

It is no coincidence the LDH was formed at this stage in Quebec history. These were the formative years of the Quiet Revolution, a period when "le grand noirceur" had finally been exorcised and the economic, social, and political modernization of the province was in full swing. Many of the LDH's founders, such as Pelletier and Trudeau, were among the leaders of the Quiet Revolution. With the Liberals' defeat of the Union Nationale in 1960, the repression associated with the Duplessis years experienced by Scott in his battle against the Padlock Act and by Casgrain in her fight for women's right to vote was a thing of the past. The potential for social change was palpable. For the first time there was a legitimate hope the state would support and not prove an obstacle to reform. The principles of the Quiet Revolution made the optimism of the LDH's founders possible.

The LDH dealt with a variety of issues in the first seven years after its birth. Each of the four case studies eventually tackled the emotionally charged question of denominational education, and yet, amazingly for an organization operating in a province where religion played a major role in education, the LDH avoided the issue. In 1967, Dr. Henry Morgentaler (soon to be famous for challenging the abortion laws) raised the issue at a meeting of the LDH. Morgentaler's concerns were the same as those raised by the BCCLA, the CCLA and the Newfoundland-Labrador Human Rights Association (NLHRA): teachers were being fired or rejected for work because they did not conform to tenets of a particular faith, and students of minority faiths were forced to expose themselves to other religions. His motion was defeated, and, for the next twenty years, the issue did not figure prominently in the group's activities.[4]

The leadership of the LDH may not have been interested in dealing with denominational education, but it fought against the inadequacies in the legal system with a passion. Several members of the LDH were already in a strong position to influence government regarding the administration of justice in Quebec. Casgrain sat on a Conseil consultatif de l'administration de la justice for the Ministry of Justice as of 1965, and Scott was chair of a government committee that examined revisions to the Civil Code. Within the LDH, a law committee was quickly formed to research current problems in the justice system. George Wesley, a lawyer and founding member of the LDH, prepared a report that revealed an estimated fourteen thousand cases awaiting trial at the Superior Court in Montreal alone, compared to 2,550 in Ontario. Some cases had to wait a remarkable four to five years before being heard, with the average wait being thirty-six months. Judges were also underpaid, with the average salary of a Superior Court judge in Canada being $17,000 compared to $22,000 in the United States. A shortage of judges led to constant delays, and economically weak litigants were at the mercy of those who were well financed and could stretch out legal proceedings for long periods of time.[5]

As a solution to the many problems plaguing the judicial system, the LDH proposed the appointment of a commission to investigate the administration of justice, and, in 1967, its lobbying paid off. Thanks largely to the efforts of the LDH, the minister of justice appointed the Prévost Commission in 1967 to report on the administration of justice in penal and criminal matters in Quebec. What emerged from the inquiry was the most comprehensive analysis of the provincial justice system ever written. Out of 253 meetings and 181 public sessions, the Prévost Commission produced a massive compendium condemning the judicial system and recommending vast changes to it.[6]

Virtually all the recommendations forwarded by the LDH in its report to the commission were accepted and included in the document. These included recommendations for operating some twenty-four-hour courts, indemnifying victims of crimes, providing more resources for the judicial system, hiring more judges and police officers, and enforcing stricter regulations on search warrants. The Ligue even recommended that the commission go beyond its mandate and inquire into the uncertainty and arbitrariness of penal sentences. This the commission did, recommending the system be reformed to impose more lenient sentences and that it focus more on rehabilitation than on punishment.[7] Many of the LDH's recommendations endorsed by the commission, including twenty-four-hour courts and an expanded judicial system, would eventually be established, although not for many years to come.

Perhaps because of their initial interest in the administration of justice, the leadership of the LDH soon turned their energies towards the question of prisoners' rights. One of the concerns raised by the Prévost Commission was the prison system's focus on punishment rather than on rehabilitation. This was clearly the case with the new psychiatric wing being planned for St. Vincent de Paul Prison in 1965. St. Vincent de Paul was a federal penitentiary with a special wing for mentally ill offenders – a wing designed to isolate particularly violent felons, including those who represented a threat to the rest of the prison population. Cells were designed for complete isolation, with no windows or views of other prisoners and with guards patrolling above looking down on prisoners. In a letter to Solicitor General Guy Favreau in 1965, professors at the McGill forensic science clinic suggested the new wing would simply encourage violence: "As spatial and social isolation become more rigorous, destructive impulses tend to intensify in some individuals, precisely the type for whom this unit is designed. These impulses find solution in three ways, often interchangeable; aggression directed against the self in self-mutilation and suicide; against others in physical violence, or in the demolition of the cell; or there is withdrawal, with mental breakdown."[8]

The LDH helped organize a coalition of groups, including the John Howard Society and the Quebec Criminological Society, to lobby the federal government to stop construction of St. Vincent de Paul. Activists with the LDH organized seminars, wrote letters, and toured the prison. Opposition was also raised to the construction of a maximum security prison, with similar isolation units at Ste-Anne-des-Plaines. Lucien Cardin, minister of justice, justified the building of a new wing on the grounds that those inmates who would be placed in it were the worst of the worst: hardened habitual criminals guilty of causing disturbances in prisons and, in some cases, murdering prison guards. In response, in 1966 a coalition of forty-eight groups, including the LDH, organized a delegation to the solicitor general.[9] The delegation failed, and the government, determined to construct both facilities, refused to back down. Nonetheless, the LDH would continue to advocate on behalf of prisoners, visiting prisons and lobbying both levels of government.

Most of these issues remained peripheral to the LDH's main concern during this period: a bill of rights for Quebec. From its founding in 1963 to the passing of the Quebec Charter of Human Rights and Freedoms in 1975, the leadership of the LDH was almost obsessive in its pursuit of a provincial bill of rights. And for good reason. Many of its leaders, particularly Frank Scott, considered it shameful that, by the early 1970s, Quebec was virtually the only province in Canada with no human rights legislation on the books.

The LDH favoured a bill of rights that, in contrast to most human rights codes, would incorporate both fundamental freedoms, such as speech and assembly, and the anti-discrimination provisions commonly found in human rights codes. In fact, by the late 1960s, Saskatchewan was the only province in Canada with a bill of rights. Since there remained some confusion regarding jurisdiction in the field of individual rights, most provinces limited their human rights legislation to actions that were clearly in their sphere of influence. Specifically, human rights codes dealt with discrimination in employment, accommodation, and services.

The LDH's vision of a provincial bill of rights was first articulated by law professor (and future parliamentary leader of the Parti Québécois) Jacques-Yvan Morin in a 1963 article published in the *McGill Law Journal*. Morin's article was later republished by the LDH, with the association's endorsement, and he was asked to chair a committee to lobby the provincial government for a bill of rights.[10] The proposed bill of rights offers a glimpse into the LDH's perception of rights during its formative years. Given Morin's disposition to construe provincial jurisdiction broadly (he challenged the assumption that only the federal government could legislate on human rights), there were articles that protected the five fundamental freedoms (speech, religion, association, assembly, and press), equality for women, and administration of justice. Surprisingly, there were provisions for the recognition of economic and social rights; Morin wanted to ensure access to a free education, a minimum salary and standard of living, as well as the right to work and to social security. The inclusion of these rights in any provincial statute would have made Quebec the most progressive province in the field; even the Saskatchewan Bill of Rights did not include such sweeping economic and social rights. In suggesting clauses for education and social rights in a provincial bill of rights, the LDH also distinguished itself from the BCCLA, which would have considered education as a question of public policy rather than of rights. Finally, the proposed bill ended with recommendations to ensure the supremacy of the legislation over all other statutes by making it impossible to amend the bill without a two-thirds vote in the National Assembly.

With Morin's draft in hand, the LDH's leaders initiated a province-wide campaign to convince the Quebec government to pass a bill of rights. This campaign mainly took the form of organizing seminars and public engagements, with prominent individuals such as Frank Scott espousing the benefits of a provincial bill of rights. These efforts bore some fruit. In Volume 5 of its extensive report, the Prévost Commission recommended that the minister of justice introduce a "Charte des droits fondamentaux de la personne humaine" to define people's rights, specify the means and recourse through which such rights could be recognized, and establish sanctions in cases where such rights were violated. The report failed to specify the contents of such a charter, but the recommendation in itself was a validation of the LDH's position. Paul Crépeau, as president of the Office for the Revision of the Civil Code, also appointed Scott (who served as chair) and Morin to a civil rights committee to propose amendments to entrench certain rights in the code. A declaration of rights in the Quebec Civil Code would complement a bill of rights by entrenching rights in private law. Their report was submitted in 1966, with ten new articles to be added to the code.

Members of the LDH were therefore at the forefront of proposing significant revisions to provincial law in order to better protect individual rights. The work of the LDH, combined with the lobbying efforts of the United Council for Human Rights (a coalition of human rights groups in Quebec), finally paid off in 1970, when the newly elected Liberal government under Robert Bourassa appointed two people to draft a bill of rights. The government asked Frank Scott and Paul Crépeau to draft a bill, which they completed in 1971. By this stage, each political party in Quebec had expressed some support for a provincial bill of rights, and most had placed it in their election platforms.[11] An election in 1970 temporarily postponed plans to enact a bill of rights.

Fresh from an election victory in 1970, the Liberals acknowledged the critical role of the LDH in raising support for a bill of rights by sending their newly appointed minister of justice to the LDH's annual meeting to announce their intention to establish greater protections for individual rights. Among the reforms Jerôme Chôquette suggested were the insertion of a declaration of human rights in the Civil Code and in a future Quebec constitution, the creation of a permanent commission for the revision of civil rights in the Civil Code, the creation of a system of legal aid, and the institution of new measures to improve the speed and efficiency of the courts. Most important, Chôquette committed himself to a provincial bill of rights to complement the Canadian Bill of Rights, which he characterized as "almost worthless."[12] This apparent success, however, achieved little. Although initially warming to the idea of a provincial bill of rights and promising to present a declaration of rights before the National Assembly, Chôquette soon refused to go ahead with the proposal. It would take another five years before he would honour his commitment to introduce a bill of rights into the National Assembly.

With human rights codes being passed across the country in almost every province, why was the Quebec government so recalcitrant? Duplessis had responded to demands for a bill of rights in the 1950s by claiming that the only thing Quebeckers needed in order to defend themselves against discrimination was the Bible.[13] Clearly, under his regime there was little chance of passing anti-discrimination legislation. But the sixties was the period of the Quiet Revolution and the blossoming of the rights revolution. Jean Lesage's Liberals had ushered in a new era of Quebec politics – one more sympathetic to the idea of state protection for individual rights, and the Union Nationale of Daniel Johnson and Jean-Jacques Bertrand was a far cry from the party under Duplessis. Both Johnson and Bertrand publicly endorsed the idea of a provincial bill of rights. And yet, successive governments in Quebec hesitated to act on this issue. The most likely explanation for this hesitation was the highly contentious issue of language rights. The entire question of language rights had proven to be a political time-bomb in the late 1960s, and a riot in the St. Leonard suburb of Montreal in 1969, followed by a divisive debate regarding the Union Nationale's Bill 63 (which provided that parents could choose the language of their children's education) simply inflamed the issue. Lesage and the Liberals were unwilling to consider a provincial bill of rights until a commission appointed under the previous government to study language issues in Quebec (the Gendron Commission) completed its report.[14] Any attempt to pass a bill of rights would invariably mire the government in a debate on language rights, and most politicians in Quebec were not interested in doing this until the timing was propitious.

For these reasons, the LDH's dream of a bill of rights for Quebec remained unfulfilled by 1970. It is interesting to note how the LDH itself continued to avoid the question of language rights. The group had failed to assert language rights in its declaration of principles, made no presentation before the Royal Commission on Bilingualism and Biculturalism, and, in 1969, avoided taking any position on Bill 63. Morin's proposal for a provincial bill of rights and the Civil Rights Committee's recommendations for the Civil Code made no mention of language rights. When the Ligue publicly endorsed Trudeau's call in the late 1960s for a constitutional bill of rights, it conveniently sidestepped any mention of his position on language rights.[15] It was also a hallmark of the LDH's activism during this period that, while in some situations it may have advocated for social and economic rights, it did not explicitly take a position in favour of collective rights. At no time did it express any support for Quebec self-determination or for the protection of the French language. This was no doubt the type of organization envisioned by Trudeau and Scott, both of whom rejected the nationalists' stand demanding special protections for the French language in Quebec.

In 1969, Claude Forget (who would later become minister of social affairs under the Liberals) resigned as president of the LDH. It was not a happy parting. Forget, who wrote an extensive discussion paper on economic and social rights on behalf of the Quebec committee for the International Year for Human Rights, accused the Ligue and its members of being incapable of accomplishing anything. He characterized the organization as composed of dilettantes and elites who had never been victimized themselves; he saw it as an anachronism that was failing to function properly.[16] Forget's embittered resignation highlighted the basic weakness in the Ligue during this early period. With limited funds and only a few dedicated volunteers, the LDH was capable of only a few minor achievements. In particular, the association had adopted a minimalist approach to rights activism and was exclusively focused on lobbying for legislative and policy reform. It had limited contact with other SMOs in the province and did not participate in the United Council for Human Rights. The LDH's early years reflected a limited vision of social change, one based on a small group of elites working the legal and political system to protect basic civil and political rights.

"Just watch me": The October Crisis, 1970

In October 1970, the nation held its collective breath as events in Quebec unfolded. The October Crisis, initiated by the kidnappings of James Cross and Pierre Laporte by the Front de libération du Québec (FLQ), was one of the most stunning events of the period. For decades it has been the subject of intense discussion in the media as well as in academic and political circles. For the second and only other time in Canadian history, the powers of the War Measures Act were employed to suspend Canadians' civil liberties during peacetime. The imposition of the War Measures Act on 16 October 1970 remains one of the most controversial human rights crises in Canadian history.

The FLQ emerged amidst Quebec's Quiet Revolution. The Liberal Party defeated the Union Nationale in 1960, and the former played a key role in a fundamental transformation of Quebec politics and society. The "grand noirceur" was replaced with a secular, technocratic, modern society. Two new separatist parties were formed in the early 1960s: the Rassemblement pour l'indépendence nationale and the Ralliement national. They were soon joined by two other organizations dedicated to an independent Quebec state: l'Action socialiste pour l'indépendance du Québec (1960) and le Comité de liberation nationale (1962).

Some Quebec nationalists, however, eschewed the political movement and favoured a radical course of action. The original members of the FLQ were drawn from the Rassemblement pour l'indépendance nationale, and they inaugurated the organization by throwing a Molotov cocktail through the window of an English radio station (CKGM) in Montreal in February 1963. Soon after, in March 1963, they fire-bombed a Canadian forces barracks and spray-painted "FLQ" on the walls. Six additional bombings rocked Montreal between March and April 1963. Wilfred O'Neil, a night watchman, became the FLQ's first victim: he was killed in a bomb attack on a Canadian forces recruiting centre in Montreal in April 1963.[17]

The FLQ wanted more than an independent Quebec nation. While in jail, Pierre Vallières, one of the ideological leaders of the FLQ, wrote a best-selling book entitled *Nègres blanc d'Amérique (White Niggers of America)*. The book, which, through the word "niggers," borrowed the imagery of the black civil rights movement to symbolize the repression and second-class status of francophones ("to be a 'nigger' in America is to be not a man but someone's slave"), was a call to arms.[18] Vallières saw the FLQ as the vanguard of a revolutionary movement comparable to movements in Algeria and Cuba that would lead to the creation of an independent socialist Quebec state.

The rise of a terrorist organization deeply influenced by socialist principles was, in part, a manifestation of broader developments within the left in Quebec. During the sixties, the labour movement in Quebec broke away from its links with the conservative Roman Catholic Church and shifted dramatically to the left. Through the unionization of public-sector workers (Quebec was the first province to permit public-sector workers to unionize), organized labour expanded considerably. Unions represented approximately 40 percent of workers in the 1960s, compared with 30 percent a decade earlier.

Hundreds of bomb attacks between 1963 and 1970 can be attributed to the FLQ. Most of the attacks were directed against federal government property (armories, mailboxes, government offices), transportation links (railways, bridges), and businesses. Various FLQ cells robbed banks to finance their operations and stole weapons from armories and dynamite from construction sites to arm themselves. The RCMP managed to infiltrate the organization in June 1963, and it arrested most of its members by August 1963. Within a few months, a new and decentralized FLQ emerged: "From then on, the FLQ was no longer a single organization, a unified movement, but a collection of more or less connected but still clearly distinct groups, a set of initials to which all supporters of political violence lay claim."[19] On 19 February 1969, the most spectacular FLQ bombing took place at the Montreal Stock Exchange. The explosion injured twenty people (there were no deaths because the FLQ sent a warning in advance). The attack was initiated by the most violent cell of the FLQ network, that of Pierre-Paul Geoffrey. He was arrested on 4 March 1969 and pleaded guilty to all the actions of his cell. Judge André Fabien, presiding over Geoffrey's trial, handed down the most severe sentence in the history of the British Commonwealth: 124 life sentences.[20]

Although the Province of Quebec had been the locus of extreme forms of violence and social unrest for almost a decade, the October Crisis began when James Cross was abducted on 5 October 1970. In response to Cross' kidnapping, the police organized one of the largest manhunts in Canadian history. Between 7 and 10 October, police carried out nearly one thousand raids and searches and arrested, questioned, and then released about fifty people.[21] The provincial government balked at submitting to the majority of the terrorists' demands, such as releasing "political" prisoners and sending the kidnappers to Cuba or Algeria with an armload of gold bullion. Five days after kidnapping Cross, another FLQ cell kidnapped Pierre Laporte.

The abduction of Pierre Laporte was a symbolic act for the socialist FLQ: Laporte was the minister of labour in the Quebec government. The kidnappings heightened tensions to new levels; they gave the impression that the FLQ was organized and capable of coordinated action. Fifty people were arrested immediately following Laporte's abduction. On 15 October, three thousand people crowded into the Paul-Sauvé arena in Montreal chanting pro-FLQ slogans. Bourassa responded to the capture of his friend and colleague by calling for negotiations with the FLQ, but within days it became clear that the two sides could not find common ground. Meanwhile, military reinforcements continued to pour into Quebec. Six thousand troops were stationed in Montreal by the evening of 15 October.[22] Soldiers lined the streets of the city, keeping watch over government buildings and some street corners.

In Ottawa, the federal cabinet discussed the possibility of employing extreme methods to deal with the second kidnapping. Recently released cabinet documents reveal that two meetings took place on 15 October, one at 9:00 a.m. and the other at 2:30 p.m., when the cabinet met to consider implementing some form of emergency legislation. Bourassa was calling for special measures from the federal government to help his embattled administration, which Trudeau interpreted to mean an amendment to the Criminal Code or special temporary emergency legislation. The cabinet security committee had earlier rejected Pelletier's recommendation to implement emergency legislation. However, Pelletier and several other ministers raised the issue again during the cabinet's first meeting on 15 October. John Greene, minister of energy, mines, and resources, could not see how the government could establish the existence of an insurrection, particularly as the security panel had not come to such a conclusion. Nonetheless, it was much less a debate than a discussion. The cabinet was unanimously behind some form of emergency legislation.[23]

The cabinet was not insensitive to the potential repercussions of invoking the War Measures Act. Trudeau was worried that the retroactive nature of the legislation would offend rights activists (an accurate prediction, in hindsight). John Turner, minister of justice, was concerned that the declaration of an apprehended insurrection and the use of emergency powers was excessive. He stressed the need to mobilize parliamentary and public support behind their decision.[24] Meanwhile, desperate to find a solution, Bourassa and Jean Drapeau (mayor of Montreal) sent a letter to Trudeau declaring their belief that an apprehended insurrection was at hand.[25] Trudeau responded by proclaiming the War Measures Act. The next day, Pierre Laporte was found in the trunk of a car, murdered by the FLQ.

The Ligue and the Crisis of 1970

The defining moment in the history of the Ligue des droits de l'homme was the October Crisis. Within a few years, the fundamental orientation of the Ligue, its organizational structure and leadership, would alter dramatically. At the initiation of the crisis, the LDH was a collection of intellectual, economic, and political elites with close ties to government, and it was concerned primarily with defending civil liberties through legal reform. Quiet backroom diplomacy was its core strategy. But by 1973, the LDH had expanded its membership base and embraced a broader conception of rights. The organization also solicited state funding to hire a permanent staff and the Ligue soon became utterly dependant on state funding. All of this could be linked to the Ligue's inability to take an effective stance during the October Crisis.

The use of the War Measures Act shocked and stunned many Canadians. Although most of the English-language papers supported the government, the Quebec media were divided over the need for such extreme measures.[26] The three major union federations in Quebec organized a common front and were among the most out-spoken critics of the federal and provincial governments. Quebec labour called on Bourassa to lift the emergency measures and criticized the state for denying bail to prisoners.[27] Civil liberties groups were formed, at the instigation of professors at McGill University and the University of Montreal, to challenge the use of emergency powers, and a thousand students and teachers attended a teach-in organized by these groups on 27 October.[28] On university campuses throughout Montreal, students organized demonstrations, expressed sympathy for the FLQ in campus newspapers, planned sit-ins, and, at one point, paralyzed the campus of the Université du Québec à Montréal. In response, concerned administrators closed down the university in the face of militant student activism.[29]

Extensive abuses of human rights were committed under the War Measures Act and the subsequent regulations (Public Order Regulations) approved by Parliament in early December. The War Measures Act empowered the police to arrest and detain individuals for an indefinite period. Two hundred and eighty-eight people were arrested on the first night. Ultimately, 497 people were detained under the War Measures Act, and police conducted 3,068 searches without warrants. Most of the raids and arrests were directed against nationalists and the political left in general.[30] The average detainee spent a week in jail (some as many as twenty-one days). Yet, the vast majority of them (87 percent) were later released and never charged with a crime. Six-two people were charged by January 1971. Within a month, half of them were released and the charges were dropped. In the end, only eighteen people were convicted of a crime arising from the crisis.[31] "The whole exercise," as Thomas Berger suggested, "reveals how unwise it is to have such extraordinary power easily available to any government."[32]

Everyone arrested under the War Measures Act was denied due process.[33] Habeas corpus (an individual's ancient right to have a judge confirm that they have been lawfully detained) was suspended. The prisoners were not permitted to consult legal counsel and many were held incommunicado. Membership in the FLQ became a criminal offence. J.N. Lyon captured the significance of this one simple fact in the following passage, which was written in 1972 for the *McGill Law Journal*:

> This was a judgement that the FLQ was guilty of seditious conspiracy, made not by a judge or a jury in a court of law but made by the Federal executive ... What this really meant was that any person who belonged to or assisted the FLQ was judged, by executive degree, to be a party to the seditious conspiracy the federal executive had found to exist ... The judiciary was reduced to the role of timekeeper, keeping track of

who attended what meetings and spoke or communicated what statements on behalf of an association. Criminal guilt was determined by executive decree.[34]

Most importantly, the crime was retroactive. A person who had attended a single FLQ meeting in the early 1960s was, by the wording of the regulations, criminally liable.[35]

The state targeted the media during the crisis. Among those arrested after the War Measures Act was declared on 16 October 1970 were several journalists and media personalities, including Louis Fournier from CKAC, Yves Fabre (a photographer from the *Journal de Montréal*), and journalist Pol Chantraine. Student newspapers, in particular, faced numerous obstacles during the crisis, and the War Measures Act was applied outside Quebec. In Ottawa, the printer of Carleton University's student newspaper decided to call the RCMP about an issue dealing with the crisis. The RCMP subsequently "allowed" the paper to print the FLQ's manifesto and commentaries on the emergency if the editors indicated on the front page that the paper did not endorse the FLQ.[36] Student newspapers in Toronto and Halifax were also confronted by their respective printers, who refused to publish the manifesto.[37] Police confiscated hundreds of copies of student newspapers at the University of Guelph for publishing the manifesto.[38] The (University of) *St. Mary's Journal* in Nova Scotia carried blank spaces where a printer refused to publish articles on the situation in Quebec, and in Saanich the police paid several visits to the editors of the University of Victoria student newspaper to "remind" them that publishing the manifesto was forbidden.[39] Meanwhile, in Quebec, authorities cautioned McGill University's student newspaper, the *McGill Daily,* against writing editorials that attacked the War Measures Act and expressed sympathy with the FLQ.[40]

Radio-Canada vice-president E.S. Hallman also warned his reporters to be cautious about reporting on the October Crisis. Michel Bourdon was suspended and then fired from Radio Canada for insubordination on 7 November 1970, and three other newspeople were dismissed from Radio Canada's News Service for lack of objectivity.[41] One scholar has suggested that "the most troubling aspect of the October Crisis was the pressure and the repeated attempts of intimidation from the Canadian Prime Minister's colleagues [with regard to the media]."[42] Gérard Pelletier, for example, phoned and visited Claude Ryan (the editor of *Le Devoir* and one of the leading critics of the federal government) and encouraged other editors to practise self-censorship. Trudeau's chief of staff, Marc Lalonde, phoned newspaper editors and discouraged others from publishing the FLQ manifesto.[43]

Pelletier vigorously denied accusations that the government was putting pressure on the media, and he insisted that the government had only warned journalists to be sure of their facts.[44] Tensions were clearly high. CBC postponed a few documentaries dealing with political crises and kidnappings, cancelled several television shows (one because the lead singer was imprisoned under the War Measures Act!), and the documentary *Testament of Lenin* was not aired out of concern it might incite the populace to violent action.[45] At one point during the crisis, the president of the Federation of Professional Journalists of Quebec compared Canada to Paraguay and castigated the federal government for censoring the publication of the FLQ manifesto.[46] Trudeau and his allies fired back and accused the media of alarming the public and giving the FLQ a partial victory by providing the organization with so much publicity. Meanwhile, the Syndicat général des communications, representing most journalists in Montreal, and the Association professional des journalistes de l'Outaouais called for changes to the regulations issued under the War Measures Act to allow greater diffusion of information.[47]

The press was not without fault. Unconfirmed rumours abounded in the pages of leading newspapers. Pierre Laporte's murder was grotesquely exaggerated: the media purported that he was tortured, cut up with knives, strangled, and had his genitals removed.[48] Raphael Cohen-Almagor concludes that "the behaviour of some organs of the French media exacerbated the crisis and forced the government to contemplate possible procedures for monitoring the media."[49] Radio stations CKLM and CKAC, for instance, broadcast FLQ communiqués before turning them over to the police (thus restricting the ability of the police to respond).[50] The crisis raised a classic free speech conflict during one of the worst crises in Canadian history.[51]

As was the case with the Padlock Act and the espionage commission, the October Crisis motivated concerned individuals to form ad hoc civil liberties associations. Within Quebec, civil libertarians joined students, workers, and others to demand the revocation of the War Measures Act. The *McGill Daily* called on students to attend a meeting to form the Comité pour la défense des droits et libertés; students congregated at McGill on 26 October to launch the group and to sign a petition to revoke the War Measures Act.[52] More than one thousand students and professors attended a teach-in at the Université de Montréal on 28 October 1970 to create a Comité Québécois pour la défense des libertés (another small meeting of two hundred people had been held earlier at the Université de Montréal on 16 October to begin setting up the organization).[53] On the same day, the Comité pour la défense de la démocratie was created in Quebec City; it was composed of professors and students at the Université Laval and unionists.[54] Another group, the Mouvement pour la défense des prisonniers politiques (MDPPQ), led by Dr. Serge Mongeau (who had been an independent candidate in the South Shore riding of Taillon in 1970 [against René Lévesque]), was revitalized by the crisis. Originally named the Comité d'aide au group Vallières-Gagnon, the group was reorganized in June 1970 as the MDPPQ. Although the police labelled the MDPPQ an FLQ front, the purpose of the organization was to raise bail and legal fees for anyone imprisoned for taking part in demonstrations for political reasons.[55] In January 1971, several thousand demonstrators took part in a protest organized by the MDPPQ, trade unions, and other left-wing groups to call for the release of the prisoners arrested since October.

A small opposition was also emerging outside Quebec. In Waterloo, the Citizens Commission of Inquiry into the War Measures Act was created in December 1970 in reaction to the seizure of a Guelph student newspaper and the arrest of a Kitchener resident for distributing a pamphlet on the FLQ. The committee, which included university professors, labour leaders, church ministers, journalists, and a former premier of Saskatchewan (Woodrow Loyd), held several public hearings in Ontario and Quebec.[56] The Peninsula Civil Rights Committee emerged in St. Catharines after the imposition of the War Measures Act. The committee quickly organized a "Quebec teach-in" at Brock University to protest the suspension of civil liberties; around three hundred attended to lend support to the committee's call to abrogate emergency powers.[57] Meanwhile, a national human rights organization was born: the Canadian Federation of Civil Liberties and Human Rights Associations. The Federation was a product of the October Crisis and would be active in promoting human rights across the country for the next twenty years.

In the midst of this maelstrom of activity, many Quebeckers eagerly awaited a response from the province's respected rights association. To the disappointment of many, however, the association failed to distinguish itself during the crisis. The LDH's first public statement was released on 19 October 1970 and was far from a clear condemnation of the government's actions. The Ligue limited its concerns to the arrest and detention of individuals for long periods of time: "La Ligue des droits de l'homme demande que les personnes accusées d'avoir commis un crime soient jugées suivant la loi et déplore le fait que, dans certains cas, on ait détenu des accusés pendant des périodes très longues, avant même que ces accusés nient été trouvé coupable. Ces injustices s'étant produites avant le 16 octobre 1970, il y a lieu de croire qu'elles se reproduisent d'autant plus aisément qu'elles seront devenues légales."

The statement condemned the use of emergency powers to deal with the situation in Quebec. However, the Ligue also expressed some sympathy for the federal government. The release acknowledged that the federal government was taking into consideration the interests of the province's citizens and using the only law available. Instead of calling for the immediate abrogation of the War Measures Act, the LDH recommended that the government work with the opposition parties in Parliament to replace the War Measures Act as soon as possible. The Ligue also put forward several other recommendations: the minister of justice should consult with the families of each detainee; if the police could not find any evidence to charge the detainee, they should be immediately released from custody; detainees should have access to legal counsel; and the government should establish a commission comprised of three eminent personalities to ensure that the detainees had access to appropriate services and supervision.

Several weeks later the government continued to detain people without charging them with a crime. And yet, the LDH maintained its diplomatic position. In a press release issued on 27 November 1970, it challenged the law's provisions for guilt by association, arrest without warrant, and detention without bail. As Trudeau predicted, the retroactive nature of the regulations passed under the War Measures Act was a particularly sore point for human rights activists, and the LDH warned the government against arresting young men who were only associated with the FLQ in its early years.

The statements issued on 19 October 1970 and 11 November 1970 were the sum total of the LDH's public declarations during the crisis.[58] No demonstrations were organized, no briefs were presented to the federal or provincial governments, no letters were sent to public officials, and no attempt was made to rally support against the legislation. Students held sit-ins and formed ad hoc civil liberties groups, the MDPPQ led rallies, and organized labour united to condemn the government's actions; the LDH, however, remained relatively silent. No action was taken to undermine the governments' position.[59] In a column published in *Le Devoir* on 12 December 1970, Claude Lemelin lambasted the Ligue for its weak response to the suspension of civil liberties during the crisis.[60] Years later, Sandra Djwa, interviewing Jacques Hébert for her biography of Frank Scott, noted that during the October Crisis the president of the LDH justified the Ligue's actions by

> pinpointing the difference in emotional climate between Quebec and Ontario when he observed the Quebec Civil Liberties Union could not take a position like that adopted by the Canadian Civil Liberties Association in Toronto, which condemned the use of the Act, because Québécois members were so conscious of living in "a climate of fear." In the Montreal group there was complete unanimity about the need to restore order, but the middle-of-the-road position they took annoyed both the moderates and the extremists.[61]

Nonetheless, the LDH was not inactive during the crisis. On 25 October 1970, the LDH formed the Comité d'aide aux personnes détenues en vertu de la loi sur les mesures de guerre (Committee to Help Persons Detained under the War Measures Act), whose mandate was to inquire into the conditions of prisoners held under the War Measures Act. This committee was unquestionably the LDH's most effective contribution to the battle against the state's zealousness in stamping out the FLQ. This initiative was consistent with the Ligue's concern with the rights of prisoners, and its goal was to focus exclusively on getting access to prisoners and helping them contact their families, evaluating the conditions of their detention, and providing some of them with legal counsel. The committee received generous funding from the CCLA ($4,000), the provincial government ($5,000), and from various individual and group donations (amounting to another $5,000).[62]

Jacques Hébert, Reverend Jacques Tellier, and Rolland Parenteau were allowed access to the prisoners and to inspect the prison. In many cases, the committee was successful in winning the early release of prisoners. The committee also created a legal aid subcommittee, led by Paul Crépeau, to provide prisoners with free access to legal counsel. It managed to convince the provincial ombudsman to investigate and consider compensating individuals who were detained but never charged (several people, for instance, lost their jobs while in jail). In addition, the committee provided financial assistance to families whose breadwinners were detained, intervened with landlords to prevent families and individuals from being evicted when rent was not paid in time, negotiated with banks and other credit institutions over loan payments, and spoke on behalf of students who missed exams. It also made several recommendations to the minister of justice relating to the unnecessary seizure of books and documents unrelated to the crisis, raised concerns regarding the unjustified treatment of certain prisoners during their imprisonment and interrogations, and complained about people who were held incommunicado. Hébert was particularly concerned that Parthenais Detention Centre, a prison designed to hold people for a few weeks at most, was being used for the long-term incarceration of people arrested during the crisis.[63] In its formal report, the committee suggested that "all the prisoners, men and women, were being held in conditions unworthy of a civilized country."[64] By the time most of the prisoners had been released, the committee had met with 130 prisoners.

The crisis lasted approximately two months.[65] Cross was released on 3 December, and his kidnappers were flown to Cuba. Laporte's killers were captured on 27 December and sent to jail (by 1982, however, most of the exiles and prisoners were back on the streets in Quebec, having been granted parole or a reduced sentence). The army left Quebec in January 1971 and the emergency powers lapsed on 30 April 1971.[66] Although the Ligue never supported the use of emergency powers, Hébert and the Ligue had carefully avoided condemning the federal government throughout the crisis. In fact, while the troops were marching out of Quebec in January 1971, Hébert reiterated his sympathy for Trudeau's position during a meeting of the Undersecretary of State's Advisory Committee on Human Rights. Hébert was invited to consult with the committee on how the federal government could involve itself in the field of human rights. He insisted that the province, not the federal government, was responsible for any human rights abuses arising out of the crisis. He did not feel "that the Federal government lacked in some way, as far as Human Rights were concerned [but that,] after all, it was not their responsibility ... People were detained in the Provincial jail, so it was, to [his] point of view, totally provincial."[67]

Several Quebeckers, though, were unwilling to allow the LDH to shrug off criticism of its weak performance during the crisis. In March 1971, twenty members of the MDPPQ and a group calling itself the Chevaliers de l'indépendance marched into Hébert's publishing house to protest the Ligue's inaction. They were also protesting the publication of Gérard Pelletier's *The October Crisis* by Éditions du Jour. With large signs stating "Hébert is a Traitor" and sporting two-by-fours, the grim-faced protestors refused to allow anyone in or out of the office, forcing Hébert to sleep there for a couple of nights to avoid a violent confrontation.[68] The protestors demanded that the LDH call a general assembly to denounce the retroactivity of the Public Order Act and the treatment of prisoners in Orsainville prison, and to provide observers during the trials of the individuals arrested during the crisis. Hébert attempted to negotiate with the protestors, but, failing to come to an accord, he eventually called the police and the sit-in was brought to an end after thirty-six hours. The conflict between Hébert and the MDPPQ soon moved to the pages of the province's leading newspapers. Not only did the incident at the publishing house receive extensive coverage but Hébert and Serge Mongeau also lashed out at each other in the pages of *Le Devoir, La Presse,* and the *Montreal Gazette,* accusing each other of cowardice and of betraying French Canadians.

The hostile encounter between the MDPPQ and the LDH had more symbolic than practical consequences. Hébert was re-elected as president of the LDH, and there were no further confrontations between the two organizations. But for many on the left, including members of the Ligue, the LDH had failed to act against the most repressive attack on civil liberties in Canada since the Second World War. Organized labour and several members of the Parti Québécois, Rassemblement pour l'indépendance nationale, MDPPQ, and other political movements were not only targets for arrest during the crisis but were also among the federal and provincial governments' most vocal critics. When the CLC presented a brief to the federal cabinet in 1971, Louis Laberge, president of the Fédération des travailleurs du Québec, entered into a shouting match with Trudeau over the War Measures Act.[69] The failure of the LDH to act more aggressively during the crisis was a particularly significant omission for a civil liberties organization. Since the 1930s, rights associations in Quebec had never hesitated to defend unpopular individuals and associations, particularly those on the militant left who were often the target of state repression, as was the case with individuals prosecuted under the Padlock Act. Even Frank Scott, a founding member of the LDH with a history for taking key civil liberties cases to the Supreme Court of Canada, openly supported the use of the War Measures Act.[70] He was joined by many other notable figures in Canada, including chief justice of the Supreme Court of Canada Samuel Freedman, future attorney-general and chief justice of Ontario James McRuer, and Canadian historian Arthur Lower (who once led the Winnipeg Civil Liberties Association).

The MDPPQ was not alone in criticizing the LDH for failing to rise to the occasion. The LDH released its third and final press release relating to the crisis in April 1971. Hébert made no attempt to counter the claims that the Ligue had been soft on the federal government, and the association reiterated its support for the federal government. Letters to the editor published in *Le Devoir* called on Hébert to resign because of his failure to position the Ligue more critically during the crisis. One individual writing to the newspaper suggested that "if your degree of patience is proportional to the level of your friendship with Mr. Trudeau, leave the union Mr. Hébert."[71] At the same time the paper's editor, Claude Ryan, pointed out that parts of the Quebec media had criticized the Ligue for its poor response to the crisis. Another article that appeared in the *Montreal Gazette* in April predicted that Hébert would face a bitter crowd at the LDH's annual general meeting the following day because the Ligue "under Hébert's leadership has been woefully negligent in doing battle against alleged injustice and abuses in this province, practically all of them stemming from the October Crisis."[72] The author hinted that Hébert's relationship with Trudeau had stayed the former's criticism of the federal government during the crisis; the two had travelled together in China in the early 1960s and had co-written a book on their experiences, and they had founded the LDH with Pelletier in 1963. Trudeau appointed Hébert to the Canadian Radio and Telecommunication Council in 1971 and, later, to the Senate. As a 1972 report prepared for the secretary of state concluded, since Trudeau "was one of the association's founding members along with Jacques Hébert, now president of La Ligue, and others, and because of the ambiguous stand taken by the association on the War Measures Act, many citizens are not convinced that the group is non-political, as such a group must be."[73]

The LDH had placed itself in a difficult position by attempting to condemn the use of emergency powers while simultaneously hedging its criticism of Trudeau's government. To make matters worse, the leadership of the LDH was dismayed to discover that Trudeau had actually gone on television and stated that the LDH actively *supported* his position during the crisis. When asked how, as a civil libertarian, he viewed the crisis, Trudeau responded in one interview that the "Civil Liberties Union of Montreal supported the government's invocation of the War Measures Act. Never forget that. It's easy when you're sitting in Toronto and Vancouver to talk about civil liberties. But the Civil Liberties Union of Montreal supported the government; don't forget that."[74] Both furious and confused by Trudeau's claim that the LDH endorsed the use of the War Measures Act, the members of the Ligue resolved at their 1971 general meeting to send a letter to the prime minister asking him to retract his comments. But Trudeau refused. He argued in his letter to Pierre Jasmin, director general of the LDH, that the LDH had acknowledged that the government was acting in the interests of the people and was working under extreme circumstances. As far as Trudeau was concerned, the LDH understood the necessity of his government's actions and supported them.[75]

Fourteen years later, the Ligue's conduct during the October Crisis continued to rankle its members. The events of October 1970 would be seen by future members of the Ligue as an abysmal failure on the part of the LDH. In a report to the administrative council in 1984, the LDH's actions in 1970 were characterized as shameful and as a failure to live up to the organization's mandate.[76] This attitude was to be a major stimulus for instigating the institutional and philosophical changes in the LDH between 1970 and 1972.

Transition Years, 1970-75

The impact of the October Crisis did not have immediate implications within the LDH. But within a few years, Maurice Champagne, a professor at the University of Montreal, would take over as director general of the LDH and lead the organization into a new era of human rights activism.

The most profound development in the history of the Ligue began with the publication of a new manifesto in September 1972. From an association of elite members with a focus on isolated cases and individual rights, the LDH began to take on the role of encouraging social transformation in Quebec. The manifesto called upon the Ligue to adapt to the changes occurring within Quebec society and to consider the unique problems facing the poor, women, the elderly, youth, and ethnic minorities. Freedoms of speech or assembly were no longer sufficient: citizens had a *right* to be better informed on ways to challenge exploitation and to participate equally in social institutions. The manifesto embraced notions of *positive* freedom. With this new mandate, economic, social, and cultural rights were given equal (if not greater) priority than were civil and political rights. First Nations, the handicapped, non-unionized workers, immigrants, families, and others fell under the new mandate. Several of the original priorities would continue to dominate the LDH's agenda: prisoners' rights, police abuse of powers, and a bill of rights for Quebec. But now, instead of concerning itself with individual rights, the LDH would focus on achieving equality by improving the social conditions within which those rights were exercised.[77]

The manifesto raised a number of concerns about social inequalities in Quebec society. Many elderly were kicked out of their homes by their children and had no place to go; they were rejected by hospitals for not being sick enough and by old-age homes for being too sick. Discrimination against women was prevalent. Children and teenagers were abused, families raised children in decaying urban environments, prisoners were held in degrading conditions, immigrants were summarily refused entry to the country and had little recourse to appeal, college students were denied freedom of opinion, and employees were dismissed for union activity. The manifesto constituted a broad attack on both specific problems and fundamental inequalities in Quebec society, and it went much further than did the civil liberties-oriented BCCLA.

The LDH's new approach to human rights activism embraced positive rights and, in turn, placed new demands on the state. In a way, its changing activism was part of the overall socio-political transformations that were occurring within the province during this period. Organized labour became increasingly radicalized, and many of the province's leading labour institutions advanced broad-based critiques of capitalist society. Of course, it was also during this period that the Quebec independence movement was maturing. By the 1970s, the movement had manifested itself most directly in the form of a new political party, the Parti Québécois. Although primarily a coalition of nationalists of varying political stripes, with a strong middle-class base of support, the Parti Québécois also began as a social democratic party with strong links to the political left. The party's membership, electoral support base, and platform were consistent with those of other social democratic parties of the period and favoured a strong, activist role for the state.

The massive expansion of organized labour, combined with the rise of the Parti Québécois and its election victory in 1976, strengthened the left in Quebec. Since the onset of the Quiet Revolution, the Quebec state had played a prominent role in the social and political life of Quebeckers. Francophones in Quebec "came to view the Quebec state as a powerful instrument capable of improving their social and economic condition and, moreover, obligated to do so."[78] The LDH's shift towards positive rights and greater demands on the state was consistent with broader developments within Quebec at this time.

With the administrative council's acceptance of the new manifesto in 1972, structural changes were introduced to make the LDH more inclusive. The elitism that had characterized the LDH since its founding was quickly shed. Membership fees, having risen to ten dollars per person in the late 1960s, were reduced to two dollars. No longer would new members have to be vetted by the administrative council. By 1972, the administrative council, once dominated by lawyers, professors, and journalists, became more representative. There were now only four lawyers, and they worked alongside criminologists, sociologists, psychologists, social workers, journalists, an ex-prisoner, and various advocates for the rights of women, youth, non-unionized workers, and others.

One of the central architects of this new orientation was Maurice Champagne. He was well educated, with a bachelor's degree from the University of Montreal (1955), a master's degree in medieval studies from the same university (1957), and a second master's degree in French literature (1965). He completed his doctorate in 1968 at l'Université de Nice (France) in child psychology. He was a professor for a short period and became the director of social studies at Collège Saint Denis until he joined the LDH full time.[79] Champagne had been elected vice-president of the LDH in 1971 and was later elected president, a volunteer position he vacated in 1972 to become the LDH's full-time director. It was Champagne who recommended and drafted the manifesto that set the stage for the group's new orientation.

It became clear early on that the manifesto's proposed new direction was not a hollow declaration. No issue made this more evident than the LDH's decision to take a position on language rights, an issue the old guard had vigorously avoided. An LDH committee on language rights reported on 12 April 1973, offering a series of principles it felt should guide the government in determining its language policies. A year later, the Bourassa government introduced Bill 22, legislation designed to protect the French language by removing, among others things, parental choice for a child's education as established in 1969's Bill 63 (language of education would now be based on a competency test). Whereas the LDH had studiously avoided taking a stance on Bill 63, it eagerly jumped into the fray in 1974. The association wanted French entrenched as the official language of Quebec and it wanted education to be used to promote the French language: two of the core objectives of Bill 22. But the LDH's position went much further. Alongside a statement acknowledging the equal rights of Aboriginals and ethnic minorities to explore their own separate cultural identities, the LDH forwarded the radical suggestion that all primary education should be in French. The justification was that, since English speakers were overprotected by the dominant North American environment, it would be just for them to cede some of their privilege to the majority in Quebec so that francophones could exercise their right to survival (the LDH's own publications were now to be printed only in French).[80] In forcing students to be educated in French, the LDH was committing what the old guard would have considered blasphemy: placing the collective interests of French society (through the preservation of the French language) over individual choice. According to the declaration, the "droits linguistiques pour la majorité français au Québec sont des droits collectifs qui ont une importance telle qu'ils peuvent justifier pleinement, à ce moment de notre histoire, des mesures qui aient pour effet de créer des obligations particulières aux individus, notamment dans les limites qu'il faut apporter au choix de la langue d'enseignement pour les parents et les jeunes." The LDH supported aspects of Bill 22 but was concerned with those parts of the bill that threatened to legalize "both in spirit and in letter those very bilingual practices that should have been curtailed in order to affirm the priority of French."[81] Bourassa criticized the LDH's proposals, attacking the association publicly on a radio show, where he used several choice epithets to describe the organization's ideas on language rights.

If taking a position on language rights hinted at a new orientation, the decision to adopt a position on the right to self-determination was proof that the LDH had abandoned its roots. Although the group shied away from going so far as to take an explicit position on independence, the LDH asserted the right of minorities to self-determination as stated in the Charter of the United Nations. In a special declaration issued in 1972, the LDH advocated that no fair negotiations for rights could take part between minority and majority unless the fundamental right to self-determination of the former was recognized by the latter.[82] The organization's new orientation was not well received in many quarters. An editorial published the next day in *Le Devoir* warned against taking such an extreme position. If the

LDH hoped to advocate a rights-based approach to self-determination, the editor argued, it would have to affirm its position on the basis of minority rights: "Ce n'est donc pas pour défendre l'indépendantisme que le Ligue affirme le droit à l'auto determination, mais c'est plutôt pour forcer tous les hommes politiques à affirmer leur respect pour les droits des minorités ... Le simple respect des droits individuels et collectifs exige qu'on laisse aux hommes et aux peuples la liberté d'évoluer comme ils l'entendent." Premier Robert Bourassa publicly condemned the LDH, saying that it was run by fanatical nationalists with unrealistic policies on language rights.[83] The LDH was clearly drawing on the rhetoric encouraged by the Parti Québécois and the current political battles raging in the province over language and education. The LDH's new orientation evolved within the context of an increasingly influential sovereignty movement, which, in 1973, had garnered the Parti Québécois 30 percent of the popular vote. Although there were no formal ties between the Parti Québécois and the LDH, they often entered into coalitions on various issues, such as calling for more government-sponsored daycare.[84]

To honour its new mandate, the LDH also formed separate offices for the elderly and women, both of which, by 1974, had floundered due to lack of interest. In contrast, the Office des droits des détenu(e)s (ODD) proved to be an impressive success. The LDH had always advocated on behalf of the rights of this unpopular class of citizens, and, while a few other rights associations took up the cause of prisoners' rights, no group did so to the extent of the LDH. In the 1960s, the LDH had lobbied against the construction at St. Vincent de Paul and Ste-Anne-des-Plaines, and in 1971 it formed a committee that successfully lobbied Chôquette to transfer Paul Rose and Bernard Lortie from Parthenais prison. Parthenais was de-signed to hold prisoners only for short periods as people awaited trial, yet these two FLQ prisoners had been held there for months. The LDH had even opposed the construction of Parthenais itself in the early 1970s, to no avail.

The ODD was an extension of this type of advocacy. It was formed as a separate office, which meant that it had its own executive and administrative council and that it did not have to answer to the administrative council of the LDH except in cases dealing with broad policy issues. Its mandate was to develop an open and accessible prison system concerned with rehabilitation and to defend prisoners' rights. The committee was chaired by Raymond Boyer, one of the individuals de-tained by the espionage commission in 1946.[85]

In the spirit of the LDH's new mandate, the ODD was far more than an exten-sion of the Ligue's previous activities in dealing with prisoners.[86] The ODD not only sought fair treatment for prisoners but also adopted the radical position of calling for the complete abolition of prisons: "L'objectif de l'ODD est l'abolition des prisons. L'emprisonment est fondée sur la discrimination et la destruction de la personne incarcérée. À courte terme, l'ODD prône des changements qui non seulement améliorent les conditions de vie des personnes détenues mais qui vont dans le sens de l'abolition."[87] Within a few years, the ODD had become an impressive success and, at times, it was more productive than the entire LDH. At a time when rights associations struggled to mobilize a dozen people in a room together for monthly meetings, anywhere from ten to fifteen people attended *weekly* meetings of the ODD, which produced a regular journal, appeared on numerous radio and television shows, and organized at least a dozen press conferences a year.[88] The amount of dedication and volunteer work engendered by the ODD would have made the leader of any social movement organization envious.

In addition to its work in spreading awareness and taking on individual dossiers, the ODD promoted coalition building among SMOs. One example of successful coalition building was the group's campaign for the closure of Parthenais. Parthenais prison (Centre de prévention de Parthenais) had been built to accommodate short-term prisoners who were awaiting trial (it was built on the tenth, twelfth, and thirteenth floors of the Quebec Provincial Police building in Montreal), yet in practice prisoners would be incarcerated for extended periods of time. The conditions were deplorable. Prisoners engaged in a hunger strike in 1974, when they complained of poor food, of being required to eat in their cells near the toilet instead of at tables, of not being able to use the telephone, of having no clean clothes and of being kept in individual cells for extended periods (sometimes days) without being allowed outside.[89] Demonstrations and protests by prisoners became a regular feature of life at Parthenais: four hunger strikes took place between 1970 and 1973, a riot erupted in 1973, and, in the same year, six prisoners mutilated themselves to protest their living conditions. In 1974, the ODD organized a seminar in collaboration with the School of Criminology at the Université de Montréal to bring together groups to collectively pressure the government to close the controversial prison. In the following year, at the initiative of the ODD, twelve associations (including the three provincial labour federations) formed a common front to call on the government to commit to the closure of Parthenais. Chôquette acquiesced to their demands but refused to offer a firm date. For the next several years, the common front remained intact and kept constant pressure on the government to close the controversial prison, only to be consistently frustrated by the state's stubborn refusal to eliminate Parthenais.

The LDH also dealt with issues of national concern, although it was unquestionably a provincial organization first and foremost. Abortion was one such issue. The Ligue's first major publication (the LDH never published a newsletter before 1982) appeared in 1974 in the form of a book entitled *La société québécoise face à l'avortement*. It provided a detailed analysis of the abortion issue in Quebec, noting attitudes and changing perceptions in Quebec society. Thanks to the 1969 omnibus bill, which decriminalized hospital-sanctioned abortions, therapeutic abortions had risen in Quebec from 534 in 1970 to 2,847 in 1972. However, only five francophone hospitals provided abortions (mostly in Montreal) compared to 133 hospitals in the rest of Canada. There was a clear hesitancy among francophone institutions to provide this service, and this was a serious problem for poor francophone women who could not afford to travel out of province for abortions.

Instead of using a pure rights-based approach by arguing that abortion was a human right in itself, the LDH characterized the issue as a question of social justice: "La Ligue ne saurait reconnaître l'avortement comme un droit mais comme une mesure d'exception légitimée par le droit à la santé et à la qualité humaine de la vie pour tous ainsi une par le droit de la femme à decider de ses maternités et à les voir faciliter par la société et l'état."[90] It went to great pains to place abortion in the context of positive rights, such as promoting gender equality (as opposed to simply being a question of individual liberty): "La discrimination systématique qui est fait à la femme, par l'absence de politiques et de services adéquats de garderies, contribue à maintenir un partage injuste des tâches et des responsabilités entre l'homme et la femme." The problem was not with the law but with the sociopolitical context of Quebec, where people knew little about abortion or its implications, had minimal education on sexuality and contraception, and had access to limited support services. It was a truly egalitarian position and contrasted sharply with the group's previous focus on negative rights.

Abortion and prisoners' rights were just a few examples of the renewed activism of the LDH during the transition years. Implementing a bill of rights in Quebec, however, remained the group's central priority. Unfortunately, Jérôme Chôquette continued to vacillate. The LDH responded by forming a committee to draft a proposed charter of human rights and freedoms for Quebec and, by February 1973, had consulted with a variety of jurists, judges, union leaders, and others on the contents of the proposed bill.[91] Its goal was to stimulate a massive public debate to pressure the government to introduce a provincial bill of rights. It was fully consistent with the group's new philosophy of a "société de participation" and would encourage greater public participation in public policy. A total of 500,000 copies of the Ligue's proposed bill were distributed across the province; *Le Devoir* and *La Presse* distributed 50,000 and 100,000 copies, respectively. *Le Soleil* carried a full-page advertisement, and 50,000 information packages were sent to individuals and organizations. Members of the executive council participated in radio shows, television programs, newspaper interviews, and various conferences to promote the proposal. By the end of 1973, the group had managed to encourage the participation of almost four hundred groups in the bill of rights debate.[92]

A proposal for a provincial bill of rights was completed by May 1973. It was evident from its proposal that the LDH had evolved since Morin's draft ten years earlier. All of the basic provisions in the Morin proposal were to be found in the new draft, with only minor variations. Unlike Morin's draft, however, this new proposal had specific provisions for economic and social rights for children, the elderly, and the handicapped. For instance, it recognized the rights of children to be treated equally with adults and for the handicapped to have equal access to public transportation. References to collective rights appear in the 1973 draft, whereas Morin focused exclusively on individual rights.[93] Finally, and most tellingly, it included language rights. The proposal would establish French as the official language of Quebec, while asserting the right of the people and government to act to protect their language. In such areas as immigration, the state was called upon to do all in its power to assure the supremacy of the French language.

Despite continued efforts to pressure the government to act, nothing developed. In a speech before the Canadian Jewish Congress in March 1974, Chôquette made it clear that "si cette Charte n'a pas été présentée jusqu'a date, c'est en large partie à cause de la difficultué de réconcilier, dans la domaine linguistique, les aspirations de la majorité français au Québec de voir exister et se développer une vie culturelle française même économique avec, ce qui est aussi important, le droit de ceux qui sont ici et qui sont déjà intégrés, dans la minorité anglophone, d'exercer leur libre choix en matière d'éducation et en matière de communication avec leurs proches ou dans leurs affaires."[94] Then, in late 1974, the Bourassa government introduced Bill 22. With the controversial issue of language rights solved for the Bourassa government, it could now move towards implementing a bill of rights.

The efforts of the LDH had clearly paid off when, in the 1974 throne speech announcing the government's intention to introduce language legislation, the government committed itself to a bill of rights.[95] By March 1974, a committee of the Department of Justice began a study on a potential bill of rights and solicited input from the LDH. Months later, on 29 October 1974, the government introduced Bill 50: Loi sur les droits et libertés de la personne. Led by Champagne, the LDH expressed both support and concern over Bill 50 before a legislative committee. In many ways, the bill was far ahead of most provincial human rights codes in Canada, and the section on the proposed human rights commission represented about 70 percent of the LDH's own recommendations, including provisions to ensure its independence by requiring it to report directly to the National Assembly.[96] But the legislation had some significant flaws. Section 60 limited the commission's investigations to cases of discrimination, whereas the LDH hoped the commission could have a broader mandate to investigate all complaints as well as to take on educational activities. There was also no provision for a right to access to information, and the LDH felt the Charter should include a clause asserting francophones' right to self-determination.

The final version of the Quebec Charter of Human Rights and Freedoms, passed in 1975, owed a great deal to the efforts of the LDH. A few months before the legislation was passed, the Quebec representative to a conference of human rights ministers in British Columbia credited the LDH with being the leading influence on Bill 50.[97] In the debate in the National Assembly on the proposed legislation, no group except the LDH was mentioned, with the official opposition citing the LDH to support its own demand for a paramountcy clause that would place the Charter above all other legislation in Quebec.[98] The first eight articles of the Charter of Human Rights and Freedoms incorporated the recommendations of the 1966 Civil Rights Committee, which Frank Scott chaired while an LDH board member. There were also specific provisions for the protection of the elderly and children in both the proposed and final draft Charter. Small changes in wording and the inclusion of new factors, such as civil status and social condition (as opposed to social origin) as prohibited bases of discrimination, emerged verbatim from the LDH brief.[99] Perhaps the LDH's greatest success was to convince the government to make the Charter a fundamental law of the province, an issue it had vigorously promoted alongside the Parti Québécois, whose parliamentary leader at the time was none other than Jacques-Yvan Morin. Chôquette vigorously opposed a paramountcy clause; he feared that the application of the Charter to existing legislation would cause widespread instability. In the end he partially relented, agreeing to insert a section to ensure that all future laws would be required to conform to the Charter (unless explicitly stated otherwise) and that two-thirds of the National Assembly would have to consent in order to make future amendments to the Charter.[100]

With the passing of a Quebec Charter of Human Rights and Freedoms, the LDH basked in what would be its greatest accomplishment. The group peaked in 1975, with high levels of funding, several full-time staff, a highly active ODD, a book-length publication on abortion, and various other public policy initiatives wherein the LDH was consulted on proposed legislation. At the same time, a fundamental ideological shift had occurred within the organization. Not coincidentally, this ideological shift was linked with the rise of French-Canadian nationalism and the Quiet Revolution. Nationalists transformed the LDH with positions on language rights and self-determination. Paralleling these developments was the strengthening of the political left in the province, symbolized not only in the ideology of the FLQ and the rising power of organized labour but also in the rise of the social democratic Parti Québécois in the 1970s.

New Orientations and Divisions, 1975-82

The passing of the Quebec Charter of Human Rights and Freedoms was the impetus for the second major transformation within the LDH since its formation in 1963. For years, the group had taken on the responsibilities of a human rights commission in Quebec. It instituted educational programs to promote awareness of rights, lobbied the government to change legislation to protect rights, and mediated rights abuses between private citizens. All these responsibilities would now be taken up by the Quebec Human Rights Commission.

With the creation of the Human Rights Commission, the Ligue also lost one of the key figures who had guided the organization along its new path: Maurice Champagne. While René Hurtubise, a Quebec judge and former president of the LDH

(1964), was appointed president, Champagne accepted the job of vice-president of the commission – further evidence of the impact of the LDH on the passing of the Charter.

In 1977, the resignation of Simonne Chartrand and Norman Caron from the staff of the LDH signalled the rising dominance of the committees within the association. With the departure of Champagne in 1975, Normand Caron had taken over as director general, with Simonne Chartrand as his assistant. By 1977, the two were gone, having been replaced by a general coordinator and researcher. The energy and dedication that Caron and Chartrand had brought to the organization dissipated with their absence, and the staff became more concerned with simply maintaining the organization (a common development in bureaucratically structured SMOs). Lacking effective leadership, the committees became responsible for most of the new initiatives. As one report suggested, after "l'année du départ de Simonne Chartrand, la permanence à l'infrastructure cessa à peu près complètement de prendre des initiatives en matière de droits, et elle se contenta de voir au maintien de la Ligue comme organisme. Par ailleurs, les comités commencèrent à se multiplier; plusieurs d'entre eux étaient très actifs et militants."[101] These were the beginnings of the core divisions that would plague the LDH in the following years as the group became increasingly decentralized – a situation made worse by the limited leadership emanating from the administrative council.

Between 1977 and 1979, a host of new committees emerged. One of these was a women's committee, which evolved into an office of women, although it never achieved the same prominence as did the ODD. In fact, it seems to have accomplished little early on except, in 1978, to convince the LDH to change its name to the Ligue des droits et libertés (the English name, Civil Liberties Union, remained unchanged) in order to remove the gendered aspect of the group's title.[102]

Committees on the handicapped, Aboriginals, workers, and academic freedom were also formed. After the provincial appeals court denied a request by the Keable Royal Commission to have access to federal government records on the RCMP, a national security committee was launched within the LDH. Jean F. Keable had been appointed by the Parti Québécois government in June 1977 to investigate allegations of wrongdoing by the RCMP. Keable consistently fought with the federal solicitor general, who used his power to block access to critical documents for reasons of national security. Opération liberté was launched by the national security committee at a colloquium in May at the University of Montreal. The colloquium brought together four hundred people representing dozens of groups, including the three large labour federations, to discuss the ways in which police were using national security to abuse individual rights. Among the concerns raised at the meeting were the use of electronic listening devices; mail opening; and the police promotion of criminal activities such as stealing arms and explosives, harassing individuals and organizations, and utilizing medical dossiers.[103] The coalition soon began publishing a newsletter, *Opération liberté*, which had an initial circulation of 100,000.

As with other initiatives during this period, the work of the national security committee was a product of the LDH's post-1972 egalitarian philosophy towards human rights advocacy. In fact, the committee went even further, proffering a radical left-wing critique of social and political institutions. In a publication entitled *Mounting Repression*, the RCMP was portrayed as an institution that defended the interests of Canadian and American capitalists. Its main purpose was to intervene against labour, undermine revolutionary movements, and harass individuals and groups that promoted socialism. The expansion of national security measures, including spying on unions and other left-wing organizations, was explained as a manifestation of the economic crisis in the capitalist system caused by the recent economic depression. There was no shortage of national security regulations for the committee to attack, such as provisions in the Federal Court Act (which allowed judges to keep certain documents inaccessible to the public if related to national security) and recently passed privacy legislation, with sections that allowed police to use wiretaps. Opération liberté was mandated to combat the emerging national security state by cementing alliances and presenting a common front against all new initiatives justified for reasons of national security.[104]

Unsurprisingly, many of the members of the national security committee were also members of the Parti Québécois.[105] Since the mid-1970s, members of the separatist party had begun playing a more prominent role in the LDH, although the association never adopted a policy of outright support for separation and did not endorse the 1980 referendum on sovereignty-association. The Parti Québécois' original platform was far more social democratic than was that of its main political rival, the Liberal Party, and thus had more in common with the post-1972 orientation of the LDH. In staking out positions on self-determination and language rights, the LDH embraced two issues that were at the core of the Parti Québécois' politics. The Ligue was thus, in some ways, a reflection of broader political developments that were occurring within Quebec.

Meanwhile, a crisis was brewing within the LDH. By 1979, the Ligue had become so decentralized that it no longer reflected the organization once run efficiently by Champagne, Caron, and Chartrand. The administrative council was providing little leadership.[106] Facing further cutbacks in 1979 in government grants, the administrative council decided to cut members of the staff. But the unionized staff members refused to accept the decision of the administrative council, and that, coupled with existing personality clashes, resulted in their deciding to quit in unison in 1979.[107] For two months the LDH was paralyzed, with the only employee being Jean-Claude Bernheim, the non-unionized ODD staff member. Only one staff person was hired in 1979, and for the next two years the LDH operated with a small budget and few employees. Divisions within the Ligue continued to hamper its ability to work collectively. Two members of the administrative council, Elizabeth Roussel and André Legault, convinced the council had become a useless body incapable of providing direction, resigned from their posts in the administrative council in 1980.[108]

As a result of the divisions and tribulations in 1979-80, the LDH was generally inactive; most of the other committees were either defunct or doing little as a result of minimal resources or lack of direction. Nonetheless, the ODD achieved a major success by helping gain the provincial vote for prisoners. Under provincial election law, prisoners were not specifically denied the vote, yet they were denied the facilities with which to exercise their democratic rights. For years the ODD had sent letters, distributed press releases, and met with government officials to demand that prisoners be given the right to vote. Finally, in 1979, the government acceded, and prisoners in Quebec were allowed to vote for the first time in the 1980 referendum.[109] Unfortunately, the vote continued to be denied to federal prisoners in federal elections, but it was nonetheless a significant victory in the battle to recognize the rights of prisoners in Quebec.

The impressive record of the ODD proved to be a mixed blessing. By the early 1980s, there was pressure on the LDH to distance itself from the ODD, particularly in the wake of the latter's charter. In 1980, the ODD published a statement of principles, which included a clause stating that prisoners had a right to escape prisons that abused inmates. Tensions between the LDH executive and the LDH finally reached a climax in the wake of a prison riot at Archambault. In July 1982, a prison riot at Archambault maximum security prison near Montreal led to the killing of three prison guards and the suicide of two prisoners. Within weeks rumours began to filter into the offices of the ODD that the guards had decided to retaliate against the inmates. The ODD called on the federal minister of justice, Robert Kaplan, to investigate and to evacuate the guards from the prison while placing the army temporarily in charge. When Kaplan chose not to investigate, the ODD shocked the country by calling in Amnesty International to investigate. According to its report, made pubic in March 1984, prisoners at Archambault were being routinely tortured. Amnesty International warned the government not to dismiss accusations that the guards beat the inmates, used tear gas, urinated on the prisoners, and forced them to provide sexual services to the guards. The report and the activities of the ODD upset many people in the legal system, from the police to the prisons guards, and a furious provincial minister of justice quietly warned the president of the LDH about the ODD's activities. Within the LDH, many members felt the ODD's actions and rhetoric had gone too far, and, combined with the previous policy statement on the right of prisoners to escape, the LDH faced the very real possibility of losing its funding from the United Way (a major source of revenue for the ODD and the LDH after 1975). Within a year, a coalition within the LDH successfully ousted the ODD, and within a few years the latter disintegrated.[110]

Despite the turmoil of the early 1980s, the LDH enjoyed a partial revival between 1980 and its twentieth anniversary in 1983. With the mass resignation of the five staff members in 1979 and their replacement with new people, tensions within the organization declined and it was able to focus its energies on securing more funding. The new staff members were able to reorganize the Ligue and place it back on its collective feet. Since 1979, the group had been haemorrhaging elected members and had had a hard time simply achieving a quorum at its meetings. The group lost its status as a charity organization because it had failed to submit reports; membership lists were lost; there was little contact with the membership; and the only two active committees were the Aboriginal committee and the ODD. By 1982, the new staff members had helped reinvigorate committees on immigration, health and social services, national security, and youth. The administrative council was finally achieving a regular quorum, and a new full-time coordinator was hired, alongside a secretary and a part-time bookkeeper. A newsletter was also organized, its purpose being to provide information to the membership on LDH activities. For twenty years, the Ligue had not bothered to publish a newsletter (most likely because its funding came from the state and not the membership), but its revival in the early 1980s led to the publication of its first official newsletter.[111] Thanks to these new efforts, the LDH was able to boast a level of activity it had lacked for several years.

The period from 1975 to 1982 proved to be the most difficult in the history of the LDH, but it managed to end on a positive note. In 1982, it hosted the first meeting in North America of the Fédération internationale des droits de l'homme, for which it was the Canadian representative. Gilles Tardif, LDH president, was elected a vice-president of the international organization. With the passing of the Charter of Rights and Freedoms in 1982, a new era opened up for the LDH – one in which the courts would play a prominent role in the defence of human rights. Most important for the organization itself, it had survived a difficult period in which its purpose and internal cohesion had come under attack, and it had emerged in 1982 on a healthy footing. A new beginning was under way for the second oldest and second largest rights association in the country.

The LDH: A Case Study in Positive Freedom

The LDH's conception of rights as positive rights, and its position as one of the largest and most active rights associations in Canada, makes it a perfect case study through which to contrast civil liberties organizations and human rights organizations. As a social movement organization and a rights association, the LDH's conception of human rights had an impact on its strategies for change, relationships with other SMOs, and its role within the Canadian Federation of Civil Liberties and Human Rights Associations. The LDH's participation in the Federation demonstrated that civil libertarians and human rights activists could find common ground. Moreover, by accepting state funding, the LDH had to contend with the same danger of cooption as did the BCCLA.

"It is evident that a totally new conception of the Ligue is now dominant": Ideological Foundations

Unlike the BCCLA, the LDH did not develop an extensive array of position papers. Nonetheless, we can clearly see the LDH's human rights philosophy in the positions the organization adopted on issues such as abortion, national security, prisoners' rights, and a provincial bill of rights. Before 1972, the LDH was primarily interested in due process rights and enshrining civil and political rights in a provincial statute. In contrast, the ODD fought for better food and sanitary conditions in prisons, defining them as human rights; and the LDH's positions on the rights of the elderly and children during the bill of rights debates in the mid-1970s were clearly at variance with its predecessors' vision.

The LDH's conception of human rights is exemplified in its fight for children's rights. On 8 November 1972, Bill 65 (the Youth Protection Act) was introduced into the National Assembly. The legislation was designed to coordinate the province's various programs for treating youths in criminal and abusive situations (current policies had remained unchanged since the original legislation had been introduced in 1950). Bill 65 was devised to provide an infrastructure for protecting children from threats to their security, health, and development. The new system would also ensure that, whenever possible, delinquent or abused children would remain in a family environment.

The LDH's central critique was that the bill provided a legal/administrative solution to a social problem. The proposed statute assigned the primary responsibility for dealing with abused and delinquent youths to the courts. In addition, a highly bureaucratic system would be established in the form of a youth protection service to supervise children who lived in a deteriorating family environment and to place children in detention centres or foster care. What was needed, according to the LDH, was a declaration of the rights of youth, more welfare funding to poor families, and more provisions for treatment and prevention rather than punishment.[112] By applying rights discourse to welfare funding and treatment, the LDH was offering a far more expansive approach to rights than was to be found in the positions developed by the BCCLA.

More than any of the other case studies, the LDH case study epitomizes the very real difference between civil liberties and human rights activism. In the early 1970s, a new cohort of activists replaced the old guard and imbued the association with a new vision for social change. This new orientation was bound to have some significant repercussions, one of which was the loss of many of LDH's founding members. Perhaps the most notable departure was that of Frank Scott, who left the administrative council in 1972 while remaining an ordinary member. In a letter to Maurice Champagne, Scott expressed concern about the association's new direction: "Since reading the last public declaration of the League I have felt that I could not honestly continue to be a member of the Council. It is evident that a totally new conception of the League is now dominant, and however valid this may appear to the present executive it is a concept which I find quite at variance with my notion of what a proper Civil Liberties Union should be. There were political statements in that declaration which I do not think we had any right to make."[113]

Under Champagne, the LDH had called for a minimum salary for workers and had attacked the government for being too secretive.[114] Scott and many of the old guard had carefully avoided statements that could be interpreted as partisan, and he feared the implications of the Ligue's crossing the boundary into politics.

Scott's alienation from the LDH was a reaction to the association's move towards advocating for positive rights. While he had always been an avowed social democrat and a determined supporter of the CCF/NDP, Scott was liberal when it came to human rights advocacy. In other words, Scott's brand of rights activism was rooted in the idea of equality of opportunity as opposed to a more expansive approach to rights activism according to which the state was expected to ensure more than simply formal equality among individuals. Scott had, for instance, helped author the Saskatchewan Bill of Rights, which offered no provisions for economic, social, or cultural rights. The LDH's call for a minimum wage, and many of the declarations within the 1972 manifesto, were clearly at variance with the organization Scott had helped found eight years earlier. His decision to leave the administrative council was thus in many ways symbolic of the Ligue's increasing shift towards *human rights* activism.

Scott found himself once again in conflict with the LDH in the wake of the association's position on language rights. In a letter to Walter Tarnopolsky in 1976, he railed against the Ligue, which he believed had been "captured by a group of extreme nationalists and separatists whose chief concern was to see that [an amended] Bill 22 was enacted and that the Charter of Human Rights, which Crépeau and I drafted, was not put into force until the language position was clarified."[115] Scott was unwilling to accept the far-reaching provisions of the LDH's position on language rights, which would have, in effect, made Quebec unilingual. When it came to language rights, Scott's position had far more in common with that of civil liberties groups than it did with that of the LDH. As noted in Chapter 7, the leader of the Canadian Civil Liberties Association shared Scott's antipathy for collective rights and for any generous interpretations of French-Canadian language rights.

State Funding

The LDH began as an organization fully funded by its members, and it deliberately chose to avoid government funding. In 1963, the more militant members of the newly formed association were determined to ensure the group's independence and autonomy, and government funding threatened to institutionalize the association and make it dependent on the state. Thus, after one year of operations, revenue amounted to only a few thousand dollars.[116] Membership in the organization fluctuated between one hundred and three hundred during this period.

One of the most profound changes within the LDH in the wake of the October Crisis involved the infusion of state funds. In the midst of the crisis, Jacques Hébert managed to secure a grant of $21,000 from the Secretary of State (presided over by Gérard Pelletier).[117] Naturally, many of the group's members were uncomfortable with the idea of accepting a federal grant, particularly since, years earlier, they had voted to refuse state funding. After an intense debate at the 1971 Annual General Meeting, the membership decided to accept the grant, but with the caveat that all future funding must be approved by the administrative council.

The infusion of state funding could not help but have a significant impact on the LDH. Up until 1970, meetings of the administrative council had taken place in Thérèse Casgrain's home or Hébert's publishing house. The Ligue had no money to hire lawyers or to fund legal cases, and hiring full-time staff was, at best, wishful thinking. Within the next five years, the LDH was able to hire a full-time director general, a secretary, an assistant to the director general, a receptionist, and a researcher. And the level of state funding was staggering, far more than was the case for most other rights associations in Canada (see Table 6.1). Between 1963 and 1969, revenues averaged around $1,200 per year. In 1971 and 1972, revenues for the association were $24,614 and $28,252, respectively, soaring to $126,395 in 1975, with the bulk coming from the federal (Secretary of State) and provincial governments (minister of justice).[118] While it is true that the BCCLA was taking in similar monies during this time period ($30,494 in 1973 and $115,426 in 1975), its grants were primarily locked into specific projects. The LDH was given core grants, which allowed the group to hire more full-time staff. In addition, the BCCLA's grants peaked in 1975 and its revenues would drop afterwards, whereas the LDH continued to enjoy a revenue base well over $100,000 for the next several years. Revenue from membership fees rose from $1,200 (1973) to $2,635 (1975) but continued to represent a minuscule portion of the group's revenues (LDH membership had risen from about 200 in 1972 to about 1,000 in 1975).[119] It was fully dependent on state funding.

Not everyone within the LDH was willing to embrace state funding. The ODD was prolific in securing funding to support its own activities. In 1972, the ODD received a major grant from the Donner Foundation ($41,000) to conduct research into the conditions of prisons in Quebec. With the support of the provincial minister of justice it conducted an extensive study of prison conditions, which, in 1976, was published as a book *(Les prisons par içi)*.[120] Thanks to the Donner Foundation and, beginning in 1975, a series of grants from the United Way, the ODD was able to operate without government funding. In fact, it became a staple position

Table 6.1

Secretary of State's human rights program grants for 1970-71

Rights association	Grant
Ligue des droits et libertés	$21,000
Alberta Human Rights Association	5,000
Association Canadienne pour les Nations Unies	200
BC Human Rights Commission	5,000
Canadian Civil Liberties Association	1,566
Civil Liberties Association, National Capital	358
Le Comité des citoyens, Sudbury, ON	1,500
CRAN	3,500
École Polyvalente Clément-Cormier	500
Elliott Lake Centre for Continuing Education	5,000
Mayor's Committee for Human Rights	300
Poor People's Conference	5,000
Saskatchewan Association on Human Rights	5,000
St. John's South End Tenants Association Inc.	3,400
United Nations Association	4,500
United Nations Association, Montreal Branch	750
Williams Lake Community Council	1,500

Source: Secretary of State Papers, LAC, RG 6, acc. 1986-87/319.

of the ODD to reject government funding (except for specific projects) in order to avoid any conflict of interest, an ironic position given that it was an office of the heavily state-subsidized LDH.[121]

One of the unexpected implications of the passing of the 1975 Quebec Charter of Human Rights and Freedoms was a financial crisis. With the establishment of a human rights commission, the Bourassa government no longer felt the need to provide generous funding to the LDH. At the same time, the federal government was reviewing its own funding program. However, the federal government's decision to withdraw its own grant had more to do with the Ligue's controversial language policy than it did with economics. In 1976, the LDH publicly accused the federal government of trying to influence its language policy by withholding financial support. There was a clear lesson to be learned: government funding was not always unconditional. A hastily convened press conference, which brought the issue to light, managed to convince the federal government to reinstate its grant.[122] What began as a major financial crisis soon settled into a reduced 1976 budget and some staff cuts. The financial crisis forced the organization to create a large membership base for the first time in its history, and by 1977 it had accumulated $37,811 in membership fees alone, almost 30 percent of the budget. The membership drive was so successful that the organization was propelled from having members in the hundreds to having more than two thousand individual members and one hundred organizational members. The LDH could now claim to be the second largest rights association in Canada, with only the CCLA enjoying a larger membership base at a little over three thousand. For at least one year, the LDH was no longer fully dependent on state funding.

In 1980, the group could boast a budget of $210,755, but it had once again managed to dip into public monies. Most of its revenue came through government grants; in 1981, the group amassed only $8,429 from members. The one exception to the group's dependence on state funding was the United Way. By the early 1980s the LDH, in addition to the ODD, was receiving substantial funding from the United Way. This source of revenue was threatened, however, when the ODD published a charter of the rights of prisoners in 1980, with a provision that suggested that, given the conditions under which they were held, prisoners had a right to escape.[123] United Way officials threatened to cut off funding unless the LDH issued a declaration retracting the clause, but the ODD and the LDH remained adamant in their stand that policies could not be dictated by outside funding donors: "La Ligue a toujours refusé qu'un bailleur de fonds, quel qu'il soit, nous dite nos lignes de conduite et nos positions. C'est le genre de compromission que nous trouvons tout à fait inacceptable. Un organisme comme le nôtre ne peut accepter d'avoir les mains liées par de telles contraintes."[124] As a result, the ODD's funds were cut off, and the Ligue itself was facing the loss of substantial funding (as much as $100,000) because of the ODD's radicalism.

SMOs thus faced enormous pressures when they accepted funding from outside agencies. But the lesson of the LDH is that private funding can be as dangerous as state funding, and dependence on either one can threaten an organization's principles and activities.

Strategies for Change

The LDH may have proffered a more expansive conception of human rights than the BCCLA, but its tactics were little different from those of its civil libertarian counterpart. After it had identified an issue, whether it was the conditions of inmates at Parthenais or abortion, the association conducted research, prepared a brief, and presented it to the relevant public body. In other cases, the organization prepared press releases, published research, organized public seminars, or formed coalitions to lobby the state. Although the group did occasionally endorse and participate in public demonstrations, even the more radical ODD did not use mass mobilization as a strategy.[125] In general, the Ligue preferred to develop a cadre of skilled activists and use their talents to lobby for change. In this sense, the LDH was a typical professional social movement organization. But whereas some groups embraced a dual strategy approach, using civil disobedience or mass mobilization to complement other, more conservative, tactics, the LDH rarely mobilized its own membership (which remained relatively small until the late 1970s).

There was also little courtroom activity. In the sixties, when the LDH focused almost exclusively on the administration of justice and legal rights, it never brought a case to court. The association had no desire to replicate any services provided by private agencies or to act as a legal aid centre. There was an attempt, in June 1970, to apply for funds through the Donner Foundation to hire staff lawyers, but it was unsuccessful.[126] Over a decade later, the Ligue continued to refrain from dedicating its resources to litigation. Whereas the BCCLA often sought out the courts for the defence of individuals' rights, the Ligue's focus on social justice was not conducive to spending precious resources on legal action. It occasionally hired lawyers to provide people with free advice and consultations. Yet this remained a marginal aspect of the group's work, and by 1982 the LDH had not directly sponsored a single case.

The National Question

For years the LDH had remained relatively aloof from other rights associations, except to produce a bilingual version of the CCLA's booklet, *Arrest and Detention,* for distribution in Quebec.[127] But during the transition years it was becoming increasingly involved with other rights associations. In 1970-71, the LDH became a leading force in the creation of the Canadian Federation of Civil Liberties and Human Rights Associations. Since the LDH was heavily state-funded, it did not share the CCLA's qualms about government funding (discussed in detail in Chapter 7). By the mid-1970s, the LDH had overtaken the BCCLA as the second largest rights association in Canada, and its presence on the Federation's board had an important symbolic role because the Ligue was the leading francophone rights association in the country. Although the LDH never hesitated to take on national issues outside the Federation, it coordinated briefs with the Federation, supported Federation initiatives, and allowed the Federation to act as its spokesperson on such key issues as the McDonald Commission.

Maintaining strong ties with other rights associations was an important aspect of the LDH's work, although it was never a high priority. For the LDH, the Federation offered the prospect of a stronger voice at the national level on those occasions when it dabbled in national issues.[128] The leaders of the LDH also saw their role as offering an alternative ideological approach to rights activism. In a predominantly anglophone organization, the LDH insisted on recognizing collective as well as social, economic, and cultural rights: "Si on rappelle que les anglophones sont surtout orientés vers la lutte pour les *libertés civiles,* l'influence de la Ligue des droits de l'homme apparâit encore plus grande quant aux *libertés de la personne*" (italics added).[129] The LDH's new cadre of leaders associated civil liberties ideology with anglophone culture. Normand Caron, Champagne's successor as director in 1975, believed that the LDH's main contribution to the national human rights movement was to challenge anglophones' definition of human rights as purely civil and political rights.[130] Years later, Lucie Lemonde, president of the LDH in the 1990s, expressed similar sentiments when reflecting upon the association's early activism: "c'était la conception anglaise des droits civils [civil liberties] qui prévalait."[131]

One of the most curious moments in the history of the Ligue directly involved the Federation. Virtually every rights association in Canada eagerly participated in the consultations of the Special Joint Committee on the Constitution in 1980-81, which led to the repatriation of the Constitution and the entrenchment of the Charter of Rights and Freedoms. The Ligue was notable by its absence. Instead of attending, the Ligue decided to participate in the Charter debates by sending a representative with the Federation's delegation to the Special Joint Committee on the Constitution. The minutes of the LDH's executive committee and the board are virtually silent on the Constitution issue. It is unlikely that Trudeau's proposed Charter of Rights and Freedoms would have been welcomed in the offices of the Ligue. The LDH had already taken a strong stand on language rights, and the Charter would have made it virtually impossible to implement the policies favoured by the Ligue. For over a decade the Ligue had fought for a provincial, not a national, bill of rights. Maurice Champagne was a vocal critic of the Charter of Rights and Freedoms, although by the 1980s he was no longer a member of the LDH's executive. Champagne believed that the Charter was designed to undermine Quebec's language legislation (Bill 101), and he feared "judiciariser les droits de la personne" by making the judiciary the final arbiter of competing rights claims. [132]

Relations with Other Social Movement Organizations

In contrast to the BCCLA, the LDH developed close relationships with numerous SMOs. The ODD formed coalitions with prisoners' rights groups to protest health conditions in prisons and the closing of Parthenais; the national security committee initiated a common front to protest human rights violations in the name of national security; and the LDH led a massive campaign for a provincial bill of rights that linked over four hundred organizations. The LDH participated in dozens of coalitions with other SMOs throughout the seventies, from protests on the anniversary of the use of the War Measures Act to advocating for daycare and the rights of youths. In doing so, the LDH was able to establish strong ties with organized labour. Members of the Quebec Federation of Labour were regularly represented on the Ligue's administrative council, and the Confédération des syndicats nationaux provided financial support to the LDH.

Once again, the Ligue's work in the field of children's rights offers a useful example. In addition to contesting the contents of Bill 65, the Ligue was opposed to the lack of public consultation in drafting the legislation. This reflected its mandate to promote community involvement in public policy. Soon after the bill was introduced, the LDH formed a youth committee and organized a public seminar, drawing together dozens of organizations from the Association des institutions pour enfants to the Service juridiques juveniles. The government agreed to send Bill 65 to a parliamentary committee, where the LDH presented a brief endorsed by 22 organizations representing 7,000 professionals and 100,000 parents. The brief was an unequivocal rejection of Bill 65 and called on the government to organize a series of public consultations on the contents of a future youth protection act.[133] A growing coalition, led by the LDH, drew together a wide range of community groups, including the Fédération des travailleurs du Québec, Confédération des syndicats nationaux, Corporation des enseignants du Québec, Association nationale des étudiants et étudiantes du Québec, Regroupement des association étudiantes univesitaires, Regroupment des organismes nationaux de loisir du Québec, Vélo-Québec, and others. After the bill was retracted, the Ligue kept the coalition active. When a new bill was introduced in 1975, without much public consultation, the LDH once again successfully led the fight to have the bill retracted. When the Youth Protection Act was finally passed in 1977, one of the bill's major advocates in the National Assembly, Pierre Marois, recognized the work of the Ligue in the five-year process leading up to the bill: "Je crois qu'il faut reconnaître l'oeuvre de pionniers qu'ont accomplie à ce niveau, des organismes comme la Ligue des droits de l'homme et d'autres groupes qui s'y sont associés pour sensibiliser l'opinion publique à la nécessité absolue de cette réforme."[134]

After 1972, the LDH had dedicated itself to promoting a "société de participation"; unlike other rights associations, it had a mandate to collaborate with other SMO. As the only rights association in Quebec, located in the second largest city in the country (home to numerous social movement organizations), and with a long-established reputation as a respected advocacy group, the Ligue was well-placed to draw together members of the community. The committee system was also conducive to building coalitions; individuals with a passion for a particular issue could form a committee and mobilize those who cared about that specific concern but who may not have been interested in working with a broad-based human rights organization. Most important, the LDH's ideology was not an obstacle to cooperating with others. By accepting a positive conception of human rights, which included economic, social, and cultural rights, the Ligue could find common ground with anyone from feminists to civil libertarians.

By the 1980s, the LDH had abandoned its roots and embraced an expansive approach to human rights activism. The LDH employed rights discourse to demand recognition of the economic, social, and cultural needs of the elderly, youth, the disabled, francophones, and others. No civil liberties association in Canada had suggested that prisoners had a right to escape because of their living conditions; that the state's violations of individual rights in the name of national security were linked to the crisis facing capitalism; or that extensive economic, social, and cultural rights should be recognized in human rights legislation. Not only did this clearly distinguish the LDH from rights associations such as the BCCLA, but it also had little in common with the first generation of rights associations in Montreal. Unlike its predecessors, the LDH had to deal with fundamental changes in the role of the state, from welfare programs to the Quiet Revolution, that shaped its agenda for a generation.

Yet, as we can see by looking at the history of the LDH, an organization dedicated to an expansive interpretation of human rights had little in the way of a grassroots following. Despite a decisive break with the past, the demographics of the LDH and its strategies for change had altered only moderately. True, the new Ligue was far less elitist than its founders had envisioned, and it was certainly willing to engage issues never considered by the first generation. By the mid-1970s, the LDH was arguably far more representative of its community than were its fellow rights associations, with ex-prisoners, women, Aboriginals, and others joining the group. But the Ligue remained dominated by educated, middle-class, white francophones. State funding provided the association with a stable financial base. Since it did not have to mobilize large numbers of people to survive, the group's activities continued to be centred around the work of a small number of skilled activists. Even the ODD, easily the most radical committee within a rights association in Canada, never developed a grassroots following. As with many professional SMOs of this period, despite the eventual necessity of building a large membership base, the LDH had a weak relationship with its membership, relating to them largely through dues and donations. The association's professed goal of promoting a "société de participation," which was manifested most clearly in its campaign for a provincial bill of rights, was a rare example of a rights association's employing a strategy that required mobilizing large segments of the population in order to promote change. It was one of the few instances in the history of the LDH when it abandoned insider tactics in favour of mass mobilization.

7
The Canadian Civil Liberties Association

On the night of 11 May 1974, undercover agents from the RCMP and the Niagara Regional Police slowly crept into the Landmark Motor Inn Hotel in Fort Erie, Ontario, in preparation for a massive drug raid. Without a warrant but under the authority of a writ of assistance authorized through the Narcotic Control Act, fifty police officers prepared to storm the hotel in search of heroin and marijuana. Although three of the officers had been recognized by drug dealers who quickly left the scene, the raid went ahead. Approximately 115 patrons were arrested and detained. All thirty-five women were herded into the women's washroom, stripped, and subjected to vaginal and anal searches; those who refused to comply were threatened with having a male officer come into the room and force the search on them. Meanwhile, only seven of the male patrons were similarly searched. With the searches completed, the raid's bounty became depressingly clear: six ounces of marijuana were found, and most of it was lying on the floor, not in people's orifices. According to a *Globe and Mail* editorial on 30 July 1974, "it is highly probable that the Niagara Regional Police has succeeded in making itself the laughing stock of its community; that is, among people who aren't afraid to go out to have a drink for fear that they'll end up stark naked and leaning spread eagled against some washroom wall."

This monumental blunder was not without serious consequences. Media coverage was extensive across Ontario, and the Toronto papers, notably the *Globe and Mail* and the *Toronto Star*, covered the story almost continually throughout May to August 1974.[1] Rights activists, led by the Toronto-based Canadian Civil Liberties Association (CCLA), called on the Ontario government to appoint an independent inquiry. A rally organized by the CCLA in June 1974 was attended by nearly one thousand people from the Niagara Falls region. Bowing to public pressure stimulated by the press and the CCLA, Solicitor General George Kerr created an inquiry chaired by Justice J.A. Pringle. Although Pringle's report would later acknowledge that, under the Narcotic Control Act, the police had the authority to raid the inn based on a mere suspicion of drug use, he called the raid "foolish" and "unnecessary." Both Pringle and Kerr called on the federal government to clarify and narrow the powers of police when searching for drugs.

The events surrounding the Fort Erie drug raid represent a central theme in the history of the CCLA. Created ten years before the Fort Erie affair, in the wake of another scandal surrounding excessive police powers, much of the early history of the CCLA was dominated by the desire to curb police abuse of powers and to see the implementation of an independent review board to oversee civilian complaints of police actions. While the BCCLA fought for the rights of drugs addicts and against censorship, and the LDH came to the defence of prisoners and lobbied for a provincial bill of rights, the CCLA dedicated its resources to campaigning against religious education in public schools, abusive police practices, and national security policies. Free speech, due process, and the rights of welfare recipients were among the other priorities guiding the CCLA agenda in its formative years. It became perhaps the most recognizable rights association in the country, particularly in the wake of its successful participation in the parliamentary hearings on the proposed Charter of Rights and Freedoms in 1980-81.

When it was founded in 1964, the CCLA had to undergo a generational shift similar to that experienced by the LDH. Although the shift was far less dramatic, the second generation of activists in the CCLA did not share their forerunners' primary concern for discrimination. The problems posed by an expanding police force in Toronto and the dangers implicit in the creation of state agencies with quasi-judicial powers captured the attention of the CCLA's new generation of activists. While the association's demographics and strategies did not fundamentally differ from those of the Association for Civil Liberties, the CCLA's leaders found themselves trying to establish a niche for an organization located in a city where, in the sixties and seventies, new SMOs emerged seemingly on a daily basis.

The history of the CCLA brings to the fore important questions about forming and sustaining an SMO. The association struggled over whether or not to accept state funding, the ideological divide between civil liberties and human rights activism, and the viability of constructing a national association. It also developed a philosophy of rights that was at variance with that of the Ligue des droits de l'homme. Whereas the LDH promoted social, economic, and cultural rights, the CCLA embraced a negative conception of freedom focused around civil and political rights. In fact, there were many significant differences between the LDH and the CCLA. The LDH was one of the key founders of the Canadian Federation of Civil Liberation and Human Rights Associations, while the CCLA sought to establish itself as the country's only viable national rights organization. As of 1970 the LDH, and most rights associations in Canada, accepted government funding; the CCLA adamantly refused to do this. Thus, the CCLA evolved into the largest group in Canada in terms of membership. The LDH occasionally had lawyers provide free advice to people off the street, whereas the CCLA brought dozens of cases to court, several of them to the Supreme Court of Canada. Finally, the CCLA exemplifies the evolving relationship between organized labour and contemporary rights associations. It is clear that, at least in the case of the Canadian Labour Congress, the nation's leading labour organization increasingly deferred to rights associations with regard to leading human rights campaigns.

"It makes the Quebec padlock law look like the Bill of Rights": First Steps, 1964-68

As the birth mother of the CCLA, Bill 99 (the Ontario Police Bill) seemed an innocuous piece of legislation. In first reading on 19 March 1964, Attorney General Frank Cass characterized the legislation as simply a series of amendments to the Police Act whose purpose was to define and clarify the powers of the Ontario Police Commission.[2] Once the press realized the contents of the legislation, however, a political controversy erupted that would only be settled with the resignation of the attorney general and the appointment of the McRuer Royal Commission on Civil Rights. The incident illustrated not only the extent to which governments could restrict fundamental freedoms but also the power of an aroused public opinion to force a government to retract legislation offensive to human rights.[3]

Bill 99 was a response to the rising threat of organized crime in Ontario. Following a provincial inquiry into organized crime, the newly established Ontario Police Commission persuaded the attorney general of the need for a continuous investigation into the impact of organized crime. Under Bill 99, the commission could arrest and detain individuals without notifying their next of kin, deny them access to legal counsel, and jail them for eight days if they refused to testify before it. Bail and the right to appeal were withheld. Should witnesses continue to frustrate the commission they could be held almost indefinitely for eight-day periods, and those who testified were subject to a $2,000 fine and a year in jail if they or anyone else revealed information presented before the commission. The new leader of the Liberals, Farquhar Oliver, called on the government to retract the bill or call an immediate election. In Ottawa, J.W. Pickersgill suggested that the bill made the Quebec Padlock Act look like the Bill of Rights.[4]

It did not take long for the media to condemn Bill 99. One *Toronto Star* editorial, which appeared on the front page within twenty-four hours of the legislation's being introduced, suggested that it was "the most offensive and dangerous legislation ever introduced in Ontario. It was brought in like a thief in the night – slipped through the Conservative caucus when only 12 members were present, and introduced to the Legislature under the pretence that it was concerned only with police pensions and other routine matters. Now that its real nature is known, the Legislature should lose no time in rejecting it."

Eventually, amendments to the legislation were introduced to clearly detail the rights of witnesses before the Ontario Police Commission, including the right to counsel, habeas corpus, and other remedies. In camera sessions could be held only at the behest of the witness.[5] A.A. Wishart replaced Cass as attorney general, and the McRuer Commission was soon appointed. However, the most enduring legacy of Bill 99 was unquestionably the creation of the CCLA.

Since the late 1950s, the Association for Civil Liberties had been effectively moribund. It existed only on paper, with Irving Himel, a prominent Toronto Jewish lawyer, as its sole member and leader. The police bill spurred Himel to reinvent the group. He brought together a collection of prominent members of the Toronto community who had an interest in civil liberties to form the Canadian Civil Liberties Association, and he transferred the remaining $10,000 from the accounts of the Association for Civil Liberties to the CCLA. The CCLA officially came into being at a meeting at Osgoode Hall on 11 February 1965, although its early years would prove, as was the case with all rights associations during this period, a struggle for simple survival.[6]

As was the case in the early years of the LDH and the BCCLA, the CCLA was a relatively elitist organization. Its president was J. Keiller Mackay, former lieutenant-governor of Ontario and famous for having presided over the *Drummond Wren* case in 1945, where he ruled that restrictive covenants were illegal.[7] Among its other more notable founding members were Professor Harry Arthurs (Osgoode Hall Law School), June Callwood (writer), Pierre Berton (writer, journalist), Abraham Feinberg (rabbi emeritus of Holy Blossom Temple), professors Edward McWhinney, Mark MacGuigan, and Bora Laskin (University of Toronto Law School), Reverend Donald Gilles (Bloor Street United Church), Ron Haggart (*Toronto Star* columnist), and lawyers Glen Howe and Sydney Midanik. Julian Porter, a young lawyer and son of Chief Justice Dana Porter of Ontario, was the part-time counsel for the organization; Himel was chair of the Board of Directors; and Doris Dodds (founder of the Ethical Education Association, which opposed religious instruction in public schools) served as the executive secretary.[8] Many of the CCLA's founders would go on to have highly distinguished careers. Bora Laskin became chief justice of the Supreme Court and Mark MacGuigan would serve as minister of justice as well as minister of external affairs under Trudeau. As with the BCCLA and the LDH, this was clearly a middle-class, Caucasian, male-dominated organization.

Members were to provide the bulk of the group's funding, although surprisingly (for a group later famous for refusing state funding) there were at least a few attempts made to secure state funding. A request by Sidney Linden to the Secretary of State for a grant in 1966 was rejected, and in 1970-71 the CCLA was awarded a small grant from the federal government ($1,500).[9] As with the BCCLA and the LDH, funding for the CCLA was initially minimal and desperate. Unlike the Association for Civil Liberties, the new group hoped to establish a permanent office with paid employees. But, in November 1966, the CCLA was forced to close its office and dismiss its staff due to lack of funds (having peaked at 330 members), only to be saved from ruin by a $10,000 operating grant from the Atkinson Foundation. After this, the group's funding improved substantially, with an $80,000 grant in 1967 from the estate of Clement Wells, which allowed them to hire a full-time general counsel.[10]

When the CCLA was created in 1964, it joined an already vigorous community of human rights activists in Ontario. Under the leadership of Alan Borovoy, a young lawyer trained at the University of Toronto, the Ontario Labour Committee for Human Rights was easily the most active of the JLC's human rights committees. As previously noted, most of the work of the labour committees centred around discrimination. The CCLA also had the advantage of operating in a province with a well-funded and active human rights commission. Ontario had been the first province to pass a human rights code and the first to employ full-time commission staff. From its inception, members of the CCLA saw themselves focusing on civil liberties issues such as censorship and due process of law, while discrimination cases were to be left primarily to the Human Rights Commission and the JLC.[11] Within a decade, the CCLA would become one of the leading defenders of individual rights in the province; however, between 1964 and 1968, it was nothing more than a small, young association struggling to survive.

The CCLA accomplished very little in its initial years. As its first act in January 1965, the group sent out letters and press releases protesting a bylaw passed by the Ontario Police Commission, which empowered police officers to censor signs used in parades and processions.[12] In April 1965, Porter and Mackay presented a brief to the McRuer Royal Commission on Civil Rights, calling for the end of religious practices in public schools, stricter regulation of electronic eavesdropping, an end to any form of government censorship, reform of the bail system (which discriminated against the poor), and compensation for victims of police abuse.[13] A few months later, the CCLA came to the defence of Dorothy Cameron, a local gallery owner who had the paintings displayed in an exhibit entitled "Eros '65" seized by police. The paintings were seized under the vague obscenity provisions of the Criminal Code, which the CCLA considered too broad and sought to challenge all the way to the country's highest court, only to have the latter deny it the right to appeal.[14] This was the first major case the CCLA took to court (it reached the Ontario Appeals Court, which ruled against Cameron) and would represent the first of many cases the organization would pursue with the help of volunteer lawyers.

Free speech issues dominated the CCLA in its early years. When violence erupted at Allan Gardens in response to a speech by a self-styled Nazi, John Beattie, city council chose to enact a bylaw that allowed it to ban public speaking permits if there was the potential for violence. Although opposed to the content of Beattie's speech, the CCLA supported his right to speak and lobbied city council to remove the bylaw. Two years later, the Ontario Police Commission passed a bylaw empowering police officers to remove people or groups from Nathan Phillips Square if they did not have the city council's permission to be there. Once again, the CCLA unsuccessfully lobbied against this limitation on free speech.[15] Finally, in the same year, the CCLA challenged a decision by the Ontario Police Commission to reroute an anti-Vietnam parade from Yonge Street to Bay Street.[16] As Alan Borovoy would later comment in reminiscing on the commission's decision, "I don't know how many of my readers have been on Bay Street or University Avenue on a Saturday, but if they have, they probably were the only ones there. In certain parts of Canada, we don't ban demonstrations, we re-route them. The demonstration becomes, as one writer put it, not an exercise in freedom of communication, but an exercise in freedom of soliloquy. You can say anything you like in your backyard or your bathtub."[17]

In its early years, the CCLA had established itself not only as a defender of free speech but also as a dedicated observer of police activities and of attempts to expand police powers. But it was a slow start. It was still a young organization with minimal staff and minimal exposure in the community. Without the Atkinson grant in 1966 and the estate grant in 1967, the CCLA could very well have folded early on. It was unusual for such a new organization, barely a few years old, to receive such generous donations, and the success of the CCLA in gaining private funding was no doubt facilitated by its being located in Ontario (the Atkinson Foundation was only for organizations in Ontario) and by its leadership, with several well-known Canadians (such as Pierre Berton and Keiller Mackay) vouching for the group. It was also in these initial years that the group established the key priorities that would guide it for the next fifteen years: free speech and police practices.

"The insane are devil possessed!" Entrenchment Years, 1968-77

Few rights associations, as is the case for many SMOs, manage to survive without the services of one particularly dedicated individual. Reg Robson in Vancouver, Maurice Champagne in Montreal, and, as will be seen in the following chapter, Biswarup Bhattacharya in St. John's, were absolutely critical in making their respective rights association viable and effective. This was no less the case with the CCLA: the hiring of Alan Borovoy in 1968 was a critical moment in its history.

Borovoy had earned a bachelor's degree and an LLB in 1956. By the time the CCLA recruited him in 1968 to be its general counsel, he had already distinguished himself with the Ontario Labour Committee for Human Rights. In 1961, he had organized activists in Halifax and attracted a great deal of attention in taking up the cause of the residents of Africville, which led to the formation of the Halifax Advisory Committee on Human Rights. A year later he was at the centre of a successful lobby to introduce legislation against racial discrimination in Ontario. When Aboriginal people from Kenora approached Borovoy about discrimination and poor government services, he organized a large protest march to City Hall, with hundreds of Aboriginals from neighbouring reserves, to demand everything from telephones to an alcohol treatment centre (which were eventually provided).

Borovoy encapsulated many of the qualities of the CCLA as an organization. He had an undying faith in the law and its ability to promote tolerance and liberty, and he focused most of his energies on briefs to the government or on seeking redress in the courts. Borovoy was a Jewish lawyer (as was Himel) with an appreciation for the plight of minorities, having himself experienced discrimination. He had lived and worked all his life in Toronto, and, although he travelled extensively, most of the issues taken on by the CCLA during this period were Ontario-centred. Finally, he was a middle-class, white male in an organization that claimed to speak on behalf of everyone in the community yet failed, for instance, to attract many women to its ranks. In 1971, out of forty-two board members and executives, only four were women. The leadership of the organization consisted primarily of lawyers, academics, journalists, unionists, and church ministers. The demographics of the CCLA would remain the same until at least the early 1980s.

Through its full-time staff the CCLA was able to attract more funding and members. In 1968, it had barely three hundred members; by 1977, it could boast more than three thousand – by far the largest rights association in the country (it would have more than five thousand by the early 1980s). The CCLA was particularly proficient with regard to gaining private grants from various foundations. In 1968, the group successfully applied to the Ford Foundation for an $85,000 grant to study due process across Canada. In 1973, the Atkinson Foundation provided another grant of $53,000 to study Aboriginal access to legal services in northern Ontario. In 1971 and 1973, the Laidlaw Foundation supplied grants of $30,000 and $45,900, respectively, to study the rights of welfare recipients. While membership fees generally covered 90 percent of the organization's expenses, these and hundreds of smaller grants allowed the CCLA to conduct extensive programs throughout Ontario and, at times, across Canada.

Soon after arriving in the CCLA, Borovoy was pleased to see the publication of a report that would bolster its advocacy in the realm of education. Since 1944, Ontario had allowed the exercise of religious practices and the teaching of religion by clergy in public schools. At the time, roughly half the population in Ontario supported this practice.[18] But by the 1960s, criticism of the use of religious exercises and teachings in schools had mounted. Increasing urbanization and secularism, rising prosperity, declining Sunday school attendance, heavy immigration (which introduced new faiths into the community), and the rising youth rebellion against parental mores all combined to undermine support for religious practices in public schools. There were also several practical reasons why people opposed the practice. Jewish organizations, for obvious reasons, objected to a system of religious instruction based on Christian theology. Teachers, many of whom felt unqualified to be teaching scripture, feared retaliation from their employers should they request an exemption, as provided for in the legislation. Students who were allowed to stand outside the classroom during the exercises were placed in the same position as were students who were being punished.

Borovoy raised all of these concerns in 1966, when he was invited by a group of universalists in the small town of Gosfield, forty-eight kilometres outside of Windsor, to call on the school board to remove religious instruction in the school. Several parents in the region had been concerned about some of the content of the instruction, with clergy going so far as to suggest that the insane were "devil possessed" and that people whose faith was strong enough could defy gravity.[19] It was a failed endeavour; the school board decided to maintain the practice. But the debate engendered a great deal of publicity in the press.

In 1967, Borovoy once again challenged the denominational education system in Ontario. J. Keiller Mackay, honorary president of the CCLA since 1965, had been appointed in 1966 by the Ontario government to lead an investigation into the implications of religious practices in Ontario schools. At the time, Borovoy was chairman of the Ontario Labour Committee for Human Rights, and he used the committee as a forum to denounce religious practices in public schools. Although the committee later concluded in favour of maintaining the Lord's Prayer, it otherwise vindicated Borovoy's position by calling for the removal of all religious practices from public schools.[20]

After Borovoy joined to the CCLA, his crusade against religious exercises in public schools in Ontario resumed. He organized a delegation to the minister of education in 1971, with sixty people representing various organizations, to demand the implementation of the report's key recommendations.[21] Petitions were organized and letters were sent to members of the government. Yet, the government remained recalcitrant, claiming that it was waiting for an alternative to present itself for teaching morality to youths in public schools. One can only speculate as to the reasons behind the Progressive Conservatives' intransigence. Many MLAs were undoubtedly concerned about the need to teach morality to children and were themselves devout Christians. At the same time, in the 1960s, Roman Catholics throughout the province had mobilized a campaign to convince the province's three political parties to support funding for the Catholic school system. Both the Liberals and the NDP were sympathetic, but the Progressive Conservatives, fearing the potential costs to the system, refused. Conscious of the strong support the Liberals already enjoyed among Catholics, it is probable that the Progressive Conservatives feared alienating Catholic voters even more if they eliminated religious practices in public schools. For a political party, an issue like prayers in schools is often best left to the status quo, lest it result in courting a negative public backlash. The government quite likely thought those whose interests were threatened (i.e., those who supported prayers in schools) were more likely to be vocal critics than were those who had been living with the practice for years. In any event, a large number of school boards had discontinued the practice in the 1970s and 1980s, making it a non-issue for many voters.[22] It was not until 1990, following one of the

CCLA's most successful Charter cases, that religious preaching in Ontario schools was finally discontinued.[23]

On the heels of the Mackay Committee's report in 1969 came the October Crisis. The CCLA soon found itself embroiled in a national crisis and shifted its efforts from Queen's Park to Parliament Hill. Whereas the LDH had failed to distinguish itself during the crisis, *Le Devoir* credited the CCLA with being one of the few groups outside Quebec to take a clear stand. As one editorial noted regarding the extensive support Trudeau enjoyed outside Quebec, at the "height of the crisis brought on by the abduction of Mr. Cross and Mr. Laporte, one had the impression that, but for a few voices crying in the wilderness, all critical reflection had practically ceased in English-Canada. The solid, almost dogmatic support which English Canadians gave to the governments' decisions (including those which contradicted their strongest traditions) was such that certain dissident voices seemed themselves frightened at times of their own isolation."[24]

In the midst of the crisis a rally of five thousand people was organized on the campus of York University in support of the federal government. The rally would leave an indelible mark on at least one of the critics in attendance who spoke out against the government: "I have never before or since been afraid of a crowd, never feared being torn from limb to limb, but that day I was frightened. The shouts from the students that interrupted my speech were frequent and hostile; the visceral hatred of the FLQ kidnappers and murderers, and, as I interpreted it, of all Québécois, was palpable."[25]

The most notable aspect of the LDH's actions during the crisis, which damned them in the eyes of many, was the group's unwillingness to take a definitive stand against the War Measures Act. This was clearly not the case with the CCLA. Three days after the War Measures Act was declared, the CCLA submitted a brief to the federal cabinet calling for its revocation, arguing that such powers had not been justified.[26] Ten days later, the CCLA appeared before the Toronto Board of Education to challenge a proposed resolution, similar to the one passed by the provincial government in British Columbia, in which teachers could be dismissed for advocating FLQ policies.[27] When the Public Order Act was passed in order to ban the FLQ and to suspend civil liberties, the CCLA returned to Ottawa with another brief outlining the same position: the government had yet to justify the need to use extraordinary powers because the Criminal Code possessed sufficient powers of arrest and detention to deal with the kidnappings.[28] Letters were sent out to members of Parliament and other organizations to garner their support. At a time when the LDH was doing little to discourage the federal government from its course of action, Borovoy met informally with Justice Minister John Turner in Ottawa in November 1970 to discuss the situation and to consider alternatives.

It is difficult to gauge how much influence the CCLA had on the decision makers in Ottawa, but it is clear that the organization had access to high-level officials and that it was one of the few vocal organizations outside Quebec that was attacking the government. A public forum was organized in November 1970, featuring Jean Paul Goyer (future solicitor general). A meeting of rights activists and scholars was convened on International Human Rights Day (10 December 1970) to discuss the implications of emergency powers, and Borovoy appeared on various television and radio shows. The October Crisis was one of the greatest threats to civil liberties in a generation, and the CCLA was swift to act.[29] When the federal government announced it was considering permanent peacetime emergency legislation, the CCLA organized a delegation to meet Turner in March 1971. Perhaps the most compelling argument presented in the brief was that it was essentially common detective work, not emergency powers, that led police to capture Laporte's kidnappers and to rescue James Cross.[30] Turner left the meeting to announce to the press that the government was no longer committed to peacetime emergency legislation.

The October Crisis was assuredly one of the most dramatic episodes in the CCLA's history, and it was the first time since its inception that the group had demonstrated its effectiveness at the national level. Soon after the crisis, the association entered a new realm of advocacy: the rights of welfare recipients. The creation of the welfare state expanded exponentially the ways in which the state interfered in the private lives of its citizens. And yet, whereas human rights associations such as the LDH embraced the idea of economic and social rights, the CCLA shared the same ideological bent as did the BCCLA – a concern for negative freedom. In other words, the CCLA dealt solely with the *administration* of welfare and the equitable treatment of recipients as opposed to the amount and the nature of welfare support.

Jennifer Smith was a thirty-year-old woman who lived in Toronto and who was trying to raise four children by herself, after having been deserted by her husband.[31] She was taking courses to complete her high school degree and had been on welfare since the mid-1960s. In 1970, Smith was stunned when she received a letter in the mail informing her that her support was being cut off because she was no longer living as a single person.[32] Denied any right to challenge the decision and having to wait until a board of review was called, Smith was typical of single mothers who were victims of a welfare system eager to cut costs. Single women suspected of having a male in the house – the infamous "man-in-the-house" rule – were denied access to welfare because it was assumed that males, as breadwinners, would provide for women. The man-in-the-house rule clearly discriminated against women. It assumed that a sexual relationship implied a financial one, and the abruptness with which recipients could be denied welfare raised the potential for numerous procedural abuses. There were also serious concerns about the tactics employed by the welfare office in determining whether women were living as single persons. During some surprise visits, inspectors would demand to know about the most intimate aspects of a recipient's relationships and, in some cases, would draw conclusions based on such weak evidence as the presence of open beer cans or a raised toilet seat.[33] In one instance, a woman was forced to hide her boyfriend in the closet when an inspector arrived unannounced. When the stowaway was discovered, the inspector demanded she explain his presence or lose her welfare support.

The man-in-the-house rule and the procedural regulations of the Department of Welfare in Toronto were two of many issues raised by the CCLA in briefs and correspondence to various ministers of family and social services. A report produced by the CCLA based on interviews with 1,002 welfare recipients across Canada revealed a host of abuses relating to the procedural rights of welfare recipients, and it became the basis of much of the organization's lobbying work throughout the seventies.[34] The amount of control exercised by the welfare department was extensive. Through welfare, the state determined how people could eat, where they could live, and what they bought and from whom. Welfare procedures at local offices departed significantly from common law requirements of due process, requiring recipients to wait for long periods for responses. Decision makers were difficult to contact, and official conduct was often characterized as demeaning. Women with illegitimate children were forced to reveal the names of the fathers in order to allow the department to seek them out and recover costs.[35] Recipients lived well below the poverty line, receiving an estimated 60 percent of the basic amount required to lead a healthy and functional lifestyle. These regulations emerged from a system that was struggling with the inherent contradiction of providing welfare while seeking to minimize costs. As the report itself suggested, a "person accused of the most heinous crimes enjoys more discernible protection of his domestic privacy than does an innocent recipient of public welfare."[36]

Through the efforts of the CCLA and anti-poverty groups in Ontario, welfare regulations were eventually narrowed through court action and lobbying. One of the few requirements attached to the Canada Assistance Plan was that provinces provide appeal boards. Ontario initially resisted, and only through pressure from various activists did the province finally establish a board of review in 1969. Although the CCLA's attempt to challenge the provincial regulations dealing with the discretion of the director of welfare and the man-in-the-house rule failed in the Ontario Court of Appeal, Jennifer Smith eventually had her benefits restored after negotiations between the CCLA and the minister.[37] In the same year that Jennifer Smith's case was resolved, the Ontario government passed the Civil Rights Law Amendment Act, which required notice in advance of any loss of benefits and allowed recipients to reply in writing to defend themselves. A few years later, an Ontario Court of Appeal ruled in 1975 that welfare officials were required to demonstrate the existence of a financial relationship between a man and a woman before cutting off benefits to single women. The man-in-the-house rule was more resilient, despite several attempts by the CCLA to defeat it in court. The rule lasted until 1986, when women's groups threatened to bring the province to court for violating the Charter, and the Ontario government decided to simply eliminate the regulation.[38]

Religious education and welfare rights are two examples of issues addressed by the CCLA's advocacy program during these years; other issues included Aboriginal rights, demonstrators' rights, abortion, and capital punishment. But no issue captured the imagination of the organization more than police abuse of powers and a new civilian complaints system. Throughout the 1970s, there was no cause upon which the CCLA remained more single-mindedly focused than the question of a civilian review board. As early as 1967, Harry Arthurs began research for the CCLA on a proposal for a new system for investigating civilian complaints against police officers in Toronto.[39] Metropolitan Toronto's police force was a recent creation, formed in 1957 with the amalgamation of thirteen municipalities. The police force employed a fairly crude complaints system, whereby citizens could raise concerns at a complaints bureau located in the force's headquarters and regular duty officers would conduct informal investigations of their colleagues. The idea of a civilian review board for complaints against police was rejected in 1968 by Attorney General and Minister of Justice A.A. Wishart because of the functional difficulties of such a system. If separate agencies existed for the enforcement of the law and the disciplining of law officers, Wishart claimed, it would inevitably lead to conflict between the two agencies and undermine the effectiveness of the system.

A year later, the CCLA presented a brief to Wishart calling for a civilian complaints system; this was followed up by another brief in 1973 to the Task Force on Policing, which was created by the province in 1972 to study the organization and effectiveness of policing in Ontario. According to the CCLA's research, of 161 individuals interviewed in seven Ontario cities, forty-one claimed they had been abused by police. Yet, only 12 percent sought redress, and most assumed it would do no good to try. The problem was simply that, in a system in which police investigated police, there was a perception of rampant cover-ups and bias against the complainant. A police commission concerned about the public image, efficiency, morale, and legal liability of the force could hardly conduct an impartial investigation. In fact, in 1972, when the Ukrainian Canadian Committee publicly accused the police of using abusive tactics against demonstrators during the visit of Soviet premier Aleksei Kosygin, the Toronto Police Commission asked the attorney general to establish an independent inquiry in order to eliminate the perception of bias on its part. Clearly, this was an acknowledgment by the police commission of the limitations of the current system. In its many briefs throughout the seventies, the CCLA called for an independent citizen advisory committee made up of members from the community to investigate complaints. Once a complaint had been received, it would be investigated and could not be withdrawn (the point being to avoid making complainants potential targets for police intimidation). If some fault were found, the committee would be empowered to conciliate and to force the police department to pay damages or call a hearing with regard to the issue. The key was to ensure a fair and open investigation and the perception of independence. This was the CCLA's enduring vision of how the relationship between citizens and police should be regulated.[40]

The vision would only be partially realized in the early 1980s, but in the 1970s there were many opportunities for the CCLA to air its grievances against the then current system of processing complaints. There were three major inquiries in the seventies alone, each of which highlighted the problems with the current system of handling complaints against the police. The Toronto Police Commission appointed Toronto lawyer Arthur Maloney to a one-man inquiry in 1974 to study complaints procedures.[41] Maloney found evidence of cover-ups and recommended the appointment of a commissioner of citizen complaints. He refused to go so far as to suggest creating a fully independent civilian system, instead preferring an outside arbitrator appointed by the Metropolitan Toronto City Council to review police activities. The investigation would remain with the police. A civilian system was rejected because it would lower police moral and increase tensions between police and citizens.

The Maloney Report helps to explain why the subject of complaints procedures could no longer be ignored. The seventies was a period in which Ontarians, as an increasingly well-educated community, possessed a heightened awareness of individual rights and were willing to seek redress when those rights were abused. Second, the widespread enforcement of criminal laws respecting drugs involved a new criminal element: mainly young, middle-class, and often vocal individuals who were increasingly brought into contact with police. Third, complaints usually arose when the police were required to enforce unpopular laws about which people in the community were ambivalent – notably, those pertaining to drinking, gambling, prostitution, and drugs. Since these crimes had no discernible victims who would push for an investigation, they could often lead to illegal searches, arrests, and sometimes outright entrapment.

In the same year (the year of the Fort Erie raid) that Maloney reviewed Toronto's police complaint system, the media was pressuring the province to take action. A series of ten hard-hitting front-page stories appeared in the *Globe and Mail* in October 1974 documenting seventeen cases of police brutality. In one case, a drug dealer claimed his police interrogators applied a stapler and mechanical claw to his genitals in order to extract a confession, while another man was kicked in the stomach so severely he nearly died later in hospital. The province appointed Justice Donald Morand, who later became the province's second ombudsman

(Maloney was the first), to head the Royal Commission into Metropolitan Toronto Police Practices. Morand investigated 114 complaints against Toronto police. The report, presented in 1976, documents a variety of illegal activities on the part of police officers, from lying under oath to hiding evidence, changing duty books, and lying to superior officers. Morand called for criminal charges to be laid in relation to eleven incidents and for a new system of processing complaints against police. Once again, the CCLA's conception of an independent civilian complaints system was rejected. Morand favoured Maloney's recommendation that the chief of police retain responsibility for imposing discipline and that the police be allowed to investigate the initial complaint.[42]

By 1977, the province had yet to act on the major recommendation of both the Maloney and Morand reports. The Toronto Police Commission had called on the provincial government to implement Maloney's recommendations to no effect. A civilian review agency, long sought after by the CCLA, remained beyond its grasp. Nonetheless, between 1968 and 1977, the CCLA established itself as the leading rights association in Ontario and one of the leading advocacy groups in the country. It was invited to meet with government ministers, to present briefs, and, through several generous grants from large foundations, to conduct important research projects that led to significant legislative reforms. In 1973, former Supreme Court justice Emmett Hall was appointed honorary president of the association, following the death of Keiller Mackay three years earlier. These were the formative years, as the CCLA worked to place itself in a position to influence key national and provincial policy issues.

Protecting People from the Police, 1977-82

Police scandals and investigations into the need for a new process for investigating complaints did not end with the Morand Report in 1976. Within a year the public was once again clamouring for reform in the face of police violence. This time it involved cases in which Toronto police were accused of physically abusing members of minority groups, notably in a series of subway beatings with racial overtones on New Year's Eve in 1976. In 1977, Walter Pitman, president of Ryerson Polytechnic Institute, was appointed by the Toronto Police Commission to head the Task Force on Human Relations. Once again, an investigation led to calls for basic reforms to the structure of the police force and recommended the implementation of a new system for processing citizen complaints (along the lines of the Maloney Report).[43] All of his recommendations were eventually adopted, and the police commission asked the provincial government to legislate for a new system of processing citizen complaints.[44]

After three major reports investigating police abuse in Toronto, it was an understatement when the chairman of the police commission suggested that "no other police force or public agency for that matter has undergone such intensive and wide-ranging scrutiny in recent years as the Metropolitan Toronto Police."[45] And it was not to end there. Two years after the Pitman Report, the Toronto police force found itself mired in another scandal following complaints by the gay community. Homosexuals became incensed following revelations that police officers were notifying school boards about public school teachers who had appeared in court on morals charges. Tensions between the police and minorities finally exploded when a black man, Albert Johnson, was shot and killed on 26 August 1979. It was the culmination of a series of police shootings over a ten-month period involving mostly members of minority groups, with at least one shooting a month. Two thousand people demonstrated in downtown Toronto in the wake of the Johnson shooting. The issue was serious enough to lead Toronto City Council to pass a motion of non-confidence in the Toronto Police Commission.[46] Gerald Emmett Cardinal Carter of the Roman Catholic Church was appointed to mediate between police and minority groups. He recommended revising police practices to include more street patrols as well as regulations against verbal abuse. Unsurprisingly, Carter called for a better procedure for handling complaints.[47]

Throughout all this, the CCLA consistently called for a civilian agency to review complaints against police. The association was present before the Maloney Commission, made representations before the Toronto Police Commission, and lobbied several provincial solicitors general. Remarkably, the CCLA was even able to make common cause with the Ontario Police Association, which supported the former's call for a fully independent civilian complaints system.[48] Throughout the seventies, a series of events continually revitalized the CCLA's dogged campaign for a civilian review system. In 1973, without provocation, Vicky Trerise, a striker on a picket line during the Artistic Woodwork labour dispute in Toronto, was dragged by her hair and beaten by police.[49] A year later, the CCLA made presentations before the Pringle Commission regarding the Fort Erie raid. Throughout 1978 and 1979, the CCLA entered into extended correspondence with two succeeding solicitors general over questions of police abuse of Aboriginal people in Kenora, following a series of investigations in which twenty people claimed they had been abused. The issue was serious enough to lead to an inquiry on the part of the Ontario Provincial Police and a debate before the Standing Committee on the Administration of Justice.[50] Following accusations of police abuse of strikers during the Boise Cascade strike in Kenora in 1979, the CCLA repeated its demands to the solicitor general to implement a new system.[51] For over a decade, the CCLA had been constantly calling for reform.

Attempting to legislate a new system for processing citizen complaints proved to be a tortuous process. As early as October 1976, John MacBeth, Ontario's solicitor general, promised legislation to improve complaints procedures. A year later, he introduced Bill 113, An Act to Amend the Police Act, to implement Maloney's recommendation for a civilian complaints commissioner. His bill died on the order paper, and another bill was not introduced until 1979, when his successor, Roy McMurtry, introduced Bill 201 to create a commissioner of citizen complaints for a three-year test period. This bill also died on the order paper, and McMurtry attempted again in May 1980 to push through similar legislation. At the time the Progressive Conservatives under William Davis were operating as a minority government, and there was intense opposition, particularly from the NDP, to the government's proposed legislation. Each piece of legislation introduced thus far by the government had simply proposed civilian oversight of the initial police investigation. A citizen complaints commissioner would review a report produced following a police investigation of the complaint and had the power to call a tribunal or impose penalties if the commissioner felt the investigation had been improperly handled. While this was consistent with Maloney's vision, it contrasted with the CCLA and the opposition NDP's idea of a fully independent civilian investigatory body. From McMurtry's perspective, since 90 percent of complaints were solved in the initial interview (either through clarifying an issue or an apology from the officer), a fully civilian system would create unnecessary burdens. Undoubtedly, McMurtry was also concerned about a possible confrontation with the police, who, with few exceptions, were adamantly opposed to a fully independent review system.[52]

While an attempt by the NDP to introduce a private member's bill failed, McMurtry's legislation was defeated by combined opposition from the Liberals and the NDP. Four attempts by the government and private members to introduce legislation to deal with civilian complaints had thus collapsed.[53] Finally, on 5 May 1981, McMurtry introduced Bill 68 to create an office of the public complaints commissioner. Two key factors paved the way for passing the legislation. First, in March 1981 the Progressive Conservatives had won a resounding victory over the Liberals and NDP, and now enjoyed a majority government. Second, in February 1981, in what was characterized as the largest police action since the October Crisis, 150 Toronto police officers raided four bathhouses and arrested hundreds of gay men. The incident sparked an outcry from the gay community and local papers regarding the police force's decision to single out homosexuals. The *Globe and Mail* characterized the raids as an "ugly action" and a clear case of discrimination against homosexuals, suggesting that "this flinging of an army against the homosexuals is more like the bully-boy tactics of a Latin American republic attacking church and lay reformers than of anything that has a place in Canada." At least two papers, the *Globe and Mail* and the *Toronto Star*, suggested that, in light of the bathhouse raids, the provincial government should implement an independent civilian system for handling complaints soon after the election.[54] All of this pressure undoubtedly encouraged McMurtry to reintroduce his police review bill in the form of Bill 68 within days of the Legislature's being recalled in May 1981.

Once again, the CCLA had used a highly public issue to call for a new system of transmitting citizen complaints. After nearly fifteen years of pressure, the CCLA finally had its wish in the form of Bill 68. Despite the failure to achieve a fully independent civilian system for handling police complaints, the CCLA could claim a partial success, after more than a decade of advocacy, in the creation of the public complaints commissioner. The entire question of police powers had been the central preoccupation of the CCLA, with its first activities directed against police censorship and limits on demonstrators. Appropriately enough, the first public complaints commissioner was none other than Sidney Linden, former general counsel and one of the founders of the CCLA. As the CCLA moved from focusing predominantly on local issues to tackling more national concerns, it would retain its interest in regulating police powers.

While 1977 to 1982 represented a culmination of the CCLA's activities in the field of police abuse, it was also a period during which the CCLA vigorously asserted itself on the national stage. Whereas in the preceding thirteen years the association, with a few exceptions, had focused its efforts on provincial and municipal issues, by 1982 the CCLA had truly made a name for itself nationally. This was done through two key events, the first being Canada's version of Watergate.

In 1976, there were revelations of extensive illegal activities being conducted by the RCMP. Among other things, police were illegally opening mail and, in 1972, had conducted an illegal raid on the office of the Agence de Presse Libre du Québec, a left-wing news agency. RCMP officers, in conjunction with the Quebec Provincial Police and the Montreal Urban Community Police force, were further responsible for secretly (and illegally) raiding the offices of the Parti Québécois and copying membership lists. Some of the force's more outrageous actions included stealing explosives and burning down a barn to prevent a meeting of the Black Panthers and suspected members of the FLQ. It was clear the RCMP had overstepped its bounds, although its actions were entirely consistent with the force's focus on separatists and socialists as a threat to national security. Within a year, federal Solicitor General Francis Fox appointed a royal commission chaired by Alberta judge David C. McDonald. The commission's final report appeared in 1981.

The history of the McDonald Commission is presented elsewhere and does not need be recounted in full here.[55] Sitting from 1977 to 1981, the inquiry conducted extensive research into the role of the RCMP, produced hundreds of briefs and individual investigations, generated massive media coverage, and even led to conflicts with the Keable Commission in Quebec. The McDonald Commission took forty-nine months to produce more than two thousand pages in three separate reports, costing $8 million and an additional $2 million for RCMP lawyers. At the heart of the commission's findings was the idea that there was an inherent contradiction within the RCMP: the belief that in order to enforce the law they had to break the law. To protect the nation from security threats, the police believed that they had to circumvent the law by opening mail and committing other abuses. Among the commission's recommendations was the creation of a civilian agency, without police powers, that would take control of the RCMP's security service. It further recommended making access to information reviewable by the Federal Court, clarifying the mandate of the RCMP, banning the infiltration of unions and political parties, establishing external investigations of RCMP activities, and ensuring greater ministerial responsibility for the force. However, it did not recommend that any specific criminal proceedings be taken against the accused police officers (although the Keable Commission did recommend prosecutions, several of which were undertaken in Quebec). The entire episode served to highlight the weak political oversight of the RCMP and, as journalist Jeff Sallot suggested in 1979, the fact that the "true test of a national security agency ... is its ability to quickly identify the real threats and not to waste its time on legitimate dissenters. This the Security Service failed to do."[56] In the end, the commission not only mobilized rights activists across the country but also stimulated a widespread public debate on the extent of police powers in Canada.[57]

The CCLA embraced the scandal surrounding illegal RCMP activities with a passion. This response was entirely consistent with the association's long-standing efforts to establish civilian checks on the operation of police forces. One of its first acts was to petition the commission for standing to allow its own lawyers to cross-examine witnesses, a request McDonald denied. Not to be discouraged, the CCLA had a representative at the commission's public hearings whose job was to produce regular reports on the commission's activities. Borovoy organized a team of researchers across the country to prepare a massive brief. After all, no issue fit more perfectly into the CCLA's mandate, and there would be no better forum for promoting reform in the relationship between the police and citizens throughout the country than the McDonald Commission. Lawyers and other volunteers were recruited from as far away as Nova Scotia and British Columbia to do research.[58] It was a testament to the CCLA's effectiveness that it was able to recruit volunteers from diverse backgrounds across the country.

There is little doubt the CCLA exploited the McDonald Commission in an attempt to establish itself as Canada's true national civil liberties association. On 16 November 1977, the CCLA sent a letter to Prime Minister Trudeau, and three days later had it published in the *Globe and Mail*. This full-page advertisement cost the organization a painful $10,000, straining its budget but ensuring that it did more than any other rights association with regard to publicly challenging the government's position on RCMP wrongdoings. Signed by such luminaries as Walter Tarnopolsky and Emmett Hall, the letter went to the heart of the issue as the CCLA perceived it: ministerial responsibility. Quoting Trudeau's own words, the letter questioned the prime minister's defending illegal RCMP activities by noting how, in some situations, the police must break the law, as in the case of entering a private residence to diffuse a bomb or speeding to catch a bank robber. According to the CCLA, none of these acts could justify the need to break into the office of a legitimate political party and copy its membership lists. The letter went on to question why the prime minister and his cabinet failed to inform themselves of the activities of the RCMP, and the CCLA accused the government of using the commission as a delaying tactic. The association called on Trudeau to prosecute all known police offenders, to inform the provincial attorneys general of all the evidence the commission had gathered, and to launch a parliamentary committee to investigate the responsibility of a minister of the Crown with regard to supervising the RCMP.

Trudeau responded with his own public letter, effectively criticizing the CCLA for quoting him selectively and justifying the need for ministers to remain aloof from the administration of the police: "I do not believe it appropriate, for example, for the government to be aware of, or involved in, either police or security investigations. The independence of these investigations, and the confidence of the public in their honesty, must not be impaired by even the suggestion of political interference ... It is necessary, I suggest, for those asking these questions to bear in mind the extraordinary techniques employed by those engaged in espionage, subversion or terrorism, as it is necessary for those answering the questions to focus on the precarious and sometimes fragile nature of our democratic process."[59]

Trudeau rejected all the CCLA's recommendations. He refused to pass on information to individual attorneys general (preferring a single investigation run by the federal government), and he left the disciplining of individual officers to the force.

The issue of ministerial responsibility was at the heart of the divide between the CCLA and the federal government. For years the CCLA had been calling for civilian review of local police forces, and, in calling for greater ministerial responsibility, the group hoped to achieve a form of civilian review of the RCMP. In contrast, Trudeau and his ministers seemed loath to take direct responsibility for RCMP law breaking. As suggested in a *Globe and Mail* editorial on 11 November 1977, the "Prime Minister and his colleagues either don't know or won't admit what Cabinet responsibility means. This has been growing more and more apparent as incidents involving the Royal Canadian Mounted Police have been revealed." According to the *Globe and Mail*, Solicitor General Francis Fox admitted to the mail opening but claimed to have known nothing about it; Justice Minister Ron Basford said there was nothing he could do but refer the issue to the McDonald Commission since the RCMP's own investigatory unit would be inappropriate; and, Postmaster Jean-Jacques Blais claimed to know nothing of the practice. Not only would the Liberals introduce a bill to legalize mail opening a couple of years later in 1979 (and, in doing so, inflame rights activists who felt this legitimized illegal police activities), but after the report was released in 1981 the new solicitor general, Robert Kaplan, would continue to maintain that, with the exception of the more egregious offences, such as barn burning, the RCMP's activities were justified.[60]

Given the consistent refusal of senior political leaders to accept responsibility and the four-year delay in the McDonald Commission's investigation, cynicism surrounding the inquiry and the belief that it was a delay tactic were understandable.

The CCLA's campaign, mixed with several public forums and no less than five briefs before the McDonald Commission, substantially increased the group's public profile.[61] It garnered four hundred new members in the first two weeks alone, following the advertisement placed in the *Globe and Mail*.[62] By the end of the year, the CCLA's work had earned it at least one thousand new members. It also engendered some negative feedback from those who came to the defence of the RCMP. The association's correspondence files are littered with letters containing such statements as: "Bullshit!! Thank God for the RCMP," "You bloody communists ... Canadians aren't with you," "You middle class humbugs," "Drop dead you bastards," and "The country's biggest collection of assholes, especially your legal counsel."

In a creative campaign to solicit public interest and to pressure the government to act, the CCLA organized a petition calling on the government to initiate proceedings against offenders. Unlike traditional petitions, this one required all signatories to pay one dollar to emphasize their support for the cause. Well-known public figures such as Margaret Atwood, Pierre Berton, Daniel G. Hill (first chair of the Ontario Human Rights Commission), Tommy Douglas, and David Lewis sat at a sidewalk booth on Yonge Street soliciting donations. The CCLA was also able to use its connections with the NDP and organized labour to solicit support by way of large mailing campaigns (thanks to various mailing lists) as well as by working with its chapters in Nova Scotia and Manitoba.[63] It netted more than $15,000, and the petition was presented to Solicitor General Kaplan in May 1980, with media coverage across the country.[64] By this time, the CCLA had five thousand paid members and thirty organizational members (mainly church, labour, and ethnic groups). In the end, the entire episode elevated the CCLA to the position of one of the government's leading critics.

While an initial report had been released in 1980 dealing with such issues as revisions to the Official Secrets Act and access to information, the final reports were not released until 1981.[65] After four years of tireless work and activism (the McDonald Commission was the group's largest expense for several years), the CCLA leadership must have been disappointed with the results. While many of the CCLA's minor recommendations, such as requiring that any proclamation of the War Measures Act be approved by Parliament within a specific time limit, were included in the commission's recommendations, the inquiry's two key recommendations were opposed by the CCLA. First, the commission did not directly recommend the prosecution of RCMP wrongdoers because, in some cases (such as illegal mail opening), it refused to investigate allegations on a case-by-case basis and considered recommendations for specific prosecutions to be beyond its jurisdiction.[66] Second, the commission suggested the creation of a civilian security agency with no police powers, a recommendation that eventually led to the formation of the Canadian Security and Intelligence Service.

In a lengthy column published in the *Globe and Mail*, Borovoy criticized the commission's central recommendation as it would divorce criminal investigations from security work.[67] Law enforcement was reactive, whereas security service was preventative. Security services gather a great deal of information on broad and vague mandates, while law enforcement agencies focus on specific crimes and gather evidence for easily identifiable crimes. Borovoy was concerned that a security service that was separate from criminal investigations would blur the lines between subversion and legitimate dissent. Criminal investigations dealt with specific crimes, whereas the vague mandate for national security often led authorities to undermine legitimate dissent. Creating a civilian agency with no policing responsibilities could exacerbate the danger of having government agents undercut legitimate dissent to "prevent" threats. For Borovoy, the problem with the RCMP was institutional, and the solution was to reintegrate criminal investigations with security services within the RCMP and establish effective civilian oversight.

The final domino fell in July 1982, when Minister of Justice Jean Chrétien decided not to initiate prosecutions against any RCMP officers. Nothing could have infuriated the CCLA, and other rights activists, more than the decision not to prosecute. In a letter to Solicitor General Kaplan, Chrétien explained that his refusal to prosecute was based primarily on the fact that the commission did not provide evidence for specific illegalities. Given the massive scope of hundreds of potential investigations, Chrétien chose not to act. In the case of illegal mail openings, the minister of justice noted how the statute of limitations made some prosecutions impossible; only those who had committed the crime more recently would be prosecuted, which the minister considered an unfair form of discrimination. He was also cognizant of the fact that, for many RCMP officers, the practice had an air of legitimacy and that many were unaware they were committing illegal acts; in addition, he did not believe the offenders acted out of personal gain. Ironically, given how many observers considered the commission a delaying tactic, Chrétien concluded his letter by noting that "it should be borne in mind that time applicable to limitation periods was running during the nearly four years of the existence of the Commission of Inquiry."[68]

Borovoy and the leadership of the CCLA were incensed. Chrétien's letter was a collection of excuses for not prosecuting RCMP officers even though, had it been civilians who had been accused of similar crimes, the government would surely have acted. In an article published in the *Toronto Star*, Borovoy called on Chrétien's successor (Mark MacGuigan, a former CCLA executive) to act on the commission's recommendations. Borovoy argued that there was no reason to refuse to prosecute simply because the statute of limitations had expired in a few cases. While it was true that the officers in question did not gain materially from their activities, it was also highly likely that some had committed these acts to curry favour with their supervisors. In addition, the commission's hearings clearly revealed that high-echelon officers knew the practice was illegal. The CCLA had been calling for prosecutions since 1977, and the government had yet to explain why it chose not to act earlier.[69]

To be sure, the McDonald Commission stands out as one of the CCLA's most important efforts. However, in many ways, it was a spectacular failure. Despite practically dominating the organization's efforts for several years, neither the reforms to the RCMP security service nor the anticipated prosecutions were realized. As well, the commission's recommended changes to the War Measures Act and the Official Secrets Act were never implemented. Yet, for the first time in its history, the CCLA had justified calling itself a national organization. It continued to lack representativeness across the country, with most of its membership being in Ontario and a few chapters being scattered across the nation, but it had asserted itself aggressively on a national issue. No other rights association came close to doing the same.

The Charter of Rights and Freedoms

By 1981, the CCLA was not only the largest rights association in the country but by far the most active. While the LDH struggled with internal disputes, the BCCLA with declining government grants, and the Federation with virtual invisibility, the CCLA thrived. It enjoyed a budget that fluctuated between $125,000 and $150,000, although it did not receive any major research grants during this time; membership fees and donations accounted for approximately 80 to 90 percent of its funding. By 1980, funds accrued from the campaign against RCMP wrongdoings had netted an impressive $54,000 (the CCLA executive had estimated that it would only be able to raise around $21,000).[70]

While the CCLA continued to promote legislative change in Ontario, in the early 1980s it geared up for one of the most important developments in Canadian history: the patriation of the Constitution. Aspects of the CCLA's role in the Charter debates are documented in a 1991 book by Borovoy entitled *Uncivil Disobedience;* however, given the recognition accorded the CCLA during the Charter debates and the Charter's contribution to helping establish the organization as a national rights association, the issue deserves some attention here.

The CCLA had a greater impact on the Charter than did any other rights association in the country. In its brief before the Special Joint Committee on the Constitution, the organization went so far as to actually oppose the passing of the Charter, suggesting that, unless significant improvements were made, the status quo would be better than the proposed legislation. The CCLA insisted on the removal of Section 1, the limitation clause, because it would allow judges to assert parliamentary supremacy, which had been the bane of the Bill of Rights.

The final draft of the Charter drew inspiration from the CCLA's brief. Section 8 was amended to ban unreasonable searches and seizures (in contrast to *illegal* searches, which could be permitted by law, thus placing a greater burden on the state to justify the search); Section 10 was changed to add the right to be informed of one's right to legal counsel upon arrest (although the actual wording was drawn from the Federation's brief); a new section on remedies for Charter violations was added; and trial by jury was entrenched. But it was the amendment to Section 1 that was to have profound repercussions. Section 1, the infamous "limitation clause," was reworded, based on submissions by the CCLA and the federal Human Rights Commission, to require any limits on constitutional rights to be "demonstrably justified." The CCLA would have preferred more stringent wording (that limits must be "necessary" instead of "demonstrably justified") but the effect was similar: the burden was now on the state to prove the need to limit a certain right. As James Kelly notes, the provinces had fought for the inclusion of Section 1 in order to protect the supremacy of the legislatures; instead, "constitutional supremacy came to characterize the draft Charter because the federal government, for a temporary but significant number of months, responded to the criticism of Canadians."[71]

In the Special Joint Committee on the Constitution's draft report to Parliament the CCLA was the only rights association mentioned. In fact, out of 95 groups that made presentations before the committee and 914 that submitted briefs, only the CCLA and 4 other groups are referred to in the report.[72] When, in January 1981, Jean Chrétien introduced his recommendations for changing the draft resolution repatriating the Constitution, the CCLA was among only nine organizations referred to as having directly influenced the revised version of the resolution. With the exception of one short reference to the BCCLA, the CCLA (not the Federation) was the only rights association referred to by the minister of justice.[73] Although not all of Chrétien's recommendations were accepted in the end, it is clear that the CCLA had a critical impact on the development of the Charter. Only the brief presented by the Canadian Bar Association received more government attention. Undoubtedly, Tarnopolsky's presence as one of the country's leading experts on constitutional rights and president of the CCLA greatly enhanced the brief's reception.

If the history of the Charter demonstrates anything, it is that many policy makers at least nominally recognized the CCLA as the leading rights association in the country. This alone did not mean that the association was a truly national rights association, only that it had greater visibility and name recognition than did any other rights association in Canada. The years between 1977 and 1982 were, therefore, the peak years in the organization's early history – a time when it established itself on the national stage while continuing to promote reform in Ontario. With Section 1 entrenched in the Constitution, the Charter would no doubt prove a bitter pill for many of the organization's members; however, for those such as

Tarnopolsky, who, in principle, supported constitutional rights, it was the ultimate victory. By 1982, with a membership of five thousand, nearly double that of the next largest association, the CCLA could truly claim to have come into its own eighteen years after its birth.

The CCLA: A Case Study in National Social Movement Organizing

In the previous two case studies, it is apparent that, despite their ideological differences, the BCCLA and the LDH had many affinities with each other. Both accepted state funding and deployed similar tactics in their advocacy. They also worked together in the Federation and decisively broke with their predecessors as new controversies erupted in the 1960s. As a civil liberties organization, however, the BCCLA was far more attuned to the CCLA than was the LDH. Ironically, the relationship between the BCCLA and the LDH was more cordial than was the relationship between the BCCLA and the CCLA. Although the experience of the CCLA adds a new layer of understanding to the relationship between rights associations and other SMOs (particularly organized labour), and to the courts as a forum for social change, the key insights we can draw from the CCLA's history involve the debate over state funding and, in particular, the failure to form a truly inclusive national rights association in Canada.

Strategies for Change

At the heart of Alan Borovoy's 1991 book on strategies for activists, *Uncivil Obedience,* is a faith in human nature and a belief that public opinion will set most wrongs right. His book emphasizes the CCLA's core tactic: convincing the media to cover a story and bringing public pressure to bear on the state or private individuals. In the sixties, for instance, the CCLA organized several surveys of employment agencies and held press conferences to show how agencies were posting racially discriminatory job advertisements. When Borovoy visited the small town of Gosfield to petition the school board to end religious practices in public schools, he had little hope the board would ever change its policy; instead, he wanted the media to cover his visit. In Gosfield the media was exposed to extremists who sought to use public schools for religious indoctrination, and the resulting headlines and editorials strengthened the CCLA's campaign.

The CCLA engaged in a variety of strategies to attract the media. Although Borovoy has often recommended that social activists employ "disruptive" tactics to get their message across (e.g., sit-ins), the CCLA itself has rarely employed grassroots mobilization and has scrupulously avoided disruptive tactics. The only exception to this rule was the occasional rally organized in conjunction with other SMOs (which had closer ties to a grassroots following). However, by the late 1990s, the CCLA had only participated in three such actions throughout its long history.

Appealing to the press therefore became one of the CCLA's core strategies. Public letters, press conferences, surveys, and, to a lesser extent, litigation were all designed to attract the media. The CCLA was also prolific in presenting briefs to various municipal councils, government officials, or regulatory bodies. It presented no fewer than forty-four briefs between 1964 and 1982. The RCMP petition, albeit the only instance of the CCLA's organizing a petition, was successful in bringing attention to illegal RCMP activities.[74] Extensive correspondence provided an additional means of convincing an organization to change its policies. Throughout the seventies, the CCLA exchanged dozens of letters with the Canadian Veterinary Medical Association in an attempt to persuade the association to stop discriminating against Asians in the provision of licences.

These tactics were appropriate for an organization that sought respectability. The CCLA, and the other rights associations in this book, did not embrace civil disobedience or mass mobilization as strategies to promote social change. Instead, the CCLA recruited "respectable" members of the community to facilitate its activism, as was the case in 1970, when, thanks to the participation of the CCLA president, former lieutenant-governor J. Keiller Mackay, the CCLA was granted a meeting with the Ontario minister responsible for the administration of welfare. The elitist nature of rights associations led them to speak on behalf of people in their community who were poorly represented within the organizations. In addition, rights associations clearly differed from many other SMOs in their unwillingness to employ dual strategies. None of the tactics associated with the American civil rights movement, including sit-ins, freedom rides, boycotts, occupying public buildings, shouting obscenities at public meetings, and dozens of other disruptive tactics was ever employed by Canadian rights associations. In an article written for the *Canadian Bar Review* in 1973, Borovoy condemned civil disobedience and suggested that violence would simply beget a similar reaction from the state.[75] However, rational public debate, the cornerstone of the CCLA's modus operandi, could only achieve so much. As Borovoy himself admitted, "the reliance on exclusively legal tactics in political disputes is likely to reduce the prospects of anything but incremental victories. The quick and radical transformation of society can rarely be achieved through the use of lawful strategies."[76]

Nonetheless, no other rights associations had more of a proclivity towards litigation than did the CCLA. Granted, the BCCLA also looked to the courts for redress. But the BCCLA was able to take on only a few cases in its first twenty years of operation, and only one of them reached the Supreme Court of Canada. No rights association had a stronger presence in the provincial appellate court and the Supreme Court in the pre-Charter era than did the CCLA. As Robert J. Sharpe and Kent Roach note, under "Laskin's liberal regime, the CCLA became a familiar presence before the [Supreme] Court."[77] Between 1964 and 1982, the CCLA provided legal counsel for twenty-three separate cases in either the County Court, the provincial superior/supreme courts, the appellate courts, or the Supreme Court of Canada. Of these cases, five reached the highest court in the country, six were argued before a provincial appellate division, two went before the Federal Court (one of them reached the Federal Court of Appeal), and the rest resided in various inferior courts. Most of the litigation occurred in Ontario, although four of the CCLA's cases during this period were outside the province.

One of the significant advantages of being located in Toronto was having access to a fairly large pool of volunteer lawyers and two major law schools. The CCLA rarely had difficulty securing free legal counsel at a time when most rights associations had trouble finding lawyers who were willing to work for free. To be sure, the organization's faith in the legal system was driven by a belief in the potential for the law to promote equal (legal) opportunity. As was the case with the BCCLA, the CCLA sought in most cases to convince the courts to aggressively apply the Bill of Rights. In other cases, the CCLA simply hoped to encourage the courts to accept the practice of interveners.[78]

An analysis of the CCLA's track record suggests that its faith in the legal system, in the pre-Charter era, was misplaced. Of twenty-three challenges, the association was successful in only one case involving access to material behind the issuance of a search warrant.[79] Otherwise the CCLA failed in each court battle, although in some cases it won in the appellate court only to be defeated in the Supreme Court. Attempts by rights activists to seek redress in the courts were therefore continually thwarted, bringing into question the ability of the courts to act as an effective forum for the defence of human rights.

Of course, the success of litigation should not be measured only in the decision handed down by the court (although several leading members of the CCLA, such as Borovoy and Harry Arthurs – who served as president of the CCLA from 1976 to 1978 – were cautiously enthusiastic about the court's potential to promote social change):[80] an SMO could also benefit from the publicity and mobilization that accompanied a major court case. Both the BCCLA and the CCLA used the legal system to politicize and to claim legitimacy for their demands. A loss in the courts could also help to soften public opinion and pave the way for a political assault.

The passing of the Charter represented a significant victory for the CCLA, an organization dedicated to using the courts to protect individual rights. By 2001, the CCLA had intervened in more Charter cases than had any other organization in Canada, with the exception of the Women's Legal Education and Action Fund. Between 1982 and 1997 alone, the CCLA had intervened in thirty-two Charter cases to the Supreme Court of Canada and was the primary litigant in two other cases. With a 63 percent success rate, the post-Charter era represented a significant transformation in the association's fortunes in court and encouraged the use of litigation as a core tactic.[81]

Ideological Foundations

As civil liberties associations, the CCLA and the BCCLA understood human rights in terms of civil and political rights; that is, they understood them in terms of negative freedom. In the field of administrative decision making, the BCCLA distinguished between the administration of social services and the content of such services, avoiding any discussion of the latter as a right. This was clearly the case with the CCLA's extensive work in the field of welfare. According to the federal government and the Toronto Social Planning Council, in the early 1970s, Ontario welfare recipients received barely 60 percent of the minimum funding they required in order to survive. Yet, when the CCLA took on the case of Jennifer Smith and provided a duty counsel in welfare offices, its goal was to improve the administration of welfare and to ensure due process: it never questioned the amount of welfare doled out by the state. In the association's voluminous report on welfare practices noted earlier, there was no mention of rampant underfunding.

Civil liberties activists mobilized to deal with the new threats posed by the welfare state, but there remained important ideological distinctions between civil liberties activists and human rights activists. A human right, for equality-seekers, involved more than simply protecting individuals from lack of unfair restraints. The LDH defended the handicapped, the elderly, youth, and prisoners – groups the CCLA generally avoided. Not only did the ODD focus on prisoners' due process rights but it also advocated for better food, wages, and, ultimately, the abolition of prisons altogether. With regard to the elderly, the LDH argued that they had a right to their own lodgings and to obtain services at home, including medical help and transportation, as well as the right to achieve a minimum standard of living and to participate in the social and cultural life of the community.

But it was more than simply a question of prioritizing rights. The BCCLA and the CCLA have been ardent defenders of free speech, and both have opposed criminalizing hate speech and censoring pornography.[82] To this day, the Newfoundland-Labrador Human Rights Association supports the censorship of pornography (and, in the late 1980s, adopted a position supporting legislation banning hate speech), as have many human rights associations.[83] Surprisingly, the LDH did not take a stance on pornography, despite the creation of an office for women in the mid-1970s with an express mandate to promote women's equality. Nonetheless, the LDH's equality-seeking agenda is evident in its 1980 campaign to, among other things, have the Criminal Code amended to prohibit accused rapists from introducing their accusers' sexual history at trial.[84] Eleven years later, the CCLA earned the ire of many equality-seekers when it successfully intervened in a case to strike down the Criminal Code's rape-shield law.

Free speech was not the only issue dividing rights associations. Since 1972, the LDH has distinguished itself as an ardent defender of the collective rights of French Canadians, including the extension of their language rights in such a way as to

make the public education system unilingually French. It was not only an assertion of the socio-cultural rights of French Canadians but also a positive understanding of human rights based on a belief that the state should actively promote
equality and not just protect liberty. In the 1970s, few civil libertarians with a pen-
chant for conceiving of human rights as negative freedoms would have seen Quebec's language laws in a favourable light. Borovoy, for instance, severely criticized
the application of Quebec's language laws in the workplace and on public signs,
characterizing it as "morally dubious," as an unwarranted encroachment on freedom of expression, and as "an affirmative action program in favour of the majority," which "contributed nothing to the legitimate protection of the French
majority."[85]

Relations with Other Social Movement Organizations

In its crusade to protect free speech, the CCLA found itself at odds with many
other SMOs, mostly notably Jewish activists and feminists. Generally, however,
the CCLA had a positive working relationship with other SMOs. Several of its
mail solicitation campaigns, sometimes numbering as many as 80,000 letters, used
the mailing lists of other groups.[86] Throughout the 1970s, Borovoy even sat on a
committee of the Canadian Jewish Congress, although the two groups did not
cooperate on joint ventures. The CCLA occasionally organized coalitions on issues
such as religious education and capital punishment, but it was not a common
strategy. The LDH was far more prolific in organizing coalitions than was the
CCLA. It is likely that the CCLA's narrow rights philosophy limited its ability to
find common ground with other SMOs, whereas the LDH, which considered
issues such as the conditions of imprisonment and the financial needs of the
elderly as human rights, found it easier to establish links with other groups.

There is no question that the CCLA was closer to organized labour than it was
to any other SMOs. Several of the leading members of the CCLA's Board of Directors were important figures in the labour movement, notably Terry Meagher
(secretary-treasurer of the Ontario Federation of Labour) and Dennis McDermott
(president of the CLC). Borovoy himself was the main link between labour and
the CCLA. He had been one of the most important figures in the JLC and in
organized labour's human rights program, and he maintained these ties when he
moved to the CCLA. He continually gave speeches and represented the CCLA at
meetings with the CLC, the Ontario Federation of Labour, and various labour
councils. It was Borovoy who convinced the CLC to hire Patrick Kerwin to work in
Kenora during the International Year for Human Rights, and for the next two
years Borovoy and the CCLA supervised his work.[87]

Labour could also count on the CCLA to come to its aid when the police abused
strikers on the picket line. In 1972, the CCLA supported striking workers from the
United Steelworkers of America by sending letters of complaint to the provincial

government when the courts repeatedly forced strikers to stay away from the picket line. Similarly, in 1973, the CCLA attacked the provincial government's proposed legislation to restrict the right of teachers to strike.[88] When Vicky Trerise was beaten by police during the Artistic Woodwork strike, the CCLA lobbied the police commission and the solicitor general for a public inquiry. Six years later, strikers accused local police of harassment and of supporting strike-breakers during the Boise Cascade Strike in Fort Francis-Kenora. In response, the CCLA sent a staff member to investigate and lobbied the solicitor general for sanctions against police.

These were just a few examples of how the CCLA cooperated with organized labour generally, and the CLC specifically. When the CLC decided in 1972 to write a primer on civil liberties to distribute to its members, it asked the CCLA, rather than the JLC, to write it. To support the CCLA's petition in 1978 on RCMP wrongdoings, the CLC endorsed the petition and distributed it to its members, encouraging them to sign-up. Several NDP clubs also endorsed the CCLA campaign and provided it with access to their mailing lists for the petition, while the United Auto Workers and the Canadian Union of Public Employees donated $1,000 each to defray the costs of the advertisement in the *Globe and Mail*.[89]

Through the JLC, organized labour had become a dominant player in the human rights movement, but by the seventies it was clear it had surrendered its position to rights associations. The decision to have the CCLA and not the JLC produce the primer was in itself an acknowledgment of the rise of the CCLA as a leader in the human rights movement. Most important, the CLC's interest in human rights activism was waning. Although the CLC's National Committee on Human Rights continued to operate, the committee was increasingly eclipsed by the activities of the Women's Bureau and no longer published its newsletter.[90] With the National Committee on Human Rights falling by the wayside, the only active branch of labour's human rights program was the JLC, and it was effectively defunct by the mid-1970s. In retrospect, the CLC's last major human rights initiative occurred in 1968, when it sent Kerwin to Kenora and organized a national conference in Ottawa. Since then, the CLC has effectively shied away from human rights advocacy. Without a doubt the CLC took an active interest in specific human rights issues such as privacy legislation, abortion, and capital punishment, presenting briefs to various parliamentary commissions. But this was a far cry from the financial commitment it had accepted with the JLC, the educational programs it had sponsored through the local labour committees in the 1960s, and taking on specific cases of discrimination.

Nothing exemplifies this reality more clearly than the fact that, with nearly a thousand submissions presented to the Special Joint Committee on the Constitution in 1980-81, organized labour was virtually absent from the proceedings. Leo Panitch and Donald Swartz blame the Quebec Federation of Labour for paralyzing the CLC in order to prevent the latter from taking part in a process that could strengthen federalism in Quebec. In fact, the CLC did submit a letter to the commission (but not a brief). The letter was short, and it simply reminded the committee about the need recognize the rights of First Nations peoples in the Constitution. This was consistent with the CLC's official statement on human rights (written in 1968) and with its work during the International Year for Human Rights, which placed Aboriginal rights at the forefront of the CLC's human rights program. Nonetheless, the CLC's limited participation in the Charter debates, and the virtual lack of any strong response from organized labour generally, was a significant omission from a movement that had been visibly active in the committees that studied a bill of rights in the 1940s and 1950s. Perhaps, as Panitch and Swartz suggest, the weak response by organized labour across the country can be accounted for by the movement's "trenchant economism [and] its subordinate consciousness to the exclusion of a hegemonic orientation."[91]

Despite the proliferation of rights associations across the country in the 1970s, the CLC and its provincial federations had little or no contact with them. In fact, except for the LDH (which had some links with Quebec unions) and the CCLA (which had only a limited working relationship with the CLC alone), rights associations had few links with the labour movement. This was an important change from the 1940s, when the labour movement worked alongside rights associations in several campaigns. Organized labour's diminished participation in the human rights movement was intimately tied to the decline of the JLC. Although discrimination, the heart and soul of labour's human rights program, was hardly eliminated, human rights commissions took over most of the labour movement's human rights work. In addition, there were more SMOs in the seventies than at any other point in Canadian history. Traditionally voiceless constituencies, from gays to the disabled, were organizing themselves. These new social movements increasingly eclipsed organized labour, either in attracting more adherents or in dominating the public agenda. Finally, the early seventies was the pinnacle of the Fordist period in Canadian history, with the welfare state fully entrenched and labour focused primarily on job security and wages for its workers. As Panitch and Swartz have pointed out, the postwar settlement "directed the efforts of union leaders away from mobilizing and organizing and toward the juridicial arena of labour boards ... These activities tended to foster a legalistic practice and consciousness in which union rights appeared as privileges bestowed by the state, rather than democratic freedoms won, and to be defended by, collective struggle."[92]

State Funding and the National Question
The creation of the CCLA in 1964 set the stage for years of conflict and headaches among activists eager to create a national rights association. In order to appreciate the complex divisions at the heart of the national question, it would be useful at

this point to review in some detail the context surrounding the CCLA's evolution towards national status.

As noted in Chapter 3, by the 1950s, the Jewish Labour Committee was the closest manifestation of a national rights association in Canada, although it did not fit the mould of a "rights association" and was on the decline by the 1960s. Another example of an organization with the potential to act as a national network of human rights advocacy was the Canadian Bar Association (CBA), a professional organization for lawyers. True, the CBA was not a genuine rights association. Human rights was just one of the many issues with which the CBA dealt, and its tactics and strategies were influenced by a myriad of other priorities.

In theory, however, the CBA had established an impressive structure to place itself at the forefront of the human rights movement. As the pre-eminent lawyers' association in the country, it had access to the legal skills necessary to advocate for human rights in a society in which human rights are defined as legal rights. Since having established a permanent civil liberties committee in 1946, the CBA encouraged the formation of civil liberties committees in all of its provincial chapters. With a national committee coordinating the work of provincial subcommittees, supported by the resources of the national network, the association was in a formidable position to take a stand on human rights issues, to influence public opinion, and to lobby governments. But throughout the sixties, the CBA's civil liberties subcommittee and its provincial counterparts failed to live up to their potential. In 1967, according to the chair of the national committee, "during the last year [this section of the CBA] has been, as usual, active in one or two provinces, mildly active in one or two others, and totally inactive in all of the others."[93] Two years later, the chair continued to lament the failure of the committee to attract enough supporters and blamed the association for not taking enough interest in human rights issues.[94]

The CBA never ignored human rights issues. During its annual meetings in the sixties and seventies there were several heated debates over abortion, capital punishment, wiretapping, youth rights, and the October Crisis. Writs of assistance were considered particularly egregious and offensive to individual liberty. Unlike a normal search warrant, whereby a judge allows a search for a specific objective after having been convinced that sufficient evidence exists for a search, these legal aberrations were provided to individual RCMP officers by judges of the Exchequer Court. A writ gave the officer to whom it was provided unrestricted power to search homes or people for illegal narcotics or violations of the Customs Act. No time limit was placed on writs: the writ lasted until the officer retired or died. Obviously, such a system was easily open to abuse. In British Columbia, for instance, municipal police would ask an RCMP officer to accompany them to an individual's home so the former could use her/his writ to search for illegal narcotics or, sometimes, simply for a fishing expedition. Writs of assistance were one of the many issues the CBA dealt with in the sixties, and it would eventually be successful in lobbying for restrictions on their use.[95] These efforts, however, were most often conducted through the executive, and the civil liberties committees were not involved. In 1970, the national civil liberties committee was totally inactive. It finally began work again in 1972, only to spend the next ten years as a minor committee in the association, conducting research and passing resolutions at annual meetings. In many provinces, such as Alberta, British Columbia, Newfoundland, and Nova Scotia, the civil liberties section attracted few members and was rarely active, sometimes going years without a meeting.[96]

Although the CBA would eventually play a prominent role in the debates on entrenching human rights in the Constitution, it never lived up to its potential as a national rights association.[97] The CBA may have constructed an impressive structure through which to engage with human rights issues, but by the sixties it was apparent that it would play only a minor role in the human rights movement.

By the late 1960s, it was becoming painfully clear that Canada still lacked any kind of national rights association. Many human rights activists in Canada could only sigh with envy when the observed the accomplishments of organizations like the American Civil Liberties Union, the Ligue des droits de l'homme in France, and the National Council for Civil Liberties in England. Kalmen Kaplansky, who, in the 1950s, had played a critical role in creating the most successful national organization to fight discrimination in Canadian history, entered the spotlight briefly once again in the late 1960s in a valiant, but ultimately unsuccessful, attempt to create a national rights association.

Before Kaplansky took action, however, another national organization dedicated to human rights issues emerged in 1967: the Canadian Human Rights Foundation. It was not an advocacy group but a national charitable organization that conducted education and research programs. The foundation received grants from government sources, including the Secretary of State (hereafter SOS) and the Canada Council, as well as from federal and provincial departments of justice. Its membership included such distinguished personalities as John Humphrey (drafted the UDHR), Justice Antonio Lamer (future justice of the Supreme Court of Canada), Professor Paul A. Crépeau (head of the Office for the Revision of the Civil Code of Québec), and Thérèse Casgrain (future senator and well-known women's rights activist).[98] However, the foundation was never designed to be a popular association with a broad membership. It was a fellowship of elites dedicated to raising money to promote human rights. According to the minutes of its founding meeting, the "purpose of the Foundation is to advance the course of Human Rights by helping to finance the work of organizations and activities in this field. It would not, however, take any stand on particular issues but would restrict itself to channelling moneys to appropriate agencies."[99] At no time could the foundation honestly be characterized as a national rights association.

Two years later came an attempt to form a true national rights association. As early as August 1968, Kalmen Kaplansky, chair of the Board of Directors of the Canadian Commission for the International Year for Human Rights, was talking about using the anniversary celebrations as a forum for creating a national rights association.[100] Only one motion materialized from the December conference in Ottawa, and this represented the culmination of a year's work across the country promoting human rights in honour of the anniversary of the Universal Declaration of Human Rights. The motion called for the formation of a Canadian council on human rights, which was to act as a national rights association made up of interested individuals and voluntary agencies. Within a few months, Kaplansky brought together many of the executive members of the Canadian Commission for the International Year for Human Rights to act as the planning and organizing committee for the council. Funding left over from the SOS grant for the International Year for Human Rights (over $17,000) was transferred to the council, and an office was established with administrative support through the Canadian Welfare Council.

Unfortunately for the Canadian Council on Human Rights, it quickly ran out of funding. A grant of $19,500 from the SOS was followed by a cessation of state funding, and the council was unable to procure money from any additional sources. During its one year of existence, its major accomplishment was to fund a report produced by Maurice Miron surveying rights associations across the country. Miron's goal was to consult with potential members on the feasibility of a national human rights organization, their willingness to participate in such an organization, and the means of financing such a group. Based on his findings, Miron recommended that the SOS provide the Canadian Council on Human Rights with a $47,500 grant to set up a national rights association that would employ a national director as well as five regional directors.[101] But the SOS's office balked at such a large financial commitment to a new organization. Nothing came of the report, and the council, devoid of government funding, became inactive and officially folded in 1970.

It would take one of the greatest crises in Canadian history to successfully mobilize rights activists to form a national organization. The October Crisis was the birth mother of the Canadian Federation of Civil Liberties and Human Rights Associations. In 1970, a collection of rights associations from Montreal, Toronto, St. John's, Edmonton, Windsor, Fredericton, and Vancouver had coordinated their efforts to publicly oppose the imposition of the War Measures Act and to lobby the federal government to rescind the emergency powers.[102] On 18 February 1971, rights associations in Ottawa, Newfoundland, and British Columbia sent a letter endorsed by ten other rights associations to Quebec's minister of justice, Jérôme Choquette, asking the government of Quebec to compensate individuals arrested under the War Measures Act.[103] These initial efforts prompted the leaders of established rights associations to consider the formation of some type of national umbrella organization to provide a unified national voice.

During the October Crisis an information network of rights associations was formed under the banner of the Union of Human Rights and Civil Liberties Associations, officially established on 30 October 1970. It had the support of groups in Vancouver, Montreal, Halifax, Fredericton, Ottawa, Edmonton, and Windsor. The union published a regular newsletter and focused its energies on applying for a grant from the SOS to hold a national conference of rights associations. At this stage, the union was not an advocacy group but, rather, an association facilitating the exchange of ideas and developing national positions on key issues.[104]

Meanwhile, the CCLA was making its own initial attempts to form a national body, but the association's efforts failed miserably. At a meeting in Toronto to conclude its research for the Ford Foundation, the CCLA proposed that groups from Vancouver, Winnipeg, and Halifax form a national group headed by the CCLA general counsel, centred in Toronto, and funded by individual membership fees. The proposal was soundly rejected because some of the other groups felt that such an organization would be easily dominated by the CCLA.[105] Don Whiteside (who worked for the SOS and was a member of the National Capital Region Civil Liberties Association) and Eamon Park of the CCLA divided bitterly over the question of government funding. Park was adamantly opposed to any kind of government funding, whereas Whiteside was equally adamant about the need for small rights associations to seek out government grants.[106] The rift represented the basic divide between the CCLA and most of the remaining rights associations in Canada, and this split would play a key role in preventing the formation of a national organization that included the largest association in the country as a member.

Why did activists seek to create a national organization? Undoubtedly ambition, egos, and a desire to enjoy the prestige of leading a national association motivated many people to take action. From the point of view of Whiteside and officials in the SOS, a national rights association would promote Canadian unity through the formation of national advocacy groups. Given the CCLA's failure to attract large numbers of French Canadians, a national federation of rights associations that included the LDH would have been an attractive funding target for the SOS. But there were also many practical reasons for creating a national group. For many, the October Crisis was a painful reminder that Canadians lacked a strong voice at the national level comparable to that of the American Civil Liberties Union or England's National Council for Civil Liberties. A national organization would be in a stronger position to engage the federal government than would provincial rights associations that were inevitably caught up in local affairs. Moreover, a national organization could share information and resources, encourage co-operation among associations, focus its efforts on Ottawa, and facilitate the exchange of ideas on tactics and strategies. A national group would also be in a much stronger position to apply for funding from the federal government and large international funding agencies such as the Carnegie, Donner, or Ford foundations. For these and many other reasons, activists were attracted to the idea of creating a Canadian rights association.

Another attempt at founding a national organization was made in 1972 at a conference of rights associations in Winnipeg. Unfortunately, the same problems arose. In this case, not only was government funding an issue, but the question of control and representation in the Federation was debated. The CCLA refused to join the Federation unless its constitution included a ban on state funding and members were given voting rights equal to the size of their membership. When no compromise could be reached, sixteen organizations formed a national organization based on principles of equal representation according to group rather than membership. On 27 June 1972, the Canadian Federation of Civil Liberties and Human Rights Associations was officially formed at a meeting in Montreal. This was the first truly national rights association in Canadian history, with representation from every province. The central aim of the organization was to liaise between rights associations and to develop national policies in the field of rights.[107] The CCLA, with its desire to ignore regional distinctions through a single national voice, would not accept such an arrangement and boycotted the new organization.[108]

Representation and funding were the core issues separating rights associations. The question of government funding was fundamentally an ideological division based on the relationship of SMOs to the state, and it had replaced the divisions between social democrats and communists, which had prevented the formation of a national association in the 1940s. Another distinction between the CCLA and the Federation was the relationship between the parent organization and its affiliates. All the organizations affiliated with the CCLA enjoyed a great deal of independence and experienced minimal interference with their internal affairs (the exception being that any position taken on a national issue, such as abortion, had to be approved by the CCLA's Board of Directors). In contrast, the Federation's constitution stated that each member retained "complete integrity and independence in regard to its existing Constitutional arrangements, policy statements, programme priorities, finances and membership."[109]

Over the next ten years, the Federation provided as much support to its affiliates as was fiscally possible, writing letters of support and working with the media to offer national credibility to a local group's campaigns. It dealt with a variety of issues, from the federal Privacy Act to, in 1975, opposing the deportation of Haitians who faced poverty and persecution at home.[110] In general, however, it was a weak advocacy group, and its major contribution was to network among rights associations. Nonetheless, in 1981, it played a critical role in the deliberations of the Special Joint Committee on the Constitution, in which the Federation, represented by members from three separate associations, presented a comprehensive brief. Among the Federation's recommendations were revisions to Section 10, dealing with legal rights upon arrest. These amendments were accepted almost verbatim in the final draft of the Charter. Its brief also expressed concerns regarding Section 7, which originally read, "Everyone has the right to life, liberty and security of the person and the right not to be deprived thereof except in accordance with the procedures established by law." By qualifying the deprivation of rights as being "in accordance with the procedures established by law," the Federation argued that any government could pass a law allowing officials to ignore these basic freedoms. Instead, as was accepted in the final draft of the Charter, the Federation recommended that the section be modified to read: "except in accordance with the principles of fundamental justice."[111]

Despite its victory before the parliamentary committee, the Federation had failed to achieve anywhere near the same public profile as the CCLA. The CCLA's brief received the most attention in the committee's draft report (in the final report reference to specific groups was omitted). In addition, when Minister of Justice Jean Chrétien introduced his suggested revisions to the government's proposal for a charter of rights and freedoms, the CCLA, not the Federation, was credited with inspiring many of the changes to the proposal.[112] This rankled Whiteside, who acknowledged, as president of the Federation in the early 1980s, his frustration with the national media's focus on the CCLA.

The Federation folded in the early 1990s after Whiteside died from cancer and several associations had stopped attending meetings (federal financial support to attend meetings had been discontinued by this time). The fall of the Federation could be attributed to a host of factors. Its shoestring budget made it impossible to hire a permanent national director, and it depended on part-time labour and volunteers. The situation was exacerbated by having the head office in Ottawa while the executive was scattered across the country. Ross Lambertson, one of the Federation's last presidents, found it "virtually impossible" to manage the organization from his home base in Victoria.[113]

Ideology, regionalism, and state funding also contributed to the demise of the Federation. It had always been a shaky coalition. Within the Federation human rights advocates were sometimes frustrated with their civil liberties counterparts, particularly with regard to free speech issues such as pornography. Civil liberties associations such as the British Columbia Civil Liberties Association had a history of conflict with egalitarians from various movements, notably feminists. As noted in Chapter 5, the BCCLA was reviled by feminists for its position on free speech, and many human rights organizations shared feminists' opposition to pornography. Regional priorities further divided the Federation: members in Montreal or Vancouver questioned the value of belonging to a national federation when their priorities were provincial.[114]

Finally, and perhaps most telling, by the late 1980s the Federation had lost its main source of revenue when the SOS refused to continue to provide core funding.[115] Between 1971 and 1978, most of the group's administrative costs were covered by a grant from the SOS. The grant was denied in 1978, however, on the basis that the department did not fund "established" community organizations. This was a serious change in federal policy regarding non-governmental organizations, and it undoubtedly played an important role in the disbanding of many SMOs in the seventies. After 1978, the SOS increasingly refused requests for core funding by groups such as the Federation, although project grants were still provided to some organizations.[116] In the context of economic recession and cutbacks in public spending (the Opportunities for Youth Program and the Local Initiatives Program were discontinued in 1977), state funding for SMOs was increasingly difficult to secure. The federal government would continue to provide funding to numerous citizens groups well into the 1980s, until the Conservatives began extensive cuts to the SOS's funding programs. These developments sealed the fate of the Federation. The founders of the Federation had never intended the organization to be supported by membership fees. It began as a product of state funding, and, in the end, the Federation was a victim of government cutbacks.

The demise of the Federation and other failed attempts to form a national rights association represent one of the more unique aspects of the history of the human rights movement in Canada. While the Federation limped through the seventies, the CCLA thrived and grew. Yet, the CCLA's claim to national status should be viewed with some scepticism.

Irving Himel's legacy to the CCLA – having founded its predecessor, the Association for Civil Liberties (which failed as a national association) – was a vision of a central body that defended against rights violations across the nation. Since its founding, the CCLA has used two strategies in its attempt to be a strong national rights association: (1) the formation of chapters across Canada and (2) engaging with national issues.

As early as 1967, the CCLA was formulating plans on how to create a framework for a national organization. Thanks to the Ford Foundation grant and the interest surrounding the International Year for Human Rights, affiliates of the CCLA emerged in eight cities across Canada: Windsor, London, Hamilton, Regina, Ottawa, Fredericton, Winnipeg, and Halifax.[117] By 1971, when Whiteside and the BCCLA were making plans to form a federation of rights associations, the CCLA had lost three chapters to disaffiliation (Ottawa, Windsor, and London). True, the CCLA participated in the negotiations leading up to the creation of the Federation, but the proposed Federation threatened the CCLA's vision of forming a single national rights association comparable to the American Civil Liberties Union.

Not only was the Federation going to accept state funding, to which the CCLA was adamantly opposed, but it would be a loosely connected federation of associations rather than a centralized agency capable of quick and coordinated action. Throughout the negotiations, the CCLA attempted to offer a counterproposal to the original federation concept. The "Arthurs proposal," as it was dubbed, would create a coordinating committee of civil liberties associations, in which every member association would be allowed to send to meetings one delegate for every one hundred members. In 1971, this would have translated into twenty delegates for the CCLA and five for the BCCLA as the next largest association (many groups would only have one or two delegates). It would be funded through a one-dollar fee per each association member, and the office would be located in Toronto, with the CCLA's general counsel as the committee's executive director. Among the committee's responsibilities would be coordinating the activities of various groups, promoting national rights campaigns, working towards establishing a permanent structure, and holding an annual conference.[118]

The result was a clash of visions between the CCLA and most of the other rights associations. From the perspective of the CCLA, if the proposed national group was to succeed without government funds, it would need a head office and a national director. Since in 1971 the CCLA was the only rights association with a full-time director and staff, and since it was centrally located in Toronto, it felt that it was the logical choice. At the same time, the leaders of the CCLA felt that it made no sense for the Prince Edward Island Civil Liberties Association, which had barely a dozen members, to have an equal vote with the CCLA, which had more than two thousand members. Most important, the CCLA refused to budge on the question of state funding, and it was evident that the BCCLA and the other future members of the Federation were unwilling to compromise on this issue. The CCLA was helpless to act.

Why did state funding lead the CCLA to reject the Federation? Several of the CCLA affiliates, including the Nova Scotia Civil Liberties Association and the Manitoba Association for Rights and Liberties, received funding from the SOS. Clearly, the CCLA had no problem working alongside state-funded organizations, but it drew the line at joining a federation dependent on government grants. None of the affiliates could claim to speak on behalf of the CCLA. However, if the CCLA joined the Federation, the latter could conceivably have deferred to the government out of fear of losing support while claiming to speak on behalf of the CCLA. This new state-funded federation challenged the CCLA's vision of what defined an effective national SMO.

Between 1964 and 1982, the CCLA had managed, at one point, to create chapters in twelve different cities across Canada. Many times Borovoy was himself directly responsible for the creation of a chapter, taking the opportunity after being paid to speak at a law school or before a particular association to mobilize locals (often law students or lawyers) to form an association. Such a process led to the creation of highly unstable and ad hoc groups, and the leadership of the CCLA remained based in Toronto. When the CCLA attempted to recruit Mark MacGuigan, one of the association's founding members, back into the fold in 1970, MacGuigan informed the association that he "would like to belong to a national civil liberties association, but I am reluctant to join the Toronto one."[119] MacGuigan refused to join the CCLA because the association's Board of Directors was predominantly from Toronto. Although, in 1982, the CCLA claimed to have eight chapters (Saint John, Timmins, Fredericton, Halifax, Hamilton, Winnipeg, Regina, and Calgary), most of them were inactive. The only affiliate on the rise by the 1980s was the Manitoba Association for Rights and Liberties, which had emerged in 1978. The Manitoba group was the sole affiliate with a full-time staff member and, thus, the only group with any kind of stability.[120]

By the 1980s the CCLA had failed to create a network of rights associations and, thus, had failed to be a truly national rights association. The vision of a centrally organized national association – one that would organize national campaigns and whose membership dues would be funnelled from its various chapters to its Toronto headquarters without state funding – never materialized.

With its failure to create a viable national association through chapters, the CCLA's only other claim to national status was its advocacy. It was not until after 1977 that the CCLA established a strong presence at the national level, but it did so effectively with its work surrounding the McDonald Commission and the Charter. However, except for a couple of campaigns involving due process and the rights of welfare recipients, the CCLA's advocacy was limited primarily to Ontario. In theory the affiliates would do the advocacy work for the CCLA as part of a national campaign, but in practice they tended to act independently and rarely coordinated at the national level. For instance, the research surrounding a report published by the CCLA in 1975, and based on interviews with welfare recipients across Canada, was the basis for the association's advocacy on welfare rights for most of the seventies. Yet, the CCLA's work was largely confined to Ontario, despite its having discovered various administrative abuses of due process in other provinces.

The main exception to the CCLA's provincial focus was six briefs presented before parliamentary committees. Combined with its work with regard to the McDonald Commission and the Charter, the CCLA could legitimately claim to be doing more work at the national level than any other rights association. This was often simply a question of resources, with groups in Vancouver and St. John's being unable to cover the expenses to fly to Ottawa. Located in Montreal, the LDH was partially active in presenting briefs to the federal government on such issues as capital punishment and immigration. In general, however, the CCLA was far more active federally with briefs on immigration, capital punishment, privacy, RCMP mail opening, prisons, the Human Rights Act, and freedom of information. Often the CCLA could claim some success, as when the federal government, in reaction to opposition from a variety of sectors, including the CCLA, chose to abandon its legislation to legalize mail opening by the RCMP. In other cases, the association was less effective, notably in its opposition to hate propaganda provisions in the federal human rights legislation. Nonetheless, as was the case with the Charter, by 1982, despite being a primarily Toronto-based association, the CCLA was a well-recognized organization with members from across Canada and a strong voice in Ottawa.

The British Columbia Civil Liberties Association, the Ligue des droits de l'homme, and the Canadian Civil Liberties Association were the largest and most dynamic rights associations in the country. All three are still active today. Each one sought to apply vague human rights principles to concrete situations; the resulting differences in ideology were informed by the historical context and the local situation facing each organization. As typical professional SMOs, they had to deal with issues such as state funding, establishing links with other organizations, creating a national organization, and developing an array of strategies for achieving their objectives. But whereas all three groups were distinct in a variety of ways, including setting up shop in different geographic regions, they did share two important qualities: each association emerged independently and each operated in a large metropolis. As noted in Chapter 5, however, among the numerous rights associations born during this period were groups created in small cities across the country in the wake of the state-sponsored programs for the International Year for Human Rights. No organization is better suited to represent these organizations than the Newfoundland-Labrador Human Rights Association.

The Newfoundland-Labrador Human Rights Association

Religion and religious institutions have historically played a more influential role in the public education system in Newfoundland than in any other province in Canada, with the possible exception of Quebec. As a result, when, in 1972, twenty-five-year-old Judy Norman refused to state her denominational affiliation on the application form, she was denied a teaching certificate. With the aid of friends and colleagues, student committees were formed at Memorial University to debate the value of a church-based education system, and supporters marched through shopping malls in St. John's, Gander, Grand Falls, and Harbour Grace with petitions demanding that Norman be granted her certificate. In the House of Assembly, the Liberal opposition's education critic, F.W. Rowe, echoed the demands of the petitioners that "academic or professional qualification be the basis for recommendation [for a teaching certificate]."[1] Progressive Conservative premier Frank Moores responded by announcing an immediate investigation into the matter by a committee of the House. Newspaper articles discussing the activities of Judy Norman and her colleagues were carried in at least eleven papers across the country. In dismissing accusations of discrimination, Reverend Geoffrey Shaw, head of the Pentecostal examining board, argued that the existing system was ideal for a province in which 98 percent of the population was Christian. He also stressed the need for children not to "be subjected to a militant atheistic Communist who might unteach Christian principles," though he had no evidence regarding Norman's political views.[2] A potentially divisive social issue quickly died away. Moores' investigation never materialized, the media soon tired of the case, and Norman began teaching for the Integrated School Board a few months later, having never declared her affiliation.[3]

A significant sidebar to this event, ignored by the media and Norman herself, was an exchange of letters between John Carter, minister of education, and Dr. Biswarup Bhattacharya, a psychiatrist at the Waterford Hospital and president of the Newfoundland-Labrador Human Rights Association (NLHRA). In response to Bhattacharya's concerns about religious discrimination in the education system, Carter countered with the contradictory response that "never has a teacher been denied a Teaching Certificate in Newfoundland on the basis of Religion ... If a teacher will agree to uphold the Christian tradition within the school system of her choice ... but the candidate for certification ought to indicate the denomination he or she wishes to teach under ... [Judy Norman] failed to assure the certifying authorities that she would not seek to undermine the religion of others."[4] In reply, Bhattacharya challenged Carter's assumptions about the value of a "Christian" education system in a multicultural society, and he dismissed the idea that non-Christians would undermine the religion of others. He claimed to have contacted civil liberties and human rights associations across the country, and all agreed that this was a case of religious discrimination: "Our [concern] lies ... with the process within which there remains a loophole which allows discrimination on religious grounds, and not accepted merit only."[5] Bhattacharya then offered Norman the services of the NLHRA in her fight to gain a teaching position. She did not respond, and the NLHRA moved on.

The Norman episode was a brief interlude in the history of the NLHRA, which was founded in the wake of the International Year for Human Rights and, unlike the LDH, has been a committed human rights organization since its inception. It was representative of the many organizations born in 1968 out of a government-based initiative. Unlike the LDH and the CCLA, there was no need for the leaders of the NLHRA to break with their predecessors. Put simply, it had none. Newfoundland certainly had no shortage of social movements throughout its long history, but no rights association emerged until the NLHRA in 1968. It was a small but vigorous organization that struggled with the same internal issues that confronted rights associations on the mainland, from developing strategies for change to applying human rights principles in campaigns at home. More than any of the other case studies, and perhaps more than any other rights association in Canada, the NLHRA embodied the debate over state funding of SMOs. It was always possible for the BCCLA and the LDH to use their location in a major city as a base for raising money; state funding unquestionably enhanced their activities, but other options were always there. For the NLHRA, state funding made its work possible. Without state funding, the history of the NLHRA would have been short indeed.

Each of the previous case studies, while active at the national level, was preoccupied with local human rights struggles, and this was no less the case with the NLHRA. While Reg Robson sat in court to defend the right of the *Georgia Straight* to advertise for "muffdivers," and Maurice Champagne packed a community hall with angry parents who were concerned about children's rights, and Alan Borovoy stood before Gosfield city council decrying religious teachings in public schools, Bhattacharya sat at a typewriter and wrote articles condemning the ineffective Human Rights Commission. In barely a dozen years, the NLHRA became an important advocate for human rights in the province, leading campaigns to improve the Human Rights Code, secularize the education system, protect protestors, defend due process in the courts, and develop teaching tools for youngsters. These campaigns dominated the agenda of one of the smallest, but most active (and lasting), rights associations in the country. However, despite its success, the NLHRA remained unsuccessful in confronting one of the most important human rights issue in Newfoundland history: denominational education.

Nineteen Sixty-Eight: International Year for Human Rights

In Ottawa, the federal government decided to make a big splash for the International Year for Human rights, which was being held to observe the 1948 signing of the Universal Declaration of Human Rights (UDHR). It would be a grand celebration of the rights revolution in Canada, and this fateful decision was to have a lasting impact on the human rights movement. John Humphrey, dean of law at McGill University and the original drafter of the UDHR, and Kalmen Kaplansky, an executive of the International Labour Organization, headed the Canadian commission for the International Year for Human Rights. Formed in 1967 and funded through the federal government's Secretary of State citizenship program, one of the commission's first tasks was to stimulate the creation of provincial human rights committees to organize conferences and educational activities to celebrate the twentieth anniversary of the UDHR. In some provinces, the 1968 celebrations were organized by the local human rights commissions, whereas in others new organizations were formed and led by community leaders. As would prove to be the case in Newfoundland, this surge of activity would lead to the formation of human rights associations across the country, many of which would stay active for another generation.[6]

The human rights committee was formed on 31 January 1968 at a public meeting initiated by the provincial government. This meeting was attended by twenty-three volunteer groups, Peter Truman of the United Nations Association of Canada, and seventy high school and university students. A cabinet committee was formed to consult with the executive and to discuss recommendations for legislative action. It consisted of G.A. Frecker, F.W. Rowe, John Crosbie, Alex Hickman, William J. Keough, Edward Roberts, and J.G. Channing. A provincial grant of $7,500, along with the composition of the committee, reflected the importance the government placed on the event. Rowe was the influential minister of education (later appointed to the Senate); Crosbie was minister of municipal affairs and housing; and Keough, the minister of labour, was a close friend of Joey Smallwood and later drafted the provincial human rights code. Members of the human rights committee spent the year speaking at school assemblies, encouraging clergy to discuss human rights in sermons, organizing a conference at Memorial University, corresponding with community groups, and planning for a national conference in December.

The efforts of the human rights committee throughout 1968 resulted in a series of recommendations to the provincial government, which included the following:

1 establishing a permanent human rights association with a $7,500 grant until it becomes independently funded

2 establishing a human rights commission to conduct research, education, and conciliation activities

3 introducing a human rights code and amend the Minimum Wage Act to eliminate differential pay between men and women

4 establishing an ombudsman's office with broad powers to include schools, universities, municipal councils, and boards

5 taking the initiative to have the United Nations Convention on the Rights of the Child and the UDHR entrenched in the Canadian Constitution

6 undertaking research to reassess the rights of minorities in Newfoundland, particularly in the case of Inuit and Indians

7 reviewing the prison system based on recommendations of the John Howard Society and expanding the scope of the legal aid system

8 reassessing the viability of the denominational school system, which currently discriminates against non-Christians.[7]

These recommendations were based on input from community groups and offer a glimpse into the human rights issues facing Newfoundland in the late 1960s. It was one of only three provinces (alongside Quebec and Prince Edward Island) that lacked comprehensive human rights legislation; every other province had enacted either a human rights code or laws dealing with discrimination in employment and accommodation. There was a clear appreciation for national and international issues, not only in the references to United Nations resolutions but also in the decision to focus on an issue – prison reform – that was gaining increasing attention across the country.[8] The Minimum Wage Act was of particular concern, and, over the next decade, the question of equal pay soon emerged as the central human rights issue for the provincial government. The recognition of discrimination against Aboriginals was significant, coming as it did from a committee sponsored by a government whose leaders dismissed the existence of racial discrimination. A year later, for example, Keough stated that he "knew of no case of racial and ethnic discrimination having taken place in this province."[9] The most controversial recommendation referred to the denominational school system. When Judy Norman created a minor stir in 1972, her complaint was directed towards discrimination in the hiring of teachers. The committee's recommendation was more far-reaching, attacking the legitimacy of a denominational education system that discriminated against non-Christians. It was a daring move, and from its inception a year later the NLHRA openly opposed the denominational school system. The provincial government, however, had no wish to deal with that issue.

The government was prepared to pass human rights legislation, though, and in May 1969, the Human Rights Code became law. According to Smallwood, this legislation was "not a Bill to establish human rights, to create them or to establish or protect them. This has been handsomely done by our forefathers ... This legislation does not create the right to free speech, because the right is already there, it does not need to do it. This does not create the right of free press ... It is already established."[10]

The bill was meant to bring together existing laws under one statute enforceable by a human rights commission. (Unlike the aforementioned human rights committee, which was independent of the government and evolved into the NLHRA, the human rights commission was a branch of the public service designed to process and adjudicate complaints.) In the debate, Clyde Wells was the only member to grasp the true essence of the new Human Rights Code: it was more akin to fair employment and fair accommodation practices acts than it was to an expansive human rights code.

The Newfoundland Human Rights Code was undeniably a weak piece of legislation. The commission was a temporary body with no permanent staff, to be called upon when needed, and beholden to the minister of labour. Regulations were included to ensure equal pay for women, but only for work done in the same establishment; a corporation or the government could continue with discriminatory wage scales, so long as men and women did not work in the same place. Only the inclusion of political opinion as a prohibited ground of discrimination could be considered progressive. Indeed, Newfoundland was the first Canadian jurisdiction to protect political opinion in its human rights jurisdiction.[11] The key weakness of the legislation, also noted by Clyde Wells, was the exemption under Section 9 for all educational institutions.[12] This exemption was a clear sign of the government's unwillingness to use the code to implement substantial change.

The first Human Rights commissioner was not appointed until March 1971. This was Gertrude Keough, wife of the recently deceased minister of labour and a former school teacher who, in an *Evening Telegram* interview, admitted to knowing little about the issues, the human rights committee, the Human Rights Code, or even her own salary.[13] This appointment further weakened the legitimacy of the commission and its ability to push the government to expand the scope of the code (Gertrude Keough served until 1981). It was not Keough but Fred Coates, the commission's full-time director, who was successful in pressuring the Treasury Board and private employers to end discriminatory wage practices.[14] Under Keough the commission did not make a single proposal for amending the Human Rights Code, even though Coates was publicly critical of such provisions as the exemption for educational institutions. In 1974, the Progressive Conservative government under Frank Moores removed the "same establishment" clause to guarantee equal pay for equal work across the board (the implementation of equal pay for work of equal value would take another generation).[15] But in the House of Commons debates it was the NLHRA, not the Human Rights Commission, that was credited for inspiring the amendment. In contrast, throughout the 1970s the chairs of human rights commissions in Ontario (Dan Hill) and British Columbia (Kathleen Ruff) were active in promoting changes to their respective provincial human rights codes, such as expanding the definition of accommodation.

Despite their weaknesses, the passing of the Human Rights Code and the creation of the Human Rights Commission were important steps in a province that was lagging behind the rest of the country with regard to anti-discrimination legislation. This legislation created a potential forum for handling complaints and for promoting awareness of human rights, and it helped eliminate gender differentials in minimum wage laws. The remaining recommendations of the human rights committee were generally ignored. Grants to the legal aid fund were increased but remained small; the decision to create an ombudsman's office was rejected; and no advances were made in prison reform or in the further reform of the denominational education system.

"The very survival of the organization depends on your generosity": The NLHRA

Interest in establishing a human rights association had waned by early 1969. At some point between December 1968 and July 1969, W.J. Noseworthy stepped down as president of the human rights committee and Dr. Biswarup Bhattacharya took control of the organization, which was now called the Newfoundland-Labrador Human Rights Association. Keough's death in 1969, and the dissolution of the cabinet liaison committee due to lack of interest, effectively severed the NLHRA's ties with the provincial government. An increasingly frustrated Bhattacharya lobbied Smallwood for continued funding, asserting that it was the "duty of the provincial government to start us off."[16] In his last recorded attempt to convince Smallwood to support the fledgling human rights group, the president of the NLHRA argued that "the very survival of the organization depends on your generosity. Perhaps it is true that we could receive money from different sources in this Province, but we feel this possibly would bind us in subtle ways to groups which may prevent us from working without bias and independently. It is our understanding that the responsibility of maintaining a Human Rights Association in the province is the joint responsibility of the government of the province and the Federal Government."[17]

There were small grants of $250 and $500 in 1969 and 1970, but these ended government financial support, and the NLHRA might well have become defunct, like similar committees in Quebec, Saskatchewan, Manitoba, Alberta, and Prince Edward Island, had it not been for Bhattacharya and his small executive.

There are few NLHRA records before 1972, but it appears that in its early years the organization concentrated on attempting to secure government funding and on lobbying for the full implementation of the Human Rights Code (provisions on equal pay were not to come into effect until 1972, the reason being to allow private enterprise to adjust its wage base).[18] With little financial support, the original members (Bhattacharya, Lilian Bouzane, James Morgan, and Rae Perlin) were forced to meet in private homes. But much as Robson in Vancouver, Borovoy in Toronto, and Champagne in Montreal helped keep their respective associations moving forward, so in St. John's Bhattacharya proved to be the leading force within the NLHRA.

The NLHRA drew members for its Board of Directors from the middle-class, educated, professional, and (except for Bhattacharya) Caucasian population of St. John's. Few women were active in the organization in the 1970s. Bouzane and Morgan, one a civil servant and the other a politician, would remain on the board until the mid-1970s, but fewer directors were now linked with the provincial government. Bhattacharya would be replaced as president by John Peddle, former general manager of the Newfoundland Association of Public Employees, until Norman Whalen, a young Liberal lawyer from St. John's, became president in 1977 and remained until 1981. Other directors included Karl Beck (college professor), Rae Perlin (artist), James Boyles (social worker), and David Kirby (professor of education at Memorial University). They were members of a newly emerged and mature middle class that had grown out of the economic boom of the post-Confederation period under Smallwood, with the expansion of public works programs, the bureaucracy, and the education system.[19] The NLHRA was able to recruit from a pool of social activists who had a shared concern with human rights issues, while the leadership of the NLHRA was active in maintaining its own continuity. Bhattacharya recruited Peddle and then Whalen to take over the presidency, and Whalen recruited William Collins, a lawyer practising in St. John's, to replace him for a short period in 1981.[20]

The group used its meagre funds in the first few years to set up a telephone line to provide legal advice and to direct complaints to the appropriate agency or organization. By the mid-1970s, the NLHRA was able to establish an office with a part-time secretary who could direct complaints to members of the board. They would review individual cases, discuss cases at monthly board meetings, and decide whether or not to redirect the case to another agency or take it on themselves. Lacking the funds for litigation, the best the NLHRA could do in most situations was to send a letter to the individual or organization the complaint had been lodged against, warning them that their actions could lead to legal sanctions or a Human Rights Commission tribunal. The complaints phoned in to the NLHRA office during this period (1968-82) were predominantly in the area of employment discrimination, although there were also calls dealing with housing discrimination, refusal to offer a service, and accusations of police abuse. In 1974, there was an average of thirty to forty calls per month. By 1980 there were over 1,500 calls annually.

There were also attempts to form chapters. As occurred in the other case studies, the NLHRA hoped to expand the movement into smaller urban areas across the province, but it was singularly unsuccessful. Chapters in Corner Brook, Labrador, and Gander all died within a few years due to their inability to organize local interest.[21]

The organization was able to take an active stance on local issues and to implement change. In 1973, the NLHRA was successful in pressuring the minister of justice to destroy police photographs of protestors taken the year before in front of the Confederation building, and it elicited a statement confirming that the RCMP was not keeping photo files on protesters.[22] When amendments to the Human Rights Code were introduced in 1974, the government credited the NLHRA with having informed most of the changes.[23] Not only did it secure an amendment to the equal pay provisions of the code but, in the same year, sex and marital status were also added to the code as prohibited grounds of discrimination.[24] In 1978-79, the NLHRA made representations to the minister of justice in a successful bid to improve conditions at the St. John's courtroom jail, and it convinced the Mutual Life Insurance Company to remove a question regarding illegal drug use from its insurance applications. During the same period, the association teamed up with residents in rural Labrador to push the provincial government to stop uranium mining due to health and environmental dangers.[25] In conjunction with its educational and referral activities, the NLHRA had demonstrated an ability to deal effectively with issues of local concern. In fourteen years, it had become a stable and legitimate voice for social activism in Newfoundland.

A great deal of the NLHRA's work involved individual complaints rather than legislative reform. For instance, on 26 October 1973, the medical records librarian at the Waterford Hospital in St. John's received a subpoena to appear in Supreme Court three days later to discuss the medical records of a specific patient. This was not a criminal matter but a divorce case, and neither the patient nor the psychiatrist was informed of the subpoena. Unsure about whether or not to accede to the request and divulge private patient information, the librarian contacted Bhattacharya, who immediately took possession of the documents and refused to hand them over to the court, arguing that the records were the property of the hospital and that requesting them was an unnecessary violation of a patient's privacy. When the Department of Justice realized it would have to take the president of the NLHRA to court, the matter was quietly dropped and the subpoena retracted. This is just one example of the type of service the NLHRA could provide on an individual basis for people unsure about their rights or the rights of others.[26]

The NLHRA could also claim some credit for the appointment of an ombudsman in 1975, although the process had been a long one. In 1969, a government committee recommended the creation of an ombudsman's office.[27] Although legislation was passed in 1970 creating the position, this legislation was not proclaimed, and an ombudsman was not appointed, until 1975. At that time Moores awarded the position to a recently defeated Progressive Conservative MP, Ambrose Peddle. The leader of the Opposition called the appointment a "filthy act of political patronage," and the NLHRA expressed concern that the appointee would not develop the position's full potential.[28] In retrospect, Peddle proved to be a weak advocate, and the NLHRA's hoped for expansion of the office's scope beyond government agencies to Crown corporations and other government businesses never materialized.[29]

Despite all its work over the past decade and the concerns the organization had raised, no human rights issue marshalled the local populace around the NLHRA and there is no evidence that the association attempted to develop a grassroots following or to mobilize people around a particular campaign. Outside the province, rights associations were able to mobilize around highly publicized events; they were able to step in and make a unique contribution. Members of the BCCLA assembled their forces to deal with the impact of the Gastown riot, while the CCLA had the Fort Erie raid and the LDH came to the defence of prisoners during the October Crisis. Many of the core developments that mobilized other rights associations were simply not an issue in Newfoundland. While the BCCLA's most important case in the seventies was undoubtedly compulsory treatment of drug addicts, Newfoundland's drug problem paled in comparison to British Columbia's. According to the LeDain Commission, in 1972, British Columbia had 4,029 illicit habitual narcotic drug users; Newfoundland had 2.[30] From its founding until 1975, the LDH wanted nothing more than a provincial bill of rights, something the NLHRA achieved within two years of its founding. Meanwhile, the CCLA had dedicated much of its early history towards establishing checks on police abuses in Toronto (and, to a lesser degree, around Ontario) and on the RCMP. Certainly Newfoundland had comparable figures for alcohol abuse and theft, but with regard to serious crime the Island was a haven of peace. Throughout the 1960s and 1970s there were no more than one or two murders a year (often none) and a violent crime rate that most often ranked the lowest or second lowest in Canada; Newfoundland's first ever bank hold-up occurred in 1967 – committed, appropriately enough, by a mainlander.[31] The type of issues that Maloney suggested brought police in contact with elements in society who were more likely to register complaints and to assert their rights were simply not occurring in large numbers in Newfoundland, where they remained well below the national average.[32] Combined with a comparatively homogenous population and limited urban congestion, police in Newfoundland were not faced with the racial and other minority complaints that led to so many investigations into police complaints procedures in Toronto (although the Status of Women Council did criticize the police for their failure to help battered women when responding to domestic disputes). The NLHRA was simply not confronted with the same human rights violations that faced activists in Canada's major urban areas.

There was thus, in Newfoundland, a marked absence of those issues that had mobilized mainland rights associations and pushed them to concentrate their efforts on constructive campaigns while motivating them to marshal public opinion and take an active stance on controversial cases. There was, however, one campaign that began for the NLHRA the day it was founded and that continued to occupy the association three decades later.

"The greatest single threat to equality of religion and freedom of worship": The Case of Denominational Education

From its inception, the NLHRA was a consistent critic of the denominational education system. In truth, concerns over the economic efficiency of maintaining multiple school systems organized along religious lines was perhaps the key motivation and justification for the elimination of the denominational system in the late 1990s. However, the history of the NLHRA offers a unique, rights-based perspective on one of the most important public debates in Newfoundland history.

Newfoundland's state-funded denominational education system was rooted in the nineteenth century. There had been sporadic criticism of the system from time to time; the Fisherman's Protective Union, for instance, voiced serious concerns about the system in the early twentieth century. The Commission of Government, in the 1940s, tried to implement reform but was rebuffed by the churches. It was to appease the churches, and Roman Catholics in particular, that the Newfoundland delegation, which was negotiating the Terms of Union with Canada, insisted on the insertion of Term 17 to protect denominational education. In addition to the Roman Catholic school system, a separate consolidated school system, composed primarily of Protestant denominations, was established by 1956. The consolidated school system formed the closest thing to the type of public education system available on the mainland. But they were few in number – twenty-four in 1956, out of a total of 1,193 schools – and served only 8 percent of the school population.[33] Nowhere else in Canada, with the possible exception of the Province of Quebec, did the churches enjoy such expansive control over education.

In 1967, the Royal Commission on Education (Warren Commission) recommended a switch to a secular education system, which Phillip McCann attributes to the influence of "United Nations policy on Human Rights and Children's Rights, and North American thinking on development of human resources in a technological age."[34] A minority report accused the majority of violating its terms of reference by considering the denominational issue, and it pointed to the Terms of Union as a constitutional protection for religious education. The government implemented some of the commission's recommendations, but the denominational system remained entrenched.

Only four years after the Warren Commission report, the birth mother of the NLHRA, the government-sponsored human rights committee, recommended abolishing the denominational education system. From its inception, and later reaffirmed in 1972, when Judy Norman was refused her teaching certificate, the NLHRA had opposed the churches' monopoly over education, seeing it as a violation of religious freedom. In 1984, the NLHRA prepared a brief on the Human Rights Code to the minister of justice, arguing that "the greatest single threat to equality of religion and freedom of worship [in Newfoundland] is the restrictive nature of the denominational education system. It is recommended that a second alternative be available for students who are not of faiths which benefit from a special constitutional privilege, or that denominational schools be prohibited from discriminating on the basis of religion. The best resolution of this issue would be an immediate court reference to seek a declaratory judgement concerning the scope of Term 17 of the Terms of Union."[35]

The then current system allowed public school teachers to be fired for not following the tenets of the faith, such as marrying outside the Church.[36] In order to vote or to be a candidate in consolidated school board elections, individuals were required to belong to either the Salvation Army, the Anglican Church, the Presbyterian Church, or the United Church (similar restrictions were applied in the Roman Catholic system). In a gathering of 120 people at Memorial University in 1987 to debate the merits of denominational education, Lynn Byrnes, who served as president of the NLHRA after 1982, stated that the system was "based on some very blatantly discriminatory policies which we feel must be changed ... If these legal rights allow such cut and dried examples of religious discrimination then the legal rights are wrong."[37]

In Ontario the CCLA was able to use the Charter of Rights and Freedoms to eliminate religious practices in public schools in the 1990s, but the situation in Newfoundland was complicated by the provisions of Term 17, which constitutionally protected the province's denominational education system. Throughout the 1980s the boundaries of denominational education actually expanded. In 1987 Pentecostals were added to the list of religious affiliations under Term 17 and were thus assured state funding for their schools and a voice in the administration of the education system. Within a few years, however, there was a clear movement to challenge the dominance of the major religions in education. Significantly, this movement was led not by the NLHRA but by the provincial government. In 1990, Premier Clyde Wells appointed a royal commission to study the efficiency and operation of the school system. In its report, *Our Children, Our Future*, the commission recommended a reduction of the churches' role in education while at the same time suggesting that the system continue to promote Judeo-Christian values.[38] After negotiations between the government and churches to reform the education system broke down, Wells chose to hold a referendum to revise Term 17 and to introduce a public school system. With 54 percent voting yes, the government was able to go ahead and amend Term 17, only to find itself blocked by the courts, who ruled that the revised Term 17 allowed the province to take over the administration of the school system but not to close down the schools themselves.[39] Frustrated at its inability to established a unified and secular public school system, the government held a second referendum under the direction of Wells' successor, Brian Tobin, to fully revise Term 17 to ensure that the churches had no say in the running of the education system. With 73 percent voting yes, Newfoundlanders finally achieved a fully secular public school system in 1997.[40]

The NLHRA was always at the forefront of the debate over denominational education. Children who were "bumped" from an over-registered enrichment program in 1982 due to their religion were rescued by members of the NLHRA, who lobbied to have increased federal funding provided to allow students entry into the program. Press releases were sent out and press conferences held throughout the 1980s calling on the government to end the discriminatory practices inherent in the education system. A fiery television debate between Lynn Byrnes of the NLHRA and Archbishop Penney on CBC in 1985 helped keep the controversy alive and promote the NLHRA's cause to a wide public audience.[41] In the same year, a group of French-Canadian parents approached the NLHRA when their children were denied entry into a French immersion program because they were of no professed religion or were non-Christian. Thanks to the intervention of the NLHRA, the federal government once again provided additional monies to hire teachers so that students could join the program. Other activities included submitting a detailed review of the provincial human rights legislation, with a section on denominational education, in 1985 and polling provincial election candidates in the same year and publishing their views on religious education.[42] By 1987, the NLHRA had also changed its position on denominational education: it now called for replacing the entire system with a secular public education system.

One tactic the NLHRA hoped to use to undermine the system involved applying to the federal government's Court Challenges Program, a fund set up to support Charter cases. In the mid-1980s, the association sought unsuccessfully to use this program.[43] Another tactic involved education, and this led to a large conference at Memorial University in 1987. Lynn Byrnes, a past-president of the association, even sought election to the local school board in an attempt to demonstrate the discrimination inherent in the system (she was denied because of her religious affiliation). When Premier Wells appointed a royal commission in 1990 to study the education system, the NLHRA presented a well-researched and sophisticated brief calling for the removal of denominational education. Basing its arguments on the need to end discrimination in education, the NLHRA claimed that the system unfairly discriminated against students by not allowing them to attend neighbourhood schools if they were not of the proper affiliation; it also discriminated against teachers by not hiring those who were not of the proper denomination; and it discriminated against citizens who were seeking election to school boards.[44] Although lacking a strong presence during the 1995 referendum, the NLHRA joined a coalition called Education First in 1997 to fight for the yes side during the second referendum. It received favourable press coverage, and Tobin worked primarily with the teachers' union and the NLHRA to rally support for his initiative.[45] It is unclear how effective the NLHRA was in mobilizing public support in gaining a 73 percent yes vote, but it did play a role in the campaign by distributing literature, organizing a public forum, and working with the press.

The NLHRA: A Case Study in State Funding

We can learn a great deal from the brief history of the NLHRA. As a member of the Federation and an articulate advocate for human rights, the group confronted the same issues as did its brethren across Canada, but from a unique perspective. A study of the NLHRA offers an opportunity to draw together some key themes explored in the previous case studies. Its utter dependence on state funding forces us to consider the broader ramifications of state funding for SMOs not just in Newfoundland but throughout the country. Moreover, the NLHRA's campaign against the denominational education system highlights the types of strategies deployed by rights associations to foment social change during this period.

Strategies for Change

The NLHRA's unrelenting campaign against the denominational education system is one example of the array of strategies employed by the association. Despite its expansive approach to human rights, the NLHRA favoured the same tactics utilized by all rights associations: preparing briefs and press releases, taking the issue to court, and conducting research. It was only the intervention of the premier that eventually spelled the end of the denominational education system. The failure of the NLHRA to mount an effective challenge to the denominational education system was symptomatic of the limits of social movement advocacy that shunned grassroots mobilization.

For decades, the NLHRA had argued that the solution to the denominational education system was to pressure the government to act, either through the courts or through legislative change such as amendments to the Human Rights Code. Yet, for over a century, attempts by various advocates to achieve legal reform had failed to transform government policy. The reality of Newfoundland politics made it unpalatable to challenge a system that, according to the chair of the Human Rights Commission in 1985, was "a fact of life in Newfoundland and is such because it is in accord with the wishes and desire of a large majority of the Province's population."[46] The NLHRA was no different from any other rights association in its focus on legal rights and state protection of religious freedom. The CCLA and the BCCLA both opposed any form of state funding for denominational education. As we have seen, a committee formed by the BCCLA in 1963 to lobby for changes to the Public Schools Act achieved little success, and the CCLA's early interventions were fruitless.[47] In each case, rights associations used political lobbying or litigation to challenge religious instruction in public schools; it was, in fact, a court challenge under the Charter in 1990, led by the CCLA, that resulted in the removal of religious practices from public schools in Ontario.[48]

In 1975, Gregory Stack was fired by a Roman Catholic school board for marrying a non-Catholic. The Newfoundland Teachers' Federation argued that this constituted dismissal without cause and was, therefore, a violation of the collective agreement. A board of arbitration supported the school board's argument that the Terms of Union protected the rights of the school boards to dismiss at will and that the collective agreement was ultra vires.[49] The Newfoundland Supreme Court overturned the decision, but the ruling did not challenge the right of the Catholic school board to fire Stack (and others) if sufficient notice and cause were given.

The NLHRA did not participate in the Stack case, but this example once again demonstrates the limitations of using the courts to promote social change. Courts in Newfoundland, British Columbia, and Ontario upheld the power of religious schools to dismiss teachers for violating tenets of the faith because religious observance was a "bona fide occupational requirement" under provincial human rights codes.[50] The NLHRA consistently sought to work through state institutions to secularize the education system and at no time attempted to develop a grassroots following or to organize a campaign to mobilize large numbers of people. The repertoire of strategies employed by rights associations was almost exclusively state-oriented. As a result, the NLHRA faced immense obstacles in dealing with what it believed to be one of the most important human rights issues of the period.

The National Question

The NLHRA helped to organize the first coordinated action among rights associations during the October Crisis, and Bhattacharya, representing the NLHRA, was one of the founding members of the Federation.[51] Through the Federation, the NLHRA was active in national rights debates. Both Bhattacharya and Whalen served on the Federation executive throughout the 1970s and 1980s, and it was Whalen who led the Federation's delegation before the Special Joint Committee on the Constitution in 1981. The success enjoyed by the Federation before the joint committee remains a small but lasting contribution to the human rights movement on the part of the NLHRA and its former leaders.

The NLHRA's association with the Federation was logical, but its effect was to divert interest in national issues with important local consequences (such as abortion or capital punishment) to another organization. In 1970, for instance, groups in Toronto, Montreal, and Vancouver sent separate letters and briefs to the federal government expressing their opposition to the War Measures Act, yet the NLHRA's only action during this crisis was to support a declaration written by the BCCLA. In Vancouver, Montreal, and Toronto, in an attempt to turn local opinion against the federal government, rights activists used the media to publicize their opposition to Trudeau's actions. The NLHRA made no comparable attempt to influence Newfoundlanders.

A similar silence greeted the McDonald Commission. Instead of taking a stand on illegal RCMP activities, the NLHRA did nothing to raise concerns in Newfoundland about RCMP wrongdoings, preferring to allow the Federation to take the lead in Ottawa. In this and many other situations, the NLHRA deferred to the Federation. As a small organization with limited resources and a mandate to concentrate on local issues, the NLHRA simply did not see national issues as a priority. The lack of Aboriginal or gay rights organizations on the Island in the seventies contributed to the lack of public debate over national human rights concerns, although the women's movement raised the abortion issue within the context of women's rights in Newfoundland as early as 1975.[52] Local issues dominated the agenda of the NLHRA; nonetheless, it maintained important links to rights associations of this era and made its own unique contribution.

Ideological Foundations

The LDH was not unique in propagating an expansive approach to human rights inclusive of economic, social, and cultural (i.e., positive) rights; human rights associations emerging from the International Year for Human Rights shared this philosophy. As a group born amidst celebrations over the anniversary of the UDHR, the NLHRA's conception of individual rights was distinct from that favoured by civil liberties groups.

Activists within the NLHRA called on the government to accept a more active role in promoting equality through programs promoting economic and social rights. While the NLHRA's contribution to the Charter debates through the Federation reflected a shared concern with due process, in Newfoundland the association was active in pushing for low-income housing and improving the conditions of foster care. Many of the leaders in the BCCLA and the CCLA would have characterized the issues identified by the NLHRA as having more to do with public policy than with human rights. In a brief before the mayor of St. John's at a conference on housing issues, the NLHRA stated that it was "concerned with two issues. The first being that monies be made available for housing to people with low incomes; the second, that housing be so built and allocated that it becomes a part of, and integrates with, the environment in which we live."[53] Throughout the 1980s, the issue of low-income housing was a priority for the association, and, drawing on the edicts of the UDHR, which called for a minimum standard of housing, the NLHRA advocated for more and better public housing in Newfoundland, often acting as a liaison between individuals who were seeking housing and government departments.[54] It also made several representations to government to improve the resources provided to foster homes. In perceiving individual rights within the context of subsidies to alleviate poverty as well as better conditions for foster children, the NLHRA deviated from civil libertarians' approach to economic and social rights, which focused on equal treatment by the state.[55]

Relations with Other Social Movement Organizations

At first glance, it is surprising how little interaction the NLHRA had with other SMOs. After all, it was an active participant in the Federation, and, as was the case with its counterpart in Montreal, the NLHRA's human rights philosophy would have made it easier to find common ground with other movements. True, St. John's did not have the extensive network of SMOs available to the Ligue in Montreal. But at least two members of the NLHRA Board of Directors, Lilianne Bouzane and John Peddle, were deeply involved in the Newfoundland Status of Women Council and the Newfoundland Association of Public Employees, respectively. As a universal idiom, human rights has the potential to draw together diffuse interests; and yet, there were no coalitions and no campaigns involving the NLHRA and feminists or the labour movement. As Peddle suggested in reflecting on the relationship between the NLHRA and the labour movement: "I really shouldn't even say trade unions ... it was really NAPE [Newfoundland Association of Public Employees] and nobody else, and basically because of the individuals involved."[56] The limited interaction is particularly surprising considering that the NLHRA and feminists shared a determination to fight for equal pay and that the NLHRA and the Newfoundland Teachers' Federation were both concerned about the rights of teachers in denominational schools.

In a city of little more than 100,000 people, coalition building was often unnecessary; interaction often occurred informally. As Bouzane pointed out, "there was a great deal of cross-fertilization ... there was only a small group of us [activists] in Newfoundland."[57] Individuals could move between various SMOs, and the limited pool of activists in St. John's made it easier to communicate, network, and cooperate among SMOs.

The historical context should also be taken into consideration. At a time when the women's movement was blossoming and feminists were drawn to new organizations dedicated to women's issues, such as the Newfoundland Status of Women Council (formed in 1972), it is unsurprising that women were attracted to these organizations instead of to the NLHRA. Bouzane was one of the few women to join the NLHRA, and she remembers it as a weak advocate for women's issues: "When I look back at the human rights organization, vis a vis [sic] the women's movement, we were a pretty mild organization. They [the government] weren't afraid of us [NLHRA] but they were afraid of the women's movement."[58] Numerous other factors militated against forming strong bonds with other SMOs. The labour movement was still small in Newfoundland when the NLHRA was founded; the public sector was not organized until the 1970s. Moreover, with the exception of denominational education, no single issue captured the imagination of the NLHRA's leaders. Peddle, who briefly served as president of the NLHRA in the late 1970s, believes that the lack of a cause to mobilize supporters further isolated the NLHRA within the community.[59] Finally, a potential labour ally, the Newfoundland Teachers' Federation, was more concerned with funding legal challenges and raising complaints under the collective bargaining agreement than it was with joining other SMOs to challenge the denominational education system.[60]

State Funding

With no financial support forthcoming from the provincial government, the NLHRA, soon after it was created, turned to the federal government. In addition to receiving project-specific grants as early as 1971 through the Opportunities for Youth and Local Initiatives programs, the NLHRA began receiving core funding from the SOS to establish an office and to hire secretarial staff in 1976.[61] Federal funding allowed the association to investigate human rights violations and to produce flyers and booklets for distribution to schools. Federal grants remain a central source of funding for the organization to the present day. At no point did membership fees provide more than 3 percent of the budget. The NLHRA was typical of a rights association located in a small city with no source of funding outside the state. And, indeed, it would forever be dependent on federal grants.

One of the central themes in the history of the rights associations, and to a degree in the history of the human rights movement in Canada generally, is state funding. A policy of restraint and respect for the independence of voluntary organizations gave way by the seventies to a new philosophy, whereby the state, notably the federal government, adopted a significant role in promoting citizenship participation through voluntary agencies. No department was more visible in the provision of grants for SMOs than the SOS. With the exception of the Canadian Civil Liberties Association, the NLHRA and most other rights association in Canada applied for and received grants from the SOS.

Unfortunately, SOS files are extremely bare and highly inaccessible. After years of access to information requests, it is still only possible to construct a partial image of the SOS's funding apparatus, and there is no explicit statement on how much funding went to specific organizations during this period. It is clear from the available evidence, however, that the NLHRA was not alone in seeking out state funding.

The federal government's interest in promoting integration and cohesive social relations among its citizens dates back at least to the Second World War, when the Nationalities Branch was created to "foster and sustain national consciousness and strengthen national unity."[62] The branch was renamed the Department of Citizenship and Immigration in the late forties, and the first grants offered by the department's Citizenship Branch were dispensed in 1951-52.[63] The branch's concern with immigration and refugees led it into the field of human rights, where it organized a seminar on human rights at the University of British Columbia, and, soon after Canada joined the United Nations Commission on Human Rights, it provided information to the Department of External Affairs on inter-group (i.e., racial or ethnic) relations in Canada.[64]

In 1962, the department began offering a limited number of grants to voluntary associations that were fostering Aboriginal and immigrant integration as well as group understanding and citizenship promotion. These grants were capped at $5,000 per year for three years and were to be used for specific projects rather than as operational funding.[65] By this prohibition the government wished to avoid getting involved in the creation and operation of voluntary groups. Grants were to be directed to established organizations.[66] As of 1964, no funds had yet been made available to rights associations, although a 1965 report entitled *A New Focus for the Citizenship Branch* recommended grants be provided for "civil liberties leagues" in Canada.[67] This report had little initial success.

In 1966, the Citizenship Branch was integrated into the SOS, and its priorities were narrowed to five areas: human rights, immigrant participation, Indian participation, travel and exchange programs, and youth. All the branch's activities and grants with respect to human rights focused on racial and ethnic integration and tolerance.

The International Year for Human Rights would prove to be a watershed for the human rights movement, and not simply with regard to the formation of new rights associations. The anniversary ushered in a new era of government largess for SMOs. In 1968, Trudeau became prime minister and Gérard Pelletier, former editor of *La Presse* and member of the Ligue des droits de l'homme, was appointed secretary of state. To celebrate the anniversary of the UDHR, the budget for the human rights program expanded exponentially: the $95,000 grant to the Canadian Commission for the International Year for Human Rights was a marked increase from the usual $5,000 annual grants. Other grants enjoyed substantial increases under Pelletier's tenure (1968-72), notably grants to Native groups and friendship centres, initially budgeted at $100,000 in 1967 and expanding to $540,000 in 1970 and $5,205,000 in 1972 (see Table 8.1). Grants for the promotion of human rights continued to remain relatively high under Pelletier, with $95,000 allocated

Table 8.1

Annual funding for Native organizations and friendship centres, 1968-81

Fiscal year	Budget	Fiscal year	Budget
1968	$175,000	1975	7,175,402
1969	378,168	1976	– *
1970	540,000	1977	8,395,000
1971	1,907,110	1978	8,657, 000
1972	5,205,000	1979	9,488,000
1973	8,436,000	1980	9,488,000
1974	9,403,633	1981	10,500 000

* Information on grants was not provided for the year 1976.
Source: Report of the Department of the Secretary of State of Canada, 1968-81.

Table 8.2

Secretary of State, Group Understanding and Human Rights Branch, annual grants, 1968-81

Fiscal year	Budget	Fiscal year	Budget
1968	$95,000 *	1975	138,395
1969	100,000 **	1976	139,132
1970	58,670	1977	995,000 ***
1971	85,000	1978	995,000
1972	80,000	1979	620,000
1973	140,000	1980	224,000
1974	225,000	1981	500,000

* International Year for Human Rights.
** The bulk of these funds went to the Canadian Council on Human Rights.
*** An additional $80,000 was made available for educational activities.
Source: Report of the Department of the Secretary of State of Canada, 1968-81.

in 1968 and $80,000 in 1972 (see Table 8.2). In his extensive study of SOS funding, Leslie Pal suggests that the federal government's generosity during this period was partially designed to counter French-Canadian nationalism by enhancing the role of the federal government in the voluntary sector and encouraging citizen participation in national debates and institutions. Trudeau and his contemporaries' desire to inaugurate a new era of participatory democracy was also a likely contributing factor to this new stage in state-SMO relations.[68]

After 1968, the SOS became the central department responsible for the federal government's human rights program. A memorandum prepared for the cabinet in October 1968 endorsed the SOS as, after years of working with external affairs on human rights issues, the only department with the experience and field officers that rendered it capable of administering a broad human rights program. The memorandum also set the stage for providing financial support for rights associations, suggesting they would support national unity by developing public attitudes conducive to equality of treatment and opportunity. Cabinet approved the memorandum in December 1968, and the SOS began dispensing grants soon thereafter.[69]

Within two years, grants were being allocated to a variety of rights associations (see Table 8.3). Several organizations apart from formal rights associations were funded under the SOS human rights program, from the Nova Scotia Association

Table 8.3

Total funding from the Secretary of State's human rights program for 1969-70

Rights association	Funding
Alberta Human Rights Association	$4,000
Atlantic Regional Human Rights Conference	600
British Columbia Civil Liberties Association	5,000
British Columbia Human Rights Council	2,500
BC Human Rights Council (regional committees)	5,000
Canada Council for Human Rights	19,500
Canadian-Asian Sikh Committee, Williams Lake, BC	1,000
University of New Brunswick Human Rights Group	250
University of PEI Student Union	300
Canadian Association for Adult Education	150
École Polyvalente de Buckingham	100
École Secondaire Immaculée-Conception	1,000
Fredericton Civil Liberties Association	250
Hamilton Growth Centre	5,000
Newfoundland-Labrador Human Rights Committee	500
Nova Scotia Association for the Advancement of Coloured People	3,500
New Brunswick Committee Project	520
Saskatchewan Association on Human Rights	1,000
Séminaire bilingue sur les Nations Unies	3,000
Sudbury Mayor's Committee on Human Rights	4,500
Toronto Christian Resources Centre	500
United Nations Association of Canada	500
Total	$58,670

Source: Report of the Department of the Secretary of State of Canada for the Year Ending 31 March 1970.

for the Advancement of Coloured People to the Toronto Christian Resource Centre. Of the 249 grants (totalling $1,082,472) provided through the Citizenship Branch in 1970 to voluntary groups, $58,670 was provided for twenty-two associations engaged in human rights activities.

Between 1970 and 1982, the operations and size of the SOS and the Citizenship Branch continued to expand. As Tables 8.1 and 8.2 demonstrate, grants to Aboriginal organizations and friendship centres reached $10,500,000 per year by 1981, and the human rights program peaked, with $995,000 allocated for 1977 (it went as low as $224,000 in 1980 but rose to $500,000 in 1981 to coincide with the Trudeau government's project to repatriate the Constitution). An average of thirty to thirty-four organizations received funding each year through this program. Under Pelletier, the branch and the SOS in general had dispensed with the classical liberal hesitancy to become implicated in the maintenance of SMOs and were generously providing the bulk of funding for many organizations. Other government programs, including the Opportunities for Youth Program and the Local Initiatives Program, became significant sources of financing for rights associations in the seventies. The NLHRA, in particular, was well placed to receive grants under the Local Initiatives Program, which had a mandate to support initiatives in economically depressed regions of Canada.

The files of the SOS and its annual reports contain a breakdown of grants to specific rights association in only one year – 1970 – as detailed in Table 8.3. Otherwise, there is no information on how much money was provided to which associations and based on what criteria. Nonetheless, other sources demonstrate the pervasiveness of such grants. Of the four case studies in this book, only the Canadian Civil Liberties Association refused to accept government grants, although in 1966 and again in 1971 it applied to the SOS for funding.[70] The NLHRA, the BCCLA, and the LDH were dependent on SOS funds (in some cases supplemented by provincial government funds as well) for maintaining staff and an office. Each association organized a variety of recruitment campaigns, but membership numbers were never high enough to provide sufficient funding for operational expenses and, in general, accounted for less than 10 percent of their budget.[71]

With the exception of a handful of groups, virtually every rights association in Canada in the seventies received funding, often quite regularly, from the state. A thorough analysis of recently released SOS files combined with interviews and archival research reveals the names of a host of other rights associations at the receiving end of state funding (listed in Table 8.4). An entire network of SMOs was, in effect, bankrolled by the federal government. In many cases, the very survival of an organization depended on the generosity of the state. The Canadian Council on Human Rights was one obvious example of a national rights association that was unable to survive without state funding.[72] As the case studies have

Table 8.4

Government funding for rights associations, 1970-82

The following is a list of groups that received funding from the Secretary of State throughout the 1970s.

Alberta Human Rights and Civil Liberties Association
Civil Liberties Association, National Capital Region
Comité pour les droits de l'homme du nord-est (NB)
Comité pour les droits de l'homme du Sud-Est (NB)
Cornwall Civil Liberties Association
Fredericton Chapter, CCLA
Kamloops Civil Liberties Society
Kitchener-Waterloo Human Rights Caucus
Lethbridge Citizens Human Rights Council
Manitoba Association for Rights and Liberties
Nova Scotia Civil Liberties Association
Prince Edward Island Civil Liberties Association
Quesnel Civil Liberties and Human Rights Association
Saskatchewan Association for Human Rights
South Okanagan Civil Liberties Association
Williams Lake Civil Liberties Association

demonstrated, however, dependence on state funding may have constrained the activities of rights associations, but it did not discourage them from challenging the state on a variety of fronts.

No organization better exemplifies a dependence on state funding than the Federation. The initial meeting that led to the formation of the Federation in Winnipeg in 1971 was funded by a $3,500 grant from the SOS.[73] From then on, SOS grants ranging up to $5,000 per year were provided to the Federation to cover the costs of its annual meetings. Operational and project funding was also provided by the SOS over the years, with individual grants as high as $50,000.[74] With membership fees capped off at $25 for each organization (later raised to $250 in the 1980s), there was no way the Federation could have covered its own expenses, much less an annual meeting, without government funding.[75] Any attempt to change the fee structure was vigorously opposed by such groups as the BCCLA, which was determined to keep the fees equal for all organizations.[76] The Federation once endeavoured to secure non-governmental funds through an application to the Donner Foundation for a $48,900 grant to study police and Native community relations.[77] The application failed, and other attempts between 1972 and 1982, including the creation of the Rights and Freedoms Foundation (a charitable wing of the Federation designed to raise funds), to encourage large private donations were equally unsuccessful. The group was clearly at the mercy of government funding. With no alternative means of support, the ability of the Federation to operate an office, hire staff, publish a newsletter, and organize annual meetings depended each year on the SOS. Not long after the federal government ceased to provide it with operational funding, the Federation ceased to exist.

The NLHRA offers a useful comparison with other rights associations because it was located in a small, geographically isolated region of the country. It was an eager participant in the Federation, which made it possible for a small organization with limited funds and far from Ottawa to participate in national debates. As a case study, the NLHRA also exemplifies the types of strategies deployed by rights associations: the development of a small cadre of skilled activists to lobby for change through the state. The NLHRA's dependence on state funding is further evidence of the potential for an SMO to be an active critic of the same institution that is keeping it afloat. State funding distinguished the second generation of rights associations from its predecessors. The economic, social, and political context of the seventies facilitated the mass funding programs that the federal government provided to SMOs and made it possible to establish and maintain groups such as the NLHRA. The first generation of rights associations did not suffer through the divisive debates over state funding, which, ultimately, with the refusal of the CCLA to join the Federation, resulted in two competing national rights associations in a country barely capable of sustaining one.

Conclusion

The 1960s and 1970s was a period of energetic social movement activism, with the arrival of a vast array of new social movement organizations representing a myriad of constituencies. During this period the rights revolution came to fruition as manifested, in part, by the explosion of civil liberties and human rights associations across the country. Rights associations were a product of an evolving human rights culture in Canada and were supported by the rising affluence of the middle class. Fuelled by an economic boom that lasted into the mid-seventies and the rise of the service sector and bureaucracies, the middle class played an increasingly prominent role in funding and leading SMOs. Linked with the rise of university enrolments in the wake of the postwar boom, rights associations drew their members and leaders from rising numbers of middle-class professionals, including journalists, lawyers, academics, social workers, and ministers. The focus on quality of life issues characteristic of many social movements of this period, such as the environmental movement and the women's movement, was distinct from the focus of working-class activism, which was rooted in attacks on capitalism and excessive individualism.

The mounting influence of Canada's middle class coincided with the expansion of the welfare state, which, in turn, motivated rights associations to act. Rights activists traditionally concerned with state suppression of rights believed that the welfare state represented a potential threat to individual liberties. Prime Minister Lester B. Pearson's declaration of a war on poverty in the 1960s symbolized not only the expanding role of the state through welfare policies but also Canadians' expectation that the state would take an active role in dealing with poverty and other social welfare issues.[1] While the CCLA and the BCCLA spent years defending welfare recipients' due process rights, members of the LDH and the NLHRA saw in the welfare state an acknowledgment of the right of citizens to certain basic social and economic resources, from low-income housing to subsidies for the disabled.

More than ever the state was intruding upon people's private lives and regulating the behaviour of its citizens. With urbanization came greater population density, more crime, and larger police forces. In 1957, the Metropolitan Toronto Police Force was created, and by 1977 it had more than five thousand members (about one thousand of them civilians); the cost of policing Toronto alone had risen from $58,129,000 in 1971 to $140,520,000 by 1977.[2] State repression of illicit drug use was at an all-time high. Not only did this translate into greater conflict between police and citizens with regard to an activity many felt should be legalized, but it also forced a clash between police and middle-class youths, who were vocal and articulate in defending their rights. Perhaps the most visible manifestations of this conflict were the Gastown Riot and the demands for a civilian review system for dealing with complaints against the police in Toronto. In these years, rights associations were active in defending youths against charges of vagrancy, drug use, and/or engaging in protests. At the same time, the growing consensus around the inviolability of human rights internationally, as manifested in the UDHR and subsequent covenants, as well as the eruption of the civil rights movement in the United States, undoubtedly played a role in inspiring and motivating human rights activists in Canada. An increasingly well-educated population, rising affluence, greater state activity, new social movement activism, the marginalization of the labour movement, urbanization, international developments, and conflicts between police and youths all contributed to the unprecedented proliferation of rights associations.

The New Anti-Liberals? Comparing Generations
Since the 1960s, a new generation of activists has been at the forefront of organizing and leading rights associations. The idea of distinctive generations is an elusive and vague concept, but if one accepts the notion that generations are an age group shaped by history, there "is no doubt that the social moment for the baby-boom generation was the sixties."[3] The history of rights associations is less a story about how human rights "evolve" than it is a story about how a particular historical context shaped social activism. Many individuals overlapped both generations. Two notable examples include Frank Scott, who was active in the LDH and its predecessors, and Kalmen Kaplansky, who continued to be a key figure in the human rights movement well into the sixties. And yet, a sense of rebellion and renewal pervaded rights associations during this period, a genuine belief that they were moving in new directions. Scott left the Ligue in the 1970s, unable to accept the new direction taken by the group's young leadership, and Kaplansky's brainchild, the JLC, was a shadow of its former self by the 1970s. The 1972 manifesto of the Ligue des droits de l'homme is the most tangible example of breaking with the past, but the Ligue was not the only rights association to be shaped by the unique wave caused by the baby boomers. Second-generation rights activists built upon the achievements of their predecessors and were intimately affected by the youth movement, the Quiet Revolution, drug use among middle-class youth, and a host of other issues that emerged when the children born in the wake of the Second World War came to maturity.

The generational divide among rights activists was best symbolized by the differing priorities of Irving Himel and his replacement, Alan Borovoy. Both were lawyers with an interest in civil liberties; both were Jewish with strong ties to organized labour and Jewish organizations; and both were dedicated to combatting discrimination in all its forms. Yet whereas one of Himel's key objectives was to secure anti-discrimination legislation in Ontario, Borovoy spent most of his time dealing with police powers and due process violations. Unlike his predecessor, Borovoy led a rights association at a time when discrimination was increasingly unacceptable, and he had the support of an emerging state human rights program in the form of a provincial human rights commission. Borovoy was in his early teens when the espionage commission was formed and had only recently graduated from law school when the Padlock Act was struck down by the Supreme Court of Canada. He never had to deal with the infighting between communists and social democrats that had divided the Toronto associations in the 1940s; rather, he had to contend with egalitarians who were hostile to his own ideology of rights, finally reaching the point at which he wrote a book denouncing egalitarians as "anti-liberals."[4]

Still, there were several important similarities between the two generations. Since the 1930s rights associations have failed to organize a grassroots following and have drawn their members primarily from among educated middle-class intellectuals. Journalists, academics, ministers, and other professionals have consistently formed the leadership structure in these organizations. By the 1960s, with the increasing accessibility of university education, this core constituency expanded dramatically, allowing rights associations to be larger and to mobilize more members. Essentially, however, the basic qualities of their members remained the same. Women continued to participate in small numbers, and there were few racial or religious minorities on the boards of rights associations. Jews have always been prominent in Toronto rights associations, yet outside Toronto few have participated in these groups.

Despite these similarities, there was one significant distinction between the demographics of each generation: the presence of French Canadians. Virtually absent from the first generation, by the 1970s French Canadians led one of the most dynamic rights associations in the country. They dominated the LDH, an association that began as a bilingual organization only to become unilingually French by 1972. The LDH was one of the founders of the Federation, and, although not to the same degree as the CCLA, it did participate in national debates.

The second generation also had the benefit of the UDHR (1948) and the Bill of Rights (1960). Although neither document had much of an impact on Canadian law, and the latter proved to be a lame duck, they had a strong symbolic value and were exploited by rights associations. Certainly the Bill of Rights, if it had any kind of an impact at all, was to begin chipping away at the idea of parliamentary supremacy. By 1970, in the wake of the first Special Joint Committee on the Constitution, parliamentary supremacy was no longer seen as a viable obstacle to entrenching human rights in the Constitution. The Bill of Rights was also often the inspiration for litigation. When the BCCLA challenged the validity of the Heroin Treatment Act, it claimed that the act violated the Bill of Rights' guarantee to equality under the law. And the CCLA often intervened in court cases to argue a violation of the Bill of Rights. At the same time, human rights activists pointed to the UDHR as a symbol of how human rights should be interpreted and applied. Rather than negative rights, human rights activists favoured positive rights, demanding more positive state action with regard to welfare, housing, and providing for the poor. Both the UDHR and the Bill of Rights were powerful tools employed by rights activists who could claim that the state was violating its obligations under one or both of those documents.

Without a doubt the single most important distinction between the two generations of rights activists involved the question of ideology. Both generations were characterized by ideological divisions, although only in the first generation did these divisions degenerate into bitter conflicts between activists. The division between communists and social democrats/liberals in the 1930s and 1940s was part of the broader divisions within the left. By the 1970s, rights associations were divided between negative and positive conceptions of rights. In Montreal, activists in the LDH saw human rights as a pathway to promoting a program of social justice. They called for the abolition of prisons; insisted on providing statutory protections for youths, the handicapped, and the elderly; and placed the debate over national security within the context of class repression. This ideological transformation was intimately linked with the Quiet Revolution and the increasingly militant left in Quebec. But it is too reductionist to account for this transformation solely in terms of the Quiet Revolution and French-Canadian nationalism. It should not be forgotten that the LDH emerged within the context of an expanding human rights movement in Canada. Rights associations such as the NLHRA, and many of the participants in the celebrations surrounding the International Year for Human Rights, embraced a positive approach to human rights. The LDH was thus part of a movement concerned with the limits of traditional notions of rights articulated by civil liberties organizations that shared their space within the human rights movement.

Divided We Stand: A National Rights Association

Bitter divisions between communists and social democrats/liberals in the 1930s and 1940s were sufficient to prevent the formation of a national rights association. The second generation of rights activists found itself equally helpless to form a truly national rights organization.

The Federation had always been a weak organization. Dependent on government funding, it soon collapsed when the state pulled the plug in the late 1980s, being left unable to pay for its newsletter and annual meetings. For nearly twenty years it had proven to be the best forum for bringing together rights associations, but it never developed a strong agenda or lobbying program, and it focused more on networking than it did on advocacy. The Federation was a pale image of the type of national rights association envisioned by its founders.

Only the CCLA challenged the Federation for the status as Canada's national rights association. By the 1970s, with chapters spanning the country and confronting important human rights violations such as the implementation of the War Measures Act and illegal RCMP activities, the CCLA was far closer to being a national rights association than was the Federation. Yet the strength of the CCLA was also its weakness. What made the Federation so weak was its decentralized model, its inability to consult with other associations quickly, and its failure to raise funds to act decisively on national issues. Most of the work was left up to individual associations. In contrast, the CCLA, as a highly centralized association, was able to act more quickly and efficiently, but in doing so it could rarely be said to represent the interests of its chapters. Most chapters could not afford to send their leaders to CCLA board meetings, and by the 1980s it was clear that most of the chapters were themselves in decline. Whereas the Federation could honestly claim to be a national association with representation from across the country, the CCLA had a weak claim through its chapters and could only point to having some members from outside Ontario. In addition, national campaigns rarely materialized. The reality was that the Toronto group spent most of its time dealing with problems in Ontario. This was continually acknowledged by other rights associations who refused to recognize the CCLA as a national association and by individuals who refused to join the association because it was Toronto-centred.

Two weak national organizations took shape during the 1970s, and neither was able to develop a viable program of action at the national level. In an era with no electronic mail and a costly long-distance telephone service, it was extremely challenging to maintain a national organization. The inability to form a national human rights and civil liberties organization is a central theme in the history of rights associations in Canada.

State Funding

When Don Whiteside sought to mobilize rights activists across Canada to form a national rights association in 1970-71, he was entreated by Eamon Park, the current chair of the Board of Directors of the CCLA, not to solicit government funding for the meeting. The two men found themselves at an impossible impasse, which would eventually cause a fundamental rift between the two national rights associations, one heavily state funded and the other autonomous. In exhorting Whiteside to refuse state funding, Park warned him that it would forever tarnish the reputation of the proposed Federation and undermine its credibility. Imagine, Park suggested, an organization supported by state funding refusing, for legitimate reasons, to take on a particular issue involving the government. No matter how justified its motivation, the group would be perceived as having backed off because of its dependence on state funding.[5]

It is clear that the CCLA was able to survive and thrive without state funding while other associations faced bankruptcy unless outside support could be secured. No issue caused more acrimony between the CCLA and other associations than the question of state funding. For the CCLA, state funding was proof of cooption by the state and an inability to effectively challenge governments when the state itself represented the greatest potential threat to civil liberties.

From the perspective of government officials, funding private voluntary agencies had a specific policy objective. Funding became a means, among other things, through which the federal government could help organizations to mobilize the public and to direct public attention to national issues in order to develop a sense of a national community, fostering a "greater allegiance to national institutions through a feeling that these institutions were open to popular forces."[6] This was clearly the case with rights associations. The human rights program was entirely consistent with Trudeau's vision of combatting Quebec separatism with rights discourse as epitomized in the Charter of Rights and Freedoms. Immediately following the October Crisis the LDH received its first major grant from the SOS, and just prior to Trudeau's introduction of a draft Charter of Rights and Freedoms the budget for the human rights program doubled from that of the previous year.

From the perspective of most rights associations, state funding often meant the difference between survival and dissolution. CCLA opponents of state funding generally shared the same three concerns. First, they believed that organizations dependent on state funding would hesitate to take their paymasters to task on controversial issues. Yet, during the period when state funding for rights associations peaked, there is no evidence that the BCCLA, the LDH, or the NLHRA ever found themselves constrained by state funds. All three organizations expanded their activities and scope exponentially over twenty years and never hesitated to challenge the government on controversial issues. While the NLHRA received most of its funding from the federal government and shied away from national issues for functional reasons, the other two associations did not hesitate to take on controversial issues involving the same governments (federal and provincial) that funded them. In fact, the one time the federal government threatened to cut off funds as a result of the LDH's language policy, a hastily convened press conference denouncing the government's tactics soon led to a renewal of the grant. While it is true that all three organizations were often constrained by project-specific grants and were unable to conduct the type of initiatives they might have desired, this was no less the case with the CCLA. The latter's focus on welfare and Aboriginal issues was no doubt intensified as a result of various project-specific grants from private foundations.

At most, one could accuse the three state-funded rights associations of making little effort to draw potential members to their ranks, whereas the CCLA continually focused on building up its membership list. The CCLA was very involved in encouraging individuals to become active in a rights association, whereas the LDH only attracted large numbers of members when its government grants were temporarily cut off. The LDH and the NLHRA did not even bother to publish a newsletter, whereas the CCLA published both *Civil Liberties* and the bi-monthly *News Notes*. At any rate, in an age of professional SMOs, when, for most middle-class adherents, placing a cheque in the mail was the sum of their participation, there is no evidence that the CCLA was able to mobilize the public in its activities more intimately than were the other associations. Except for the petition campaign, several public forums, and the Fort Erie demonstration, the CCLA hardly stands out among its contemporaries with regard to mobilizing the public to participate in its activities.

·The CCLA also enjoyed several core advantages that any Toronto group invariably has over other organizations in Canada. First, located in the country's largest and richest city, the association had access to a wide base of support. Most of its membership drives involved large mail solicitation campaigns that were facilitated through lists acquired from unions, church groups, the NDP, and others, many of whom were located in Toronto or throughout Ontario. Even by 1982 the vast majority of the association's membership was located in Toronto, including its Board of Directors and its Board of Advisors. The availability of a large base of support allowed the group to hire full-time employees whose job was to enlist new members, an advantage that groups in isolated and small cities could never match. With a large and stable membership base, the CCLA was a much more attractive recipient for a grant from various private foundations than were rights associations that might use the funds to secure staff. Second, the CCLA had access to the Atkinson Foundation, which helped it to stave off financial crises in 1967 and 1973. Third, much of the association's success in acquiring funding was attributable to its elite leadership, which included notable figures such as Keiller Mackay, Pierre Berton, and June Callwood. Organizations located in St. John's or Saskatoon could not hope to match these advantages.

In addition, as noted earlier, Eamon Park assumed that any group that received state funding would be perceived as being biased in favour of the state if it failed to take on a key rights issue, even if it had legitimate reasons for not doing so. Of course, it is impossible to disprove a negative. However, there is no evidence that any of the three state-funded associations were openly criticized for inaction with regard to a major issue or that they lost members due to inaction. Only the LDH was publicly lynched for not doing enough during the October Crisis; however, this incident occurred before the association received its federal grant. Compared to the CCLA, all three associations, either individually or through the Federation, were vocal critics of the government. On only one issue – illegal RCMP activity and the Macdonald Commission – was the CCLA clearly more active than were the associations discussed in the other case studies. But this reflected the regionalization of rights associations and their preference, when it came to national issues, for working through the Federation.

Finally, Donald Smiley (a director of the CCLA) once asked how one can ever expect bold and imaginative leadership leading to significant social change from state-funded associations. There is undoubtedly some validity to Smiley's criticism. Rights associations dependent on state funding did not seek to mobilize large numbers of adherents. All three state-funded associations employed the same tactics, mainly litigation, education, press releases, letter-writing campaigns and briefs to parliamentary committees – in order to pursue their agenda. Yet was this any different from the CCLA? The CCLA was not the only rights association to organize a protest; the LDH did the same on the anniversary of the War Measures Act, and the BCCLA raised a picket in front of the Pacific National Exhibition. Perhaps the only truly imaginative campaign pursued by the CCLA in its early history involved the petition on illegal RCMP activity. Otherwise, there is no evidence that a group not funded by the state provided more imaginative leadership than did groups funded by the state. In fact, as a civil liberties association, the CCLA embraced a more limited vision of human rights than did the LDH and the NLHRA. When the LDH revolutionized its operations in 1972, after it began receiving government grants, it became more militant, adopting positions on language rights and self-determination and taking on new issues such as the rights of the elderly and children. State funding did not dampen its activism but enhanced it. Granted, the most radical wing of the LDH was the only privately funded subcommittee of the association, the prisoners committee. Nevertheless, when the prisoners committee suggested in its Charter of Prisoners' Rights that prisoners were justified in trying to escape because of the harsh conditions of jails, the United Way pulled its funding. Thus even private funding could threaten to adversely affect a group's ideals.

Rights Activism in the Age of Protest

Rights associations in Canada are typical of the professional SMOs. Government and private funding expanded considerably in the 1970s and played a key role in allowing rights associations to thrive. They were also supported by a membership base with which they had little contact except through membership dues and donations. Middle-class professionals dominated these organizations, and the media were key tools for expanding their membership base as well as for promoting their cause to a wider audience. With regard to their advocacy, rights associations also depended a great deal on experts, whether this involved placing BCCLA board members on the stand to testify to the literary merits of the *Georgia Straight* or using the LDH's academic experts to study the conditions of prisons across Quebec. Finally, while rights associations did not *constitute* the human rights movement, they formed an important dynamic within it. Campaigns such as the CCLA's petition on illegal RCMP activities, the LDH's bill of rights crusade, the NLHRA's public debates on denominational education, and the BCCLA's free speech campaigns were designed, in part, to reach out to adherents of the human rights movement and to encourage them to join the association or support their cause. Many of these qualities are attributable to most, if not all, rights associations.

Scholars who have studied SMOs have identified a myriad of strategies employed by these organizations. Since the 1960s, an important feature of social movement activism has involved the use of dual strategies, including alternatives to working through state institutions. In the age of protest, social movement activists raised the spectre of mass mobilization, from rallies to sit-ins, as well as alternative forms of protest, including civil disobedience or the formation of subcultures, to promote social change. Yet it is a distinguishing feature of rights associations that, with the exception of a few rare instances, they did not favour such strategies. All of the associations identified in this book, the sole criteria being that they self-identified as civil liberties or human rights organizations (with no partisan or constituency affiliation), depended largely on what some social movement scholars have characterized as "conservative" tactics. Rights associations shied away from grassroots mobilization with the same alacrity that tenants unions employed mass rent strikes or civil rights activists used sit-ins.[7] The repertoire of tactics available to SMOs was extensive, but rights associations limited themselves primarily to briefs, publications, litigation, the development of position papers, and sending observers to protest marches.

It is interesting to note, as Ross Lambertson has pointed out in his exhaustive study of the first generation of rights activists, that such tactics have always been the hallmark of rights associations in Canada: "Much of the impact of these organizations came from reasoned argument and moral suasion, rather than from brute political power; for the most part they did not represent many votes or sources of campaign funds, nor could they mount huge demonstrations or threaten the authorities with violence in the streets."[8]

No single element can explain this development. The strategies embraced by rights associations were informed by a confluence of factors. Rights associations have rarely been led by the same oppressed peoples whom they were defending; many SMOs tend to focus their activities on state institutions by virtue of their own hierarchically organized bureaucratic structure; professional SMOs have little direct interaction with their members; and state funding allows SMOs to forgo the mobilization of large numbers of constituents. Most important, it is essential to appreciate the impact of rights discourse in conjunction with these other forces. The idea of human rights encourages the perception of social change as legal change and, when combined with these other factors, further motivates rights associations to focus their efforts on state institutions. Human rights, after all, are primarily realized through the state.

Despite the case studies' limited repertoire of strategies, rights associations exploited rights discourse in order to advance the interests of the vulnerable and the powerless. In Vancouver, the BCCLA articulated a forceful defence of free speech for an unpopular newspaper; in Quebec, the unique needs of the handicapped, youths, and the elderly were explicitly recognized in the provincial Bill of Rights, while individuals associated with a brutal act of terrorism discovered that, even in the midst of a crisis, they would not be left completely to the mercy of the state; in Toronto, poor single mothers dependent on welfare ascertained that they could question the government's arbitrary policies and seek redress; and, in St. John's, the NLHRA played a key role in getting equal pay for women through amendments to the human rights code.

But seeking social change through state institutions can often be a bitter and frustrating enterprise. The history of rights associations abound with examples of failed attempts to use conservative tactics to protect individual rights. These organizations often found themselves unable to deal with the core controversies they themselves identified, including abusive drug laws, police violence, and denominational education. Perhaps the most successful association was the LDH, which managed to convince the Quebec government to implement expansive human rights legislation (never mind that Quebec was the last province to do so). And yet, even the LDH faced severe obstacles, including national security regulations that prevented individuals from seeking redress from state abuse of fundamental freedoms. For many human rights activists, institutional barriers simply proved too difficult to overcome.

According to some critics, the problems facing some rights associations are of their own making and have to do with their minimalist approach to human rights. Irwin Cotler, a future federal Liberal minister of justice, suggested in the early 1990s that, at the time, "a disproportionate number of NGOs deal[t] with matters pertaining to political and civil rights, while the cause of economic, social and cultural rights appear[ed] to be under-represented among the NGOs."[9] Around the same time, Laurie Wiseberg, a founder and former executive director of Human Rights Internet (an international research centre based in Ottawa), advanced a similar criticism about the limited scope of human rights activism in Canada: "Yet [human rights associations] have, by and large, not delved into the structural causes of [human rights] violations, and they have, by and large, not devoted the same degree of attention to economic and social rights."[10] Michael Ignatieff believes "that social and economic inequality, the focus of so much socialist pas-sion when I was a student, has simply disappeared from the political agenda in Canada and most other capitalist societies."[11]

Civil liberties associations refused to embrace positive notions of human rights, and any engagement with social rights was conceived in terms of negative free-dom. Borovoy, for instance, has accused feminists of violating liberal principles by promoting egalitarianism. In *The New Anti-Liberals,* Borovoy attacked the Women's Legal Education and Action Fund's support for a blanket rape-shield law. A woman's sexual history is relevant if, according to Borovoy, she has a history of exhorting men by threatening to accuse them of rape. He then goes on to attack feminists for undermining free speech through political correctness and accuses the National Action Committee on the Status of Women of violating equal oppor-tunity by encouraging employers to favour women in certain professions over equally qualified men. Borovoy's concerns echo similar positions adopted by the BCCLA in these areas, particularly with regard to employment equity and por-nography. The conception of rights adopted by civil libertarians reflected a con-cern with *individual* responsibility and *individual* freedom, and they did not attempt to counteract systemic or structural inequalities.

By proffering a limited conception of rights based on negative freedom, the BCCLA and the CCLA, and the other civil liberties groups in Canada, were blind to systemic inequality. If advocating for proper training, health, and education in order for individuals to be free and equal is to recognize systemic inequalities, then human rights associations had a greater capacity to challenge systemic in-equalities than did civil liberties associations. It is noteworthy that the LDH and the NLHRA considered low-income housing and the economic needs of the elderly as *rights* and not simply as privileges of the welfare state. In addition, they sided with feminists against civil libertarians on issues such as pornography. The LDH and the NLHRA did not adopt a minimalist approach to human rights.

As critics of human rights activism have indicated, however, even an expansive approach to human rights can function as a camouflage for inequality. Ignatieff suggests that rights talk "can capture civil and political inequalities, but it can't capture more basic economic inequalities, such as the ways in which the economy rewards owners and investors at the expense of workers."[12] Judy Fudge contends that rights discourse forces feminists to abandon discourses of power for a dis-course of equal rights (a gender-neutral idiom that has been used to undermine many of the achievements of the women's movement). Rights discourse does not threaten systemic inequality in the way that feminists threaten private power, so-cialists threaten capitalism, or gay liberationists threaten heterosexuality.[13] Human rights is a universal idiom that offers the same remedy to problems that require different solutions. In other words, if rights discourse leads activists to focus too much on the state and does not address abuses at the substate, social level, then it is incapable of confronting systemic inequality.

Looked at in this light, it is difficult to see how the strategies deployed by human rights associations could undermine systemic inequality. If one assumes that structural inequalities cannot be dealt with through the legal and political system but must, instead, challenge the foundation of the system and other forms of power, then rights associations were, at best, reformers. The women's movement provides an ideal illustration of this. One of the first books produced by the women's liberation movement in Canada, *Women Unite!*, published in 1972, introduced women's liberation by distinguishing it from reformers' concern with equal rights: "The philosophy of the women's rights groups is that civil liberty and equality can be achieved *within* the present system, while the underlying belief of women's liberation is that oppression can be overcome only through a radical and fundamental change in the structure of our society."[14] Women Against Pornography, a grassroots feminist organization in British Columbia in the early 1980s, rejected legislative action as a solution to pornography: "We do not believe that, in a patriarchy, such legislation can be made to serve the interests of women. We believe censorship legislation is ineffective (by definition and enforcement) in a patriarchy."[15] Even the Vancouver Status of Women Council, a liberal-feminist organization, employed dual strategies. It may not have organized pickets of pornography stores alongside Women against Pornography, but it hosted night courses for women, consciousness-raising groups, and vigils. Moreover, the Vancouver Status of Women Council acknowledged the limits of legal reform: "People who expect [law] to change the status of women in society or alter their socio-economic status ... are insane ... What is necessary is an overall change in the attitude of people and that has to be done through education and through women actually doing the jobs people thought they would never do."[16]

Leaders of rights associations, from Reg Robson to Maurice Champagne, were certainly not dogmatic about legal reform or unaware of structural inequalities. Nonetheless, rights associations did not deploy strategies for dealing with systemic inequality. By embracing the state as a vehicle for social change, rights associations hobbled their ability to achieve their own goals. It is true, as many defenders of litigation have pointed out, that rights talk can highlight injustices and legitimize demands for change. But it is an uphill battle, which, more often than not, proved to be an unsuccessful strategy. "Law generally," as one Canadian scholar of social movement activism points out, "is a system of rules designed to secure and maintain the existing social order ... law plays a very important role in regulating and controlling dissent."[17]

The LDH and the NLHRA embraced a broader conception of rights, but the two organizations deployed strategies for change focused on legal change. Undoubtedly a key reason for this lay in the nature of rights associations: most SMOs engage with the state. But innumerable SMOs have historically employed dual-strategies, working both inside and outside the system. Rights associations did not. SMO strategies are guided by the ideas and ideologies that inform their vision for social change. The one idea that linked all rights associations in Canada, their vision for social change that led them to embrace conservative strategies for change, was human rights.

Notes

Chapter 1: Introduction

1 William K. Carroll, "Social Movement and Counterhegemony: Canadian Contexts and Social Theories," in *Organizing Dissent: Contemporary Social Movements in Theory and in Practice*, ed. W.K. Carroll (Toronto: Garamond Press, 1997), 4.

2 Evelyn Kallen, *Ethnicity and Human Rights in Canada: A Human Rights Perspective on Ethnicity, Racism and Systemic Inequality* (Don Mills: Oxford University Press, 2003), 12.

3 Jack Donnelly, *Universal Human Rights in Theory and Practice* (New York: Cornell University Press, 2003), 1.

4 Ronald Dworkin, *Taking Rights Seriously* (Cambridge: Harvard University Press, 1977), 272-73.

5 In the exercise of their own rights, human beings cannot violate the rights of others; thus human rights principles are not absolute. Evelyn Kallen provides a useful and more detailed discussion of universal human rights principles in Chapter 1 of her book on ethnicity and human rights. See Kallen, *Ethnicity and Human Rights in Canada*.

6 Walter Tarnopolsky, *The Canadian Bill of Rights* (Toronto: Carswell Company, 1966), 3.

7 George Williams, *Human Rights under the Australian Constitution* (Melbourne: Oxford University Press, 1999), 7.

8 *Reference re Alberta Statutes*, [1938] S.C.R. 100.

9 One of the first and most influential discussions on negative and positive liberty was developed by Isaiah Berlin. See Isaiah Berlin, *Four Essays on Liberty* (London: Oxford University Press, 1969).

10 Jerome Bickenback, *Physical Disability and Social Policy* (Toronto: University of Toronto Press, 1993), 37.

11 Berlin, *Four Essays on Liberty*, 7; Maurice Cranston, *What Is a Human Right?* (New York: Basic Books, 1973), 124.

12 Ross Lambertson, *Repression and Resistance: Canadian Human Rights Activists, 1930-1960* (Toronto: University of Toronto Press, 2005), 8-9.

13 Ron Hirschl, "'Negative' Rights vs. 'Positive' Entitlements: A Comparative Study of Judicial Interpretations of Rights in an Emerging Neo-Liberal Economic Order," *Human Rights Quarterly* 2 (2000): 1071-72.

14 Rosalie Silberman Abella, "From Civil Liberties to Human Rights: Acknowledging the Differences," in *Human Rights in the Twenty-First Century: A Global Challenge*, ed. K.E. Mahoney and P. Mahoney (London: Martinus Nijhoff Publishers, 1993), 67.

15 Irving Dillard, ed., *The Spirit of Liberty: Papers and Addresses of Learned Hand* (New York: Knopf, 1954), 189-90.

16 Some of the more notable studies examining rights activism from a state or court-centred perspective include: Elizabeth M. Schneider, "The Dialectic of Rights and Politics: Perspectives from the Women's Movement," *NYU Law Review* 589 (1986): 589-62; Louis Henkin, *The Age of Rights* (New York: Columbia University Press, 1990); Michael W. McCann, *Rights at Work: Pay Equity Reform and the Politics of Legal Mobilization* (Chicago: Chicago University Press, 1994); Rainer Knopff and F.L. Morton, "Canada's Court Party," in *Perspectives on*

Canadian Constitutional Reform, Interpretation, and Theory, ed. A.A. Peacock, 63-87 (Don Mills: Oxford University Press, 1996); Miriam Smith, *Lesbian and Gay Rights in Canada: Social Movements and Equality-Seeking, 1971-1995* (Toronto: University of Toronto Press, 1999); Mary L. Dudziak, *Cold War Civil Rights: Race and the Image of American Democracy* (Princeton and Oxford: Princeton University Press, 2000).

17 Joe Foweraker and Todd Landman, *Citizenship Rights and Social Movements: A Comparative Statistical Analysis* (Toronto: Oxford University Press, 1997) 33.

18 Smith, *Lesbian and Gay Rights in Canada*, 75.

19 James Walker, *"Race," Rights and the Law in the Supreme Court of Canada: Historical Case Studies* (Waterloo: Wilfrid Laurier University Press, 1997), 320-21.

20 Martha Minow, *Making All the Difference: Inclusion, Exclusion and American Law* (Ithaca: Cornell University Press, 1990).

21 Knopff and Morton, "Canada's Court Party."

22 Tom Warner, *A History of Queer Activism in Canada* (Toronto: University of Toronto Press, 2002).

23 Gary Teeple, *The Riddle of Human Rights* (New York: Humanity Books, 2005), 101.

24 Nelson Lichtenstein, *State of the Union: A Century of American Labor* (Princeton: Princeton University Press, 2002), 209-10.

25 Walker, *"Race," Rights and the Law*.

26 Minow, *Making All the Difference*, 307.

27 Teeple, *Riddle of Human Rights*, 118.

28 Karl Manheim, *Essays on the Sociology of Knowledge* (New York: Oxford University Press, 1953), 291. For a discussion of generation as a historical concept, refer to: Anthony Esler, *Generations in History: An Introduction to the Concept* (n.p., 1982); Doug Owram, *Born at the Right Time: A History of the Baby Boom Generation* (Toronto: University of Toronto Press, 1996).

29 Esler, *Generations in History*, 44.

30 James Walker and Constance Backhouse have demonstrated the advantages of the case study approach for historical inquiry in their own work on key legal cases in Canada dealing with race. See Walker, *"Race," Rights and the Law*; Constance Backhouse, *Colour-Coded: A Legal History of Racism in Canada, 1900-1950* (Toronto: University of Toronto Press, 1999).

31 Some of the leading works that have discussed the evolution of human rights legislation and norms in Canada, but focus their discussion on the state, include: Ramsay Cook, "Canadian Civil Liberties in Wartime" (MA thesis, Queen's University, 1955); D.A. Schmeiser, *Civil Liberties in Canada* (Toronto: Oxford University Press, 1964); Tarnopolsky, *The Canadian Bill of Rights;* Ian A. Hunter, "The Origin, Development and Interpretation of Human Rights Legislation," in *The Practice of Freedom: Canadian Essays on Human Rights and Fundamental Freedoms*, ed. J.P. Humphrey and R.S.J. Macdonald, 77-110 (Toronto: Butterworth, 1979); Michael Horn, *League for Social Reconstruction* (Toronto: University of Toronto Press, 1980); Walter Surma Tarnopolsky, *Discrimination and the Law in Canada* (Toronto: De Boo, 1982); Robert O. Matthews and Cranford Pratt, eds., *Human Rights in Canadian Foreign Policy* (Kingston and Montreal: McGill-Queen's University Press, 1988); Evelyn Kallen, *Label Me Human: Minority Rights of Stigmatized Canadians* (Toronto: University of Toronto Press, 1989); Rainer Knopff, *Human Rights and Social Technology: The New War on Discrimination* (Ottawa: Carleton University Press, 1989); Christopher MacLennan, *Toward the Charter: Canadians and the Demand for a National Bill of Rights, 1929-1960* (Montreal and Kingston: McGill-Queen's University Press, 2003, 1996); William A. Schabas, "Canada and the Adoption of the Universal Declaration of Human Rights," *McGill Law Journal* 43 (1998): 403-41. Recent work by Ross Lambertson, Miriam Smith, James Walker, Ruth Frager, and Carmela Patrias (among others) has sought to challenge this trend. See Smith, *Lesbian and Gay Rights*

in Canada; James Walker, "The 'Jewish Phase' in the Movement for Racial Equality in Canada," *Canadian Ethnic Studies* 1 (2002): 1-23; Lambertson, *Repression and Resistance;* Ruth Frager and Carmela Patrias, "'This is our country, these are our rights': Minorities and the Origins of Ontario's Human Rights Campaigns," *Canadian Historical Review* 1 (March 2001): 1-35.

Chapter 2: Canada's Rights Revolution

1 Ross Lambertson, "The Dresden Story: Racism, Human Rights, and the Jewish Labour Committee of Canada," *Labour/Le Travail* 47 (Spring 2001): 75.

2 Some examples include: Tarnopolsky, *The Canadian Bill of Rights;* Henkin, *The Age of Rights;* Michael Ignatieff, *The Rights Revolution* (Toronto: House of Anansi Press, 2000); Donnelly, *Universal Human Rights in Theory and Practice;* Teeple, *Riddle of Human Rights.*

3 For further reading on these issues, refer to: Schmeiser, *Civil Liberties in Canada;* Tarnopolsky, *The Canadian Bill of Rights;* Ramsay Cook, "Canadian Freedom in Wartime," in *His Own Man: Essays in Honour of A.R.M. Lower,* ed. W.H. Heick and R. Graham (Montreal and Kingston: McGill-Queen's University Press, 1974), 35-54; Thomas Berger, *Fragile Freedoms: Human Rights and Dissent in Canada* (Toronto: Clarke-Irwin, 1981); Tarnopolsky, *Discrimination and the Law in Canada;* Walker, *"Race," Rights and the Law in the Supreme Court of Canada;* Ignatieff, *The Rights Revolution;* Lambertson, *Repression and Resistance;* Frager and Patrias, "'This is our country, these are our rights.'"

4 Ross Lambertson explores the use of international treaties by domestic activists. See Lambertson, *Repression and Resistance.* The case studies in this work also explore how domestic activists used Canada's international obligations to bolster their activism.

5 Marc Bossuyt, "International Human Rights Systems: Strengths and Weaknesses," in *Human Rights in the Twenty-First Century: A Global Challenge,* ed. K.E. Mahoney and P. Mahoney (London: Martinus Nijhoff Publishers, 1993), 247. Writing in the late 1980s, Louis Henkin points out the impressive accomplishments of the international human rights movement in only forty years: "Human rights are in the constitution of virtually every state. All states have recognized the idea of human rights and have accepted their articulation in the Universal Declaration; most states are parties to some of the principal international instruments, and at least half of the world's states (including most of the major powers, but not the United States) are parties to the principal, comprehensive covenants. Although the UN human rights program is still politicized, its human rights bodies – the Human Rights Commission and its Subcommission on Discrimination and its work group – increasingly consider charges of violation by more countries and seek to bring about improvement. Regional human rights systems, in Europe and also in Latin America, are at work and have contributed to significant ameliorations in the condition of human rights in various countries." See Henkin, *The Age of Rights,* 26-27.

6 Walker, *"Race," Rights and the Law in the Supreme Court of Canada,* 15, 32.

7 The decision to avoid the American experience with a bill of rights was "not surprising if one considers the traditions and training of those who were lawyers amongst the Fathers of Confederation. If they were asked what our fundamental freedoms included, they would have referred to speech, press, religion, assembly, association, probably such legal rights as right to habeas corpus and to a fair public trial. Perhaps they would have stressed the rule of law in its terms as a principle of the British constitution, and perhaps they would have emphasized freedom of contract and rights to property." See Walter Tarnopolsky Papers, speech before the Conference, Library and Archives of Canada (hereafter LAC), MG 31, E55, vol. 31, f. 14. For a fuller discussion of Canada's constitutional history and terminology, refer to Tarnopolsky, *The Canadian Bill of Rights;* Walker, *"Race," Rights and the Law in the Supreme Court of Canada.*

8   His resolution called for a "bill of rights protecting minority rights, civil and religious liberties, freedom of speech and freedom of assembly; establishing equal treatment before the law of all citizens, irrespective of race, nationality or religious or political beliefs; and providing the necessary democratic powers to eliminate racial discrimination in all its forms." See Canada, *Hansard Parliamentary Debates* (hereafter *Hansard*), vol. 1, 1945, 900.

9   Canadian Bar Association, *Yearbook of the Canadian Bar Association and the Minutes and Proceedings of Its Twenty-Seventh Annual Meeting* (Ottawa: National Printers Limited, 1944); Canada, 1960, *Proceedings of the Special Committee on Human Rights and Fundamental Freedoms.*

10   A.V. Dicey, *Introduction to the Study of the Law of the Constitution* (London: St. Martin's Press, 1962), 39-40.

11   *Hansard*, vol. 4, 1947, 3214-16.

12   Ibid., 3215.

13   Bill of Rights Act (Alberta), *S.A.* 1946, c. 11.

14   Saskatchewan Bill of Rights Act, *S.S.* 1947, c. 35.

15   Carmela Patrias, "Socialists, Jews, and the 1947 Saskatchewan Bill of Rights," *Canadian Historical Review* 2 (2006): 265.

16   Ibid., 276.

17   Canada, 1960, *Proceedings of the Special Committee on Human Rights and Fundamental Freedoms.*

18   Copy of agenda for meeting of civil liberties organizations, 28 December 1946, J. King Gordon Papers, LAC, MG 30, C241, vol. 19, f. 15

19   For further information on Canada's role at the United Nations in the passing of the Universal Declaration of Human Rights, see Schabas, "Canada and the Adoption of the Universal Declaration of Human Rights."

20   The federal committees are discussed in detail in: MacLennan, *Toward the Charter;* Dominique Clément, "Spies, Lies and a Commission, 1946-8: A Case Study in the Mobilization of the Canadian Civil Liberties Movement," *Left History* 2 (2001) 53-79; Lambertson, *Repression and Resistance.*

21   Canada, 1960, *Proceedings of the Special Committee on Human Rights and Fundamental Freedoms.*

22   Ibid.

23   Following the limited success of the 1947 and 1948 committees, Roebuck decided to force the government to act by introducing into the Senate a bill to create a federal bill of rights. He soon retracted the bill, following an agreement that would see the implementation of a Senate committee to recommend how the Canadian government could act to better protect rights in Canada and to consider a draft bill of rights.

24   Arthur Roebuck to Irving Himel, 28 June 1950, Arthur Roebuck Papers, LAC, MG 32, C68, vol. 1, f. 23.

25   Canada, 1960, *Proceedings of the Special Committee on Human Rights and Fundamental Freedoms.*

26   *Hansard*, vol. 5, 1960, 5651.

27   Ibid., 5666.

28   The Bill of Rights passed in 1960 was comparable to provincial legislation in Saskatchewan (1947), Alberta (1972), and Quebec (1975). Each was a regular statute, vulnerable to override by a future Parliament or legislature. All four referred to the five basic freedoms: religion, speech, assembly, association, and press. The Saskatchewan, Quebec, and federal bills provided for protection against arbitrary arrest and detention, while the Alberta, Quebec, and federal bills required equality before the law and the right to not be deprived of property without due process of law. Each piece of legislation, as well as Stewart and Diefenbaker's

motions, encompassed some form of due process rights. See Bill of Rights Act (Alberta), c. A-14; Canadian Bill of Rights, *S.C.* 1960, c. 44; Saskatchewan Bill of Rights, c. 35.

29 Cited by Hazen Argue in *Hansard*, vol. 5, 1960, 5667.

30 Anne F. Bayefsky, *Canada's Constitution Act of 1982 and Amendments: A Documentary History* (Toronto: McGraw-Hill Ryerson Limited, 1989), 54.

31 Canada, 1972. *Special Joint Committee of the Senate and House of Commons on the Constitution of Canada: First Report*, 18-19.

32 James B. Kelly, *Governing with the Charter: Legislative and Judicial Activism and Framers' Intent* (Vancouver: UBC Press, 2005), 48.

33 For background on the history of the Charter of Rights and Freedoms and the Bill of Rights movement in Canada, including the role played by Trudeau and the political left, see Alan C. Cairns, *Charter versus Federalism: The Dilemmas of Constitutional Reform* (Montreal and Kingston: McGill-Queen's University Press, 1992); Michael Mandel, *The Charter of Rights and the Legislation of Politics in Canada* (Toronto: Thompson Educational Publishing, 1994); MacLennan, *Toward the Charter;* Rainer Knopff and F.L. Morton, *The Charter Revolution and the Court Party* (Peterborough: Broadview Press, 2000); Kelly, *Governing with the Charter.* Peter Russell links the Charter project with Trudeau's mission to undermine the Quebec independence movement. See Peter Russell, "The Political Purposes of the Canadian Charter of Rights and Freedoms," *Canadian Bar Review* 1 (1983): 30-54. On the question of whether or not the Charter represents the Americanization of Canadian political culture, see Paul Nesbitt-Larkin, "Canadian Political Culture: The Problem of Americanization," in *Crosscurrents: Contemporary Political Issues,* ed. M. Charlton and P. Barker, 4-21 (Toronto: ITP Nelson, 1998).

34 The only comparable anti-discrimination legislation passed in Canada prior to the 1944 Ontario Racial Discrimination Act would be the 1793 Upper Canada anti-slavery law (superseded in 1833 by Imperial Statute), the 1932 Ontario amendment to the Insurance Act to prevent discrimination against race or religion, and Manitoba's 1934 amendments to the Libel Act to prohibit group libel or the promotion of racial antipathy. See "Speech before the Conference of Human Rights Ministers in Victoria," 8 November 1974, Walter Tarnopolsky Papers, LAC, MG 31, E55, vol. 31, f. 14,

35 Tarnopolsky, *Discrimination and the Law in Canada,* 27.

36 Manitoba (1953), Nova Scotia (1955), New Brunswick (1956), British Columbia (1956), and Saskatchewan (1956) passed fair employment practices legislation, and Quebec became the seventh province to ban discrimination in employment in 1964. The first Fair Accommodation Practices Act was passed in Ontario in 1954, with Saskatchewan (1956), New Brunswick (1959), Nova Scotia (1959), Manitoba (1960), and British Columbia (1961) soon doing the same. British Columbia enacted a more restricted statute in 1961, while Quebec avoided passing fair accommodation practices legislation entirely but did add a section to the Hotels Act to forbid discrimination in hotels, restaurants, and camping groups. See Tarnopolsky, *Discrimination and the Law in Canada,* 27-28.

37 *Winnipeg Free Press,* 2 September 1960, 19 November 1960.

38 British Columbia, Department of Labour, 1953-69, *Annual Report.*

39 Frank Scott to Gordon Dowding, 20 September 1964, Frank Scott Papers, LAC, MG 30, D211, vol. 47.

40 *Robertson and Rosetanni v. The Queen* (1963), 42 D.L.R. (Supreme Court of Canada).

41 *Attorney General of Canada v. Lavell; Isaac v. Bédard,* [1970] S.C.R.

42 In a commentary on the *Lavell* case that same year, Peter Hogg suggested that there was no need in Ritchie's argument to "construe the vague phrase 'equality before the law' as requiring such a radical result as the abolition of laws enacted by the federal Parliament which employed a racial classification when the use of that classification is essential to the validity

of the law under the British North America Act. It is much more plausible to construe the guarantee of equality as not intended to disturb the federal principle: inequalities between the laws of different legislative bodies within the federation should be deemed not to be inconsistent with equality before the law." See Peter Hogg, "Case and Comments," *Canadian Bar Review* 2 (1974): 268.

43 *Smythe v. The Queen*, [1971] S.C.R.

44 Karl A. Friedmann, "The Ombudsman," in *The Practice of Freedom: Canadian Essays on Human Rights and Fundamental Freedoms*, ed. R. St. J. Macdonald and John P. Humphrey, 337-58 (Toronto: Butterworth and Co., 1979), 344.

45 Nova Scotia (1971), Saskatchewan (1972), Ontario (1975), Newfoundland (1975), and British Columbia (1977) passed legislation creating the office of the ombudsman in the 1970s. Newfoundland passed legislation in 1970 for the creation of an ombudsman's office, but a quick change in government led to the legislation's remaining unproclaimed. An ombudsman was not appointed until 1975 (and was eliminated in the 1990s). British Columbia also delayed the appointment of its ombudsman. See Friedmann, "The Ombudsman," 347.

46 Ontario, 1968, *Report of the Royal Commission Inquiry into Civil Rights.*

47 J. Patrick Boyer, *A Passion for Justice* (Toronto: The Osgoode Society for Canadian Legal History, 1994), 303.

48 Nova Scotia followed Ontario in 1962 with its own human rights act but did not appoint a full-time director until 1967. Similar legislation was passed by Alberta (1966), New Brunswick (1967), British Columbia (1969), Prince Edward Island (1968), and Newfoundland (1969). Manitoba passed its human rights code in 1970, Quebec in 1975, and the federal government in 1977. Saskatchewan, Newfoundland, and Prince Edward Island delayed establishing full-time commissions until 1972, 1974, and 1975, respectively (the Saskatchewan commission enforced various anti-discrimination statutes before the code was passed in 1979). Human rights commissions in Canada were notoriously underfunded and understaffed. A 1968 report by D.A. Coupland of the Canadian Labour Congress discussing human rights legislation noted not only the lack of resources and staff but also the fact that there were some weaknesses with the provisions in the legislation itself. None of the statutes contained political opinion as a category for discrimination (Newfoundland was the first province to include political opinion in its human rights legislation in 1969), and Coupland noted that, in Quebec, women could still not belong to a union if their husbands objected. See "An Analysis of Human Rights Legislation in Canada," October 1968, Canadian Labour Congress Papers, LAC, vol. 647, f. 13.

49 In 1984, the Social Credit government in British Columbia disbanded the Human Rights Commission. In 1994, the NDP reintroduced the Commission only to have the Liberal government disband it again in 2002.

50 Walker, "The 'Jewish Phase' in the Movement for Racial Equality in Canada, 1."

51 Ibid., 1.

52 Canada, Secretary of State, 1977, *Annual Report of the Department of the Secretary of State.*

53 Tarnopolsky, *The Canadian Bill of Rights*, 4.

54 Owram, *Born at the Right Time*, 221.

55 For an overview of the women's movement, see Nancy Adamson, *Feminist Organizing for Change: The Contemporary Women's Movement in Canada* (Toronto: University of Toronto Press, 1988), 55. Becki Ross has written a detailed history of LOOT. See Becki Ross, *The House That Jill Built: A Lesbian Nation in Formation* (Toronto: University of Toronto Press, 1995).

56 According to Tom Warner, in the early 1970s "women's centres and organizations were frequently unhappy places for lesbians." It was not uncommon for centres to refuse to hang banners or advertise lesbian initiatives out of fear of alienating their members. Warner, *A History of Queer Activism in Canada*, 79.

57 Kallen, *Label Me Human: Minority Rights of Stigmatized Canadians,* 168.

58 Warner, *A History of Queer Activism in Canada,* 68-69.

59 The years 1970 to 1974 in particular "stand out as a golden age of activism ... [T]he foundation for political and social activism was firmly laid, enabling the efforts of the next several years to concentrate on discrimination in employment – and housing, breaking down loneliness and isolation, and dispelling notions of sin, sickness and deviance." In 1978, the National Gay Rights Coalition was renamed the Canadian Lesbian and Gay Rights Coalition (with twenty-seven member groups across Canada), which became defunct in 1981. See Warner, *A History of Queer Activism in Canada,* 94.

60 References to Native political organizations do not include band councils or individual tribes.

61 Of the other two national organizations, the National Indian Youth Council of Canada (1965) was reorganized and changed its name to the National Native Student Association in 1969, and the Canadian Metis Society (1969) organized Natives from the four western provinces.

62 David Long, "Culture, Ideology, and Militancy: The Movement of Native Indians in Canada, 1969-91," in *Organizing Dissent: Contemporary Social Movements in Theory and in Practice,* ed. W.K. Carroll, 151-70 (Toronto: Garamond Press, 1997), 121.

63 The protest is covered extensively by the *Standard Freeholder* newspaper throughout December 1968.

64 Long, "Culture, Ideology, and Militancy," 130.

65 Robin Winks, *The Blacks in Canada: A History* (Montreal and Kingston: McGill-Queen's University Press, 1997), 458.

66 According to Dorothy Moore, the Nova Scotia Association for the Advancement of Coloured People was founded in 1946 and "began to work on removing the various barriers which kept Blacks from participating in society; they stressed the need for improvements in education, and publicised and resisted specific instances of discrimination such as segregated seating arrangements in cinemas. This organization, together with the Church, can be viewed as the main leaders of the Black community well into the 1960s." See Dorothy Emma Moore, "Multiculturalism: Ideology or Social Reality?" (PhD diss., Boston University, 1980), 395.

67 Gus Wedderburn to David Orlikow, 24 February 1969, Jewish Labour Committee Papers (hereafter JLC), LAC, MG 28, V75, vol. 41, n. 1.

68 Black activists were becoming increasingly assertive during the 1960s and employed unconventional tactics to have their message heard. As Dorothy Moore notes, there were "one or two street demonstrations, a concert tour by the Freedom Singers from the southern United States, and increasingly serious 'rap sessions' which involved three visits by Black Panthers, the Stokeley Carmichael visit, and the formation of a group called the Afro-Canadian Liberation Movement. By this time, older members of the Black community, as well as the Whites, were thoroughly alarmed about the possibility of violence erupting from such events." See Moore, "Multiculturalism," 396-401.

69 Leslie Pal, *Interests of State: The Politics of Language, Multiculturalism, and Feminism in Canada* (Montreal and Kingston: McGill-Queen's University Press, 1993), 14.

70 Warner, *A History of Queer Activism in Canada,* 131.

71 Ibid., 160.

72 *Women Unite! An Anthology of the Canadian Women's Movement* (Toronto: Canadian Women's Educational Press, 1972), 9.

73 Ross, *The House That Jill Built,* 181.

74 Walker, *"Race," Rights and the Law in the Supreme Court of Canada,* 302.

75 Jack Donnelly has advanced one of the most sustained criticisms of the positivist school of human rights (which asserts that human rights derive their legitimacy from the state) by

arguing that the foundation of human rights is to be found in human morality. See Donnelly, *Universal Human Rights in Theory and Practice.*

76 Cynthia Williams, "The Changing Nature of Citizen Rights," in *Constitutionalism, Citizenship and Society in Canada,* ed. A. Cairns and C. Williams (Toronto: University of Toronto Press, 1985), 124.

77 Ignatieff also suggests that Canada's rights culture is unique because Canada is one of the few countries that has legislated on how to break the federation apart. See Ignatieff, *The Rights Revolution,* 7-8.

78 Ibid., 89, 118.

Chapter 3: The Forties and Fifties

1 Frank Scott, *Essays on the Constitution: Aspects of Canadian Law and Politics* (Toronto: University of Toronto Press, 1977), 71.

2 A recent spate of literature has explored the role of minorities and victims of discrimination in mobilizing support for anti-discrimination legislation in Canada. See MacLennan, *Toward the Charter*; Walker, "The 'Jewish Phase' in the Movement for Racial Equality in Canada"; Stephanie D. Bangarth, "'We are not asking you to open wide the gates for Chinese immigration': The Committee for the Repeal of the Chinese Immigration Act and Early Human Rights Activism in Canada," *Canadian Historical Review* 3 (2003): 395-422; Lambertson, *Repression and Resistance*; Patrias, "Socialists, Jews, and the 1947 Saskatchewan Bill of Rights"; Frager and Patrias, "'This is our country, these are our rights.'"

3 Scott, *Essays on the Constitution,* 50.

4 J. Petryshyn, "A.E. Smith and the Canadian Labour Defense League" (PhD diss., University of Western Ontario, 1977), iv.

5 Larry Hannant, *The Infernal Machine: Investigating the Loyalty of Canada's Citizens* (Toronto: University of Toronto Press, 1995), 222.

6 Canada, 1950, *Proceedings of the Special Committee on Human Rights and Fundamental Freedoms*; Berger, *Fragile Freedoms,* 121.

7 Ross Lambertson has noted that the initiative to create the first CCLU in Montreal actually predated the Padlock Act. But the organization did not get off the ground until the Padlock Act mobilized people to take action. See Lambertson, *Repression and Resistance,* 47-48.

8 Ross Lambertson, "Activists in the Age of Rights: The Struggle for Human Rights in Canada, 1945-60" (PhD diss., University of Victoria, 1998), 38-39.

9 Cook, "Canadian Freedom in Wartime," 38.

10 Reg Whitaker and Gary Marcuse, *Cold War Canada: The Making of a National Insecurity State, 1945-1957* (Toronto: University of Toronto Press, 1994), 7-8.

11 Cook, "Canadian Freedom in Wartime," 220-22.

12 Canadian Civil Liberties Association, copies of agent reports from rally and newspaper coverage, 1942, Royal Canadian Mounted Police Papers, LAC, RG 146, vol. 2883.

13 Lambertson, *Repression and Resistance,* 94-96.

14 Lambertson, "Activists in the Age of Rights," 40-41.

15 For further information on the divisions among social democrats and communists, see Bryan Palmer, *Working Class Experience: Rethinking the History of Canadian Labour, 1800-1991* (Toronto: McClelland and Stewart, 1992). For information on the divisions among social democrats and communists within the human rights movement, see Clément, "Spies, Lies and a Commission, 1946-8"; Lambertson, *Repression and Resistance*; Dominique Clément, "'It is not the beliefs but the crime that matters': Post-War Civil Liberties Debates in Canada and Australia," *Labour History* (Australia) 86 (May 2004): 1-32.

16 Norman Penner, *The Canadian Left: A Critical Analysis* (Scarborough: Prentice-Hall of Canada, 1977), 158.

17 For more information on the Oriental experience in British Columbia, see W. Peter Ward, *White Canada Forever: Popular Attitudes toward Orientals in British Columbia* (Montreal and Kingston: McGill-Queen's University Press, 1990).

18 Walker, *"Race," Rights and the Law in the Supreme Court of Canada,* 20.

19 Ibid.

20 Scott, *Essays on the Constitution,* 192.

21 Lambertson, "Activists in the Age of Rights," 95.

22 As quoted in MacLennan, *Toward the Charter,* 38.

23 The Cooperative Committee for Japanese Canadians was able to raise thousands of dollars to fund a challenge to the Supreme Court of Canada and, following its defeat, to the Judicial Committee of the Privy Council in England. In court, the committee argued that the orders referred only to aliens and not to British citizens and that any attempt to banish nationals based on their racial origin was a violation of international law. There were also questions raised about the vagueness of the term "Japanese race." In a unanimous decision passed down on 20 February 1946, the Supreme Court found the orders intra vires the powers of the federal government under the War Measures Act, except in the case of wives and children under sixteen years of age, which the court could not bring itself to condone for deportation. See *In the Matter of a Reference as to the Validity of Orders in Council for the 15th Day of December 1945 (PC7355, 7356, 7357), in Relation to Persons of the Japanese Race,* [1946] S.C.R. 248.

24 MacLennan, *Toward the Charter,* 48-49.

25 Ibid., 52.

26 Walker, *"Race," Rights and the Law in the Supreme Court of Canada,* 31.

27 MacLennan, *Toward the Charter,* 99.

28 Berger, *Fragile Freedoms,* 93.

29 Amy Knight has recently produced an excellent history of the Gouzenko affair and its aftermath. See Amy Knight, *How the Cold War Began: The Gouzenko Affair and the Hunt for Soviet Spies* (Toronto: McClelland and Stewart, 2005).

30 Gouzenko remained under the protection of the RCMP for the next several months; nothing was said publicly of the defection, and no one was arrested after PC6444 was passed. When the War Measures Act was revoked in December 1945 and special wartime powers continued under the National Emergency Transition Powers Act to deal with postwar reconstruction, only two sets of orders-in-council continued in operation: PC6444 and the deportation orders. However, PC6444 and the defection remained top secret, and when John Diefenbaker asked Minister of Justice Louis St. Laurent in January 1946 if any other orders-in-council passed under wartime powers were still in operation, St. Laurent replied negatively. He would later claim, after the defection became public, to have forgotten about PC6444. See Whitaker and Marcuse, *Cold War Canada,* 58.

31 Initially, King avoided making it public that they had a Russian defector. From the moment of Gouzenko's defection, King was loath to go public, concerned it would damage already shaky relations between the USSR and the West. He eventually announced the defectors' nationality following the presentation of an interim report by the espionage commission in March 1946.

32 Back, Badeau, Nora, and Grey were codenames assigned to the suspects. See E.K. Williams to Mackenzie King, top-secret memorandum, 5 December 1945, LAC, Records of the Department of Justice, RG 13, vol. 2119, 2121.

33 E.K. Williams to Mackenzie King, top-secret memorandum, 5 December 1945, Royal Canadian Mounted Police Papers, LAC, RG 146, vol. 2883.

34 The conditions under which the prisoners were held and the commission's procedures are explored in the following: Canada, 1946, *Report of the Royal Commission to Investigate the*

Disclosures of Secret and Confidential Information to Unauthorized Persons; June Callwood, *Emma Woikin* (Toronto: University of Toronto Press, 1988); and Gordon Lunan, *The Making of a Spy* (Toronto: Robert Davies Publishing, 1995).

35 David Shugar to John Diefenbaker, 9 March 1946, John Diefenbaker Papers, LAC, MG 26-M, vol. 82, 65326.

36 Lucie Laurin's research on the Montreal CCLU suggests that the stress of the Padlock Act and the Defence of Canada Regulations effectively strangled the organization. However, Larry Hannant has recently argued that the leaders of the Montreal CCLU suspended its operations as part of the communists' strategy of supporting the government in its war effort following the German invasion of the USSR. See Lucie Laurin, *Des luttes et des droits: Antécédants et histoire de la Ligue des droits de l'homme de 1936-1975* (Montréal: Éditions du Meridien, 1985), 35; Hannant, *The Infernal Machine,* 236-37.

37 Clément, "Spies, Lies and a Commission, 1946-48."

38 Copy of agenda for meeting of civil liberties organizations, 28 December 1946, J. King Gordon Papers, LAC, MG 30, C241, vol. 19, f. 15; copy of speech and agenda for civil rights rally, 27 January 1947, Arthur Roebuck Papers, LAC, MG 32, C68, vol. 1, f. 15.

39 Frank K. Clarke, "Debilitating Divisions: The Civil Liberties Movement in Early Cold War Canada, 1946-48," in *Whose National Security? Surveillance and the Creation of Enemies in Canada,* ed. G. Kinsman (Toronto: Between the Lines, 2000), 177.

40 Records of the Department of External Affairs, LAC, RG 25, vol. 2081, f. AR 13\13; Records of the Department of Justice, LAC, RG 13, vol. 2119, vol. 2121; John Diefenbaker Papers, LAC, vol. 82, 65442.

41 For further details on the debate in Parliament, see Dominique Clément, "The Royal Commission on Espionage and the Spy Trials of 1946-9: A Case Study in Parliamentary Supremacy," *Journal of the Canadian Historical Association* 11 (2000): 151-72.

42 Lambertson, "Activists in the Age of Rights," 171.

43 Palmer, *Working Class Experience,* 291.

44 *Hansard,* 1946, vol. 1, 92; *Hansard,* 1947, vol. 2, 1330-33.

45 *R. v. Mazerall* [1946] 2 Criminal Reports (Ontario High Court).

46 For more information on the spy trials, see Clément, "Royal Commission on Espionage and the Spy Trials of 1946-9."

47 *Toronto Daily Star,* 16 April 1946.

48 Gallup Poll of Canada: The Canadian Institute of Public Opinion, July 1949, CIP191.

49 Paul Axelrod, *Scholars and Dollars: Politics, Economics and the Universities of Ontario, 1945-1980* (Toronto: University of Toronto Press, 1982).

50 Walker, "The 'Jewish Phase' in the Movement for Racial Equality in Canada," 1.

51 Frager and Patrias, "'This is our country, these are our rights,'" 17-18.

52 Each of the labour committees held an annual Race Institute conference, a conference promoting tolerance among workers in unions, and distributed pamphlets and networked with various other bodies like the Canadian Association for Adult Education. See Lambertson, "The Dresden Story."

53 Palmer, *Working Class Experience,* 266.

54 Lambertson, "The Dresden Story," 48-49.

55 Ibid., 62-64.

56 Lambertson, "Activists in the Age of Rights," 316-17.

57 Lambertson, *Repression and Resistance,* 258.

58 Speaking to a Montreal audience in 1972, Michael Rubinstein, current president of the Jewish Labour Committee, said that the original purposes of the human rights committees of the Trades and Labour Council and Canadian Congress of Labour in 1948 were the following:

"Le principal objectif de ces comités était d'entreprendre une activité éducative au niveau de la section locale, ainsi que dans la collectivité elle-même, d'organiser des conférences sur les droits de l'homme, en vue de promouvoir a l'intérieur du mouvement syndical un sentiment de compréhension et de sympathie envers les problèmes des groupes minoirtaires, de protéger les syndiqués et les syndicats eux-mêmes d'être victimes de la bigoterie et de la discrimination. Enfin, le dernier objectif était d'organiser une activité et de promouvoir un appui et un intéret dans une action législative contre tout type de discrimination." See Discourse prononcé par Michael Rubinstein, à la conférence provinciale pour un code des droits de l'homme tenue à Montréal, 2 December 1972, LAC, JLC, MG 28, V75, vol. 38, f. 1.

59 Summary Report of the NCHR, 26 July 1961, LAC, JLC, MG 28, V75, vol. 13, f. 12,

60 Tom Mombourquette to Sid Blum, 11 October 1957, LAC, JLC, MG 28, V75, vol. 40, f. 7.

61 Canadian Labour Reports, vol. 15, no. 12, December 1960.

62 *The Journal*, 1 November 1979.

63 National Committee on Human Rights, CLC, Special Budget for International Year for Human Rights, 1968, Jewish Labour Committee Papers, LAC, MG 28, V75, vol. 10, f. 3; Pat Kerwin, interviewed by author, 2 July 2003.

64 National Committee on Human Rights, Ontario Labour Committee for Human Rights Papers, LAC, MG 28, I173, vol. 1, f. 20, n.d.

65 Kerwin, interview.

66 Scott, *Essays on the Constitution*, 356.

67 Alan Borovoy to Max Awner, 21 January 1966, Ontario Labour Committee for Human Rights Papers, LAC, MG 28, I73, vol. 6, f. 2.

68 Dalhousie University, *The Condition of the Negroes of Halifax City, Nova Scotia: A Study* (Halifax: Dalhousie University, 1962).

69 Alan Borovoy, interviewed by author, 12 March 2004.

70 David Orlikow to Michael Rubinstein, 4 July 1968, LAC, JLC, MG 28, V75, vol. 10, f. 8.

71 A detailed discussion on the evolving demographics of Canada's Jewish community is available in Robert J. Brym, "The Rise and Decline of Canadian Jewry?" in *The Jews in Canada*, ed. R.J. Brym, W. Shaffir, and M. Weinfeld, 22-38 (Toronto: Oxford University Press, 1993).

72 Walker, "The 'Jewish Phase' in the Movement for Racial Equality in Canada," 12.

Chapter 4: Social Movement Organizations

1 To be fair, not all new social movement scholars are directly critical of the study of social movement organizations, but this particular school of thought has inspired a flurry of studies that almost completely disregard the role of organizations in the study of social movements. Some of the leading studies examining the non-organizational aspect of social movements since the 1960s include: William A. Gamson, *The Strategy of Social Protest* (Homewood: Dorsey Press, 1975); Alain Touraine, *The Voice and the Eye: An Analysis of Social Movements* (Cambridge: Cambridge University Press, 1978); Joseph Gusfield, *The Culture of Public Problems* (Chicago: University of Chicago Press, 1981); Alberto Melucci, *Nomads of the Present: Social Movements and Individual Needs in Contemporary Society* (Philadelphia: Temple University Press, 1982); Hank Johnston, Enrique Larana, and Joseph R. Gusfield, eds., *New Social Movements: From Ideology to Identity* (Philadelphia: Temple University Press, 1994); Hank Johnston, Enrique Larana, and Bert Klandermans, eds., *Social Movements and Culture: Social Movements, Protest, and Contention* (Minneapolis: University of Minnesota Press, 1995).

2 R.A. Cloward and F.F. Piven, *Poor People's Movements: How They Succeed, Why They Fail* (New York: Pantheon, 1977); Mayer N. Zald and John D. McCarthy, *The Dynamics of Social*

Movements: Resource Mobilization, Social Control and Tactics (Cambridge: Winthrop Publishers, 1979); Mayer Zald and John D. McCarthy, eds., *Social Movements in an Organizational Society* (New Brunswick: Transaction Publishers, 1987); Jo Freeman and Victoria Johnson, eds., *Waves of Protest: Social Movements since the Sixties* (Toronto: Rowman and Littlefield Publishers, 1999); Gerald F. Davis, Doug McAdam, W. Richard Scott, and Mayer N. Zald, eds., *Social Movements and Organization Theory* (New York: Cambridge University Press, 2005).

3 Mayer Zald and John D. McCarthy, "The Future of Social Movements," in *Social Movements in an Organizational Society*, ed. M. Zald and J.D. McCarthy, 29-31 (New Brunswick: Transaction Publishers, 1987); Mayer Zald and John D. McCarthy, "The Trend of Social Movements in America: Professionalization and Resource Mobilization," in *Social Movements in an Organizational Society*, ed. Mayer Zald and John D. McCarthy, 337-91 (New Brunswick: Transaction Publishers, 1987).

4 Zald and McCarthy, "The Future of Social Movements," 323.

5 In the case of the women's movement, Freeman contends that "before any social movement could develop among women, there had to be created a structure to bring potential feminist sympathizers together." See Jo Freeman, "On the Origins of Social Movements," in *Social Movements of the Sixties and Seventies*, ed. J. Freeman (New York and London: Longman, 1983), 2, 18.

6 The major exception to this rule is the rights associations that emerged as a result of the International Year for Human Rights. These are discussed in Chapter 8.

7 Zald and McCarthy, "The Future of Social Movements," 339.

8 Ross, *The House That Jill Built*, 54.

9 Carroll, "Social Movement and Counterhegemony," 161.

10 Miriam Smith, "Interest Groups and Social Movements," in *Canadian Politics in the 21st Century*, ed. M. Whittington and G. Williams (Toronto: Thomson Nelson, 2004), 219-20.

11 Naomi Black, "The Canadian Women's Movement: The Second Wave," in *Changing Patterns: Women in Canada*, ed. S. Burt, L. Code, and L. Dorney, 80-101 (Toronto: McClelland and Stewart, 1993).

12 Magnusson details some of the strategies the Raging Grannies have adopted to promote a culture of pacifism: "Their weapon is as harmless and powerful as the Amnesty letter: song and dance. They perform as a group at peace rallies and other suitable occasions, dressing up in Victorian costumes and singing songs of peace and social protest. At times, they act out their protests theatrically: once they sang their peace songs to an American submarine from a canoe. On another occasion, they rented a caleche, rode up to the gates of the naval base, and asked to put flowers on the guns. On yet another, they journeyed with other peace activists to a small island in Nanoose Bay, north of Victoria, and pelted it with oyster shells, in symbolic protest against the shelling of an unoccupied Hawaiian Island during a Canadian naval exercise." See Warren Magnusson, "Critical Social Movements," in *Canadian Politics: An Introduction to the Discipline*, ed. A.-G. Gagnon and J.P. Bickerton (Peterborough: Broadview Press, 1990), 533.

13 Joseph R. Gusfield, "Social Movements: The Study," in *International Encyclopedia of the Social Sciences*, vol. 14, ed. D. Stills (New York: Macmillan, 1968); Gamson, *The Strategy of Social Protest*; David P. Gillespie, "Conservative Tactics in Social Movement Organizations," in *Social Movements of the Sixties and Seventies*, ed. J. Freeman, 262-76 (New York and London: Longman, 1983); Roberta Ash Garner and Mayer N. Zald, "Social Movement Organizations: Growth, Decay and Change," in *Social Movements in an Organizational Society*, ed. M. Zald and J.D. McCarthy, 293-318 (New Brunswick: Transaction Publishers, 1987); Stephen W. Beach, "Social Movement Radicalization: The Case of Poor People's Democracy in Northern Ireland," *Sociological Quarterly* 3 (Summer 1977): 305-18.

Chapter 5: The BC Civil Liberties Association

1 Statistics on Freedomite activities available in Simma Holt, *Terror in the Name of God: The Story of the Doukhobours* (Toronto: McClelland and Stewart, 1964), 8.

2 The Fraternal Council of the Sons of Freedoms was the leadership council of the sect, a group that provided moral and theocratic guidance.

3 This number does not include the many small chapters formed by various rights associations that only lasted for a few years.

4 A Brief Historical Analysis of the Development of Human Rights and Civil Liberties Associations in Canada, 6 June 1972, Kalmen Kaplansky Papers, LAC, MG 30, A53, vol. 7, f. 3.

5 *Civil Liberties* (published by the Canadian Civil Liberties Association) 2, 1 (August 1970).

6 Ibid., September 1969.

7 There is no evidence to indicate who called the meeting and why, although the initiative is linked to a decision by a group of academics and lawyers to support those Sons of Freedom charged with conspiracy. See Annual General Meeting Minutes and Agendas/Annual Reports, 1963, BCCLA, Law Society of British Columbia Archives (hereafter LSBCA), vol. 3, f. 25.

8 Holt, *Terror in the Name of God,* 269-70.

9 *BC Civil Liberties Newsletter,* 28 February 1963, 6 June 1963, RCMP Papers, LAC, RG 146, vol. 2888.

10 When the NDP was finally elected in 1972 under David Barrett, and until its defeat in 1975, the BCCLA could boast closer ties with the provincial government through its former board members than any other civil liberties group in Canada. Norman Levi held a variety of cabinet posts, including municipal affairs, and Alex McDonald was appointed attorney general. BCCLA revenues jumped from $28,000 in 1971 to $145,000 in 1974. The budget increase was largely due to special projects grants from the federal and provincial governments. See Financial Committee Reports and Statements, 1971-74, BCCLA, LSBCA, vol. 4, f. 17-21.

11 Annual General Meeting Minutes and Agendas/Annual Reports, 1963, BCCLA, LSBCA, vol. 3, f. 5.

12 *Vancouver Sun,* 20 December 1962.

13 *Democratic Commitment* (quarterly newsletter of the BCCLA) 1 (December 1967).

14 Ibid., no. 2, February 1968.

15 Ibid., no. 12, October 1969.

16 The judge held that the bylaw fell under the authority of the Municipal and Health Acts. See BCCLA press release, 1971, LSBCA, BCCLA, vol. 19, f. 8.

17 *Democratic Commitment* 1 (December 1978); (February 1979).

18 A useful overview of censorship in British Columbia throughout the twentieth century may be found on an internet site entitled "Censorship in British Columbia: A History" (http://www.bcpl.gov.bc.ca/bcla/ifc/censorshipbc/intro.html). Most of the incidents documented on the site involve Canada Customs' and the RCMP's seizure of obscene material. In addition, it was not uncommon for school boards and/or individual libraries to ban obscene or offensive material.

19 British Columbia, *Vancouver Charter,* 1953.

20 Mark M. Krotter, "The Censorship of Obscenity in British Columbia: Opinion and Practice," *University of British Columbia Law Review* 1 (1970): 125-27.

21 *Vancouver Sun,* 28 May 1969, 5 June 1969.

22 *National Newsletter* 1, 4 (December 1972).

23 L.A. Powe Jr., "The *Georgia Straight* and Freedom of Expression in Canada," *Canadian Bar Review* 2 (1970): 414; Minutes of the annual general meeting, 1970, LSBCA, BCCLA, vol. 3, f. 16; publicity policy/press releases, 1972-74, LSBCA, BCCLA, vol. 2, f. 19; activities and

function of the BCCLA, 1973-75, LSBCA, BCLLA, vol. 2, f. 1; press release by the BCCLA, 1971, LSBCA, BCLLA, vol. 19, f. 8; Krotter, "Censorship of Obscenity in British Columbia," 127-28.

24 *Democratic Commitment* 13 (February 1970).

25 The regulation read as follows: "No political activity of any kind whatsoever shall be carried out or suffered to be carried out by the Exhibitor within the area of the Exhibition. Without prejudice to the generality of the foregoing, no political party, program, theory, interest or idea of any nature whatsoever, and either of a local, national or international nature, shall be promoted, opposed, protested, or in any way whatsoever publicised or permitted to be publicised by an Exhibitor within the Exhibition area. Partisan activity of all kinds is prohibited." See *Democratic Commitment* 5 (August 1968).

26 BCCLA papers and newspaper coverage only provide partial details on the Pacific National Exhibition affair. Most of the information, including the mediation by Tom Campbell, was covered by the Canadian Broadcasting Corporation's daily television news. See Canadian Broadcasting Corporation, transcripts of daily news coverage, February 13-15, 1969.

27 Canada, 1970. *The Uncertain Mirror: Report of the Special Senate Committee on Mass Media.*

28 Krotter, "Censorship of Obscenity in British Columbia," 125.

29 Jean Barman, *The West beyond the West: A History of British Columbia* (Toronto: University of Toronto Press, 1991), 315.

30 Charles Campbell and Naomi Pauls, *The Georgia Straight: What the Hell Happened?* (Vancouver: Douglas and McIntyre, 1997), 32-33.

31 *Georgia Straight,* "2,000 Issues and Counting," 20-27 April 2006.

32 *Democratic Commitment* 1 (December 1967); Powe, "The *Georgia Straight* and Freedom of Expression in Canada."

33 *Democratic Commitment* 6 (October 1968).

34 Campbell and Pauls, *The Georgia Straight,* 3.

35 Minutes of the annual general meeting, 1970, LSBCA, BCCLA, vol. 3, f. 17; Powe, "The *Georgia Straight* and Freedom of Expression in Canada," 427.

36 Canada, *The Uncertain Mirror.*

37 *The Grape,* 23 May-5 June 1971.

38 Norman Levi, interviewed by author, 25 June 2002.

39 *Regina v. McLeod and Georgia Straight Publishing,* [1970] 73 W.W.R. [Western Weekly Reports] (British Columbia Court of Appeal).

40 Krotter, "Censorship of Obscenity in British Columbia," 136, 51.

41 Canada, *The Uncertain Mirror.*

42 Powe, "The *Georgia Straight* and Freedom of Expression in Canada," 433.

43 *Vancouver Sun,* 14 December 1973.

44 Press releases, War Measures Act, n.d., LSBCA, BCCLA, vol. 19, f. 26.

45 According to an announcement in the *Vancouver Sun,* using statistics from the Audit Bureau of Circulation, the paper sold 233,156 daily issues and had an estimated reading audience of 700,000, twice as many as the next size competitor (in the west) and three times as many as the top-rated television show in Vancouver. See *Vancouver Sun,* 1 October 1970.

46 *Globe and Mail,* 27 October 1970; *Montreal Star,* 20 October 1970; *Vancouver Sun,* 26 October 1970.

47 Peter Birdsall and Delores Broten, *Mind War: Book Censorship in English Canada* (Victoria: CANLIT, 1978).

48 *Democratic Commitment* 17 (April 1971).

49 *Vancouver Sun,* 20 October 1970.

50 The regulation read as follows: "That it is declared as public policy that no person teaching or instructing our youth in educational institutions receiving Government support shall continue in the employment of the educational institution if they advocate the policies of Le

Front de Liberation du Quebec, or the overthrow of democratically elected governments by violent means." See *Jamieson et al. v. Attorney General of British Columbia*, [1971] 5 W.W.R. 600 (British Columbia Supreme Court).

51 It was also around this time that Ronald Kirby, a philosophy professor at the University of Victoria, issued a press release supporting the FLQ and blaming Trudeau for Laporte's murder. See *Montreal Star*, 22 October 1970; *Vancouver Sun*, 22-23 October 1970.

52 *Vancouver Sun*, 24 October 1970; *Province*, 24 October 1970.

53 *Jamieson et al. v. Attorney General of British Columbia*.

54 *Democratic Commitment* 18 (July 1971).

55 AGM Minutes and Agendas, 1970, LSBCA, BCCLA, vol. 3, f. 16.

56 Minutes of the Board of Directors, 16 April 1976, LSBCA, BCCLA, vol. 1, f. 5.

57 British Columbia, 1971, *Report on the Gastown Riot*.

58 *Vancouver Sun*, 9 August 1971.

59 *Vancouver Sun*, 12 August 1971.

60 *Province*, 10 August 1971.

61 *Vancouver Sun*, 8 August 1971.

62 *Province*, 13 August 1971.

63 *Vancouver Sun*, 2 October 1971.

64 In a letter to the editor, the president of the BCCLA, Reg Robson, noted that the BCCLA's position was "that [the Gastown Riot] must be viewed in the context of the overall relationship between our police forces and the wider community they serve." See the *Province*, 14 August 1971.

65 Court cases, re "Police, Gastown Riots, the Police, and the Community: Implications of the Report of the Commission of Inquiry by Mr. Justice Dohm," December 1971, LSBCA, BCCLA, vol. 17, f. 2.

66 Columbia, *Report on the Gastown Riot*.

67 *Province*, 8 October 1971.

68 *Vancouver Sun*, 7 October 1971.

69 *Democratic Commitment* 10 (February 1976).

70 P.J. Giffen, Shirley Endicott, and Sylvia Lambert, *Panic and Indifference: The Politics of Canada's Drug Laws* (Ottawa: Canadian Centre on Substance Abuse, 1991), 359, 89.

71 One reason for not proclaiming Part 2 was the legislation's questionable constitutionality. Part 2 could have been challenged as a law providing for health care, a provincial responsibility. See Giffen, Endicott, and Lambert, *Panic and Indifference*, 396.

72 Giffen, Endicott, and Lambert, *Panic and Indifference*, 495.

73 Canada, 1973, *Final Report of the Commission of Inquiry into the Non-Medical Use of Drugs* (hereafter LeDain Inquiry).

74 Fearing such a move would convince people the drug was safe, another minority report, this one by Ian Campbell, recommended a fine for possession of cannabis. Campbell was convinced that cannabis should continue to be criminalized. See Canada, LeDain Inquiry.

75 Marcel Martel, *Not This Time: Canadians: Public Policy and the Marijuana Question, 1961-1975* (Toronto: University of Toronto Press, 2006).

76 *Vancouver Sun*, 30 October 1960, 21 November 1970.

77 Press Releases (1969-74), letter to Hon. John C. Monroe from the BCCLA, 13 August 1969, LSBCA, BCCLA, vol. 19, f. 28.

78 Reg Robson to Alex MacDonald, 6 December 1973, LSBCA, BCCLA, vol. 18, f. 6, Summary Conviction Act (1973-8).

79 British Columbia, Heroin Treatment Act, 1979.

80 Heroin Treatment Act – Reasons for Judgement (1979) – copy of brief by BCCLA in appeals case on HTA, June 1979, LSBCA, BCCLA, vol. 18, f. 17.

81 British Columbia, *Debates of the Legislative Assembly,* 1978, 2284.

82 Ibid., 2250.

83 Ibid., 2276.

84 Ibid., 2286.

85 Ibid., 2258-60.

86 *Vancouver Sun,* 15 June 1978.

87 The Social Credit government introduced extensive cuts to its human rights program soon after returning to power. Funding to groups like the BCCLA was eliminated, and the staff and resources of the Human Rights Commission were reduced. The Human Rights Act remained intact until 1984, when the Social Credit government removed the "reasonable cause" section (introduced by the NDP), which had allowed for a more expansive application of the legislation. See Warner, *A History of Queer Activism in Canada,* 154.

88 British Columbia, *Debates of the Legislative Assembly,* 1978, 2258-60, 2270, 2701; *Vancouver Sun,* 19 June 1978.

89 There was no doubt about the validity of the federal law. In *R. v. Hauser* the Supreme Court upheld the Narcotic Control Act under Parliament's residual powers. See *R. v. Hauser,* [1979] S.C.R. 984.

90 *Schneider v. R.* (1980), 37 B.C.L.R. (British Columbia High Court).

91 *Schneider v. R.* (1981), 22 B.C.L.R (British Columbia Appeals Court).

92 Financial Committee Reports and Statements, 1971-82, LSBCA, BCCLA, vol. 4, f. 1-21.

93 Ibid.

94 Local Initiatives Project – Community Information Project (May 1974), Report to the Board (December 1974) and list of inquiries for 1974, LSBCA, BCCLA, vol. 16, f. 16-17.

95 The recommended amendment read as follows: "All public schools shall be conducted on strictly secular and non-sectarian principles. No religious dogma or creed shall be taught, and no religious practices shall be observed. Nothing in this section shall be interpreted to prohibit the academic study of religion in all its aspects wherever it is appropriate within the school curriculum." See Religion in Public Schools, 1968-73, LSBCA, BCCLA, vol. 11, f. 41.

96 Letter from J.A. Spragg (BCFT) to Vaughan Lyon (United Church), 11 August 1958, Records of the British Columbia Teachers' Federation.

97 British Columbia Teachers Federation, "Religious Exercises in Schools: Consultative Committee Report, 1964," Records of the British Columbia Teachers' Federation.

98 British Columbia Teachers Federation, "Report of the Committee on Religious Education in Public Schools," compiled by A.P. Hewett, Gordon Inglis, and D.G. Steeves, 5 December 1968, Records of the British Columbia Teachers' Federation.

99 Religion in Public Schools, 1968-73, letter from British Columbia Teachers Federation to Hardin, 5 March 1969, LSBCA, BCCLA, vol. 11, f. 41.

100 *Democratic Commitment* 1 (February 1981).

101 By 1974, the group was receiving four thousand calls per year, and, in 1975, it received five thousand calls to the head office. Field workers in 1975 received seven thousand calls, although not all of these inquiries dealt with civil liberties issues. See *Democratic Commitment* 30 (February 1974); 1 (February 1975).

102 *Vancouver Sun,* 20 December 1962.

103 Court cases re. Police/Schuck, correspondence between BCCLA and lawyer Marvin Starrow, LSBCA, BCCLA, vol. 17, f. 7.

104 Legal Defence Fund Expenditures (1979-83), LSBCA, BCCLA, vol. 18, f. 19.

105 Phil Bryden, "Public Interest Intervention before the Courts," in *Liberties,* ed. J. Russell, 81-99 (Vancouver: New Star Books, 1989).

106 *Jamieson et al. v. Attorney General of British Columbia.*

107 Levi, interview.

108 Annual Reports, 1968, LSBCA, BCCLA, vol. 3, f. 19.
109 Reg Robson to Alan Borovoy, 7 August 1970, CCLA, LAC, R9833, vol. 4, f. 2.
110 *Democratic Commitment* 18 (July 1971).
111 Apart from representatives of the Regina and Winnipeg chapters, the CCLA Board of Directors had only two members from western Canada.
112 Hugh Keenleyside to Eleanor Meslin, 25 May 1973, LSBCA, BCCLA, vol. 1, f. 25.
113 *Democratic Commitment* 30 (February 1974).
114 Ibid., no. 1, February 1976.
115 The position papers discussed in this section are all available at Position Papers, LSBCA, BCCLA, vols. 8-12. The BCCLA's position papers are also available online at http://www.bccla.org.
116 William Black, interviewed by author, 20 June 2002.
117 The following is a breakdown of habitual criminal convictions by 1968: Nova Scotia 6, Quebec 7, Ontario 16, Manitoba 14, Saskatchewan 6, Alberta 13, and British Columbia 75.
118 John Dixon, "The Porn Wars," in *Liberties*, ed. J. Russell, 24-29 (Vancouver: New Star Books, 1989), 26.
119 John Russell, interviewed by author, 23 December 2004.
120 In 1969, the BCCLA and the British Columbia Federation of Labour were vocal critics of the provincial Human Rights Act. Ten years later, the BCCLA and numerous women's groups called for the resignation of the members of the provincial human rights commission, who were considered ineffective and ignorant of the province's human rights legislation (*Vancouver Sun*, 21 April 1979). For further examples of issues linking the BCCLA with other social movement organizations, see Dominique Clément, "An Exercise in Futility? Regionalism, State Funding and Ideology as Obstacles to the Formation of a National Social Movement Organization in Canada," *BC Studies* 146 (Summer 2005): 63-91.
121 Walker, "The 'Jewish Phase' in the Movement for Racial Equality in Canada."

Chapter 6: La Ligue des droits de l'homme

1 The founding members discussed the possibility of developing a national infrastructure. There were plans to open an office in Toronto and Quebec City, and the Law Society of Manitoba requested affiliation. None of the branches, however, ever materialized. Minutes of founding meeting of the LDH, 29 May 1963, Frank Scott Papers, LAC, MG 30, D211, vol. 46; Letter to Jean Louis Gagnon (no author), May 1963, Université du Québec à Montréal (hereafter UQAM), Service des archives et de gestion des documents (hereafter SAGD), Fond Ligue des droits et libertés (hereafter LDL), 24P4c/3; *Globe and Mail*, 15 February 1963.
2 Minutes of the administrative council, 7 February 1966, UQAM, SAGD, LDL, 24P1/5.
3 Lambertson, *Repression and Resistance*, 246.
4 Minutes of the administrative council, 19 January 1967, UQAM, SAGD, LDL, 24P1/5.
5 *Dans la province de Quebec, quatorze mille causes attendent la justice*, report written by George Wesley on judicial reform, 1962, UQAM, SAGD, LDL, 24P6b/1.
6 Québec, Commission d'enquête sur l'administration de la justice en matière criminelle et pénal au Québec, 1968, *La société face au crime*.
7 Mémoire de la Ligue des droits de l'homme, 18 May 1967, Archives Nationales du Québec, Fonds de la Commission d'enquête sur l'administration de la justice en matière criminelle et pénale, E142, f. 1960-01-521.
8 Letter from professors at McGill's forensic psychiatric institute to Guy Favreau, 31 May 1965, UQAM, SAGD, LDL, 24P9d/6.
9 *Face à la justice* 4, 6 (November-December 1981); Lucien Cardin to Joseph Cohen, 4 November 1965, UQAM, SAGD, LDL, 24P9d/6; E.W. Kenrick to L.T. Pennell, 22 March 1966, UQAM, SAGD, LDL, 24Pd/6.

10 Letter from Jacques Hébert to LDL members, 12 March 1964, UQAM, SAGD, LDL, 24P2a/4.
11 Conference resolution on a human rights act for Quebec, 2 December 1972, LAC, JLC, MG 28, V75, vol. 38, f. 1.
12 *Montreal Star*, 26 May 1970.
13 Discours pronounce par Michael Rubinstein, à la conférence provinciale pour un code des droits de l'homme tenue à Montréal, 2 December 1972, LAC, JLC, MG 28, V75, vol. 38, f. 1.
14 When the LDH confronted Chôquette about his 1970 promise to introduce a bill of rights, he refused to do so until after the Gendron commission submitted its report. According to the minutes of the meetings of the LDH's administrative council, Scott was among those who, for political reasons, accepted the need to delay the introduction of a bill of rights due to the explosive potential of the language issue. See minutes of the administrative council, 5 April 1972, UQAM, SAGD, LDL, 24P1/8.
15 Minutes of the administrative council, 8 February 1968, UQAM, SAGD, LDL, 24P1/5.
16 International Year for Human Rights working paper by Claude Forget, 2-3 November 1968, Canadian Labour Congress Papers, LAC, MG 38, I103, vol. 648, f. 1; Minutes of the administrative council, 13 March 1969, UQAM, SAGD, LDL, 24P1/5.
17 Jean-Francois Cardin provides a comprehensive summary of the FLQ's attacks and bombings. See Jean-François Cardin, *Comprendre octobre 1970: Le FLQ, la crise et le syndicalisme* (Montréal: Éditions du Méridien, 1990), app. 2. Also see Louis Fournier, *FLQ: The Anatomy of an Underground Movement* (Toronto: NC Press, 1984), chaps. 9-12.
18 Pierre Vallières, *White Niggers of America* (Toronto: McClelland and Stewart, 1971), 21.
19 Fournier, *FLQ*, 44.
20 *Globe and Mail*, 2 April 1969; *Le Devoir*, 2 April 1969; Fournier, *FLQ*, 150-53.
21 Fournier, *FLQ*, 221-22.
22 Bernard Dagenais, *La crise d'octobre et les médias: Le miroir à dix faces* (Outremont: VLB Éditeur, 1990), 69.
23 In fact, three days later, the cabinet discussed the possibility of having police officers stationed at every radio and television station to prevent the press from "mishandling" any information related to the crisis. See Privy Council Office, LAC, RG 2, series A-5-a, vol. 6359, 15 October 1970, 18 October 1970.
24 Privy Council Office, LAC, RG 2, series A-5-a, vol. 6359, 15 October 1970, 18 October 1970.
25 In an interview with CBC in 1975, Bourassa admitted that he never truly believed an actual insurrection was at hand but that he had used that specific language to provide an incentive and justification for the federal government to use the War Measures Act. See Mannon Leroux, *Les silences d'octobre: Le discours des acteurs de la crise de 1970* (Montréal: VLB Éditeur, 2002), 74-75.
26 Cardin, *Comprendre octobre 1970*, 94; Dagenais, *La crise d'octobre et les médias,* 141; *Evening Telegram,* 19 October 1970; *Globe and Mail,* 20 October 1970; *Vancouver Sun,* 19 October 1970.
27 Cardin, *Comprendre octobre 1970*, 126-27.
28 *Globe and Mail*, 27 October 2005; Éric Bédard, *Chronique d'une insurection appréhendée: Le crise d'octobre et le milieu universitaire* (Sillery: Les Éditions du Septentrion, 1998), 125, 34-38.
29 UQAM remained closed until 21 October 1970. Éric Bédard provides a detailed examination of student protest during the crisis in Bédard, *Chronique d'une insurection appréhendée.*
30 Among those arrested were separatists and people active in organizations of the left, including leftists elements within the Parti québécois, Comité d'action politique, Mouvement pour la défense des prisonniers politiques du Québec, Front d'action politique, and others. Approximately 20 to 30 percent of those arrested were militant unionists. See Cardin, *Comprendre octobre 1970,* 81-82.

31 Canada, *Hansard Parliamentary Debates,* vol. 3, 3 February 1971, 3034; Berger, *Fragile Freedoms,* 209.

32 Berger, *Fragile Freedoms,* 209.

33 *Les orders,* directed by Michel Brault, was released in 1974. The film is based on testimony from people detained under the War Measures Act and explores the experiences of the people who were arrested and imprisoned but never charged.

34 J.N. Lyon, "Constitutional Validity of Sections 3 and 4 of the Public Order Regulations, 1970," *McGill Law Journal* 1 (1972): 140.

35 The use of the War Measures Act was challenged (unsuccessfully) in court (*Gagnon and Vallières v. The Queen* (1971), 14 C.R.N.S. 321). Herbert Marx provides a fuller discussion of the legal ramifications of the use of emergency legislation in Herbert Marx, "The 'Apprehended Insurrection' of October 1970 and the Judicial Function," *UBC Law Review* 1 (1972): 55-69.

36 *Globe and Mail,* 19 October 1970.

37 *Varsity,* 16 October 1995 ("25 Years after the October Crisis"); Submission to the Honourable John Turner, Minister of Justice, Re. Emergency Powers, 29 March 1971, Canadian Civil Liberties Association Papers (hereafter CCLA), LAC, R9833.

38 Submissions to the Commission of Inquiry Concerning Certain Activities of the Royal Canadian Mounted Police re Emergency Powers and the War Measures Act, 3 October 1979, CCLA, LAC, R9833, vol. 19, f. 6; Alan Borovoy to A. Neler, 26 October 1970, CCLA, LAC, R9833, vol. 123, f. 3.

39 *Globe and Mail,* 27 October 2005 ("Former Editor Recalls Frightening Fight for Liberty").

40 Bédard, *Chronique d'une insurection appréhendée,* 118-19.

41 Daniel LaTouche, "Mass Media and Communication in a Canadian Political Crisis," in *Communications in Canadian Society* (Don Mills: Addison-Wesley Publishers, 1983), 202-3; Dagenais, *La crise d'octobre et les médias,* 163.

42 Guy Lachapelle, "The Editorial Position of *Le Devoir* during the October Crisis," *Quebec Studies* 1 (1990/91): 5.

43 Lachapelle, "Editorial Position of *Le Devoir,*" 5; Raphael Cohen-Almagor, "The Terrorists' Best Ally: The Quebec Media Coverage of the FLQ Crisis in October 1970," *Canadian Journal of Communication* 2 (2000): 251-84.

44 Canada, *Hansard Parliamentary Debates,* vol. 1, 4 November 1970, 873.

45 Ibid., vol. 4, 3 March 1971, 3906.

46 Dagenais, *La crise d'octobre et les médias,* 164.

47 Ibid., 151-52.

48 Dagenais, *La crise d'octobre et les médias,* 29-31.

49 Cohen-Almagor is emphatic that the Quebec media, particularly CKLM and CKAC, acted irresponsibly: "I have studied the relationships between terrorism and the media for many years and cannot think of a better example of irresponsible media behaviour ... Journalists broke almost every ethical norm that is accepted during hostage taking episodes." He, as well as Arthur Siegel, argues that most of the print and radio media in Quebec were sympathetic to the FLQ's objectives until the death of Pierre Laporte. See Cohen-Almagor, "The Terrorists' Best Ally," 275; Arthur Siegel, *Politics and the Media in Canada* (Toronto: McGraw-Hill Ryerson Limited, 1983), 223-31.

50 Siegel, *Politics and the Media in Canada,* 224.

51 In the words of Michel Roy, assistant editor-in-chief of *Le Devoir,* this "auto-censure ... des organismes, des entreprises de presse, par souci d'équilibre et par crainte d'être mal jugés par les pouvoirs politiques et les divers pouvoirs publics; par crainte d'indisposer ce public qui en grande majorité est acquis aux politiques du gouvernement parce qu'il a peur, parce que l'insécurité le rapproche du pouvoir." See Dagenais, *La crise d'octobre et les médias: Le miroir à dix faces,* 164.

52 Bédard, *Chronique d'une insurection appréhendée*, 122-23.
53 *La Presse,* 27 October 1970; Presentation du Comité québécois pour la défense des libertés, n.d., CCLA, LAC, R9833, vol. 123, f. 3; N. Cloutier, T. Daly, and R. Spry, *Action: The October Crisis of 1970* (Montreal: National Film Board, 1974). Bédard, *Chronique d'une insurection appréhendée,* 138; People's Democratic Rights Committee, protests and demonstrations (Quebec), 9 February 1971, Royal Canadian Mounted Police Papers, LAC, RG 146, vol. 2991.
54 *La Presse,* 27 October 1970.
55 Fournier, *FLQ,* 203.
56 Presentation du Comité québécois des liberté, n.d., CCLA, LAC, R9833, vol. 123, f. 3; Citizens Commission of Inquiry into the War Measures Act, press release, 16 April 1971, CCLA, LAC, R9833, vol. 6, f. 23; Fournier, *FLQ,* 203; Dagenais, *La crise d'octobre et les médias,* 163.
57 *St. Catharines Standard,* 3 November 1970; *Niagara Falls Review,* 11 November 1970; Peninsula Civil Rights Committee, surveillance report, 11 November 1970, Royal Canadian Mounted Police Papers, LAC, RG 146, vol. 3439.
58 Another press release on 1 April 1971, however, reiterated the LDH's position that the government had an obligation to protect itself. Press releases for 19 October 1970, 11 November 1970, and 1 April 1971, Frank Scott Papers, LAC, MG 30, D211, vol. 46.
59 It is interesting to note that the BCCLA, in its official declaration on the crisis, did not call for the total revocation of the War Measures Act but, rather, only that the abuse of civil liberties be kept to a minimum. Letter from the BCCLA to Pierre Elliott Trudeau, 23 October 1970, LAC, CCLA, R9833, vol. 123, f. 3.
60 Guy Lachapelle, *Claude Ryan et la violence du pouvoir: Le Devoir et la crise d'octobre 1970 ou le combat de journalistes démocrates* (Sainte-Foy: Presses de l'Université Laval, 2005), 120-21.
61 Sandra Djwa, *The Politics of Imagination: The Life of F.R. Scott* (Toronto: McClelland and Stewart, 1987), 417.
62 Most of this money went to support families with members in jail. See Rapport final du Comité d'aide aux personnes arrêtés en vertue des lois d'urgence, de la LDH, 1971, Frank Scott Papers, LAC, MG 30, D211, vol. 46.
63 Investigation report, 18 December 1970, Royal Canadian Mounted Police Papers, LAC, RG 146, vol. 2888.
64 *Montreal Star,* 23 December 1970.
65 For a reading list on the October Crisis, visit http://www.HistoryOfRights.com/sources.html.
66 Maloney, "A Mere Rustle of Leaves," 82.
67 Minutes of the Undersecretary of State's Advisory Committee on Human Rights, 25 January 1971, UQAM, SAGD, LDL, 24P2b/14.
68 At one point during the standoff, an agitated Frank Scott, walking with a cane and screaming at the protestors, forced his way past the armed men to reach Hébert in his office. Hébert described the incident in an interview a few years later: "He came in, right in, and there was this Reggie Chartrand and the other bouncers that were there with big sticks and he was pushing them around. They allowed it because he was Frank Scott. You know? They couldn't hit him on the head. So he came into the office and he was shouting 'Get out of my way. Who said that I won't get into this place? ... He was raging mad with his cane, tearing apart the signs in front of bouncers with big sticks and he didn't care ... God, he is a man of courage. He just came to comfort me and to make sure that I was okay. That I didn't need anything. And to say that he was solidaire with me and that I could count on him." See Djwa, *The Politics of Imagination,* 417-18.
69 Kerwin, interview.
70 Djwa, *The Politics of Imagination,* 416.
71 As quoted in an article appearing in the *Montreal Gazette,* 5 April 1971.

72 *Montreal Gazette,* 5 April 1971.
73 Civil Liberties and Human Rights Associations, Report on Voluntary Organizations by Gilles Thériault and Michael Swinwood, 10 March 1972, LAC, CCLA, R9833, vol. 4, f. 3.
74 Transcripts of interview with Pierre Trudeau on CBC television show *Weekend,* 16 May 1970, UQAM, SAGD, LDL, 24P6/2.
75 Pierre Trudeau to Pierre Jasmin, 13 July 1971, Frank Scott Papers, LAC, MG 30, D211, vol. 47.
76 Mémoire au conseil administration sur l'état de la ligue, 5 April 1984, UQAM, SAGD, LDL, 24P6f/4.
77 Ligue des droits de l'homme, *Les droits de l'homme dans la société actuelle: Manifeste* (Montréal: Ligue des droits de l'homme, 1972).
78 Kenneth McRoberts, *Quebec: Social Change and Political Crisis* (Don Mills: Oxford University Press, 1993), 173.
79 Curriculum vitae of Maurice Champagne, UQAM, SAGD, LDL, 24P2a/12.
80 Les québécois ont le droit de survivre: Position de la Ligue sur les droits linguistiques au Québec, 26 May 1974, UQAM, SAGD, LDL, 24P6g/1.
81 Transformation or Repeal of Bill 22, 27 May 1974, UQAM, SAGD, LDL, 246g/1.
82 La negation du droit à l'autodetermination dans la campagne electorale: Declaration spéciale du conseil d'administration de la Ligue des droits le l'homme, 13 October 1972, UQAM, SAGD, LDL, 24P6q/1.
83 Minutes of the administrative council, 30 May 1974, UQAM, SAGD, LDL, 24P1/10.
84 *Le Jour,* 27 June 1975.
85 Raymond Boyer had his own encounter with injustice, which may have encouraged his interest in joining a rights association. In 1946, he was one of the suspects arrested and held incommunicado in the Rockliffe Barracks by the espionage commission; he was convicted and sentenced to two years in jail for conspiracy to violate the Official Secrets Act. See Office des droits des détenus, LDH Statutes, 1973, UQAM, SAGD, LDL, 24P9a/1.
86 Most of the group's early work dealt with individual cases. With about two hundred separate dossiers per year, the group would receive complaints from prisoners and, in turn, contact the officer in charge, send a letter to the institution, or call for an injunction or court hearing with regard to a particular case. These usually involved illegal transfers, lack of medical treatment, segregation, or abuse of power by parole officers. There was also an educational aspect to its work, through press conferences and working with the media. See *Face à la justice* 4, 6 (November-December 1981); Summary of LDH activities, UQAM, SAGD, LDL, 24P9a/19.
87 *Face à la justice* 1, 2 (March-April 1978).
88 Jean-Claude Bernheim, interviewed by author, 26 June 2005.
89 Declaration of inmates at Parthenais during a hunger strike, 9 July 1974, UQAM, SAGD, LDL, 24P9d/4.
90 Ligue des droits de l'homme, *La première des lois au Québec: La charte et la Commission québécois des droits de l'homme* (Montréal: n.p., 1974).
91 The process by which the LDH stimulated a widespread public debate over the bill of rights is detailed in Ligue des droits de l'homme, *La première des lois au Québec.*
92 Programme d'animation sur le projet de charte et de commission québécois des droits de l'homme, October 1973, UQAM, SAGD, LDL, 24P1/8.
93 The proposed Article 5 in the LDH draft read as follows: "Les rapports qui s'établisse dans la société québécois entre les personnes, les groupes, les organismes et les pouvoirs publics, constituent l'une des principales conditions d'exercice des droits individuels et collectifs." See Ligue des droits de l'homme, Mémoire de la Ligue des droits de l'homme à la Commission parlementaire de la justice sur la loi project de loi 50 (Montréal: Ligue des droits de l'homme, 1975).

94 "Pourquoi une charte québécois des droits de l'homme?" speech by Chôquette before the CJC, 31 March 1974, UQAM, SAGD, LDL, 24P12/8.

95 Québec, *Journal des débats*, vol. 15, no. 1, 1974, p. 1.

96 Bilan de Maurice Champagne, sur ses trois années à la Ligue des droits à titre de directeur général, présenté à l'occasion de l'assemblée général annuelle des membres du 28 mai 1975, Frank Scott Papers, LAC, MG 30, D211, vol. 47.

97 *Le Devoir*, 12 November 1998; *Le Devoir*, 17 June 2000; Conference of Human Rights Ministers, 7-8 November 1974, Walter S. Tarnopolsky Papers, LAC, MG 31, E55, vol. 31, f. 14.

98 Québec, *Journal des débats*, vol. 15, no. 71, 1974, pp. 2755, 2761, 2822.

99 Ligue des droits de l'homme, Mémoire de la Ligue des droits de l'homme à la Commission parlementaire de la justice sur la loi project de loi 50 (Montréal: Ligue des droits de l'homme, 1975).

100 In 1982 the Charter would be amended to apply to all laws in Quebec.

101 Mémoire au conseil administrative sur: L'état de la Ligue, 5 April 1984, UQAM, SAGD, LDL Papers, 24P6f/4.

102 Minutes of the administrative council, 7 November 1978, UQAM, SAGD, LDL, 24P1/14; "Les droits et libertés sur la Côte Nord: Recherche action presentée par le Comité régional Côte Nord de la Ligue des droits et libertés," 1979, SAGD, LDL, 24P3/4.

103 *Opération liberté* 1, 1 (1978).

104 "Mounting Repression: Its Meaning and Importance in Canada and Quebec," UQAM, SAGD, LDL, 24P6k/23.

105 Mémoire au conseil administrative sur: L'état de la Ligue, 5 April 1984, UQAM, SAGD, LDL, 24P9f/4.

106 In his May 1979 letter of resignation as a member of the staff, Jocelyn Lauzon noted the "absences de leadership au sein du conseil d'administration, la démobilisation de certains de ses membres (démissions, absences aux réunions, etc) et sans doute aussi l'incomprehension des rôles et fonctions de certains membres de la permanence, ont amené à la Ligue et ce progressivement, une lourdeur de fonctionnement et les problèmes qui y sont inhérents." See Jocelyn Lauzon, letter of resignation, 29 May 1979, UQAM, SAGD, LDL, 24P1/15.

107 Letter from the LDL union of employees to the administrative council, 21 February 1979, UQAM, SAGD, LDL, 24P1/15; Minutes of the annual general meeting, 27 September 1980, 24P1/38.

108 Letters of resignation by Elizabeth Roussel and André Legault, 25 February 1980, UQAM, SAGD, LDL, 24P1/16. The LDH's problems were highlighted in a 1980 proposal by Marianne Roy, president of the ODD, that the LDH transform itself into a federation. According to Roy, the committees would form the membership and leadership of the organization and have their own budgets and staff. Her proposal was successfully opposed by staff members, who pointed out that such a system would result in each of the eleven committees making separate applications for funds to government agencies, with little coordination or direction. Despite this apparent victory for unity, the Ligue was wounded by the departure of its recently formed disability rights committee. Frustrated with the association's inability to act and its sinking budget, which was taking the committee's finances with it, the committee formally dissociated itself from the LDH in February 1980 and became an independent organization. See LDL: Une fédération ou un mouvement?, 1980, UQAM, SAGD, LDL, 24P4c/6; Letter from the disability rights committee to the administrative council, 10 February 1980, UQAM, SAGD, LDL, 24P1/16.

109 *Face à la justice*, 4, 6 (November-December 1981); Hélène Dumont to Rod Blaker, 24 March 1975, UQAM, SAGD, LDL, 24P9b/7.

110 *Globe and Mail*, 24 March 1984, 2 April 1984; Bernheim, interview.

111 Une affrontment qui ne doit pas perdurer: A declaration from the staff of the Ligue des droits et libertés, n.d., Archives nationale du Québec, fonds Ligue des droits de l'homme, f.S7, SS6, D2/1.

112 Ligue des droits de l'homme, Mémoire de la Ligue des droits de l'homme à la Commission parlementaire sur le project de loi de la protection de la jeunesse (Montréal: Ligue des droits de l'homme, 1973). Legislation dealing with youth crime had been introduced in 1972 and 1975. In both cases, some of the concerns raised by the LDH included access to legal counsel, informing youths under arrest of the charges, offering lawyers to youths brought before tribunals, and providing youths with greater access to education. See Québec, *Journal des débats*, no. 184, 1975, B-6316.

113 Letter from Frank Scott to Maurice Champagne, 30 May 1972, Frank Scott Papers, LAC, MG 30, D211, vol. 47.

114 *Le Devoir*, 17 March 1972.

115 Letter from Frank Scott to Tarnopolsky, 30 January 1976, Walter Tarnopolsky Papers, LAC, vol. 14, f.5.

116 Statement of revenue for LDH, 1964, Frank Scott Papers, LAC, MG 30, D211, vol. 46.

117 Minutes of the administrative council, 12 November 1970, UQAM, SAGD, LDL, 24P1/6.

118 Financial statements of the LDH, 31 December 1973, 31 December 1974, 31 December 1975, UQAM, SAGD, LDL, 24P5/12.

119 The files of the LDH provide little information on the group memberships. However, in 1974, a short list of some of these group members was mentioned at the annual meeting. The following groups were included in this list: Société Saint-Jean-Baptiste; l'Association du Québec pour les déficients mentaux; Conseil des syndicats nationaux; Association des enseignements secondaire; Association des chefs de police et pompiers de la province du Québec; Mouvement national des québécois; Fédérations des médecins omnipraticiens du Québec; Centre international de criminologie comparée; Association des institutions de niveux pré-scolaire et élémentaire du Québec. See minutes of the annual general meeting, 22 February 1974, UQAM, SAGD, LDL, 24P1/32.

120 *National Bulletin/Bulletin nationale* 3, 2 (March 1974). Pierre Landreville, Astrid Gagnon and Serge Desrosiers, *Les prisons par ici: Droits des détenus au Québec* (Montréal: Editions Parti-Pris, 1976).

121 *Face à la justice* 4, 6 (November-December 1981).

122 LDH Press release, 25 November 1976, UQAM, SAGD, LDL, 24P5/2; Minutes of the administrative council, 13 October 1973, 24P1/9.

123 Minutes of the administrative council, 18 August 1980, UQAM, SAGD, LDL, 24P1/16.

124 Press release, 10 May 1984, UQAM, SAGD, LDL, 24P9f/4.

125 Bernheim, interview.

126 Minutes of the administrative council, 30 June 1970, UQAM, SAGD, LDL, 24P1/5.

127 Minutes of the administrative council, 23 April 1970, UQAM, SAGD, LDL, 24P1/5.

128 The Federation spoke on behalf of the LDH on the most important rights issue of the period – the creation of a constitutional bill of rights – although the fact that the Charter was designed to counter the language policies the LDH favoured undoubtedly discouraged the organization from becoming involved in the consultation process.

129 Minutes of the administrative council, 5 December 1977, UQAM, SAGD, LDL, 24P1/13.

130 Minutes of the administrative council, 5 December 1977, UQAM, SAGD, LDL, 24P1/13.

131 *Le Devoir*, 12 November 1998.

132 Ibid.

133 Letter from Maurice Champagne to participants of the Sunday on youth rights, 14 December 1975, UQAM, SAGD, LDL, 24P6c/4.

134 Québec, *Journal des débats*, vol. 19, no. 123, 1977, p. 4324.

Chapter 7: The Canadian Civil Liberties Association

1 The key theme in the Toronto coverage was the decision to strip all the women and only a few of the men. Images of women being stripped and subjected to invasive searches made for sensational headlines throughout May to August. Among the papers that covered the raid and the subsequent inquiry between July and August 1974 were the *Fort Erie Times Review,* the *St. Catharines Standard,* the *Simcoe Reformer,* the *Chronicle Journal,* the *Peterborough Examiner,* the *Intelligencer* (Belleville), the *Moncton Transcript,* the *Hamilton Spectator,* the *Brantford Expositor,* and the *Montreal Star.*

2 Ontario, *Official Reports,* vol. 58, 1797.

3 Tarnopolsky, *The Canadian Bill of Rights,* 57-58.

4 It is interesting to note that the 2,230-page report of the Ontario Police Commission, upon which the legislation was supposedly based, did not call for as invasive a piece of legislation as was presented by Cass to the legislature. Notably, it was Cass's department that decided to deny bail, counsel, and the right to appeal. See *Toronto Star,* 20 March 1964.

5 Ontario, *Official Reports,* vol. 82, 2616-23.

6 Harry Arthurs, interviewed by author, 13 March 2004; Joint Submission of the Canadian Civil Liberties Association and the Canadian Civil Liberties Education Trust to the Ford Foundation for a Grant-In-Aid of an Ongoing Programme in the Field of Civil Liberties and for Special Assistance for "Due Process in Canadian Criminal Law: A Programme for Reform," circa 1968, June Callwood Papers, LAC, MG 31, K24, vol. 18, f. 16.

7 *Re. Drummond Wren* (1945), O.R. 778 (Ontario High Court). Himel recruited Mackay himself, having already established a working relationship with the former lieutenant-governor by 1964. Arthurs, interview.

8 *Globe and Mail,* 8 January 1965.

9 The letter is not dated, but another source, a report written for the Secretary of State in 1972, claims the request was made in 1966. Judy LeMarsh to Sidney B. Linden, n.d., Secretary of State Papers, LAC, RG 6, vol. 661, f. 2-4-7; Civil Liberties and Human Rights Associations: Report on Voluntary Organizations by Gilles Thériault and Michael Swinwood, 10 March 1972, LAC, CCLA, R9833, vol. 4, f. 3; Secretary of State grants, citizenship development, 1970-71, Secretary of State Papers, LAC, RG 6, acc. 86-87/319, f. 4-15-1.

10 Minutes of the executive committee, 3 October 1967, LAC, CCLA, R9833, vol. 2, f. 11.

11 Some of the CCLA's former members have suggested that one reason Himel was asked to resign from his position as chair of the Board of Directors was because of his desire to focus on discrimination issues, notably anti-semitism. Discrimination campaigns clashed with the desire of the new members of the association to focus on free speech and other fundamental freedoms, such as freedom of religion and association. Organizing and directing the new association fell into the hands of Doris Dodds and, later, Sydney Midanik, until Alan Borovoy arrived in 1968. Arthurs, interview; Borovoy, interview.

12 Public letter and press release from CCLA to Police Commission on Metropolitan Toronto, 21 January 1965, June Callwood Papers, LAC, MG 31, K24, vol. 18, f. 3.

13 Submission of the Canadian Civil Liberties Association to the Royal Commission on Civil Rights, 30 April 1965, June Callwood Papers, LAC, MG 31, K24, vol. 18, f. 15.

14 *Civil Liberties* 1, 2 (1965); *Cameron v. R.* (1965), 62 D.L.R. (Supreme Court of Canada).

15 D.J. Dodds and Julian Porter to Chairman Charles O. Bick, 5 May 1965, B.J. Shoemaker to D.J. Dodds, 10 March 1965, A.A. Wishart to D.J. Dodds, 16 March 1965, LAC, CCLA, R9833, vol. 25, f. 10, R9833; *Civil Liberties,* 19 December 1967.

16 Alan Borovoy to C.O. Bick, 9 October 1968, LAC, CCLA, R9833, vol. 14, f. 34, R9833; *Toronto Star,* 17 October 1967; C.O. Bick to Alan Borovoy, 22 October 1968, LAC, CCLA, R9833, vol. 25, f. 10, R9833.

17   Alan Borovoy, *When Freedoms Collide: The Case for Our Civil Liberties* (Toronto: Lester and Orpen Denny's, 1988), 31.

18   A poll taken in 1944 found that 49 percent of the Ontario public favoured religious exercises, that 44 percent were opposed, and that 7 percent were undecided. For a history of religious practices in Ontario public schools, see Ontario, 1969. *Religious Information and Moral Development: The Report of the Committee on Religious Education in the Public Schools of the Province of Ontario.*

19   Submission to Gosfield South School Board from a Delegation of Parents re Religious Education in Public Schools, 1966, Jewish Labour Committee Papers, LAC, MG 28, V75, vol. 43, f. 13.

20   Ontario, *Religious Information and Moral Development.*

21   *Civil Liberties* 5, 1 (1972).

22   The history of the separate school system in Ontario is examined in R.D. Gidney, *From Hope to Harris: The Reshaping of Ontario's Schools* (Toronto: University of Toronto Press, 1999).

23   *Canadian Civil Liberties Association v. Ontario [Attorney General]* (1990), 71 O.R. (Ontario Court of Appeals).

24   *Le Devoir,* 3 April 1971; *Le Devoir,* 1 February 1971.

25   J.L. Granastein, "Changing Positions: Reflections on Pierre Trudeau and the October Crisis," in *Trudeau's Shadow: The Life and Legacy of Pierre Elliott Trudeau,* ed. Andrew Cohen and J.L. Granatstein (Toronto: Vintage Canada, 1998), 297-98.

26   Submission to the Government of Canada re the War Measures Act, 19 October 1970, June Callwood Papers, LAC, MG 31, K24, vol. 19, f. 1.

27   According to the CCLA brief, educational institutions required the free exchange of ideas and the willingness to play devil's advocate, and the resolution threatened to undermined the basic need for open discussion in schools. See Submission to Board of Education, City of Toronto, the Resolution Requiring Discharge for Advocating FLQ Policies, 29 October 1979, LAC, CCLA, R9833, vol. 14, f. 3.

28   Submission to the Government of Canada re The Public (Temporary Measures) Act, 7 November 1970, LAC, CCLA, R9833, vol. 18, f. 6.

29   One of the consequences of the CCLA's campaign against the War Measures Act, and further proof of the support Trudeau's actions enjoyed in English Canada, was the loss of hundreds of members and donations. At one point, Borovoy estimated the CCLA had lost between $5,000 to $10,000 due to its controversial position on the War Measures Act. See *Civil Liberties* 3, 1 (1971); Alan Borovoy to Roger Baldwin, n.d., LAC, CCLA, R9833, vol. 181, f. 12; Borovoy, interview.

30   Canadian Civil Liberties Association, *Submission to the Honourable John Turner, Minister of Justice, Re. Emergency Powers,* 29 March 1971.

31   The name Jennifer Smith is the author's creation. The woman's real name has been concealed, as is required by access regulations.

32   Alan Borovoy to John Yaremko, 4 January 1971, LAC, CCLA, R9833, vol. 15, f. 2.

33   Extracts from a letter from the CCLA to John Yaremko, Minister of Social and Family Services, 15 June 1970, June Callwood Papers, LAC, MG 31, K24, vol. 18, f. 6.

34   The study interviewed a total of 1,002 recipients as follows: Toronto 445, Hamilton 106, Halifax 151, Winnipeg 132, Fredericton 93, and Regina 75.

35   There were several reasons, both practical and psychological, why a woman with an illegitimate child did not want to name the father. For instance, in several cases the woman in question had married or had moved in with another man and did not want to involve the father of one her children in her current life. In the study conducted by the CCLA, thirty-seven women stated that they were told to name the father, and thirty-two did so. See

Canadian Civil Liberties Association, *Welfare Practices and Civil Liberties: A Canadian Survey* (Toronto: Canadian Civil Liberties Education Trust, 1975).

36 Canadian Civil Liberties Association, *Welfare Practices and Civil Liberties.*

37 *Civil Liberties*, 2, 1 (1969).

38 Ibid.; *Globe and Mail*, 2 April 1975; *Globe and Mail*, 19 September 1986.

39 News notes, 19 December 1967, LAC, CCLA, R9833, vol. 12, f. 22.

40 Canadian Civil Liberties Association, *Submission to the Task Force on Policing in Ontario*, 21 September 1973; Submission to Arthur A. Wishart, Attorney General of Ontario, re Police Practices in Ontario, 1969, June Callwood Papers, LAC, MG 31, K24, vol. 8, f. 17; Submission to Arthur Maloney re Metropolitan Toronto Review of Citizen-Police Complaints Procedure, n.d., LAC, CCLA, R9833, vol. 14, f. 7; Submission to the Pringle Commission re Fort Erie Raid, 1974, LAC, CCLA, R9833, vol. 14, f. 7.

41 According to Maloney, "dissatisfied complainants, even though few in number, can in conjunction with the media greatly impair the regard in which the police are held by the public. As a consequence, there must be a procedure available for resolving complaints in a manner that will inspire public confidence in the police force. In the interest of maintaining the police-public relationship at a high level, justice must not be done but must be seen to be done." See Arthur Maloney: The Metropolitan Toronto Review of Citizen-Police Complaint Procedure, 12 May 1975, Daniel G. Hill Fonds, LAC, MG 31, H155, vol. 12, f. 6.

42 Ontario, 1976, *Royal Commission into Metropolitan Toronto Police Practices.*

43 Walter Pitman, *Now Is Not Too Late* (Toronto: Metropolitan Toronto Police Force, 1978).

44 Toronto, Metropolitan Board of Police Commissioners, 1980. Chairman's Report.

45 Metropolitan Board of Police Commissions, Chairman's Report, 23 January 1975, LAC, CCLA, R9833, vol. 126, f. 17.

46 Richard L. Henshel, *Police Misconduct in Metropolitan Toronto: A Study of Formal Complaints* (Toronto: LaMarsh Research Programme on Violence, 1983), 10.

47 Metropolitan Board of Police Commissioners, Chairman's Report, 1980.

48 Alan Borovoy to Roy McMurtry, 3 December 1979, LAC, CCLA, R9833, vol. 15, f. 8.

49 Alan Borovoy to George Kerr, 25 May 1974, LAC, CCLA, R9833, vol. 15, f. 5.

50 Alan Borovoy to George Kerr, 1 May 1978, Walter Tarnopolsky Papers, LAC, MG 31, E55, vol. 3, f.1.

51 Alan Borovoy to Roy McMurtry, 15 September 1979, LAC, CCLA, R9833, vol. 15, f. 8.

52 Arthurs, interview.

53 *Globe and Mail*, 27 October 1976; Ontario, Official Reports, 1977, no. 64 and 1979, no. 133, p. 5374; Ontario, Journals of the Legislative Assembly, 10 June 1980, pp. 133-34.

54 *Globe and Mail*, 10 February 1981, 28 February 1981; *Toronto Star*, 18 February 1981.

55 Jeff Sallot, *Nobody Said No: The Real Story about How the Mounties Always Get Their Man* (Toronto: James Lorimer and Company, 1979).

56 Sallot, *Nobody Said No*, 179.

57 Robert Dion, *Crimes of the Secret Police* (Montreal: Black Rose Books, 1982).

58 Alan Borovoy to Walter Thompson, 15 December 1978, LAC, CCLA, R9833, vol. 109, f. 8; Pat Reed to Helen Cainer, 12 November 1977, LAC, CCLA, R9833, vol. 109, f. 8.

59 Pierre Elliott Trudeau to Walter Tarnopolsky, 21 December 1977, Walter Tarnopolsky Fonds, LAC, MG 31, E55, vol. 2, f. 22.

60 *Canadian Lawyer*, November 1981; *Globe and Mail*, 27 August 1981.

61 Canadian Civil Liberties Association, Submission to the Commission of Inquiry Concerning Certain Activities of the Royal Canadian Mounted Police: Priorities and Procedures for the Commission's Proceedings, 30 January 1978; Submission to the Commission of Inquiry Concerning Certain Activities of the Royal Canadian Mounted Police re Public Disclosure and the Official Secrets Act and Submissions to the Commission of Inquiry Concerning

Certain Activities of the Royal Canadian Mounted Police re Emergency Powers and the War Measures Act, 3 October 1979, June Callwood Papers, LAC, MG 31, K24, vol. 19, f. 6; Submission to Commission of Inquiry Concerning Certain Activities of the RCMP re Toward a Charter for the RCMP, 17 April 1980, LAC, CCLA, R9833, vol. 109, f. 1; Submission to Commission of Inquiry Concerning Certain Activities of the Royal Canadian Mounted Police re Submissions of Commission Counsel, 24 July 1980, LAC, CCLA, R9833, vol. 108, f. 9.

62 CCLA news notes, March 1978, Walter Tarnopolsky Papers, LAC, MG 31, E55, vol. 3, f. 1.

63 RCMP Wrongdoing Petition Campaign: Progress Report, 4 January 1979, LAC, CCLA, R9833, vol. 107, f. 17.

64 The following papers covered the story on 15 May 1980: *Ottawa Journal, Le Journal de Québec, Times News* (Thunder Bay), *Barrie Examiner, Oshawa Times, Prince George Citizen, Stratford Beacon Herald, North Bay Nugget, Sudbury Star, St. Catharines Standard, Charlottetown Guardian,* and *Hamilton Spectator.*

65 Canada, 1979, *Security and Information;* Canada, 1981, *Freedom and Security under the Law: Commission of Inquiry Concerning Certain Activities of the Royal Canadian Mounted Police;* Canada, 1981, *Certain RCMP Activities and the Question of Governmental Knowledge.*

66 In their third report, the commissioners suggested "it is not within our jurisdiction to advise the federal Attorney General or provincial Attorney General whether, in any particular situation, there should or should not be a prosecution, because that is a matter solely within the discretion of Attorneys General." See Canada, *Certain RCMP Activities,* 503.

67 *Globe and Mail,* 24 September 1981. In general, the CCLA and the CLC cooperated and adopted similar positions on many of the same issues, but in the case of the security service the two groups found themselves at odds. The CLC supported the idea of a civilian security system divorced from the RCMP. Given the bitter history between organized labour and the RCMP, it is not surprising that the CLC wanted to remove from the police force the broad mandate for investigating subversion.

68 Jean Chrétien to Bob Kaplan, 20 July 1982, Walter Tarnopolsky Papers, LAC, MG 31, E55, vol. 3, f. 7.

69 *Toronto Star,* 12 February 1983.

70 Financial reports, 1977 to 1982, LAC, CCLA, R9833, vol. 1, f. 42; Minutes of the annual general meeting, 1978 to 1982, LAC, CCLA, R9833, vol. 1, f. 10 to 13; Minutes of the Board of Directors, 19 March 1980, LAC, CCLA, R9833, vol. 1, f. 41.

71 Kelly, *Governing with the Charter,* 65.

72 The following rights associations made presentations to the committee: the BCCLA, the Federation, the British Columbia Council for Human Rights, the Calgary Civil Liberties Association, the Manitoba Association for Rights and Liberties, the South Okanagan Civil Liberties Association, and the Canadian Human Rights Foundation. There is a brief mention of the BCCLA in the final report but only in reference to a word it suggested removing from one of the clauses. See Special Joint Committee on the Constitution, 1980-81 Papers, First Draft Report, LAC, RG 14, D4, acc. 90-91/119, box 59.

73 Chrétien credited the CCLA with reference to changes on the limitation clause (s. 1), search and seizure (s. 8), being detained by police (s. 9), the right to be informed of the right to counsel (s. 10), admissibility of evidence (s. 26), and remedies (new section). See Canada, 1981, *Proceedings of the Special Joint Committee on the Constitution.*

74 According to Borovoy, "permanent alliances can undermine everyone's agenda. It is wise to remember that coalitions are created among constituencies that have different as well as common objectives. Thus, these groups should create only temporary and ad hoc alliances. In the political, unlike the sexual, arena, promiscuity is a distinct virtue." See Alan Borovoy, *Uncivil Disobedience: The Tactics and Tales of a Democratic Agitator* (Toronto: Lester Publishing, 1991), 73.

75 In the same piece, Borovoy acknowledged that, for the poor and others without a voice in public debate (such as politicians), the use of disruptive tactics might be necessary and legitimate. But the CCLA never engaged in such activities. See Alan Borovoy, "Civil Liberties in the Imminent Hereafter," *Canadian Bar Review* 1 (1973): 93-106.

76 Borovoy, *Uncivil Disobedience*, 13.

77 Laskin challenged the traditional procedures of the Supreme Court by allowing more interveners to appear before it. See Robert J. Sharpe and Kent Roach, *Brian Dickson: A Judge's Journey* (Toronto: University of Toronto Press, 2003), 383.

78 One file in the CCLA Papers (vol. 191, f. 11) contains dozens of letters from various lawyers across Ontario, and some from lawyers outside the province, volunteering to litigate Charter cases on behalf of the CCLA. This was in response to a general letter sent out to lawyers across Canada. Only once has the CCLA had to pay legal fees, and even in that case it was a miserly sum. This was during the hearings of the Morand Commission, when the CCLA asked a local lawyer to attend the hearings on a regular basis to represent it and to report on the committee's activities. Given the enormous time commitment required, the CCLA felt obligated to pay the individual for her time, although the association could afford very little. See LAC, CCLA, R9833, vol. 191, f.11; Borovoy, interview.

79 News Notes, June 1981, Walter Tarnopolsky Papers, LAC, MG 31, E55, vol. 3, f. 5.

80 Arthurs, interview; Borovoy, interview.

81 Knopff and Morton, *Charter Revolution and the Court Party*, 25, 66.

82 Submission to Senate Standing Committee on Legal and Constitutional Affairs re Legislation on Hate Propaganda, 22 April 1969, LAC, CCLA, R9833, vol. 32, f. 23. Nearly a decade later, the CCLA opposed the inclusion of a section on hate propaganda in the proposed federal human rights legislation. See Submission to House of Commons Standing Committee on Justice and Legal Affairs Re the Federal Government's Human Rights Bill from CCLA, 28 April 1977, LAC, CCLA, R9833, vol. 51, f. 19.

83 Jerry Vink, interviewed by author, 11 March 2002. The Newfoundland-Labrador Human Rights Association did not develop position papers until the mid-1980s, but the positions adopted since then on issues such as hate propaganda are available on its website at http://www.nlhra.org.

84 A cornerstone of the LDH's campaign on the rape legislation involved distributing "coupons" in *La Presse* and other newspapers for individuals to fill out and mail to their federal government representatives. Over two thousand of the LDH's coupons were received in Ottawa. See Petition campaign materials, 1980, UQAM, SAGD, LDL, 24P7b/26.

85 Alan Borovoy, *The New Anti-Liberals* (Toronto: Canadian Scholars Press, 1999), 132-39. The CCLA organized a forum to debate Quebec's language law in Toronto in 1977, with Camille Laurin (the Parti québécois' chief spokesperson for the language legislation) defending the legislation. In 1982, the association considered intervening to challenge the language laws but decided to hold off because it had few resources in Quebec to support the case. See Posters and minutes of the executive committee, 1977, 1982, LAC, CCLA, R9833, vol. 141, f. 13 and vol. 1, f. 43.

86 Minutes of the Board of Directors, 1 March 1978, June Callwood Papers, LAC, MG 31, K24, vol. 18, f. 3.

87 Kerwin, interview.

88 Alan Borovoy to Dalton Bales (Attorney General of Ontario), 25 May 1972, LAC, CCLA, R9833, vol. 15, f. 3; Alan Borovoy to Thomas Wells, 17 December 1973, LAC, CCLA, R9833, vol. 15, f. 4.

89 Jim MacDonald to Alan Borovoy, 7 February 1972, LAC, CCLA, R9833, vol. 15, f. 3; Dennis McDermott to Ranking Officers of Affiliated Organizations, 15 August 1978, LAC, CCLA, R9833, vol. 109, f. 8; RCMP Wrongdoing Petition Campaign, Progress Report, 4 January 1979,

LAC, CCLA, R9833, vol. 107, f. 17; Alan Borovoy to Dennis McDermott, 15 December 1977, LAC, CCLA, R9833, vol. 183, f. 2.

90 Kerwin, interview.

91 Leo Panitch and Donald Swartz, *From Consent to Coercion: The Assault on Trade Union Freedoms* (Aurora: Garamond Press, 2003), 149-50. Submission from the CLC, n.d., Special Joint Committee on the Constitution Papers (1980-81), LAC, RG 14, D4, acc 90-91/119, box 62, wallet 10.

92 Panitch and Swartz, *From Consent to Coercion*, 20.

93 Canadian Bar Association, *Yearbook*, 1967, 273.

94 Ibid., 1969, 298.

95 Ibid., 1940, 86.

96 Black, interview; Walter Thompson, interviewed by author, 1 June 2003; Ed Webking, interviewed by author, 26 August 2003; Norman Whalen, interviewed by author, 4 April 2002.

97 For more information on the Canadian Bar Association's position on constitutionally entrenched rights, see Canadian Bar Association Committee on the Constitution, *Towards a New Canada* (Ottawa: Canadian Bar Foundation, 1978).

98 *Human Rights* (published by the Canadian Human Rights Foundation), 2 (October 1976).

99 None of the civil liberties and human rights group under study here received any grants from the Canadian Human Rights Foundation. See minutes of the Board of Directors for the Canadian Human Rights Foundation, 17 December 1968, Frank Scott Papers, LAC, MG 30, D211, vols. 44-45.

100 Kaplansky to Tarnopolsky, 12 August 1968, Kalmen Kaplansky Papers, LAC, MG 30, A53, vol. 6, f. 12.

101 Of the eighty-eight activists interviewed, seventy-three were in favour of a national organization and only four were against (eleven did not respond). See Maurice Miron, *A Canadian Organization for Human Rights: Report of a Canada-Wide Survey* (Ottawa: Canada Welfare Council, 1970).

102 Annual General Meeting of the National Capital Region Civil Liberties Association, 27 March 1971, Canadian Labour Congress Papers, LAC, MG 28, I103, vol. 662, f. 16.

103 Report of the National Capital Region Civil Liberties Association, February 1971, Canadian Labour Congress Papers, LAC, MG 28, I103, vol. 662, f. 16.

104 Nicholas Pawley to members of the Union of Human Rights and Civil Liberties Associations, 30 October 1970, UQAM, SAGD, LDL, 24P2b/12.

105 National Capital Region Civil Liberties Association executive committee report, 4 January 1971, Canadian Labour Congress Papers, LAC, MG 28, I103, vol. 662, f. 16.

106 Eamon Park to Don Whiteside, 18 November 1970, UQAM, SAGD, LDL, 24P2b/9; Don Whiteside to Eamon Park, n.d., UQAM, SAGD, LDL, 24P2b/9.

107 *National Bulletin/Bulletin nationale* 1, 2 (1972).

108 *Democratic Commitment* 17 (April 1971), LSBCA, BCCLA; *Democratic Commitments* 21 (July 1972), LSBCA, BCCLA; *Democratic Commitments* 22 (August 1972), LSBCA, BCCLA.

109 *National Newsletter* (the Federation) 1, 2 (1972).

110 Ligue des droits de l'homme, *Loi sur la protection de la vie privée, Bill C-176* (Montréal: Ligue des droits de l'homme, 22 June 1973); *National Bulletin* 3, 3 (1974); *Rights and Liberties* 16 (January 1975).

111 Webking, interview; Canada, Proceedings of the Special Joint Committee on the Constitution of Canada, 1980-81, Brief of the Canadian Federation of Civil Liberties and Human Rights Associations, RG 14, D4, acc 90-91/119, box 62, wallet 10.

112 Special Joint Committee on the Constitution 1980-81, Draft First Report, Papers, LAC, RG 14, D4, acc. 90-91/119, box 5, wallet 1.

113 Ross Lambertson, interviewed by author, 26 August 2003.

114   According to James Dybikowski (BCCLA Board of Directors, 1970-75, and president, 1977-79) and John Russell (BCCLA executive director, 1980-88), the Federation was never a priority for the BCCLA. In fact, the BCCLA rarely devoted much energy to working through the Federation. James Dybikowski, interviewed by author, 1 December 2004; Bert Riggs, interviewed by author, 15 July 2003; Russell, interview; Vink, interview; Webking, interview.

115   Norville Getty, interviewed by author, 14 October 2003; Vink, interview; Webking, interview.

116   Minutes of the Board of Directors, 11 September 1978, LSBCA, BCCLA, vol. 1, f. 4.

117   Minutes of the annual general meeting, memorandum, 1 December 1967, LAC, CCLA, R9833, vol. 1, f. 1.

118   Arthurs proposal, 1971, LAC, CCLA, R9833, vol. 6, f. 14.

119   Mark MacGuigan to Sydney Midanik, 6 August 1970, LAC, CCLA, R9833, vol. 181. f. 2.

120   In Halifax, for instance, Walter Thompson, a young lawyer and president of the Nova Scotia Civil Liberties Association in the 1970s, continued to correspond with the CCLA's head office in the 1980s; but the Nova Scotia chapter had, for all intents and purposes, become defunct years earlier. The CCLA had established a sound financial relationship with only one rights association in Canada, the Hamilton Civil Liberties Association, which provided 20 percent of its membership dues to the head office (the Hamilton group became defunct sometime in the early 1980s). See minutes of the Executive Committee, 13 April 1978, LAC, CCLA, R9833, vol. 2, f. 22; Thompson, interview.

Chapter 8: The Newfoundland-Labrador Human Rights Association

1   Newfoundland, *Hansard,* 1972, 4126.

2   *Star Weekly* (Toronto), 12 August 1972.

3   Ibid.

4   John Carter to Biswarup Bhattacharya, 29 January 1972, Centre for Newfoundland Studies (hereafter CNS), Newfoundland-Labrador Human Rights Association Papers (hereafter NLHRA), f. 2.08.001.

5   Biswarup Bhattacharya to John Carter, 5 July 1972, CNS, NLHRA, f. 2.08.001.

6   For more information on the proliferation of location rights associations in Canada, see http://www.historyofrights.com.

7   Correspondence between human rights committee and Smallwood, February 1967-December 1968, Joseph Smallwood Papers, CNS, f. 3.29.101 (human rights).

8   Prison reform was discussed extensively throughout the December conference on human rights in Ottawa, and it was a priority for many rights associations, most notably the LDH. See International Year for Human Rights, Canadian Commission, *Report of the Proceedings: National Conference on Human Rights and Activities of the Canadian Commission* (Ottawa: International Year for Human Rights, Canadian Commission, 1969).

9   Newfoundland, *Hansard,* vol. 9, 1969, 3639.

10   Ibid., 3648.

11   British Columbia followed Newfoundland's lead in 1973 by incorporating political opinion as a prohibited form of discrimination, and Manitoba (1974), Prince Edward Island (1975), and Quebec (1975) soon did the same. See Tarnopolsky, *Discrimination and the Law in Canada,* 320-21.

12   There is no evidence in the NLHRA Papers (and nothing discerned from interviews) that indicates why Memorial University was also exempted. It seems to have simply been included as a side product of broad wording in the legislation, which exempted all educational institutions. In addition, over the years government officials have often linked the code with Canada's obligations under the UDHR. In reality, the code had little in common with the UDHR, given the former's almost exclusive focus on employment issues. It is more likely, and this was suggested by Keough himself at first reading, that the code

reflected the conventions of the International Labour Organization. See Newfoundland, *Hansard,* vol. 1, 1969, 3; Newfoundland, *Hansard,* vol. 9, 1969, 3677-78.

13 *Evening Telegram,* 9 July 1971.

14 Fred W. Coates, interviewed by author, 11 March 2002.

15 Newfoundland, An Act Further to Amend the Newfoundland Human Rights Code, 1974,

16 *Alternate Press,* 27 May 1971.

17 Bhattacharya to Smallwood, 2 September 1971, Joseph Smallwood Papers, CNS, f. 3.29.101 (human rights).

18 Correspondence between human rights committee and Smallwood, February 1967-December 1968, Joseph Smallwood Papers, CNS, f. 3.29.101 (human rights); *Alternate Press,* vol. 1, nos. 1-3; *Evening Telegram,* 9 July 1971.

19 James Overton, "Towards a Critical Analysis of Neo-Nationalism in Newfoundland," in *Underdevelopment and Social Movements in Atlantic Canada,* ed. R. Brym and R.J. Sacouman (Toronto: New Hogtown Press, 1979), 237.

20 Interviewed by author: Lillian Bouzane, 13 March 2002; William Collins, 10 April 2002; John Peddle, 12 April 2002; Norman Whalen, 4 April 2002.

21 Whalen, interview.

22 There is some debate over what role the NLHRA actually played in the decision to destroy the files. The *Evening Telegram* article and the NLHRA leaders claim that dossiers on individuals were being maintained and that the efforts of the latter led to their destruction, while the minister at the time, T. Alex Hickman, denied the existence of the dossiers and claimed to have destroyed the photos prior to meeting with the association. See *Evening Telegram,* 23 October 1973.

23 Newfoundland, *Hansard,* 1974, vol. 3, 8728-30.

24 An Act Further to Amend the Newfoundland Human Rights Code, *S.N.* 1974, c. 114.

25 Mutual Life Insurance Company of Canada application form, filled out by Norman Whalen, 5 January 1979, CNS, NLHRA, f. 2.04.016; Whalen, interview.

26 *Rights and Freedoms* 2, 4 (1973).

27 Newfoundland, *Hansard,* 1969, vol. 1, 3.

28 Friedmann, "The Ombudsman," 356n20.

29 Vink, interview; The Role of the Ombudsman, CNS, NLHRA, f. 2.05.021.

30 Canada, 1973, *Final Report of the Commission of Inquiry into the Non-Medical Use of Drugs.*

31 A thorough analysis of crime reporting and statistics is available in William O'Grady, "Criminal Statistics and Stereotypes: The Social Construction of Violence in Newfoundland," in *Violence and Public Anxiety: A Canadian Case,* ed. E. Leyton, W. O'Grady, and J. Overton, 1-108 (St. John's: Institute of Social and Economic Research, 1992).

32 According to Elliott Leyton, in Newfoundland by "1977 there were fifteen reported rapes (and God knows how many unreported), 333 assaults of all kinds, thousands of cases of theft and wilful damage, hundreds of breaches of the Narcotic Control Act, 179 forgeries, and even a kidnapping and an extortion case: a long way from the alcoholic little city proffering the occasional punchup or brutal seduction attempt." See Elliott Leyton, "Drunk and Disorderly: Changing Crime in Newfoundland," in *Contrary Winds: Essays on Newfoundland Society in Crisis,* ed. R. Clark, 76-88 (St. John's: Breakwater, 1986).

33 Schmeiser, *Civil Liberties in Canada,* 185.

34 Phillip McCann, "Denominational Education in the Twentieth Century in Newfoundland," in *The Vexed Question: Denominational Education in a Secular Age,* ed. W.A. McKim (St. John's: Breakwater, 1988), 95.

35 Outline of Provincial Human Rights Code Analysis, 1984, CNS, NLHRA, f. 2.06.004.

36 The exemption for educational institutions in the Human Rights Code had consequences outside of protecting denominational education from accusations of religious discrimination.

In 1978, Marlene Webber, a professor in the School of Social Work at Memorial University, was dismissed because her "political activities have indicated considerable divergence from the philosophy and purposes of the School [as has her] involvement both on and off campus with a political movement [communism] which is totally inimical to and destructive of the system upon which our government is based." Such a clear violation of academic freedom and the right to political opinion was immune from the Human Rights Code as a result of the general exemption for educational institutions. See NLHRA Press Release on Marlene Webber, n.d., CNS, NLHRA, f. 2.04.001.

37 Quoted in *Evening Telegram*, 1 April 1987.

38 Newfoundland, 1992, *Our Children, Our Future: Report of the Royal Commission of Inquiry into the Delivery of Programs and Services in Primary, Elementary, Secondary Education.*

39 *Evening Telegram*, 1 August 1997.

40 In the words of the editor of the *Evening Telegram*, the voters supported the yes side because many "were simply fed up with court battles and endless wrangling over the shape of education compromise that we ended up with (and yet it displeased enough people to bring the matter to court). And they simply wanted to harness all the province's educational resources in a single school system, eliminating any wasteful dollars spent on duplication that might be better spent in the classroom." See *Evening Telegram*, 3 September 1997.

41 Riggs, interview.

42 Summary, Involvement with Denominational Education System, n.d., CNS, NLHRA, f. 2.04.007.

43 *Evening Telegram*, 10 December 1985.

44 Private records of the NLHRA, *NLHRA Policy Manual.*

45 *Evening Telegram*, 30 July 1997.

46 Quoted in Mark Graesser, "Public Opinion on Denominational Education: Does the Majority Rule?," in *The Vexed Question: Denominational Education in a Secular Age*, ed. W.A. McKim (St. John's: Breakwater, 1988), 35. While the Human Rights Commission lobbied the provincial government to make changes to the Human Rights Act in such areas as sexual orientation, it avoided the question of denominational education because the latter was explicitly exempted from the legislation. It was not until the 1990s that it began organizing public forums to discuss the denominational education system; and, in one case, it successfully defended a janitor who had been fired from a local high school for not sharing the religious beliefs that dominated his place of employment. According to the commission, only teachers could be fired for their religious affiliation. See Riggs, interview.

47 The resolution passed at the 1964 British Columbia Teachers' Federation Annual General Meeting read as follows: "Be it Resolved that the following resolution be added to Section 19 of the Policy Handbook: 'That the Federation recommend that religious exercises be discontinued in British Columbia schools.'" See British Columbia Teachers' Federation Records Management, Religious Exercises in the Schools, Consultative Committee Report; Background Position Papers, Religion in Public Schools, LSBCA, BCCLA, vol. 11, f. 41.

48 *Canadian Civil Liberties Association v. Ontario* [Attorney General].

49 *Stack v. Roman Catholic School Board* [1979] 23 Newfoundland and Prince Edward Island Reports 221 (Newfoundland Supreme Court).

50 Newfoundland Teachers' Association Papers, CNS, Newfoundland Teachers' Association Journals, vol. 70, no. 2, Spring 1982.

51 Report of the National Capital Region Civil Liberties Association, February 1971, LAC, CLC, MG 28, I103, vol. 662, f. 16.

52 By 1975, the St. John's Status of Women Council openly supported pro-choice and was a member of the Canadian Association for Repeal of the Abortion Law. See Sharon Grey Pope and Jane Burnham, "The Modern Women's Movement in Newfoundland and Labrador," in

Pursuing Equality: Historical Perspectives on Women in Newfoundland and Labrador, ed. L. Kealey (St. John's: Institute of Social and Economic Research, 1993), 203.

53 Brief in respect to housing, submitted to the mayor and councillors of St. John's through the Conference on Housing, n.d., CNS, NLHRA, f. 2.04.011.

54 Riggs, interview.

55 Vink, interview.

56 John Peddle, interviewed by author, 12 April 2002.

57 Lillian Bouzane, interviewed by author, 13 March 2002.

58 Bouzane, interview.

59 Peddle, interview.

60 Dominique Clément, "Searching for Rights in the Age of Activism: The Newfoundland-Labrador Human Rights Association, 1968-1982," *Newfoundland Studies* 2 (Spring 2003): 347-72.

61 The paucity of documentation available for the organization's early period makes it impossible to determine exactly when it began receiving financial grants; however, as early as 1969 the NLHRA received a $250 grant from the SOS (and by 1972 the amount had risen to $3,000) to hire a part-time administrator. Grants from the SOS were made available in the following amounts: $16,576 (1976), $22,411 (1977), $15,000 (1978), $17,900 (1979), $9,930 (1980), and $21,280 (1983). See Budgets and financial statements of the NLHRA, 1972-82, CNS, NLHRA, f. 1.03.001; Report of the Department of the Secretary of State of Canada for the Year Ending 31 March 1970.

62 Memorandum to Cabinet, Confirmation of Citizenship Branch Role, February 1968, Department of the Secretary of State, LAC, RG 6, vol. 661, f. 2-2-4.

63 Pal, *Interests of State,* 85.

64 Memorandum to Cabinet, Confirmation of Citizenship Branch Role, February 1968, Department of the Secretary of State, LAC, RG 6, vol. 661, f. 2-2-4.

65 Secretary of Treasury Board (no name) to G.F. Davidson (Deputy Minister of Citizenship and Immigration), 31 September 1962, Department of the Secretary of State Papers, LAC, RG 6, vol. 661, f. 2-2-4.

66 Despite the regulation, two organizations were granted sustaining grants: the Canadian Citizenship Council and the Indian-Eskimo Association, each receiving $15,000. See Pal, *Interests of State,* 107.

67 *A New Focus for the Citizenship Branch,* August 1965, Department of the Secretary of State Papers, LAC, RG6, vol. 661, f.2-2-4.

68 Pal, *Interests of State.*

69 Memorandum to Cabinet, October 1968, Secretary of State Papers, LAC, RG 6, acc. 1986-87/319, vol. 145, f. 17-1.

70 Judy LaMarsh to Sidney B. Linden, Department of the Secretary of State, LAC, RG 6, vol. 661, f.2-4-7; Citizenship Development Grants, 1970-71, Department of the Secretary of State, LAC, RG 6, acc. 1986-87/319, vol. 4-15-1.

71 Financial records, 1977, UQAM, SAGD, LDL Fonds, 24P5/12.

72 A report commissioned by the group concluded that "none of the possible private sources of funding were willing to commit themselves and that most of the militant groups [were] operating on a shoe-string budget. It would appear obvious, therefore, that such a national organization could come into being only through massive public support." See minutes of the meeting of the executive committee of the Canada Council on Human Rights, 18 April 1970, Kalmen Kaplansky Papers, LAC, MG 30, A53, vol. 7, f. 1.

73 Reg Robson to Jacques Hébert, 10 September 1971, UQAM, SAGD, LDL, 24P2b/16.

74 One of the Federation's advantages was having Don Whiteside as treasurer and, later, as president. He had worked for the SOS in the Citizen Rights and Freedoms Section as a

senior planning officer with strategic planning while he was active in the Civil Liberties Association National Capital Region, and thus, was highly familiar with government funding programs.

75 Most of the Federation's members were unable to pay the expense of a flight to the annual general meeting. If it had not been for government grants, many of the associations would never have attended the meeting, the most important event of the year for the Federation. Designed primarily as a networking agency among rights associations, the meeting was as crucial as was the newsletter with regard to communicating among groups. At one point, the BCCLA, the Federation's second largest member behind the LDH, notified the Federation that it would be unable to send a delegate to the meeting without government support. See minutes of the executive council, 3 April 1978, LSBCA, BCCLA, vol. 2.

76 Minutes of the executive council, 3 April 1978, LSBCA, BCCLA, vol. 2.

77 *National Bulletin* 2, 4 (1973).

Chapter 9: Conclusion

1 Tom Kent, Pearson's policy secretary and key advisor, was inspired by the American call for a "war on poverty," and he convinced the prime minister to adopt the term in the mid-1960s. See James Struthers, *The Limits of Affluence: Welfare in Ontario, 1920-1970* (Toronto: University of Toronto Press, 1994), 219.

2 Ontario, 1977, *Report of the Royal Commission on Metropolitan Toronto.*

3 Owram, *Born at the Right Time*, 159. Anthony Esler coined the expression "an age group shaped by history." See Esler, *Generations in History*, 44.

4 Borovoy, *The New Anti-Liberals.*

5 Eamon Park had also served as the chair of the Toronto and District Labour Council Human Rights Committee in the early to mid-1960s. See Eamon Park to Don Whiteside, 18 November 1970, SAGD, UQAM, LDL, 24P2b/9.

6 Pal, *Interests of State*, 251.

7 Although Alan Borovoy has advocated the use of various "disruptive" tactics, from sit-ins to boycotts, and employed them on occasion when he was with the JLC, it is important to appreciate that he did not employ such tactics when he was with the CCLA. In his book on tactics for social activists, Borovoy explores various possible strategies for legal disruption and has often suggested that other groups employ such tactics but that the CCLA did not. David Orlikow, a long-time human rights activist and a former director of the JLC, recognized the distinction between groups like the CCLA and the JLC when Borovoy consulted him about working for both groups in the late 1960s: "From the point of view of our work, I think it is important to keep in mind that the work is to the largest extent financed by the Jewish Labour Committee and Canadian Jewish Congress. These two organizations are primarily interested in human relations, with particular emphasis on race, color and religion. Civil liberties issues could often be unpopular and I can conceive of your work in civil liberties not having the approval of these organizations. Similarly, in the field of civil liberties, the people or organizations to whom you would be responsible and who would be financing the work, might not be able to endorse our activities." See David Orlikow to Alan Borovoy, Ontario Labour Committee for Human Rights Papers, LAC, MG 28 I173, vol. 8, f. 8.

8 Lambertson, *Repression and Resistance*, 381.

9 Irwin Cotler, "Human Rights as the Modern Tool of Revolution," in *Human Rights in the Twenty-First Century: A Global Challenge*, ed. K.E. Mahoney and P. Mahoney (London: Martinus Nijhoff Publishers, 1993), 19.

10 Laurie S. Wiseberg, "Human Rights Nongovernmental Organizations," in *Human Rights in the World Community: Issues and Action*, ed. R.P. Claude and B.H. Weston (Philadelphia: University of Pennsylvania Press, 1992), 380.

11 Ignatieff, *The Rights Revolution,* 20.

12 Ibid. Ron Hirschl has studied constitutional jurisprudence in Canada, New Zealand, and South Africa and has concluded that, even in 2000, a minimalist approach to human rights pervades these three countries: "My systematic analysis of these three countries' records of constitutional rights jurisprudence reveals a clear common tendency to adopt a narrow conception of rights, emphasizing Lockean individualism and the dyadic and anti-statist aspects of constitutional rights." See Hirschl, "'Negative' Rights vs. 'Positive' Entitlements," 1095-57.

13 Latin American scholar Maxine Molyneux has suggested that human rights policies have failed to close the gap between rhetoric and the material realities of women's lives in Latin America. Rights strategies are viewed by many Latin American feminists as a form of Western hegemony designed to camouflage rising inequality. Judy Fudge's analysis of feminist activism in the post-Charter era in Canada reveals how the Charter has put feminists on the defensive, forcing them to adopt the language of equal rights to the detriment of feminist discourses about power. According to Fudge, men "have used the Charter to challenge welfare legislation providing benefits to sole support mothers, child support provisions, the procedures for regulating the adoption of children born to single women, and sexual assault provisions in the Criminal Code. And an astonishing number of the challenges brought by men have been successful; male complainants are making and winning ten times as many equality claims as women." In two provocative articles in *Human Rights Quarterly,* Neil Stammers suggests that human rights abuses occur at the substate, social level; social rights are violated by private economic agencies, and the rights of women are violated by men. Human rights activism has historically been oriented towards the state, but such an approach can be highly misleading if the obligation to deal with human rights abuses lies with agencies that lack the power to solve the problem. The institutionalization of human rights may thus only provide protections for human rights in a form that does not threaten existing power structures. See Judy Fudge, "The Effect of Entrenching a Bill of Rights upon Political Discourse: Feminist Demands and Sexual Violence in Canada," *Journal of the Sociology of Law* (1989): 449-50; Neil Stammers, "A Critique of Social Approaches to Human Rights," *Human Rights Quarterly* 3 (1995): 488-508; Neil Stammers, "Social Movements and the Social Construction of Human Rights," *Human Rights Quarterly* 4 (1999): 980-1008; Maxine Molyneux and Sian Lazar, *Doing the Rights Thing: Rights-Based Development and Latin American NGOs* (London: ITDG Publishing, 2003).

14 *Women Unite! An Anthology of the Canadian Women's Movement* (Toronto: Canadian Women's Educational Press, 1972), 9. Becki Ross, in one of the few exhaustive studies of a radical women's organization in Canada, offers the same distinction. In her discussion of the Lesbian Organization of Toronto's clashes with the International Women's Day coalition, Ross notes that "in both 1978 and 1979, lesbian feminists criticized the way in which a civil-rights approach to lesbianism revealed the coalition's liberal-individualistic approach to the terrain of sexual politics. By directing its inventory of anticapitalist and antipatriarchal demands at the state, the coalition reduced lesbian oppression to the rights of lesbian mothers in child-custody battles and the inclusion of anti-discrimination protection in the Ontario Human Rights Code." See Ross, *The House That Jill Built,* 181.

15 University of Victoria Archives, Women against Pornography Papers, Women against Pornography Manifesto, vol. 1, f. 9.

16 Janet Beebe, *Update on the Status of Women in British Columbia* (Vancouver: Vancouver Status of Women, 1978), 12.

17 Byron Sheldrick, *Perils and Possibilities: Social Activism and the Law* (Halifax: Fernwood Publishing, 2004), 37.

Bibliography

Archival Sources

Centre for Newfoundland Studies (CNS)
Keough, William J., Papers
Newfoundland and Labrador Federation of Labour
Newfoundland-Labrador Human Rights Association Papers, Coll. 111
Newfoundland and Labrador Teachers' Association
Smallwood, Joey, Papers, Coll. 075

Library and Archives Canada (LAC)
Callwood, June, Papers, MG 31, K24
Canada.
–. Department of External Affairs, RG 25
–. Department of Finance, RG 19
–. Department of Justice, RG 13
–. Privy Council Office, RG 2
–. Royal Canadian Mounted Police/Canadian Security Intelligence Service, RG 146
–. Secretary of State, RG 6
Canadian Bar Association, MG 28 I169
Canadian Civil Liberties Association Papers, R 9833
Canadian Labour Congress Papers, MG 28, I103
Diefenbaker, John, Papers, MG 26-M
Gordon, J. King, Papers, MG 30, C241
Hill, Daniel G., Papers, MG 31 H 155
Jewish Labour Committee Papers, MG 28, V75
Kaplansky, Kalmen, Papers, MG 30, A53
Ontario Labour Committee for Human Rights, MG 28, I173
Roebuck, Arthur, Papers, MG 32 C68
Scott, Frank R., Papers, MG 30, D211
Special Joint Committee on the Constitution Papers (1980-81), RG 14, D4
Tarnopolsky, Walter Surma, Papers, MG 31 E55,

Law Society of British Columbia Archives (LSBCA)
Canadian Bar Association, BC Section

Public Archives of Nova Scotia (PANS)
Nova Scotia Civil Liberties Association, MG 20, vol. 625
Nova Scotia Human Rights Association, MG 20, vol. 421

Service des archives et de gestion des documents, Université du Québec à Montréal (UQAM)
Fond du Ligue des droits et libertés, 24P
Quebec Federation of Labour Papers, 100P

Miscellaneous Archives
British Columbia Civil Liberties Association Papers (Rare Books and Special Collections, Simon Fraser University)
British Columbia Federation of Labour (Rare Books and Special Collections, University of British Columbia)
British Columbia Teachers' Federation Files (not archived)
Canadian Broadcasting Corporation, Television and Radio Archives
Fonds de la Commission d'enquête sur l'administration de la justice en matière criminelle et pénale, E142 (Archives Nationale du Québec)
Montreal City Council Papers (Montreal City Archives)
Newfoundland-Labrador Human Rights Commission Files

Interviews
Arthurs, Harry, 13 March 2004
Bernheim, Jean-Claude, 26 June 2005
Bouzane, Lillian, 13 March 2002
Black, William, 20 June 2002
Borovoy, Alan, 12 March 2004
Braybrooke, David, 30 May 2003
Coates, Fred, 11 March 2002 (telephone)
Collins, William, 10 April 2002
Dickson, Gary, 4 April 2003
Dybikowski, James, 1 December 2004
Gagnon, Théo, 11 November 2003 (telephone)
Getty, Norville, 4 October 2003 (telephone)
Giesbrecht, William, 25 February 2003
Keeping, Janet, 19 March 2004 (telephone)
Kerwin, Patrick, 2 July 2003
Lambertson, Ross, 26 August 2003 (telephone)
Levi, Norman, 25 June 2002
Macdonald, Alex, 18 June 2002 (telephone)
Peddle, John, 12 April 2002
Riggs, Bert, 15 July 2003
Russell, John, 23 December 2004
Thompson, Walter, 1 June 2003
Vink, Jerry, 11 March 2002
Webking, Ed, 26 August 2003 (telephone)
Whalen, Norman, 4 April 2002

Websites
Canada's Rights Movement: A History. http://www.historyofrights.com
Alberta Civil Liberties Association. http://www.aclrc.com
British Columbia Civil Liberties Association. http://www.bccla.org
Canadian Civil Liberties Association. http://www.ccla.org
Civil Liberties Association, National Capital Region. http:// www.civil-liberties.ncf.ca
Ligue des droits et libertés. http://www.liguesdesdroitsqc.org
Manitoba Association for Rights and Liberties. http://www.marl.mb.ca
Newfoundland-Labrador Human Rights Association. http://www.nlhra.org

Government Documents

British Columbia. Commission of Inquiry into the Gastown Riot. *Report on the Gastown Inquiry.* Victoria: Commission of Inquiry into the Gastown Riot, 1971.

Canada. *Certain RCMP Activities and the Question of Governmental Knowledge (Third Report): Commission of Inquiry Concerning Certain Activities of the Royal Canadian Mounted Police.* Ottawa: Commission of Inquiry Concerning Certain Activities of the Royal Canadian Mounted Police, 1981.

–. *Final Report of the Commission of Inquiry into the Non-Medical Use of Drugs.* Ottawa: Information Canada, 1973.

–. *Freedom and Security Under the Law (Second Report): Commission of Inquiry Concerning Certain Activities of the Royal Canadian Mounted Police.* Ottawa: Commission of Inquiry Concerning Certain Activities of the Royal Canadian Mounted Police, 1981.

–. *Report of the Royal Commission Appointed under Order in Council P.C. 411 of February 5, 1946 to Investigate the Facts Relating to and the Circumstances Surrounding the Communication by Public Officials and Other Persons in Positions of Trust, of Secret and Confidential Information to Agents of a Foreign Power.* Ottawa: Edmond Cloutier, 1946.

–. *Report of the Royal Commission on the Status of Women in Canada.* Ottawa: Royal Commission on the Status of Women, 1970.

–. *Security and Information (First Report): Commission of Inquiry Concerning Certain Activities of the Royal Canadian Mounted Police.* Ottawa: Commission of Inquiry Concerning Certain Activities of the Royal Canadian Mounted Police, 1979.

–. Department of Indian Affairs and Northern Development. *Statement of the Government of Canada on Indian Policy.* Ottawa: Department of Indian Affairs and Northern Development, 1969.

–. Parliament. Senate. Special Senate Committee on Human Rights and Fundamental Freedoms. *Minutes of Proceedings and Evidence.* Ottawa: King's Printer, 1950.

–. Parliament. Senate and House of Commons. Special Joint Committee of the Senate and House of Commons on the Constitution of Canada. *Final Report.* 28th Parliament, 4th session. Ottawa: Queen's Printer, 1972.

–. Parliament. Senate and House of Commons. Special Joint Committee of the Senate and House of Commons on the Constitution of Canada. *Minutes of Proceedings and Evidence.* 32nd Parliament, 1st session. Hull: Supply and Services Canada, 1980-81.

–. Parliament. Senate and House of Commons. Special Joint Committee on Human Rights and Fundamental Freedoms. *Minutes of Proceedings and Evidence.* Ottawa: King's Printer, 1947-48.

Duchaîne, Jean-François. *Rapport sur les événements d'octobre 1970.* Québec: Ministère de la Justice, 1980.

International Year for Human Rights, Canadian Commission. *Report of the Proceedings, National Conference on Human Rights and Activities of the Canadian Commission for International Year for Human Rights.* Ottawa: Canadian Commission, 1968.

Newfoundland. *Our Children, Our Future: Report of the Royal Commission of Inquiry into the Delivery of Programs and Services in Primary, Elementary, Secondary Education.* St. John's: Queen's Printer, 1992.

–. *Report of the Royal Commission on Education and Youth.* St. John's: Royal Commission on Children and Youth, 1967.

–. *Report of the Royal Commission on Labour Legislation in Newfoundland and Labrador.* St. John's: Queen's Printer, 1972.

Ontario. Commission of Inquiry into the Confidentiality of Health Information. *Report of the Commission of Inquiry into the Confidentiality of Health Information.* Toronto: Commission of Inquiry into the Confidentiality of Health Information, 1980.

–. Committee on the Healing Arts. *Highlights of the Report of the Committee on the Healing Arts.* Toronto: Committee on the Healing Arts, 1970.

–. Committee on Religious Education in Public Schools. *Religious Information and Moral Development: Report.* Toronto: Ontario Department of Education, 1969.

–. Royal Commission Inquiry into Civil Rights. *Report.* Toronto: Queen's Printer, 1968-71.

–. Royal Commission on Metropolitan Toronto. *Report of the Royal Commission on Metropolitan Toronto.* Toronto: Royal Commission on Metropolitan Toronto, 1977.

–. Royal Commission into Toronto Police Practices. *Report of the Royal Commission into Metropolitan Toronto Police Practices.* Toronto: Royal Commission into Toronto Police Practices, 1976.

–. Task Force on Policing in Ontario. *Report to the Solicitor General.* Toronto: The Task Force on Policing in Ontario, 1974.

Pitman, Walter. *Now is Not Too Late: Report Submitted to the Council of Metropolitan Toronto by the Task Force on Human Relations.* Toronto: Municipality of Metropolitan Toronto, 1977.

Québec. Commission d'enquête sur des opérations policières en territoire québécois. *Rapport de la commission d'enquête sur des opérations policières en territoire québécois.* Québec: Ministère de la Justice, 1981.

–. Commission d'enquête sur la crime organisé. *Rapport official: La lutte au crime organisé.* Montréal: Commission d'enquête sur la crime organisé, 1976.

–. Commission of Enquiry into the Administration of Justice on Criminal and Penal Matters in Quebec. *Crime, Justice and Society.* 5 vols. Quebec: Official Publisher, 1968.

Task Force on Canadian Unity. *A Future Together: Observations and Recommendations.* Hull: Supply and Services Canada, 1979.

Secondary Sources

Abella, Rosalie Silberman. "From Civil Liberties to Human Rights: Acknowledging the Differences." In *Human Rights in the Twenty-First Century: A Global Challenge*, ed. Kathleen E. Mahoney and Paul Mahoney. London: Martinus Nijhoff Publishers, 1993.

Acker, Alison, and Betty Brightwell. *Off Our Rockers and into Trouble: The Raging Grannies.* Vancouver: Touchwood Editions, 2004.

Adamson, Nancy, Linda Briskin, and Margaret McPhail. *Feminist Organizing for Change: The Contemporary Women's Movement in Canada.* Toronto: University of Toronto Press, 1988.

Anderson, Donald. "The Development of Human Rights Protections in British Columbia." MA thesis, University of Victoria, 1986.

Badar, Mohamed Elewa. "Basic Principles Governing Limitations on Individual Rights and Freedoms in Human Rights Instruments." *International Journal of Human Rights* 7, 4 (2003): 63-92.

Bailey, Peter H. *Human Rights: Australia in an International Context.* Sydney: Butterworths, 1990.

Bangarth, Stephanie. "The Politics of Rights: Canadian and American Advocacy Groups and North America's Citizens of Japanese Ancestry, 1942-49." PhD diss., University of Waterloo, 2004.

–. "We are not asking you to open wide the gates for Chinese immigration: The Committee for the Repeal of the Chinese Immigration Act and Early Human Rights Activism in Canada." *Canadian Historical Review* 84, 3 (2003): 395-422.

Barman, Jean. *The West beyond the West: A History of British Columbia.* Toronto: University of Toronto Press, 1991.

Beach, Stephen W. "Social Movement Radicalization: The Case of Poor People's Democracy in Northern Ireland." *Sociological Quarterly* 18, 3 (1977): 305-18.

Bédard, Éric. *Chronique d'une insurection appréhendée: Le crise d'Octobre et le milieu universitaire.* Sillery: Les Éditions du Septentrion, 1998.

Berlin, Isaiah. *Four Essays on Liberty.* London: Oxford University Press, 1969.

Berger, Thomas. *Fragile Freedoms: Human Rights and Dissent in Canada.* 2nd ed. Toronto: Irwin Publishing, 1982.

Berger, Thomas. *One Man's Justice: A Life in the Law.* Vancouver and Toronto: Douglas and McIntyre, 2002.

Bialystok, Franklin. "Neo-Nazis in Toronto: The Allan Gardens Riot." *Canadian Jewish Studies* 4-5 (1996): 1-38.

Bickenback, Jerome. *Physical Disability and Social Policy.* Toronto: University of Toronto Press, 1993.

Borovoy, Alan. "Civil Liberties in the Imminent Hereafter." *Canadian Bar Review* 51, 1 (1973): 93-106.

–. *The New Anti-Liberals.* Toronto: Canadian Scholars Press, 1999.

–. *Uncivil Disobedience: The Tactics and Tales of a Democratic Agitator.* Toronto: Lester Publishing, 1991.

–. *When Freedoms Collide: The Case for Our Civil Liberties.* Toronto: Lester and Orpen Dennys, 1988.

Botting, Garry. *Fundamental Freedoms and Jehovah's Witnesses.* Calgary: University of Calgary Press, 1993.

Boyer, J. Patrick. *A Passion for Justice.* Toronto: University of Toronto Press, 1994.

Brodie, Janine, Shelley Gavigan, and Jane Jenson. *The Politics of Abortion.* Toronto: Oxford University Press, 1992.

Brym, R., and R.J. Sacouman, eds. *Underdevelopment and Social Movements in Atlantic Canada.* Toronto: New Hogtown Press, 1979.

Buechler, Steven M. *Social Movements in Advanced Capitalism: The Political Economy and Cultural Construction of Social Activism.* New York: Oxford University Press, 2000.

Buergenthal, Thomas. "The Normative and Institutional Evolution of International Human Rights." *Human Rights Quarterly* 19, 4 (1997): 703-23.

Bushnell, Ian. *The Captive Court: A Study of the Supreme Court of Canada.* Montreal and Kingston: McGill-Queen's University Press, 1992.

Calhoun, Craig. "New Social Movements of the Early Nineteenth Century." *Social Science History* 17, 3 (1993): 385-427.

Callwood, June. *Emma Woikin.* Toronto: University of Toronto Press, 1988.

Campbell, Charles, and Naomi Pauls. *The Georgia Straight: What the Hell Happened?* Vancouver: Douglas and McIntyre, 1997.

Campbell, Laurie. "The Royal Commission on Inquiry into the Confidentiality of Health Records in Ontario and Access to Government Information." MA thesis, Carleton University, 1999.

Campbell, Tom. *The Left and Rights: A Conceptual Analysis of the Idea of Socialist Rights.* London: Routledge and Kegan Paul, 1983.

Cairns, Alan C. *Charter versus Federalism: The Dilemmas of Constitutional Reform.* Montreal and Kingston: McGill-Queen's University Press, 1992.

Cairns, Alan C., and Cynthia Williams, eds. *Constitutionalism, Citizenship and Society in Canada.* Toronto: University of Toronto Press, 1985.

Cardin, Jean-François. *Comprendre Octobre 1970: Le FLQ, la crise et le syndicalisme.* Montréal: Éditions du Méridien, 1990.

Carroll, William K., ed. *Organizing Dissent: Contemporary Social Movements in Theory and in Practice, Studies in the Politics of Counter-Hegemony.* Toronto: Garamond Press, 1997.

Carroll, William K., and R.S. Ratner. "Old Unions and New Social Movements." *Labour/LeTravail* 35 (Spring 1995): 195.

Cherwinsky, W.J.C., and Gregory Kealey, eds. *Lectures in Canadian Labour and Working Class History.* St. John's: Committee on Canadian Labour History, 1985.

Christman, John. "Liberalism and Positive Freedom." *Ethics* 101, 2 (1991): 343-59.

Chunn, Dorothy E., Susan B. Boyd, and Hester Lessard. *Reaction and Resistance: Feminism, Law, and Social Change.* Vancouver: UBC Press, 2007.

Clark, Rex, ed. *Contrary Winds: Essays on Newfoundland Society in Crisis.* St. John's: Breakwater, 1986.

Clark, Roger S. "Human Rights Strategies of the 1960s within the United Nations: A Tribute to the Late Kamleshwar Das." *Human Rights Quarterly* 21, 2 (1999): 308-41.

Claude, Richard Pierre, and Burns H. Weston, *Human Rights in the World Community: Issues and Action.* 2nd ed. Philadelphia: University of Pennsylvania Press, 1992.

Clawson, Dan. *The Next Upsurge: Labor and the New Social Movements.* Ithaca and London: ILR Press, 2003.

Clément, Dominique. "An Exercise in Futility? Regionalism, State Funding and Ideology as Obstacles to the Formation of a National Social Movement Organization in Canada." *BC Studies* 146 (Summer 2005): 63-91.

–. "'I Believe in Human Rights, Not Women's Rights': Women and the Human Rights State, 1969-1984." *Radical History Review* 101 (Spring 2008): 107-29.

–. "It Is Not the Beliefs but the Crime That Matters: Post-War Civil Liberties Debates in Canada and Australia." *Labour History* (Australia) 86 (2004): 1-32.

–. "The Royal Commission on Espionage and the Spy Trials of 1946-9: A Case Study in Parliamentary Supremacy." *Journal of the Canadian Historical Association* 11 (2000): 151-72.

–. "The Royal Commission on Espionage, 1946-8: A Case Study in the Mobilization of the Early Civil Liberties Movement." MA thesis, University of British Columbia, 2000.

–. "Searching for Rights in the Age of Activism: The Newfoundland-Labrador Human Rights Association, 1968-1982." *Newfoundland Studies* 19, 2 (2003): 347-72.

–. "Spies, Lies and a Commission, 1946-8: A Case Study in the Mobilization of the Canadian Civil Liberties Movement." *Left History* 7, 2 (2001): 53-79.

Cloward, R.A., and F.F. Piven. *Poor People's Movements: How They Succeed, Why They Fail.* New York: Pantheon, 1977.

Cmiel, Kenneth. "The Recent History of Human Rights." *American Historical Review* 109, 1 (2004): 117-35.

Cohen, Andrew, and J.L. Granatstein, eds. *Trudeau's Shadow: The Life and Legacy of Pierre Elliott Trudeau.* Toronto: Vintage Canada, 1998.

Cohen, G.A. "On the Currency of Egalitarian Justice." *Ethics* 99, 4 (July 1999): 906-44.

Cohen-Almagor, Raphael. "The Terrorists' Best Ally: The Quebec Media Coverage of the FLQ Crisis in October 1970." *Canadian Journal of Communication* 25, 2 (2000): 251-84.

Coleman, William D. *The Independence Movement in Quebec, 1945-1980.* Toronto: University of Toronto Press, 1984.

Confederation of National Trade Unions. *Quebec Labour: The Confederation of National Trade Unions Yesterday and Today.* Montreal: Black Rose Books, 1972.

Cook, Ramsay. "Canadian Civil Liberties in Wartime." MA thesis, Queen's University, 1955.

Cottrell, Robert C. *Roger Nash Baldwin and the American Civil Liberties Union.* New York: Columbia University Press, 2000.

Courtis, M.C. *Attitudes to Crime and the Police in Toronto: A Report on Some Survey Findings.* Toronto: Centre of Criminology, University of Toronto, 1970.

Cranston, Maurice. *What Is a Human Right?* New York: Basic Books, 1973.

Crosbie, John (with Geoffrey Stevens). *No Holds Barred: My Life in Politics.* Toronto: McClelland and Stewart, 1997.

Dagenais, Bernard. *La crise d'octobre et les médias: Le miroir à dix faces.* Outremont: VLB Éditeur, 1990.

Dean, Malcolm. *Censored! Only in Canada: The History of Film Censorship – The Scandal Off the Screen.* Toronto: Virgo Press, 1981.

Dion, Robert. *Crimes of the Secret Police.* Montreal: Black Rose Books, 1982.

Djwa, Sandra. *The Politics of Imagination: The Life of F.R. Scott.* Toronto: McClelland and Stewart, 1987.

Donnelly, Jack. *The Concept of Human Rights.* London and Sydney: Croom Helm, 1985.

–. "Human Rights, Democracy and Development." *Human Rights Quarterly* 21, 3 (1999): 608-32.

–. *Universal Human Rights in Theory and Practice.* 2nd ed. Ithaca and London: Cornell University Press, 2003.

Drinan, Robert F. *The Mobilization of Shame: A World View of Human Rights.* New Haven: Yale University Press, 2001.

Dudziak, Mary L. *Cold War Civil Rights: Race and the Image of American Democracy.* Princeton and Oxford: Princeton University Press, 2000.

Egerton, George. "Entering the Age of Human Rights: Religion, Politics, and Canadian Liberalism, 1945-50." *Canadian Historical Review* 85, 3 (2004): 451-79.

Ferrin, Scott Ellis, Sharon A. Gibb, E. Vance Randall, and Ellen Stucki. "From Sectarian to Secular Control of Education: The Case of Newfoundland." *Journal of Research on Christian Education* 10, 2 (2001): 411-30.

Fillmore, Charles K. *In Darkest Ottawa.* Vancouver: Rose, Cowan and Latta, 1954.

Fournier, Louis. *FLQ: The Anatomy of an Underground Movement.* Toronto: NC Press, 1984.

Foweraker, Joe, and Todd Landman. "Individual Rights and Social Movements: A Comparative and Statistical Inquiry." *British Journal of Political Science* 29, 2 (1999): 291-322.

Frager, Ruth A., and Carmela Patrias. "This Is Our Country, These Are Our Rights: Minorities and the Origins of Ontario's Human Rights Campaigns." *Canadian Historical Review* 82, 1 (2001): 1-35.

Fraser, Graham. *René Lévesque and the Parti Québécois in Power.* 2nd ed. Montreal and Kingston: McGill-Queen's University Press, 2001.

Freeman, Jo, ed. *Social Movements of the Sixties and Seventies.* New York and London: Longman, 1983.

Freeman, Jo, and Victoria Johnson, eds. *Waves of Protest: Social Movements since the Sixties.* Toronto: Rowman and Littlefield Publishers, 1999.

Freeman, Michael. *Freedom or Security: The Consequences for Democracies Using Emergency Powers to Fight Terror.* Westport: Praeger, 2003.

Fudge, Judy. "The Effect of Entrenching a Bill of Rights upon Political Discourse: Feminist Demands and Sexual Violence in Canada." *Journal of the Sociology of Law* 17 (1989): 445-63.

Gamson, William A. *The Strategy of Social Protest.* Homewood: Dorsey Press, 1975.

Gaze, Beth, and Melinda Jones. *Law, Liberty and Australian Democracy.* Sydney: The Law Book Company, 1990.

Gibson, Frederick W. *Queen's University.* Vol. 2, *1917-1961.* Kingston: Queen's University Press, 1983.

Gidney, R.D. *From Hope to Harris: The Reshaping of Ontario's Schools.* Toronto: University of Toronto Press, 1999.

Giffen, P.J., Shirley Endicott, and Sylvia Lambert. *Panic and Indifference: The Politics of Canada's Drug Laws.* Ottawa: Canadian Centre on Substance Abuse, 1991.

Gillespie, William. "A History of the Newfoundland Federation of Labour, 1936-1963." MA thesis, Memorial University of Newfoundland, 1980.

Girard, Philip. *Bora Laskin: Bringing Law to Life.* Toronto: University of Toronto Press, 2005.

Godfrey, Stuart. *Human Rights and Social Policy in Newfoundland, 1832-1982.* St. John's: Harry Cuff Publications, 1985.

Gwynn, Richard. *Smallwood: The Unlikely Revolutionary.* Toronto: McClelland and Stewart, 1999.

Habermas, Jurgen. "Remarks on Legitimation through Human Rights." *Philosophy and Social Criticism* 24, 2/3 (1998): 157-71.

Hannant, Larry. *The Infernal Machine: Investigating the Loyalty of Canada's Citizens.* Toronto: University of Toronto Press, 1995.

Harvison, C.W. *The Horsemen.* Toronto: McClelland and Stewart, 1967.

Heick, W.H., and Roger Graham, eds. *His Own Man: Essays in Honour of A.R.M. Lower.* Montreal and Kingston: McGill-Queen's University Press, 1974.

Henkin, Louis. *The Age of Rights.* New York: Columbia University Press, 1990.

Henshel, Richard L. *Police Misconduct in Metropolitan Toronto: A Study of Formal Complaints.* Toronto: LaMarsh Research Programme on Violence, 1983.

Herman, Didi. *Rights of Passage: Struggles for Lesbian and Gay Legal Equality.* Toronto: University of Toronto Press, 1994.

Hiller, James, and Peter Neary. *Twentieth-Century Newfoundland: Explorations.* St. John's: Breakwater, 1994.

Hirschl, Ron. "Negative Rights vs. Positive Entitlements: A Comparative Study of Judicial Interpretations of Rights in an Emerging Neo-Liberal Economic Order." *Human Rights Quarterly* 22 (2000): 1060-98.

Holt, Simma. *Terror in the Name of God: The Story of the Doukhobours.* Toronto: McClelland and Stewart, 1964.

Hospers, John. *Libertarianism: A Political Philosophy.* Los Angeles: Nash Publishing, 1971.

Howe, R. Brian. "The Evolution of Human Rights Policy in Ontario." *Canadian Journal of Political Science/Revue canadienne de science politique* 24, 4 (1991): 783-802.

Humphrey, John P., and R.St.J. Macdonald, eds. *The Practice of Freedom: Canadian Essays on Human Rights and Fundamental Freedoms.* Toronto: Butterworth, 1979.

Ignatieff, Michael. *Human Rights as Politics and Idolatry.* Princeton: Princeton University Press, 2001.

–. *The Rights Revolution.* Toronto: House of Anansi Press, 2000.

Ishay, Micheline R. *The History of Human Rights: From Ancient Times to the Globalization Era.* Berkeley: University of California Press, 2004.

James, Matt. *Misrecognized Materialists: Social Movements in Canadian Constitutional Politics.* Vancouver: UBC Press, 2006.

Johnston, Hank, and Bert Klandermans, eds. *Social Movements and Culture: Social Movements, Protest, and Contention.* Vol. 4. Minneapolis: University of Minnesota Press, 1995.

Johnston, Hank, Enrique Larana, and Joseph Gusfield, eds. *New Social Movements: From Ideology to Identity.* Philadelphia: Temple University Press, 1994.

Johnston, Hugh. *Radical Campus: Making Simon Fraser University.* Vancouver: Douglas and McIntyre, 2005.

Jones, Peter. "Human Rights, Group Rights, and People's Rights," *Human Rights Quarterly* 21, 1 (1999): 80-107.

Kallen, Evelyn. *Ethnicity and Human Rights in Canada.* 2nd ed. Toronto: Oxford University Press, 1995.

Kallen, Evelyn. *Label Me Human: Minority Rights and Stigmatized Canadians.* Toronto: University of Toronto Press, 1989.

Kamenka, Eugene, and Alice Erh-Soon Tay, eds. *Human Rights*. London: E. Arnold, 1978.

Kaplan, William. *State and Salvation: The Jehovah's Witnesses and Their Fight for Civil Rights*. Toronto: University of Toronto Press, 1989.

Kealey, Greg. "State Repression of Labour and the Left in Canada, 1914-20: The Impact of the First World War." *Canadian Historical Review* 73, 3 (1992): 281-314.

Kealey, Linda, ed. *Pursuing Equality: Historical Perspectives on Women in Newfoundland and Labrador*. St. John's: Institute for Social and Economic Research, 1993.

Kim, Ki Su. "J.R. Smallwood and the Negotiation of a School System for Newfoundland, 1946-8." *Newfoundland Studies* 11, 1 (1995): 53-74.

Knight, Amy. *How the Cold War Began: The Gouzenko Affair and the Hunt for Soviet Spies*. Toronto: McClelland and Stewart, 2005.

Knopff, Rainer, with Thomas Flanagan. *Human Rights and Social Technology: The New War on Discrimination*. Ottawa: Carleton University Press, 1989.

Knopff, Rainer, and F.L. Morton. *The Charter Revolution and the Court Party*. Peterborough: Broadview Press, 2000.

Kostash, Myrna. *Long Way from Home: The Story of the Sixties Generation in Canada*. Toronto: James Lorimer and Company, 1980.

Kunnemann, Rolf. "A Coherent Approach to Human Rights." *Human Rights Quarterly* 17, 2 (1995): 323-42.

Kymlicka, Will. *Liberalism, Community, and Culture*. Oxford: Clarendon Press, 1989.

–. *Multicultural Citizenship: A Liberal Theory of Minority Rights*. Oxford: Clarendon Press, 1995.

Lambertson, Ross. "Activists in the Age of Rights: The Struggle for Human Rights in Canada, 1945-60." PhD diss., University of Victoria, 1998.

–. "The Black, Brown, White and Red Blues: The Beating of Clarence Clemons." *Canadian Historical Review* 85, 4 (2004): 755-76.

–. "The Dresden Story: Racism, Human Rights, and the Jewish Labour Committee of Canada." *Labour/Le Travail* 47 (Spring 2001): 43-82.

–. *Repression and Resistance: Canadian Human Rights Activists, 1930-1960*. Toronto: University of Toronto Press, 2004.

Landau, Tammy. *Public Complaints against the Police: A View from the Complainants*. Toronto: Centre of Criminology, University of Toronto, 1994.

Landman, Todd. "Measuring Human Rights: Principle, Practice and Policy." *Human Rights Quarterly* 26, 4 (2004): 906-31.

Landreville, Pierre, Astrid Gagnon, and Serge Desrosiers. *Les prisons par ici: Droits des détenus au Québec*. Montréal: Editions Parti-Pris, 1976.

Langer, Rosanna L. *Defining Rights and Wrongs: Bureaucracy, Human Rights, and Public Accountability*. Vancouver: UBC Press, 2007.

Lauren, Paul Gordon. *The Evolution of International Human Rights: Visions Seen*. Philadelphia: University of Pennsylvania Press, 1998.

Laurin, Lucie. *Des luttes et des droits: Antécédants et histoire de la Ligue des droits de l'homme de 1936-1975*. Montréal: Éditions du Meridien, 1985.

Leane, G.W.G. "Enacting Bills of Rights: Canada and the Curious Case of New Zealand's 'Thin' Democracy." *Human Rights Quarterly* 26 (2004): 152-88.

Leroux, Manon. *Les silences d'octobre: Le discours des acteurs de la crise de 1970*. Montreal: VLB Éditeur, 2002.

Leyton, Elliot, O'Grady, William and Overton. James. *Violence and Public Anxiety: A Canadian Case*. St. John's: Institute of Social and Economic Research, 1992.

Lichtenstein, Nelson. *State of the Union: A Century of American Labor*. Princeton and Oxford: Princeton University Press, 2002.

Ligue des droits de l'homme. *La société québécois face à l'avortement*. Ottawa: Editions Leméac Inc., 1974.

Ligue des droits et libertés. *Défendons nos libertés: Pas de police dans les syndicats*, 1979.

Lilly, Mark. *The National Council for Civil Liberties: The First Fifty Years*. London: Macmillan, 1984.

Lunan, Gordon. *The Making of a Spy*. Toronto: Robert Davies Publishing, 1995.

Luxton, Meg. "Feminism as a Class Act: Working-Class Feminism and the Women's Movement in Canada." *Labour/Le Travail* 48 (Fall 2001): 63-88.

Lyon, J.N. "Constitutional Validity of Sections 3 and 4 of the Public Order Regulations, 1970." *McGill Law Journals* 18, 1 (1972): 136-44.

MacDowell, Laurel Sefton. *Renegade Lawyer: The Life of J.L. Cohen*. Toronto: University of Toronto Press, 2001.

MacGuigan, Mark R. "The Development of Civil Liberties in Canada." *Queen's Quarterly* 72, 2 (1965): 270-88.

MacLennan, Christopher. "Toward the Charter: Canadians and the Demand for a National Bill of Rights, 1929-1960." PhD diss., University of Western Ontario, 1996.

–. *Toward the Charter: Canadians and the Demand for a National Bill of Rights, 1929-1960*. Montreal and Kingston: McGill-Queen's University Press, 2003.

Macpherson, C.B. *The Rise and Fall of Economic Justice and Other Papers*. New York: Oxford University Press, 1985.

Mahoney, Kathleen E., and Paul Mahoney, eds. *Human Rights in the Twenty-First Century: A Global Challenge*. London: Martinus Nijhoff Publishers, 1993.

Mandel, Michael. *The Charter of Rights and the Legalization of Politics in Canada*. Toronto: Thompson Educational Publishing, 1994.

Marquis, Greg. "From Beverage to Drug: Alcohol and Other Drugs in 1960s and 1970s Canada." *Journal of Canadian Studies* 39, 2 (2005): 57-79.

–. *Policing Canada's Century: A History of the Canadian Association of Chiefs of Police*. Toronto: University of Toronto Press, 1993.

Martel, Marcel. *Not This Time: Canadians, Public Policy, and the Marijuana Question, 1961-1975*. Toronto: University of Toronto Press, 2006.

Matthews, Robert O., and Cranford Pratt, eds. *Human Rights in Canadian Foreign Policy*. Kingston and Montreal: McGill-Queen's University Press, 1988.

McCann, Michael W. *Rights at Work: Pay Equity Reform and the Politics of Legal Mobilization*. Chicago: Chicago University Press, 1994.

McInnis, Peter S. *Labour Confrontations: Shaping the Postwar Settlement in Canada, 1943-1950*. Toronto: University of Toronto Press, 2002.

McKim, William A., ed. *The Vexed Question: Denominational Education in a Secular Age*. St. John's: Breakwater, 1988.

McMahon, Maeve, and Richard V. Ericson. *Policing Reform: A Study of the Reform Process and Police Institution in Toronto*. Toronto: University of Toronto, Centre of Criminology, 1984.

McRoberts, Kenneth. *Quebec: Social Change and Political Crisis*. 3rd ed. Don Mills: Oxford University Press, 1993.

McWhinney, Edward. *Canada and the Constitution, 1979-1982: Patriation and the Charter of Rights*. Toronto: University of Toronto Press, 1982.

Melucci, Alberto. *Nomads of the Present: Social Movements and Individual Needs in Contemporary Society*. Philadelphia: Temple University Press, 1982.

Minow, Martha. *Making All the Difference: Inclusion, Exclusion and American Law*. Ithaca and London: Cornell University Press, 1990.

Molyneux, Maxine, and Sian Lazar. *Doing the Rights Thing: Rights-Based Development and Latin American NGOs*. London: ITDG Publishing, 2003.

Molyneux, Maxine, and Shahra Razavi. *Gender Justice, Development and Rights*. Geneva: UNRISD, 2003.

Moore, Dorothy Emma. "Multiculturalism: Ideology or Social Reality?" PhD diss., Boston University, 1980.

Neary, Peter. *Newfoundland in the North Atlantic World, 1929-1949*. Montreal and Kingston: McGill-Queen's University Press, 1996.

Noel, S.J.R. *Politics in Newfoundland*. Toronto: University of Toronto Press, 1971.

O'Brien, Patricia. *Out of Mind, Out of Sight: A History of the Waterford Hospital*. St. John's: Breakwater Books, 1989.

Oestreich, Joel E. "Liberal Theory and Minority Group Rights." *Human Rights Quarterly* 21, 1 (1999): 108-32.

Offe, Claus. "Challenging the Boundaries of Institutional Politics: Social Movements since the 1960s." In *Changing Boundaries of the Political: Essays on the Evolving Balances between the State and Society, Public and Private in Europe*, ed. Charles S. Maier, 63-105. New York: Cambridge University Press, 1987.

Orend, Brian. *Human Rights: Concept and Context*. Peterborough: Broadview Press, 2002.

Ornstein, Michael D., and Michael H. Stevenson. "Elite and Public Opinion before the Quebec Referendum: A Commentary on the State in Canada," *Canadian Journal of Political Science* 14, 4 (1981): 745-74.

Owram, Doug. *Born at the Right Time: A History of the Baby Boom Generation*. Toronto: University of Toronto Press, 1996.

Pal, Leslie A. *Interests of State: The Politics of Language, Multiculturalism, and Feminism in Canada*. Montreal and Kingston: McGill-Queen's University Press, 1993.

Palmer, Bryan. "Renegades: J.L. Cohen, Bill Walsh, and the Tragedies of the Canadian Left." *Journal of Canadian Studies* 37, 1 (2002): 207-24.

–. *Working-Class Experience: Rethinking the History of Canadian Labour*. Montreal and Kingston: McGill-Queen's University Press, 1992.

Patrias, Carmela. "Socialists, Jews, and the 1947 Saskatchewan Bill of Rights." *Canadian Historical Review* 87, 2 (2006): 265-92.

Pelletier, Gérard. *The October Crisis*. Toronto: McClelland and Stewart, 1971.

Penner, Norman. *The Canadian Left: A Critical Analysis*. Scarborough: Prentice-Hall of Canada, 1977.

Petersen, Klaus, and Allan C. Hutchinson eds. *Interpreting Censorship in Canada*. Toronto: University of Toronto Press, 1999.

Petryshyn, J. "Class Conflict and Civil Liberties: The Origins and Activities of the Canadian Labour Defence League, 1925-40." *Labour/Le Travail* 10 (Autumn 1982): 39-63.

Petryshyn, Jaroslav. "A.E. Smith and the Canadian Labour Defense League." PhD diss., University of Western Ontario, 1977.

Powe, L.A., Jr. "The Georgia Straight and Freedom of Expression in Canada." *Canadian Bar Review* 48, 2 (1970): 410-38.

Rankin, Harry. *Rankin's Law: Collections of a Radical*. Vancouver: November House, 1975.

Rebick, Judy. *Ten Thousand Roses: The Making of a Feminist Revolution*. Toronto: Penguin Canada, 2005.

Richardson, James L. "Contending Liberalisms: Past and Present." *European Journal of International Relations* 3, 1 (1997): 5-34.

Ross, Becki L. *The House That Jill Built: A Lesbian Nation in Formation*. Toronto: University of Toronto Press, 1995.

Rouillard, Jacques. *Histoire du syndicalisme au Québec: Des origines à nos jours*. Montreal: Boréal, 1989.

Rowe, Frederick W. *Education and Culture in Newfoundland*. Toronto: McGraw-Hill Ryerson, 1976.

Rubinstein, Leonard S. "How International Human Rights Organizations Can Advance Economic, Social, and Cultural Rights: A Response to Kenneth Roth." *Human Rights Quarterly* 26, 4 (2004): 845-65.

Russell, John, ed. *Liberties*. Vancouver: New Star Books, 1989.

Russell, Peter H. "The Political Purposes of the Canadian Charter of Rights and Freedoms." *Canadian Bar Review* 61 (1983): 30-54.

Ryan, Claude, ed. *Le Quebec qui se fait*. Montréal: Editions Hurtubise HMH, 1971.

Salkany, Roger E. *The Origin of Rights*. Vancouver: The Carswell Company Limited, 1986.

Sallot, Jeff. *Nobody Said No: The Real Story about How the Mounties Always Get Their Man*. Toronto: James Lorimer and Company, 1979.

Saywell, John T. *The Lawmakers: Judicial Power and the Shaping of Canadian Federalism*. Toronto: University of Toronto Press, 2002.

–. *Quebec 70: A Documentary Narrative*. Toronto: University of Toronto, 1971.

–. *The Rise of the Parti Québécois, 1967-1976*. Toronto: University of Toronto Press, 1977.

Schabas, William A. "Canada and the Adoption of the Universal Declaration of Human Rights." *McGill Law Journal* 43 (1998): 403-41.

Schmeiser, D.A. *Civil Liberties in Canada*. Toronto: Oxford University Press, 1964.

Scott, Frank R. *Civil Liberties and Canadian Federalism*. Toronto: University of Toronto Press, 1959.

Scott, Frank. *Essays on the Constitution: Aspects of Canadian Law and Politics*. Toronto: University of Toronto Press, 1977.

Sharpe, Robert J., and Kent Roach. *Brian Dickson: A Judge's Journey*. Toronto: University of Toronto Press, 2003.

Sheldrick, Byron. *Perils and Possibilities: Social Activism and the Law*. Halifax: Fernwood Publishing, 2004.

Shestack, Jerome J. "The Philosophic Foundations of Human Rights." *Human Rights Quarterly* 20, 2 (1998): 201-34.

Skebo, Suzanne. "Liberty and Authority: Civil Liberties in Toronto." MA thesis, University of British Columbia, 1968.

Smith, Jackie, Ron Pagnucco, and George A. Lopez. "Globalizing Human Rights: The Work of Transnational Human Rights NGOs in the 1990s." *Human Rights Quarterly* 20, 2 (1998): 379-412.

Smith, Miriam. *Civil Society? Collective Actors in Canadian Political Life*. Peterborough: Broadview Press, 2005.

–. *Group Politics and Social Movements in Canada*. Peterborough: Broadview Press, 2007.

–. *Lesbian and Gay Rights in Canada: Social Movements and Equality-Seeking, 1971-1995*. Toronto: University of Toronto Press, 1999.

Stammers, Neil. "A Critique of Social Approaches to Human Rights." *Human Rights Quarterly* 17, 3 (1995): 488-508.

–. "Social Movements and the Social Construction of Human Rights." *Human Rights Quarterly* 24, 4 (1999): 980-1008.

Stasiulis, Daiva Kristina. "Race, Ethnicity and the State: The Political Structuring of South Asian and West Indian Communal Action in Combating Racism." PhD diss., University of Toronto, 1982.

Stenning, Philip C., ed. *Accountability for Criminal Justice: Selected Essays*. Toronto: University of Toronto Press, 1995.

Stein, Janice Gross, ed. *Uneasy Partners: Multiculturalism and Rights in Canada*. Waterloo: Wilfrid Laurier University Press, 2007.

Struthers, James. *The Limits of Affluence: Welfare in Ontario, 1920-1970.* Toronto: University of Toronto Press, 1994.

Tarnopolsky, Walter Surma. *The Canadian Bill of Rights.* 2nd ed. Toronto: McClelland and Stewart Limited, 1978.

–. "The Critical Century: Human Rights and Race Relations." *Transactions of the Royal Society of Canada* (series 9, vol. 20, 1982).

–. *Discrimination and the Law.* Toronto: Richard DeBoo Limited, 1982.

–. "The Supreme Court of Canada and the Canadian Bill of Rights." *Canadian Bar Review* 57, 4 (1975): 626-39.

Teeple, Gary. *The Riddle of Human Rights.* New York: Humanity Books, 2005.

Tetley, William. *The October Crisis, 1970: An Insider's View.* Kingston and Montreal: McGill-Queen's University Press, 2006.

Touraine, Alain. *The Voice and the Eye: An Analysis of Social Movements.* Cambridge: Cambridge University Press, 1978.

Trofimenkoff, Susan Mann. *The Dream of a Nation: A Social and Intellectual History of Quebec.* 2nd ed. Montreal and Kingston: McGill-Queen's University Press, 2002.

Vallières, Pierre. *White Niggers of America.* Toronto: McClelland and Stewart, 1971.

Waldron, Jeremy, ed. *Nonsense upon Stilts: Bentham, Burke and Marx on the Rights of Man.* London and New York: Methuen, 1987.

Walker, James. "The Jewish Phase in the Movement for Racial Equality in Canada." *Canadian Ethnic Studies* 34, 1 (2002): 1-23.

–. *Race, Rights and the Law in the Supreme Court of Canada: Historical Case Studies.* Toronto: Wilfrid Laurier University Press, 1997.

–. "The Rights Revolution: Lessons from the Maritimes." Stewart MacNutt Memorial Lecture, University of New Brunswick, 9 October 2003.

Walker, Samuel. *In Defence of American Liberties: A History of the ACLU.* New York: Oxford University Press, 1990.

Ward, W. Peter. *White Canada Forever: Popular Attitudes toward Orientals in British Columbia.* Montreal and Kingston: McGill-Queen's University Press, 1990.

Warner, Tom. *A History of Queer Activism in Canada.* Toronto: University of Toronto Press, 2002.

Whitaker, Reg. "Apprehended Insurrection? RCMP Intelligence and the October Crisis." *Queen's Quarterly* 100, 2 (1993): 383-406.

Whitaker, Reg, and Gary Marcuse. *Cold War Canada: The Making of a National Insecurity State, 1945-1957.* Toronto: University of Toronto Press, 1994.

Williams, George. *Human Rights under the Australian Constitution.* Melbourne: Oxford University Press, 1999.

Winks, Robin. *The Blacks in Canada: A History.* 2nd ed. Montreal and Kingston: McGill-Queen's University Press, 1997.

Woodcock, George, and Ivan Avakumovic. *The Doukhobours.* Toronto: Oxford University Press, 1968.

Zald, Mayer, and John D. McCarthy, eds. *The Dynamics of Social Movements: Resource Mobilization, Social Control and Tactics.* Cambridge: Winthrop Publishers, 1979.

–. *Social Movements in an Organizational Society.* New Brunswick: Transaction Publishers, 1987.

Index

Printed and bound in Canada by Friesens

Set in Helvetica Condensed and Minion by Artegraphica Design Co. Ltd.

Copy editor: Joanne Richardson

Proofreader: Tara Tovell